JOURNAL FOR THE STUDY OF THE OLD TESTAMENT
SUPPLEMENT SERIES
111

JSOT Press
Sheffield

Yahweh and the Sun

Biblical and Archaeological Evidence
for Sun Worship in Ancient Israel

J. Glen Taylor

Journal for the Study of the Old Testament
Supplement Series 111

Copyright © 1993 Sheffield Academic Press

Published by JSOT Press
JSOT Press is an imprint of
Sheffield Academic Press Ltd
343 Fulwood Road
Sheffield S10 3BP
England

Typeset by Sheffield Academic Press
and
Printed on acid-free paper in Great Britain
by Biddles Ltd
Guildford

British Library Cataloguing in Publication Data

Taylor, J. Glen
    Yahweh and the Sun: Biblical and
    Archaeological Evidence for Sun Worship
    in Ancient Israel.—(JSOT Supplement
    Series, ISSN 0309-0787; No. 111)
    I. Title II. Series
    230

    ISBN 1-85075-272-9

CONTENTS

PREFACE

This book is a slightly revised version of my doctoral dissertation entitled 'Solar Worship in the Biblical World' which was submitted to the Graduate School of Yale University in the Spring of 1989. As may be judged from the title of that work, I had at one time planned to cover more territory than sun worship in ancient Israel, but found the material pertaining to ancient Israel so vast that I never got beyond it.

I am sometimes asked about the relationship between my work and that of Mark Smith, also from Yale and one who has similarly written on the topic of sun worship. Although I have known of Mark's general interest in the topic (and he of mine) since the time I began researching and writing my doctoral dissertation late in 1985, I left Yale in January of 1986 and had no interaction with his work apart from reading his short review of the book by Stähli in *JBL* 106 of 1987 and his 'Seeing God in the Psalms' in *CBQ* 50 of 1988, the latter of which he kindly sent me in advance of its publication. Apart from this, my work in preparation for the dissertation was done independently of Smith. In preparation for this present modest revision, I have of course had access to Smith's *The Early History of God*, which has clarified some things for me and has made it possible to assume a greater familiarity on the part of readers with the general idea that an 'idolatrous' phenomenon could be at the same time 'Yahwistic'.

Although I like to consider myself one of the early recent proponents of this rather different way of looking at the relationship between Yahweh and the other deities, the major works of Saul Olyan (who studied Asherah) and Mark Smith (who studied several deities in general), have of course appeared well in advance and independently of mine.

Far more importantly, I trust that the book will be of help in better understanding several passages in the Scriptures of the Old Testament and the way in which God and his ways have been revealed to humankind through them.

J. Glen Taylor
Wycliffe College
University of Toronto, Canada

ACKNOWLEDGMENTS

I owe a great deal to many who have assisted with this project, originally a Yale dissertation (1989). I am very grateful to Robert R. Wilson who first suggested the topic and to Marvin H. Pope, my adviser. Both were immensely supportive and helpful.

Most of the archaeological research was done at the Albright Institute in Jerusalem with the generous help of a G.A. Barton fellowship from the American Schools of Oriental Research. I am grateful to Seymour Gitin, Thomas Levy and other members of the staff at the Albright for their kind assistance and support and to others in Jerusalem who were generous with their time and expertise as well (particularly Ruth Amiran, Jonas Greenfield, Ruth Hestrin, Emile Puech and Yigal Shiloh). Others in Jerusalem at the time (1986) who kindly offered their assistance included Philip Davies, Philip King and Lawrence Stager. I am grateful also to the Ecole biblique for granting me the privilege of access to their outstanding library facility, and to the staff of the Israel Museum and the Israel Antiquities Authority for allowing me to peruse artefacts and publish photographs.

In Toronto, Paul Dion, Donald Redford, A.D. Tushingham, S.D. Walters and, especially, J.S. Holladay, have been generous with their time and knowledge. Israel Ephal, visiting scholar from Jerusalem, helped me with more than one article in modern Hebrew and was helpful in other ways as well. Dr Douglas Staley helped me with the mathematical portion of my research on orientation. Nell de Boer volunteered her time for proofreading and Vicky Gale ably provided the drawings.

I am grateful also for the editorial comments of Gerald Sheppard, John Webster, and Shelley Schneider, and for the support of David Clines of JSOT Press.

Finally, I should like to thank my wife and colleague, Dr Marion Ann Taylor. To Marion and our children, David, Catherine and Peter, I dedicate this book with love and affection.

J. Glen Taylor

LIST OF PLATES

(Photographs Courtesy Israel Antiquities Authority)

1   a. Taanach cult stand, discovered by Paul Lapp during the 1968 excavations at Tell Taanach (late tenth century BCE). Front view of stand as originally found.

   b. Taanach cult stand. Front and side view of stand (with parts reconstructed; cf. pl. 1a).

   c. Tier three (from top) of Taanach cult stand (cf. pls. 1a and 1b).

   d. Top tier of Taanach cult stand showing quadruped below sun disk (cf. pl. 1a).

2   Royal Judaean jar handle with rosette (late seventh century BCE).

3   Side view of horse with cornucopia-shaped 'disk' between its ears, Jerusalem Cave 1 (seventh century BCE).

4   Front view of horse with cornucopia-shaped 'disk', Jerusalem Cave 1; cf. pl. 3 (same horse).

5   Horse figurine from Iron II period showing typical odd-shaped object between its ears (Holland's 'forelock' type) and noseband.

6   Horse figurine from Iron II period showing abrupt disk-like ending to prominent mane and bridle.

7   Horse figurine from Iron II period showing prominent mane.

8   Horse figurine from Iron II period with odd-shaped headpiece and mane ending abruptly.

LIST OF FIGURES

(Drawings by Vicky Gale, Toronto, Canada)

8   Rider and horse, both broken, Jerusalem Cave 1 (seventh century BCE). Side view showing pie-shaped 'disk', 'disk' support, and other trappings on the horse's nose and cheeks.

9   Horse with headless rider, Tomb 106, Lachish (late seventh to early sixth centuries BCE).

10 Head and neck fragment of horse with 'disk' and bridle pieces, Hazor (mid eighth century BCE).

11 Horse figurine from Amathus, Cyprus, with rider and 'disk' (Cypro-Archaic Period) (cf. A.C. Brown and W.W. Catling, *Ancient Cyprus* [Oxford: Ashmolean Museum, 1975], p. 53).

ABBREVIATIONS

AASOR	Annual of the American Schools of Oriental Research
AB	Anchor Bible
ABRL	Anchor Bible Reference Library
AJSL	*American Journal of Semitic Languages and Literatures*
ANEP	J.B. Pritchard (ed.), *Ancient Near East in Pictures*
ANET	J.B. Pritchard (ed.), *Ancient Near Eastern Texts*
ANRW	*Aufstieg und Niedergang des römischen Welt*
AOAT	Alter Orient und Altes Testament
ArOr	*Archiv orientální*
ARW	*Archiv für Religionswissenschaft*
ATANT	Abhandlungen zur Theologie des Alten und Neuen Testaments
ATD	Das Alte Testament Deutsch
BA	Biblical Aramaic
BA	*Biblical Archaeologist*
BARev	*Biblical Archaeology Review*
BASOR	*Bulletin of the American Schools of Oriental Research*
BDB	F. Brown, S.R. Driver and C.A. Briggs, *Hebrew and English Lexicon of the Old Testament*
BETL	Bibliotheca ephemeridum theologicarum lovaniensium
Bib	*Biblica*
BJS	Brown Judaic Studies
BZAW	Beihefte zur *ZAW*
CAD	*The Assyrian Dictionary of the Oriental Institute of the University of Chicago*
CTM	*Concordia Theological Monthly*
DH	The Deuteronomistic History
DSS	Dead Sea Scrolls
EA	El-Amarna (followed by tablet number)
EAEHL	M. Avi-Yonah and E. Stern (eds.), *Encyclopedia of Archaeological Excavations in the Holy Land*
EI	*Eretz-Israel*
EncMik	*Ensîclôpediâ Miqra'it*
FOTL	The Forms of the Old Testament Literature
FRLANT	Forschungen zur Religion und Literatur des Alten und Neuen Testaments
GKC	*Gesenius' Hebrew Grammar*, ed. E. Kautzsch, trans. A.E. Cowley

HBD	Harper's Bible Dictionary
HDB	J. Hastings (ed.), *A Dictionary of the Bible*
HSM	Harvard Semitic Monographs
HSS	Harvard Semitic Studies
HTR	*Harvard Theological Review*
HTS	Harvard Theological Studies
HUCA	*Hebrew Union College Annual*
IB	*Interpreter's Bible*
ICC	International Critical Commentary
IDB	G.A. Buttrick (ed.), *Interpreter's Dictionary of the Bible*
IDBSup	*IDB*, Supplementary Volume
IEJ	*Israel Exploration Journal*
ISBE	G.W. Bromiley (ed.), *International Standard Bible Encyclopedia*
JAOS	*Journal of the American Oriental Society*
JARCE	*Journal of the American Research Center in Egypt*
JB	Jerusalem Bible
JBL	*Journal of Biblical Literature*
JEA	*Journal of Egyptian Archaeology*
JEOL	*Jaarbericht...ex oriente lux*
JJS	*Journal of Jewish Studies*
JNES	*Journal of Near Eastern Studies*
JNSL	*Journal of Northwest Semitic Languages*
JPOS	*Journal of the Palestine Oriental Society*
JPS	The Jewish Publication Society
JPSV	Jewish Publication Society Version
JSOTSup	*Journal for the Study of the Old Testament*, Supplement Series
KAI	H. Donner and W. Röllig, *Kanaanäische und aramäische Inschriften*
KAR	*Keilschrifttexte aus Assurs religiösen Inhalts*
KAT	Kommentar zum Alten Testament
KB	L. Koehler and W. Baumgartner (eds.), *Lexicon in Veteris Testamenti libros*
KJV	King James Version
KTU	M. Dietrich, O. Loretz and J. Sanmartin (eds.), *Die keilalphabetischen Texte aus Ugarit*
LÄ	*Lexicon der Ägyptologie*
LCL	Loeb Classical Library
MIO	*Mitteilungen des Instituts für Orientforschung*
NASB	New American Standard Bible
NBD	*New Bible Dictionary*
NCB	New Century Bible
NEB	New English Bible
NICOT	New International Commentary on the Old Testament
NIV	New International Version

OBO	Orbis biblicus et orientalis
OCD	*Oxford Classical Dictionary*
OIP	Oriental Institute Publications
OLA	Orientalia lovaniensia analecta
OLP	*Orientalia lovaniensia periodica*
OLZ	*Orientalische Literaturzeitung*
Or	*Orientalia*
OrAnt	*Oriens antiquus*
OTG	Old Testament Guides
OTL	Old Testament Library
OTS	*Oudtestamentische Studiën*
PEQ	*Palestine Exploration Quarterly*
PIA	Publications of the Institute of Archaeology, Tel Aviv University
RA	*Revue d'assyriologie et d'archéologie orientale*
RAI	Rencontre assyriologique internationale
RB	*Revue biblique*
RevScRel	*Revue des sciences religieuses*
RivB	*Rivista biblica*
RS	Ras Shamra (followed by tablet number)
RSO	*Rivista degli studi orientali*
RSV	Revised Standard Version
SBLDS	Society of Biblical Literature Dissertation Series
SBLMS	Society of Biblical Literature Monograph Series
SBT	Studies in Biblical Theology
SOTSMS	Society for Old Testament Study Monograph Series
StudOr	*Studia orientalia*
TA	*Tel Aviv*
THAT	E. Jenni (ed.), *Theologisches Handbuch zum Alten Testament*
TOTC	Tyndale Old Testament Commentaries
TynBul	*Tyndale Bulletin*
UF	*Ugarit-Forschungen*
UT	C.H. Gordon, *Ugaritic Textbook*
VT	*Vetus Testamentum*
VTSup	*Vetus Testamentum*, Supplements
WBC	Word Biblical Commentary
WMANT	Wissenschaftliche Monographien zum Alten und Neuen Testament
WTJ	*Westminster Theological Journal*
ZA	*Zeitschrift für Assyriologie*
ZAW	*Zeitschrift für die alttestamentliche Wissenschaft*
ZDMG	*Zeitschrift der deutschen morgenländischen Gesellschaft*
ZDPV	*Zeitschrift der Deutschen Palästina-Vereins*

Chapter 1

INTRODUCTION

A claim often made within the old Myth and Ritual School of Old Testament interpretation was that solar elements formed an integral part of ancient Israelite religion. Until recently, however, the influence of this claim has been confined largely to the School because of what many scholars consider to be a paucity of evidence in support of the notion.

At least two studies in the 1980s kindled (or rekindled) the interests of mainline scholars of the Old Testament and ancient Israelite religion as the extent to which solar elements might have played a role in Hebrew religion: an article by Morton Smith called 'Helios in Palestine' and a short monograph by H.-P. Stähli entitled *Solare Elemente im Jahweglauben des Alten Testaments*.[1] When added to what has appeared thus far in the 1990s[2] it is safe to say that interest in the relationship between Yahwism and solarism has revived.

The issue of course is not whether sun worship was practised in ancient Israel; several biblical passages leave little room for doubt that sun worship was a well-known phenomenon, practised even within the context of the temple.[3] Rather, the question has two aspects: the nature of sun worship in general, and the relationship (if any) between the cults of the sun and of Yahweh in particular.

---

1. M. Smith, 'Helios in Palestine', *EI* 16 (1982), pp. 199-214; H.-P. Stähli, *Solare Elemente im Jahweglauben des Alten Testaments* (OBO, 66; Freiburg: Universitätsverlag, 1985). See also M.S. Smith, 'The Near Eastern Background of Solar Language for Yahweh', *JBL* 109 (1990), pp. 29-39.

2. In addition to the present work, see, for example, M.S. Smith, *The Early History of God: Yahweh and the Other Deities in Ancient Israel* (New York: Harper & Row, San Francisco, 1990), pp. 115-24.

3. See respectively, 2 Kgs 23.11; Ezek. 8.16. Other passages that refer explicitly to sun worship are Deut. 4.19; 17.3; Jer. 8.2; Job 31.26. Several other passages refer to the worship of the Host of Heaven, often related to the worship of the sun.

Beyond the general accord that sun worship took place in ancient Israel, there is at present no consensus about its nature. This lack of consensus centres around such issues as whether sun worship was early or late, tangential and sporadic or deeply entrenched and unremitting, autochthonous or foreign.

The last issue is particularly interesting because of the important questions that it raises. For example, within the past decade Hermann Spieckermann[1] has challenged the widely accepted view of J.W. McKay and M. Cogan that the horses and chariots of the sun in the Jerusalem temple did not arise under the influence of Assyria.[2] Moreover, whereas Spieckermann has led some scholars to believe again that the royal Jerusalem sun cult was Assyrian,[3] other possibilities remain such as Syro-Palestinian[4] or, a view argued for in this book, Israelite (at least from a practical perspective).

Probably the most provocative issue related to the nature of sun worship in ancient Israel, however, is the specific claim that Yahweh was identified with the sun.[5] For example, according to one proponent of this view, H.-P. Stähli, the following evidence supports such an association: (1) theophoric personal names in which the verb *zārah*, 'rise', normally used of the sun, is predicated of Yahweh; (2) Ps. 84.12 [11] in which Yahweh is called *šemeš*, 'sun'; (3) the solar emblems on the royal Judaean *'lmlk'* jar handles (that is a two-winged sun disk and a four-winged scarab); (4) correspondences between Hebrew *ṣdq*, 'righteousness', and concepts which in Egypt

1. H. Spieckermann, *Juda unter Assur in der Sargonidenzeit* (FRLANT; Göttingen: Vandenhoeck & Ruprecht, 1982).

2. J. McKay, *Religion in Judah under the Assyrians* (SBT, 2/26; Naperville, IL: A.R. Allenson, 1973), pp. 32-35; M. Cogan, *Imperialism and Religion* (SBLMS, 19; Missoula, MT: Scholars Press, 1974).

3. The influence of Spieckermann on recent exegesis of 2 Kgs 23.11 is evident, for example, in the commentary of E. Würthwein, *Die Bücher der Könige: 1.Kön. 17–2.Kön.25* (ATD, 11, 2; Göttingen: Vandenhoeck & Ruprecht, 1984), p. 459.

4. McKay, *Religion in Judah*, pp. 32-35.

5. J. Morgenstern and G. Ahlström are among the more prominent earlier proponents of a direct association between Yahweh and the sun. Many of Morgenstern's ideas about Yahweh and the sun are drawn together in his work entitled *The Fire upon the Altar* (Chicago, IL: Quadrangle Books, 1963). (For specific studies of Morgenstern, see later in this study.) In the case of Ahlström, see, for example, his *Psalm 89: Eine Liturgie aus dem Ritual des leidenden Königs* (Lund: C.W.K. Gleerup, 1959), p. 86.

and Mesopotamia are linked with the sun god[1]; and (5) references to both Heliopolis and Jerusalem as 'city of righteousness'.[2]

To be sure, no justice has been done to Stähli's case for a close link between Yahweh and the sun by offering a list so brief and partial. Even on the basis of this partial list, however, there are many points that one might wish to challenge. Moreover, it is fair to say that, on the whole, the book falls short of offering a fully convincing case for extensive overlapping between the cults of Yahweh and the sun.[3] This is not to say, however, that several of the points raised by Stähli (along with other points which he does not include) do not merit serious consideration.

Prevailing uncertainty regarding the relationship between the worship of Yahweh and the sun in ancient Israel may be illustrated further by noting a number of incongruities and interpretive and methodological problems. To cite a general example, studies prior to the 1980s that sought to establish the presence of a sun cult within ancient Israelite religion are impressive by virtue of their sheer numbers as well as the great variety of arguments which each adduces. At the same time, however, many of these studies have often been judged unimpressive by virtue of the presence of what many have referred to as 'fanciful' exegesis and conclusions which far exceed the evidence.[4] Similarly, whereas there is a considerable amount of archaeological evidence which is potentially relevant to the issue—for example, horse figurines bearing 'sun disks', the royal *lmlk* jar handles, seals from the Achaemenid period depicting bulls with sun disks[5]—this evidence has not always been considered or dealt with

1. For example, the fact that 'righteousness' precedes Yahweh in Ps. 85.14 [13] is compared with Egyptian literature in which Maat goes before the sun god Re (Stähli, *Solare Elemente*, p. 45).

2. Respectively, Isa. 19.18 and 1.26 (Stähli, *Solare Elemente*, pp. 39-45).

3. See, among others, my review of Stähli's book in *JAOS* 111 (1991), pp. 128-31.

4. For criticisms, see for example, McKay, *Religion in Judah*, pp. 114-15 n. 78; Johann Maier, 'Die Sonne im religiösen Denken des antiken Judentums', *ANRW*, II, 19/1, p. 351; and, in the case of Morgenstern (against whom the criticism of fanciful exegesis is perhaps most often levelled), Stähli, *Solare Elemente*, pp. 6-7.

5. Examples of other possibly suggestive data are eastward facing temples at Arad, Beer-sheba, and Lachish (including the so-called Solar Shrine). (For

judiciously. Moreover, even among professional archaeologists of Syria-Palestine there are differences of opinion about how to assess these and other archaeological data that possibly suggest the presence of solar elements within the cult. Finally, although Stähli has attempted to demonstrate the presence of a conflict between Yahweh and the sun within the history of Israelite religion, his work, some fifty pages in length, is more a helpful introduction to the problem of the interrelationship between the cults of Yahweh and the sun than an exhaustive treatment of the subject.

Although these factors are perhaps sufficient alone to justify a fresh study of the role of sun worship in ancient Israel, a number of other considerations call for the study as well. To date there has been no full-scale study devoted solely to the problem of sun worship in ancient Israel.[1] Moreover, even though scholars have often used archaeological evidence in discussing possible points of interaction between a sun cult in ancient Israel and the cult of Yahweh, to my knowledge this evidence has never been scrutinized as a whole with a view to addressing this problem in the history of Israelite religion. The same situation prevails in the case of the biblical evidence.

It is the purpose of this book, then, to study the archaeological and biblical evidence that bears on sun worship in ancient Israel, and to focus in particular on the relationship between the cult of Yahweh and worship of the sun. Moreover, since during the course of research I found that relationship to be quite close (even to the extent that the sun was identified with Yahweh), this study is also in effect an early attempt to articulate some of the more important aspects of the nature and history of what Zimmerli has already tentatively called a 'solar interpretation of Yahweh'.[2]

---

references, see the discussion of temple orientation offered in the next chapter.)

1.   The few studies that have been done on solar elements in Hebrew religion tend to focus either on a later period or on an early period while nonetheless drawing in large measure from evidence of that later period. A case of the former is the work of Maier ('Die Sonne') which devotes only three pages to biblical material and some sixty to early and talmudic Judaism. Cases of the latter are the works of Smith ('Helios in Palestine') and, to a lesser extent, Stähli (*Solare Elemente*).

2.   W. Zimmerli, *Ezekiel I* (trans. R.E. Clements; Hermeneia; Philadelphia: Fortress Press, 1979 [1969]), p. 244. (Zimmerli prefaced his remark with the word 'possibly'.)

The book contains four chapters, including this Introduction and the Conclusion. Chapter 2 is a study of archaeological evidence that is possibly suggestive of a relationship between the worship of the sun and the worship of Yahweh in ancient Israel. Chapter 3 is a study of the biblical evidence and includes an examination of the following: (1) all passages explicitly referring to the worship of the sun; (2) passages or topics that seem helpful for discerning at least in broad terms the nature and history of solar Yahwism.

Chapter 2

ARCHAEOLOGICAL EVIDENCE

Among the rich insights that archaeology can provide is its own portrait of sun worship in ancient Israel. This portrait, clear and bright in some places, faint and almost unintelligible in others, must be weighed carefully for its contribution to the understanding of the relationship between Yahweh and the sun in ancient Israel.

The purpose of this chapter is to examine carefully the archaeological evidence that has been used (or, in the case of neglected evidence, should be used) to contribute to the present state of the question concerning the presence of solar elements within ancient Israelite religion. Each line of evidence is examined in turn, starting with a tenth-century cult stand from Taanach.

A Cult Stand from Tell Taanach

Important artefactual evidence suggestive of the presence of sun worship in ancient Israel is a cult stand found during the 1968 excavations at Tell Taanach, on the southern side of the Valley of Jezreel, some five miles southeast of Megiddo. The stand will be considered in some detail.[1]

---

1. Discussions of this stand may be found in the following sources: W.G. Dever, 'Asherah, Consort of Yahweh? New Evidence from Kuntillet 'Ajrûd', *BASOR* 255 (1984), p. 33 n. 24; A.E. Glock, 'Taanach', *EAEHL* 4 (1978), p. 1147; *idem*, 'Taanach', *IDBSup*, pp. 855-56; R. Hestrin, 'Canaanite Cult Stand', in J.P. O'Neill (ed.), *Treasures of the Holy Land: Ancient Art from the Israel Museum* (New York: Metropolitan Museum of Art, 1986), pp. 161-63; *idem*, 'The Cult Stand from Ta'anach and its Religious Background', in E. Lipiński (ed.), *Studia Phoenicia V: Phoenicia and the East Mediterranean in the First Millennium B.C., Proceedings of the Conference Held in Leuven from the 14th to the 16th of November 1985* (OLA, 22; Leuven: Peeters, 1987), pp. 61-77; P.W. Lapp, 'A Ritual Incense Stand from Taanak', *Qadmoniot* 2 (1969), pp. 16-17 [Hebrew];

Description

First, a description of the stand is in order (see pls. 1a, 1b). The item is made of clay and is slightly more than half a metre in height. This tall rectangular stand is hollow and divided into four separate tiers, each of which depicts a cultic scene with crudely fashioned figures: animals, deities, and architectural features clearly characteristic of a temple (for example, on the top tier, free-standing columns and what appear to be altars). Unlike the front and sides, the back of the stand bears no images, but is smooth and contains two roughly square-shaped holes which remind one of fenestration typical in other cult stands.[1]

At the front and centre in the bottom tier (tier four, numbered from the top down) is a nude female figurine with arms outstretched, each extending to the ears of lions (perhaps lionesses[2]) which stand on either side of her and the sides of whose bodies are portrayed on the sides of the stand.[3] Lions identical to those found on this fourth or bottom tier (and in a similar flanking position) are found on the second tier from the top and between these lions and at the centre is a pair of ibex with legs extending into a 'tree of life'. No central figure analogous to the nude female in tier four or the sacred tree in tier two is found on the third tier, but, like these other tiers, there is on either side of this central (vacant) section a pair of animals, this time winged sphinxes/cherubim, again with body sides portrayed on the sides of the tier (see pls. 1a–1c). On the top or first tier, a pair of voluted columns stands where the flanking animals were found on each of the three

idem, 'The 1968 Excavations at Tell Ta'annek', *BASOR* 195 (1969), pp. 42-44; W.A. Maier, III, *'Ašerah: Extrabiblical Evidence* (HSM, 37; Atlanta: Scholars Press, 1986), p. 168; and, most recently, Smith, *Early History of God*, pp. 19-20. (An earlier version of the present discussion appeared in the form of an article entitled 'The Two Earliest Known Representations of Yahweh', in L. Eslinger and J.G. Taylor (eds.), *Ascribe to the Lord: Biblical and other studies in memory of P.C. Craigie* [JSOTSup, 67; Sheffield: JSOT Press, 1988], pp. 557-66; cf. also J.G. Taylor, 'Yahweh and Asherah at Tenth Century Taanach', *Newsletter for Ugaritic Studies* 37-38 [April–October 1987], pp. 16-18.)

    1.   For a photo, see Hestrin, 'Cult Stand from Ta'anach', p. 64, fig. 3.

    2.   Hestrin, relying on the analysis of E. Černov (but see p. 32 n. 2 below), judges the animals portrayed on the sides of both tiers two and four to be lionesses rather than lions because of the absence of a mane ('Cult Stand from Ta'anach', p. 65; see also p. 31 n. 2 below.)

    3.   See Hestrin, 'Cult Stand from Ta'anach', p. 66, fig. 4.

tiers below. At the centre of this top tier is the side view of a loping quadruped above which is a winged sun disk (see pl. 1d). On each of the two sides of this tier is a side view of a winged griffin (cf. pl. 1b).[1] Finally, at the very top of this stand and immediately above tier one is a shallow square-shaped basin with rims decorated on the outside with button-like emblems.

Archaeological and Historical Background
The cult stand was found at the bottom of a cistern shaft in the cultic area in the southwest quadrant of the tell.[2] Due to a soft layer of silt below, the stand survived remarkably well a fall of ten metres down the shaft and a subsequent downpour of collapsed bedrock into which the cistern was originally cut.[3] A cylindrical cult stand, chalices and sherds (all of which were found lying in the same silt deposit as the present cult stand) identify all of these objects with a nearby cache of cultic objects dating to the late tenth century BCE and covered by a destruction layer attributed to the campaign of Shishak.[4] This nearby cache, discovered five years earlier by Lapp, was found in a storeroom which, together with a virtually empty room to the north and probably an olive press two metres to the east of the storeroom, are all that remains of the cultic area.[5] Objects in the storeroom include the following: a mould for the mass production of a female figurine bearing a tambourine,[6] at least sixty 'loom weights',[7] spindle

---

1. See Hestrin, 'Cult Stand from Ta'anach', p. 63, fig. 2.
2. Lapp, '1968 Excavations', p. 42.
3. Lapp, '1968 Excavations', p. 42; *idem*, 'Ritual Incense Stand', p. 16.
4. P.W. Lapp, 'The 1963 Excavation at Ta'annek', *BASOR* 173 (1964), p. 28; *idem*, '1968 Excavations', p. 42; *idem*, 'Ritual Incense Stand', p. 16.
5. On the archaeological context of the cultic area, see Lapp, '1963 Excavation', pp. 26-32, 35-39; *idem*, 'Taanach by the Waters of the Megiddo', *BA* 30 (1967), pp. 17-27.
6. R. Amiran ('A Note on Figurines with "Disks"', *EI* 8 [1967], pp. 99-100 [English summary, p. *71]) has argued that female figurines traditionally thought to be clasping a tambourine should properly be regarded as clasping a sun disk in light of the discovery at Nimrud of an ivory plaque with a disk which she identifies as a sun disk. Indeed, the finds at Nimrud attest to the presence of a winged sun disk with a female head (e.g. M.E.L. Mallowan, *Nimrud and its Remains* [2 vols.; London: Collins, 1966], p. 497, figs. 392-94). However, the Nimrud female (known only on a plaque and not as a figurine) bears little resemblance to the female figurines clasping sun disks/tambourines. Moreover, these same discoveries at

whorls, storage jars containing grain, 140 astragali of sheep or goats,[1] bowls, cooking pots, a censer, at least seven knife blades, a sickle blade, eight stone pestles, several stelae, a mace head, a toggle pin, a stand and beads.[2]

Although it is possible that some of these features served a domestic purpose, it is preferable to see the objects in the storeroom and the olive press as facilities for the production (and perhaps sale) of items needed within the cult.[3] Thus understood, the 'loom weights' and numerous spindle whorls could reflect the use of priestly garb, and the olive press could indicate equally well the need of oil for lamps, grain offerings or both.[4] The various cooking pots suggest consumption and the knives intimate sacrifice or circumcision (or both).[5] The figurine mould is also well suited to the interpretation that the stand was part of a major cultic installation.[6]

Nimrud also attest to the widespread representation of females bearing tambourines (R.D. Barnett, *A Catalogue of the Nimrud Ivories* [London: British Museum Publications, 2nd edn, 1975], pls. 16-17). Finally, D.R. Hillers ('The Goddess with a Tambourine', *CTM* 41 (1970), pp. 606-19) has responded adequately to several criticisms of the notion that these figurines bear tambourines and points further to one unambiguous case from Tell el-Farah (north) in which a female figurine has the right hand extended over the round object as if to strike it like a tambourine (Hillers, 'Goddess with a Tamourine', p. 98, fig. 5). At present, then, it is best to consider the female as bearing a tambourine rather than a sun disk or some other object.

7.   L.E. Stager and S.R. Wolff, 'Production and Commerce in Temple Courtyards', *BASOR* 243 (1981), p. 98. J.P. Dessel informs me that the identification of these items as loom weights is uncertain.

1.   That the astragali are those of pigs should no longer be maintained (see, for example, Stager and Wolff, 'Temple Courtyards', p. 100 n. 7).

2.   Lapp, '1963 Excavation', pp. 28, 35-37; Glock, 'Taanach', p. 1147.

3.   See Stager and Wolff, 'Temple Courtyards', pp. 98-100.

4.   Stager and Wolff ('Temple Courtyards', pp. 98-100) note the use of holy garb at Kuntillet 'Ajrûd, and argue for the presence of other olive installations used for the purposes stated above at Dan, and, probably, Tell el-Farah (north).

5.   Lapp, 'By the Waters', p. 25.

6.   According to Lapp ('By the Waters', p. 23), assuming that the basin-like structure (now thought to be the olive press) and the incense stand found earlier by E. Sellin are associated with the cache (which Lapp elsewhere states as being probable), 'it seems preferable to envision an entire building devoted to cult rather than a few rooms with stored cult material in an otherwise secular building'. The judgment that the olive press and nearby cultic remains at Taanach likely reflect a large-scale

A second factor relating to the context concerns the role of Taanach in the late tenth century. According to 1 Kgs 4.12, Taanach was the headquarters for Baana, the administrator who was directly respons-ible to Solomon for the administration of the king's fifth district which also included most of the plain of Jezreel as far east as Beth-shan and a good deal of the western Jordan valley south of Beth-shan.[1] Thus, although it may be that there is no more connection between this cult centre and Solomon beyond this indirect administrative link, it is possible that the cult centre at Taanach functioned under royal administrative sanction.

Interpretation

The interpretation advocated in the present study is as follows. First, Y. Yadin's suggestion[2] that the tiers represent temple scenes is almost certainly correct; his view can be supported from the box- or building-like shape of each tier, and, more importantly, from the free-standing pillars flanking the quadruped-and-sun on the top tier (that is, tier one). Moreover, the pillars on the top tier, which are clearly an architectural feature, set a clear precedent for also under-standing the lions or cherubim in the same flanking position in the tiers below as architectural features, an interpretation clearly support-able from the fact that both free-standing pillars and large animal orthostats are characteristic of Syro-Palestinian temple architecture.[3] The pillars, lionesses and cherubim on these tiers thus 'house' the deities represented by the winged sun above the quadruped (tier one), the sacred tree (tier two) and the nude female (tier four).[4]

Secondly, as noted already, there is general agreement that the same deity, Asherah, is represented in tiers two and four; the figures of the sacred tree with ibex in tier two and the nude female in tier four are

---

cultic installation has also been expressed by L.E. Stager (personal communication).

1. Y. Aharoni, *The Land of the Bible* (Philadelphia: Westminster Press, rev. edn, 1979), p. 313.

2. Cited in Lapp, '1968 Excavations', p. 44.

3. See further Lapp, '1968 Excavations', p. 44. For a few examples, see *ANEP*, figs. 644, 646-47, and Y. Yadin *et al.*, *Hazor I* (Jerusalem: Magnes, 1958), pls. 29-30, 181.

4. The problem of the absence of a deity in tier three will be addressed later in this section.

two common ways of representing Asherah.[1] Moreover, as Dever has noted, Asherah is referred to as the 'lion-lady',[2] and this corresponds extremely well with the lionesses chosen to flank the deity on these two tiers. Furthermore, to make it clear to the observer that the same deity is represented on tiers two and four, albeit in two different ways, the lioness pairs flanking the deity on each of these tiers are almost identical.[3] Thus, although the sacred tree (clearly Asherah) and the nude female might independently represent different deities (in the case of the nude female, Astarte, for example), the only deity likely to be represented as *both* nude female and sacred tree, in each case flanked by virtually identical pairs of lionesses, is Asherah.

To this point in time the identity of the deities represented on tiers one and three has proved problematic. The following observations, based on the structure of the stand itself, are consonant with the view that the deity represented on these two tiers is in fact Yahweh. Tiers three and one are examined in turn.

In tier three (see pl. 1c) there is an exception to a clear pattern noted in all other tiers. Unlike the other tiers, it contains no representation of a deity between the architectural features appropriate for that deity (as was seen, for example, in the case of Asherah between the lioness orthostats on tiers two and four). In tier three, then, the deity one expects to find between the two cherubim is notably 'absent'. Moreover, as a close examination of the stand reveals, the central deity is not just missing, but in fact was never portrayed. In view of the pattern just observed, the following question may be asked: What west-Semitic deity might be represented at Israelite Taanach in the late tenth century BCE by an 'invisible' deity posed between two cherubim? A clear answer, of course, is immediately apparent: 'Yahweh of Hosts who dwells (between) the cherubim'.[4] Consideration

---

1. See, for example, Hestrin, 'Cult Stand from Ta'anach', pp. 67-71, 74. Further on Asherah, see J. Day, 'Asherah in the Hebrew Bible and Northwest Semitic Literature', *JBL* 105 (1986), pp. 385-408, esp. 403-406; Maier, *'Ašerah*; and S.M. Olyan, *Asherah and the Cult of Yahweh in Israel* (SBLMS, 34; Atlanta: Scholars Press, 1988).

2. Dever, 'Consort of Yahweh?', p. 33 n. 24; cf. Hestrin, 'Cult Stand from Ta'anach', pp. 67-71.

3. The same argument has been made independently by Hestrin, 'Cult Stand from Ta'anach', p. 77.

4. In light of the present interpretation, the words of T. Mettinger regarding the

of the structure of the stand, its Yahwistic context,[1] and its iconography, then, strongly suggest that tier three is an iconographic
representation of Yahweh of Hosts, the unseen God who resides
among the cherubim, the earliest 'representation' of Yahweh known in
the archaeological record.

Finally, how is tier one to be interpreted (pl. 1d)? No interpretation
can be offered without determining first the identity of the quadruped
below the winged sun disk, and here a debate arises about whether
the animal is a calf or an equid.[2] For example, according to
R. Hestrin of the Israel Museum, the quadruped on the top tier is a
calf[3] (which she interprets as Baal-Hadad).[4] However, upon consulting
two experts in the study of large mammals, C.S. Churcher and

aniconic God in ancient Israel are noteworthy: 'The official cult was early [that is,
early monarchic, the time of the Taanach cult stand] aniconic: over the cherub throne
and ark, the god of Israel was enthroned in unseen majesty. The place usually
occupied by the deity is empty' (T. Mettinger, 'The Veto on Images and the
Aniconic God in Ancient Israel', in H. Biezas [ed.], *Religious Symbols and their
Functions* [Uppsala: Almqvist & Wiksell, 1979], p. 27).

    1.   On the basis of Judg. 1.27 a few scholars (e.g. J.H. Tigay, *You Shall Have
No Other Gods* [HSS, 31; Atlanta: Scholars Press, 1986], pp. 92-93) have raised
the notion that the cult stand might have belonged to a 'Canaanite' population rather
than an Israelite group, as W.G. Dever and others maintain. However, as A. Mazar
has noted recently, although some of the unconquered cities mentioned in Judg.
1.27-35 and Josh. 13.2-6 show the presence of Canaanite culture with elements
characteristic of the Sea Peoples in the Iron I Period, Taanach is not among them. In
Mazar's words, 'at Taanach the Canaanite city seems to have been destroyed at the
end of the Late Bronze Age and replaced by an Israelite village' (A. Mazar,
Archaeology of the Land of the Bible [ABRL; Doubleday: New York, 1990],
p. 333). In short, I am aware of no dispute among archaeologists concerning the
essentially Israelite character of Taanach by the *late* tenth century, the time of the cult
stand (cf. Josh. 12.21a, 21.25a; 1 Kgs 4.12). Whilst this does not rule out entirely
the possibility that the shrine might still belong to some Canaanite enclave within the
city, the imagery of tier three of an invisible deity in association with two cherubim
is, at least to my mind, unmistakably characteristic for an *Israelite* group of the early
monarchic period.

    2.   The opinion of Lapp ('1968 Excavations', p. 44) and Hestrin (for which see
the next footnote), for example, is that it is a calf; the view of Glock ('Taanach',
p. 1147) is that the animal is an equid.

    3.   Hestrin, 'Cult Stand from Ta'anach', p. 67 n. 7.

    4.   Hestrin, 'Canaanite Cult Stand', pp. 161-63; *idem*, 'Cult Stand from
Ta'anach', p. 75.

P.W. Physick-Sheard,[1] each judged independently and with a reasonable degree of certainty that the animal was an equine creature rather than a bovine animal.[2] On the basis of anatomical[3] and other

1. The former is Professor of Zoology at the University of Toronto and of Vertebrate Paleontology at the Royal Ontario Museum, Toronto, and has published a number of articles that consider the depicting of large mammals in ancient Near Eastern art. The latter is Professor in the Department of Clinical Studies at the Ontario Veterinary College, University of Guelph, Ontario, and a specialist in large mammals such as cows and horses. Both were given a four-by-six-inch photograph of the front panel of the top tier (pl. 1d), as well as a photo of the whole stand (courtesy of the Israel Antiquities Authority).

2. Note, for example, the prominent hooves, and tail not roped and hairy only at the end as on a calf, but hairy to the croup as on a horse. The following are important excerpts from the written evaluation of Physick–Sheard: 'The animal on the stand has a tail whose fullness from the base would suggest a member of the equidae... [Regarding the ears,] their relatively erect position would be most compatible with an equine rather than a bovine. Ears on all ungulates are positioned laterally... The animal appears to have rather a long muzzle and a strong angle to the jaw, features which are more prominent features of equidae than bovidae. The flat upper part of the head from forehead to muzzle also implies an equid... In summary... the impression given on general examination is that of a calf. However, critical evaluation of several individual features and some interpretation leads me to suggest that this is an equine figure, though somewhat crude.' (Physick-Sheard's statement, 'the impression given on general examination is that of a calf', was probably made in deference to those who regard the animal as a young bull.) Regarding the opinion of Hestrin (personal communication) that the bony protrusion of the head above the eyes is typical in depictions of calves in ancient Near Eastern art, this protrusion appears to be simply the breadth of the forehead shown in an attempt to portray more than a simple side view of the head as is indicated by the depiction of both ears.

    Even if the quadruped were a calf, an association with Yahweh would by no means be ruled out, a point argued in an earlier version of this research read at the Albright Institute and also expressed by D.N. Freedman in a letter written on 26 January 1988: 'Even if the animal in question were a bull, that would hardly weaken the case for identification with Yahweh, whose animal symbols, especially in the northern kingdom, were precisely "calves," that is, immature bulls (hence the absence of horns)'. (Freedman adds, 'I think you are right that only Asherah is represented in this stand, and the male deity is Yahweh'.)

3. Hestrin admits, 'Some scholars have suggested in discussions that it [the "bull"] should be identified as a horse', but responds, 'but an important element—the mane—is missing' ('Cult Stand from Ta'anach', 67 n. 7). The response, however, is based upon *one* criterion, the mane, which could have been omitted in a crude portrayal (note that only on assumption that the animals on tiers two and four are

fairly objective considerations,[1] then, the animal may be judged to be an equid, a view supported by all the animal experts who have examined the stand thus far.[2]

When the less popular view that the animal is an equid is now taken seriously, there arises a clear and rather obvious biblical parallel to the Yahwistic scene on the top tier of the stand, 2 Kgs 23.11, part of the description of the Deuteronomistic reform programme:

> And he [Josiah] removed the horses that the kings of Judah had dedicated to the sun, at the entrance to the house of the Lord, by the chamber of Nathan-melech the chamberlain, which was in the precincts; and he burned the chariots of the sun with fire.[3]

More will be said about 2 Kgs 23.11 in the next chapter; suffice it to observe here that the scene depicted on the top tier of the cult stand is remarkably similar to the scene described in this passage. Points of commonality include a monarchic Israelite context, association with a shrine (in each case with two free-standing pillars, and association more specifically with the 'entrance'[4] of the shrine), and the

---

'lionesses' can one argue that manes were not similarly left off the *lions*). In either case, as the preceding footnote makes clear, a combination of several factors strongly favours the identification of the animal in question as a horse.

1.   For one thing, based upon the well-known solar affinities of the griffin, a sun horse is more likely to appear in association with it than a young bull. (By contrast, Hestrin's case for a link between the griffin and Baal ['Cult Stand from Ta'anach', p. 76] is somewhat tenuous [but see ahead notes on the griffin].) And secondly, several problems have been raised recently with the notion, implied by Hestrin's analysis, of a close link between Baal and Asherah in the Iron Age (see, for example, Olyan, *Asherah and the Cult of Yahweh*, pp. 38-61). Rather, the evidence at present points towards an affinity between Yahweh and Asherah in the same period.

2.   Although Hestrin ('Cult Stand from Ta'anach', p. 65 n. 5) strongly implies indebtedness to Professor E. Černov of the Hebrew University for the identification of the animal as a 'calf', Černov denies ever having examined any of the animals on the stand (oral communication).

3.   RSV. The Hebrew text reads: *wayyašbēt 'et hassûsîm 'ašer nāt*ᵉ*nû malkê yᵉhûdâ laššemeš mibbō' bêt YHWH 'el liškat nᵉtan melek hassārîs 'ašer bapparwārîm wᵉ'et markᵉbôt haššemeš śārap bā'ēš.*

4.   2 Kgs 23.11 locates the horse at the *mibbō'* 'entrance' to the temple (on which see the discussion in Chapter 3). Similarly, the free-standing pillars (to which Hestrin compares the pillars Jachin and Boaz of the Solomonic temple) situate the horse in the cult stand at a point just outside the temple. Note also that the forehead, muzzle, and left-front leg appear to place the Taanach horse in front of the pillars and

prominence of a horse or horses in relation to a cult involving the sun. When in the case of the Taanach cult stand one adds to these affinities with 2 Kgs 23.11 less obvious imagery relating specifically to chariots of the sun[1] as well as other imagery linking the stand with the temple of Solomon (that is, tier three), it is reasonable to suppose that the top tier of the Taanach cult stand is a precursor from Solomonic times of a Yahwistic solar rite that has been attested so far for the Jerusalem temple only as late as the seventh century BCE.[2]

There are other reasons for supposing that tier one is a cultic scene in which Yahweh is represented by the sun. First, in light of the Yahwistic context in which the stand was found, it is logical to suppose that there would be in the top (and thus, presumably, the most important) tier[3] a cultic scene representing Yahweh. Secondly, that Yahweh is featured on top of the stand is suggested by the structure of the stand; since the same deity (Asherah) is represented on alternate tiers two and four, one naturally expects the pattern of alternation to continue through the representation of the same deity (Yahweh) on the other pair of alternate tiers, one and three.[4] Thirdly, as is well known,

---

not between them. Thus, whereas the sun itself was perhaps thought to reside in the temple, the equid is outside, at the entrance to the temple.

1. I refer to the presence of griffins on the sides of the top tier which were understood to draw the chariot of the sun god (E.R. Goodenough, *Jewish Symbols in the Greco-Roman Period* [13 vols.; Bollingen Series, 37; Princeton, NJ: Princeton University Press, 1953–1968), VIII, p. 145). (Further on the griffin, see notes ahead.) At any rate, the presence of the imagery of a chariot drawing the sun god akin to that found in 2 Kgs 23.11 appears to be assured by the presence of the griffin as well as the equid.

2. Although scholars often attribute the presence of the horses and chariot(s) to Manasseh, DH itself attributes these solar apparatuses to the 'kings' (plural) of Judah, implying a long-standing tradition. (DH of course seems to implicate Manasseh wherever possible, but not here.) (See further the discussion of sun worship in DH, Chapter 3.)

3. Interestingly, Hestrin also assumed the top tier to be the most important, though indicative of Baal ('Cult Stand from Ta'anach', pp. 75, 77). Her statement, 'the winged sun-disk symbolized the supreme god in the Mesopotamian, Hittite and Canaanite pantheons' ('Cult Stand from Ta'anach', p. 75) might apply no less in the case of the God of Israel.

4. The pattern of alternation may be even more specific: just as Asherah was portrayed 'in person' and in symbol on the alternate tiers four and two respectively, so, too, Yahweh is depicted 'in person' and in symbol on the alternate tiers three and one.

the pairing of Yahweh and Asherah (or asherah, but in either case a reference to the deity) is attested at a later period on inscriptions from both Kuntillet 'Ajrûd[1] and Khirbet el-Qôm.[2] Fourthly, the earliest written testimony to the nature of Yahwism in the area of Taanach, Judges 5, shows evidence of an intense struggle with mythological notions associated with Canaanite deities and goes so far as to describe Yahwism in astral (though not specifically solar) terms (cf. the sun disk in tier one).[3] Finally, in view of the presence of both Yahweh and Asherah on the other tiers of this stand, not to have Yahweh portrayed on the top and most prominent tier would be strange indeed. Thus, whilst it may be difficult to recognize Yahweh in this depiction which predates Deuteronomistic censoring (compare 2 Kgs 23.11 nonetheless), there are good reasons to identify him with the imagery on the top tier of the Taanach stand.

A final means of testing this interpretation of the top tier is offered by the griffin, the animal chosen to complete the scene with horse, temple entrance and sun. Are the mythological connotations associated with the griffin consistent with the view that the top tier represents a deity with a solar character? The following overview suggests that they are.

Attested in Mesopotamia as early as the beginning of the third millennium BCE, and represented later across the ancient Near East

---

1.   The bibliography on these inscriptions and the controversy they have generated are now immense. On the reading of the *'šrth* at Kuntillet 'Ajrûd as 'his [that is, Yahweh's] Asherah [or, perhaps preferably, asherah]', see the recent overviews of Olyan, *Asherah and the Cult of Yahweh*, pp. 23-37, and Smith, *Early History of God*, pp. 85-88.

2.   See for example Dever, 'Consort of Yahweh?', pp. 21-22, 30-32. On the reading *lyhwh* and *l'šrth* in the el-Qôm inscription, see, for example, A. Lemaire, 'Les inscriptions de Khirbet el-Qôm et l'ashérah de YHWH', *RB* 84 (1977), pp. 597-608; J. Naveh, 'Graffiti and Dedications', *BASOR* 235 (1979), pp. 27-30.

3.   Judg. 5.20. (Note also the mention of 'new gods' in v. 8 and the specific mention of 'sun' in v. 31 which, though probably later than the poem itself, was clearly deemed appropriate.) On the presence of Canaanite imagery in the Song of Deborah, see, for example, P.C. Craigie, 'Deborah and Anat: A Study of Poetic Imagery (Judges 5)', *ZAW* 90 (1978), pp. 374-81; S.G. Dempster, 'Mythology and History in the Song of Deborah', *WTJ* 41 (1978), pp. 33-53; J.G. Taylor, 'The Song of Deborah and Two Canaanite Goddesses', *JSOT* 23 (1982), pp. 99-108; and S. Ackerman's paper, 'Baal, Anat and the Song of Deborah', read at the 1990 Annual Meeting of the Society of Biblical Literature.

and the Graeco-Roman world, the griffin[1] conveyed a broad range of notions.[2] Fortunately for the present purpose, the context in which the griffins occur on the Taanach cult stand limits the range of probable significances to two. First, Börker notes that in Syria the griffin is associated with fertility, as evidenced for example in the portrayal of a griffin on a bowl from Ugarit.[3] This association is possibly relevant to the cult stand in view of the presence on tiers two and four of Asherah, a goddess associated with fertility. Secondly, the griffin has a clear and widespread affinity with solar deities,[4] including the notion,

1. Among the more important works on the early history and significance of the griffin are the following: W. Barta, 'Der Greif als bildhafter Ausdruck einer altägyptischen Religionsvorstellung', *JEOL* 23 (1973–74), pp. 335-57; A.M. Bisi, *Il grifone: Storia di un motivo iconografico nell'antico oriente meditteraneo* (Studi semitici, 13; Rome: Centro di studi semitici, 1965); J. Börker, 'Greif', *Reallexicon der Assyriologie*, III, pp. 633-39; Ingeborg Flagge, *Untersuchungen zur Bedeutung des Greifen* (Sankt Augustin: H. Richarz, 1975). On the role of the griffin in Egypt, see E. Eggebrecht, 'Greif', *LÄ* 2 (1977), pp. 895-96. For a convenient summary of the griffin as a Jewish symbol, see also Goodenough, *Jewish Symbols*, VIII, pp. 142-46.

2. See especially Barta, 'Der Greif', pp. 348-57; Börker, 'Greif', pp. 636-39; and Flagge, *Untersuchungen*. In addition to the ideas conveyed by the griffin, the beast also attends or represents the following deities: Osiris, Seth and Horus in the Egyptian realm; and Sol-Helios, Dionysius, Nemesis and (especially) Apollo in the Graeco-Roman world.

3. Börker ('Greif', p. 638) also mentions that in Crete the griffin is associated with the *potnia thērōn*, 'mistress of wild beasts'.

4. For example, W. Barta ('Der Greif', p. 356) argues that in ancient Egypt the griffin, the mightiest beast on earth and unrivalled recompenser, was thought to be the incarnation of the sun deity and the executor of this god's will on earth. Barta bases his conviction primarily on a demotic papyrus of the second century CE in which this identification is made, but he also feels that this identification existed in earlier periods as well. For the text, see W. Spiegelberg (ed.), *Der ägyptische Mythus vom Sonnenauge nach dem leidener demotischen Papyrus I 384* (2 vols.; Strassburg: R. Schultz, 1917), pp. 38-41 (cols. 14.13–15.24). When this evidence is combined with the witness of the cult stand which puts the sun and griffin together in the same temple scene, it is reasonable to judge that here the griffin plays one of its known roles in association with the solar deity, such as protector, 'executor of the will of the sun god' or even symbol of the sun itself (cf. Eggebrecht, 'Greif', p. 895).

Many scholars of course have drawn attention to an association between griffins and the solar deity in Greek mythology, where griffins are most commonly associated with Apollo. That Apollo was eventually identified with the sun god is

though attested so far only at a later period, of drawing the chariot of the sun god. This is even more relevant because the griffin shares the top tier with an equid and the sun. Thus, if my interpretation is correct that the top tier portrays a deity with solar traits, a griffin is precisely the kind of animal that we might expect to complete the scene conveyed on the top tier.[1]

In my judgment, then, the iconography of the Taanach cult stand is an early monarchic representation of Yahweh and Asherah, the former of whom is conveyed alternatively by means of an invisible deity posed between two cherubim, classical imagery of the temple in biblical tradition, and by means of the sun along with one of the horses that drew it in a chariot, imagery reluctantly admitted by DH (but to its credit) for the temple of Yahweh in 2 Kgs 23.11. While I do not expect this interpretation to be widely accepted without reference to evidence adduced elsewhere in this book, at this early point in the present study it is perhaps worth asking, in the case of 2 Kgs 23.11, what deity other than Yahweh would be drawn by the 'chariots of the sun'—not a recent innovation of Manasseh, at least according to v. 11—at the entrance to his own temple? And similarly in the case of the Taanach cult stand, what deity other than Yahweh would be represented on the top tier of the cult stand, have his cult symbols form an alternate representation to the imagery of an invisible god who resides among the cherubim, and be paired with Asherah?

unquestioned, resulting, for example, in the widespread confusion of Apollo and Helios, the latter of whom came to be associated with griffins as well. Although most classical scholars today doubt that Apollo should ever have been identified with the sun, it is sufficient for the present purposes to note that this understanding not only prevailed in Hellenistic and imperial times but can be traced back to as early as the fifth century BCE (see, for example, H.J. Rose and C.M. Robertson, 'Apollo', *OCD*, p. 82). The connection between Apollo and griffins is thus suggestive and, when combined with the Egyptian evidence (as well as a possible solar origin for the common association of griffins with both light and passage to the life beyond), the conviction of many scholars that there was an important and ancient connection between the griffin and the solar deity seems justified.

1.   In fairness to the view of Hestrin that the top tier represents Baal-Hadad, one of the griffin's roles in Mesopotamia included drawing the chariot of the weather god Adad (Börker, 'Greif', p. 636). However, particularly if I am right that the animal at the front of the top tier is not a young bull (and perhaps even if I am wrong), then there is little reason apart from this attested role for believing that Baal is represented on this cult stand.

To conclude, the cult stand discovered by the gifted young archaeologist P. Lapp in 1968 apparently bears witness to yet another cult of Yahweh and Asherah, this time at a large-scale cultic centre which perhaps functioned under (at least indirect) royal administrative sanction during the reign of Solomon.[1] If the hypothesis offered here is correct, the Taanach cult stand implies a solar interpretation of Yahweh (tier one) and, in turn, a rather direct association between this understanding of Yahweh and the epithet 'Yahweh of Hosts', the invisible god who dwells among the cherubim (tier three).

A Terracotta Equid from Hazor

Another artefact that might imply the presence of solar elements in ancient Israelite religion is a terracotta figurine which was found in an Israelite stratum at Hazor. This small figurine portrays an animal with a disk-like symbol on its forehead (see fig. 1).[2] According to Y. Yadin, the chief excavator of Hazor, the figurine is either a horse (Yadin's early view)[3] or a bull (his later opinion).[4] In the event that the former view is correct, Yadin claims that this figurine is indicative of the sun cult known to have connections with horses and chariots.[5] In the event that the latter is correct, Yadin argues that this must be the bull of the weather god, Hadad, whom Yadin identifies as the deity with circle-and-cross on its breast standing on a bull in area H, dated to the end of the thirteenth century BCE. Once again it becomes important to determine whether or not the animal is an equid.

In the opinion of both C.S. Churcher and P.W. Physick-Sheard

1. Cf. 1 Kgs 4.12 in context. Since the stand was found underneath an ash layer dating to the campaign of Shishak, it is also possible (but less likely) that this cult stand dates to early in the reign of Jeroboam I.

2. For a drawing and photo of the figurine, see Y. Yadin *et al.*, *Hazor II* (Jerusalem: The Magnes Press of the Hebrew University, 1960), pls. 103.9 (drawing), 163.12, 13 (photographs). For photographs, see, for example, Y. Yadin, *Hazor: The Head of all those Kingdoms* (The Schweich Lectures of the British Academy, 1970; London: Oxford University Press, 1972), pl. 19c; *idem*, *Hazor: The Rediscovery of a Great Citadel of the Bible* (New York: Random House, 1975), p. 186.

3. Yadin, *Great Citadel of the Bible*, p. 189.

4. Yadin, *Great Citadel of the Bible*, p. 189.

5. Yadin, *Great Citadel of the Bible*, p. 189.

(whom I consulted also regarding the top tier of the Taanach cult stand), there can be little or no room for doubt that the animal is an equid and not a bovine creature. Thus Churcher's judgment, based upon examination of several photographs including the large scale colour enlargement in Yadin's popular work on Hazor was that the animal was 'not at all likely' to be a bull or cow, but was rather an equid. The similar analysis of Physick-Sheard is as follows:

> There is no doubt in my mind that this is a sculpture of part of a horse's head. The erect and dorsal position of the ears and relatively lateral placement of the eyes together with the flat line of the forehead are to me equine features.[1]

Moreover, although Yadin was later inclined towards the view that the animal was a bull because of the triangular marking on this animal's forehead found on depictions of cows or bulls in ancient Near Eastern art,[2] he fails to account for the two inscribed dots in the middle of the triangle on the Hazor figurine which are uncharacteristic of bull depictions and which in fact rule out the possibility that the triangle represents a colour mark on the beast.[3] Rather, the two dots suggest that the triangular marking represents a trapping, for which there is an extremely close parallel on a horse figurine from Samaria.[4] The trapping on the Samarian horse dangles from below the brow band of its bridle and is positioned between the eyes as is the case with the animal from Hazor. The presence of a brow band on the animal from

1.   Excerpt from a letter written on 19 November 1986. So sure was Physick-Sheard that the Hazor figurine was a horse that he thought that the request to identify the animal was my way of testing the validity of his judgment regarding the animal on the top tier of the Taanach cult stand.

2.   Yadin, *Great Citadel of the Bible*, p. 189; *idem, Head of all those Kingdoms*, pp. 145-46 n. 1. That the sun disk as incised disk-and-cross on this horse is similar to that found on the deity associated with the bull Hadad in Area H at an earlier date can be explained simply on the basis of continuity in the expression of a common motif (that is, the sun disk) at the same site.

3.   Even if the triangular-shaped object were to denote a mark on the animal, a colour patch on the forehead of a horse, a blaze, is at least as common on a horse as it is on a cow or bull.

4.   See E. Mazar, 'Archaeological Evidence for the "Cows of Bashan" who Are in the Mountains of Samaria', in B. Akzin *et al.* (eds.), *Festschrift: Rëuben Hecht* (Jerusalem: Korén Publishers, 1979), pp. 151-52. (I am indebted to J. Magness-Sweeney for directing my attention to this figurine.)

Hazor is significant in itself; not only does it offer a perfect parallel to the horse figurine from Samaria (as well as another),[1] but it indicates that the animal in question is wearing a bridle. Since *bovidae* are not controlled by means of a bit and reins (which a bridle holds in place), the animal must be a horse.[2] Moreover, the presence of trappings on the animal also indicates that the equid either bore a rider or, more likely in view of the absence of a rider and the presence of the cult symbol of the sun,[3] drew a chariot, presumably that of the sun god.

The archaeological context must be examined in order to determine further the significance of this artefact. This piece was found in a complex of rooms located some five metres west of a casemate wall of the Upper Citadel, and just south of a large city gate.[4] The complex of rooms, consisting of an eastern and western unit, underwent three changes in floor plan over a period of some sixty years between about 945 and 885 BCE, when the last of these phases, 9A, was destroyed by Ben-Hadad of Aram.[5] The presence of domestic items in the rooms suggested to Yadin that the complex was a dwelling, which, in view of its strategic location (that is, near the city gate) and its large number of small rooms, he judged tentatively to be a 'barracks'.[6] The horse figurine with disk was found in Room 217b, in the southeastern part of the western unit of this complex.[7] Assuming that each of the three

1. See J.W. Crowfoot, G.M. Crowfoot and K.M. Kenyon, *The Objects from Samaria* (Samaria-Sebaste: Reports of the Work of the Joint Expedition in 1931–1933 and of the British Expedition in 1935, no. 3; London: Palestine Exploration Fund, 1954), p. 77, fig. B.2.

2. For example, of the figurines of two horses and of two cows/bulls from Deir 'Allā published by H.J. Franken ('The Excavations at Deir 'Allā', *VT* 10 [1960], pl. 15), both horses (much like the Hazor horse in appearance) wear a brow band, as does the Hazor figurine, whereas neither bull/cow bears a brow band, but only a nose band. Moreover, I was not able to find a single case in which a cow or bull was portrayed with a brow band. As is the case today, it appears, then, that the brow band was used for holding the bridle of a horse securely, but was not necessary on a halter which is used simply to lead the animal.

3. A common sun symbol, the cross in a circle is attested in as far away contexts as Scandinavia (J.R. Bram, 'Sun', in M. Eliade [ed.], *Encyclopedia of Religion* [New York, MacMillan, 1987], XIV, p. 134).

4. Yadin, *Head of all those Kingdoms*, pp. 142-43; cf., pls. 27A, B.

5. Yadin, *Head of all those Kingdoms*, p. 143.

6. Yadin, *Head of all those Kingdoms*, p. 144.

7. Yadin, *Head of all those Kingdoms*, p. 143, fig. 33; p. 144 n. 1.

phases between Stratum 10B and Stratum 8 had a life of roughly twenty years, the object, dating to the middle of these three phases (Stratum 9B), would then belong to some time between about 925 and 905 BCE, either at the end of the reign of Solomon or during the rule of Jeroboam I. The domestic context, then, suggests that this figurine is a manifestation at the end of the tenth century, or the beginning of the ninth, of some aspect of personal religion. Moreover, that the figurine perhaps belonged to an individual associated with the king's army suggests also that the object might reflect a popular religious notion associated specifically with royal religion, although this is little more than a guess on the basis of context.

Not only the context but also the previous study of the Taanach cult stand sheds light on the significance of the figurine. The cult stand provides further support for Yadin's initial and independent judgment that the figurine from Hazor attests to the presence of a sun cult associated with the horse and chariot. Moreover, since the cult stand bears imagery similar to that on the figurine, and comes from a similar context (that is, northern, Yahwistic and of similar date), it provides a context for understanding the nature of that sun cult. In light of that context it is reasonable to suppose that the disk-bearing horse figurine from Hazor attests further to the presence in the north of a solar element within Yahwism of the late tenth century in which Yahweh was associated with the sun and drawn by an equid. Whereas at Taanach these elements existed within the context of public worship at a large-scale sanctuary perhaps under royal administrative sanction, at Hazor these elements are further attested within the context of private religious devotion, but, again, with possible links with royal religion.

A Solar Symbol for the Royal Israelite Seal?

In an article that appeared in 1970, A.D. Tushingham[1] claimed that a seal of a winged scarab which he had acquired and some nine seal impressions found likely in association with the palace complex at Samaria bore the 'State Seal of the kingdom of Israel...the

---

1. A.D. Tushingham, 'A Royal Israelite Seal (?) and the Royal Jar Handle Stamps (Part One)', *BASOR* 200 (1970), pp. 71-78; *idem*, 'A Royal Israelite Seal (?) and the Royal Jar Handle Stamps (Part Two)', *BASOR* 201 (1971), pp. 23-35.

four-winged flying scarab with sun-balls clasped between fore and hind legs'.[1] In support of his case, Tushingham cites the following evidence: (1) the possibly royal palatial context in which impressions from Samaria were found;[2] (2) the lack of an inscription on the seal/seal impressions, suggestive that the owner of the seal was a known entity such as royalty (which in turn would explain why no seal or impression belonging to a named king of Israel or Judah has ever been found);[3] (3) the presence of the winged scarab on the royal Judaean '*lmlk*' jar handles, the occurrence of which together with another emblem, the two-winged sun disk, can be explained on the basis of the assumption that the four-winged emblem was the old symbol of the northern kingdom and the two-winged emblem that of the southern kingdom.[4]

A. Millard challenged Tushingham's claim to have found the royal Israelite seal on the following grounds: (1) the location of the nine impressions in association with the palace at Samaria provides no conclusive evidence concerning either the prevalence or the provenance of the impressions; (2) on the analogy of Assyrian royal seals, the Israelite seal would probably have been inscribed, but could be uninscribed if the significance of the emblem chosen was 'unmistakably regal' which the winged scarab is not; and (3) Tushingham's assumption that the royal emblems on the *lmlk* jar handles had been out of use in the period of Assyrian vassalage and thus required the reminder *lmlk*, '(pertaining) to the king', when reissued is very doubtful because Assyrian policy did not require of its vassal states the revocation of their national emblems.[5]

In spite of the many suggestive arguments of Tushingham, there is, following Millard, insufficient evidence to identify with any degree of certainty the four-winged scarab as the royal emblem of the kingdom of Israel.[6] However, although the four-winged solar emblem cannot

1. Tushingham, 'Royal Israelite Seal (Part One)', p. 77.

2. Tushingham, 'Royal Israelite Seal (Part One)', p. 74.

3. Tushingham, 'Royal Israelite Seal (Part One)', pp. 76-78.

4. Tushingham, 'Royal Israelite Seal (Part One)', pp. 77-78; *idem*, 'Royal Israelite Seal (Part Two)', pp. 23-35.

5. A.R. Millard, 'An Israelite Royal Seal?', *BASOR* 208 (1972), pp. 5-9.

6. See Millard, 'Israelite Royal Seal?' In spite of the validity of Millard's criticisms, it is nonetheless striking that the seal is uninscribed. However, beyond this Tushingham's only evidence for the seal as a royal Israelite emblem is the

be accepted at present as the symbol of Israel, its function as a royal
emblem of Judah, clearly evident from the royal jar handles of the
southern kingdom, is relevant and will thus be examined in the
discussion of these jar handles that follows.

The *lmlk* Jar Handles and the Royal Emblem
of the Kingdom of Judah

First discovered in Jerusalem by Captain Charles Warren on 19
January 1869, jar handles of the so-called *lmlk* type have generated a
lengthy discussion.[1] Most of the discussion to this point has focused on
the date of these jar handles and on the particular purpose which the
jars served. Of greater relevance for this study, however, is the
iconography of the jar handles: a two-winged sun disk and a four-
winged scarab (see, for example, figs. 2 and 3 respectively). These
emblems are potentially relevant because they are both solar in
character and yet clearly denote the royal emblem of the kingdom of
Judah. How did the adoption of these emblems as royal Judaean come
about, and had the emblems lost their solar significance by the time of
adoption? This two-pronged question cannot be answered decisively,
but considerable progress can be made towards understanding the
context and significance of the emblems through the following careful
re-examination of the evidence.

Samarian provenance (only hearsay in the case of the seal), and the presence of a
four-winged scarab on the royal jar handles of the southern kingdom. As will be
shown in the next section of this chapter, that one of the two emblems on the Judaean
jar handles is the old symbol of the northern kingdom is only one possible way of
explaining the presence of the two emblems. Although R. Younker's identification of
the Ammonite emblem as possibly royal lends some (indirect) force to Tushingham's
contention that the Samarian seal is royal, Younker simply assumes the validity of
Tushingham's interpretation, making no reference at all to the criticisms of Millard.
(See R.W. Younker, 'Israel, Judah, and Ammon and the Motifs on the Baalis Seal
from Tell el-'Umeiri', *BA* 48 [1985], pp. 173-80.)

1.   The bibliography on these handles is enormous. For a bibliography citing
many of the more important articles, see Nadab Na'aman, 'Hezekiah's Fortified
Cities and the *LMLK* Stamps', *BASOR* 261 (1986), pp. 19-21. For a bibliography
of works between 1950 and 1969, see P. Welten, *Die Königs-Stempel: Ein Beitrag
zur Militärpolitik Judas unter Hiskia und Josia* (Abhandlungen des Deutschen
Palästinavereins; Wiesbaden: Otto Harrassowitz, 1969), pp. 192-94.

Scholarship to Date and Background

Recent scholarship has helped to clarify much about the jar handles that was once hotly debated. For example, recent excavations of Stratum 3 at both Lachish and Tel Batash now indicate that the four- and the two-winged emblems are contemporaneous and date to just prior to the campaign of Sennacherib in 701 BCE. The jars were thus issued during the reign of Hezekiah and probably for the purpose of preparing key military centres for the onslaught of 701.[1] Moreover, neutron activation analysis suggests that the jars, made of the same clay, were produced in the same workshop[2] and 'private' seal impressions which sometimes occurred in conjunction with the royal impressions probably belonged to officials who oversaw the manufacture, preparation or distribution of the jars.

There appeared at about the time of Josiah and extending to at least the time of the Babylonian exile the same jar type with what appears to be another royal emblem of Judah, a rosette, which differs from the previous two royal emblems in bearing neither a geographical name nor the inscription *lmlk*, '(pertaining) to the king (that is, "royal")' (see pl. 2).[3] Finally, three remaining problems, each addressed to some extent below, include the simultaneous use of both the four- and the two-winged emblem, the use of so common a symbol as the uninscribed rosette as a 'third' royal emblem, and the lack of a

1. Mazar, *Archaeology*, p. 458.

2. H. Mommsen, I. Perlman and J. Yellin, 'The Provenience of the *lmlk* Jars', *IEJ* 34 (1984), pp. 89-113.

3. According to A. Mazar (oral communication) there is 'no question' that the rosettes replaced the winged emblems on the royal storage jars. Jar handles with rosettes first appeared at the end of the seventh century and occur on jars which are clearly a development from the style of jars with four- and two-winged emblems. See further, B. Mazar, T. Dothan and I. Dunayevsky, *En-Gedi: The First and Second Seasons of Excavations: 1961–1962* ('Atiqot, 5, English Series; Jerusalem: Department of Antiquities and Museums, 1966), p. 34; Y. Yadin, 'The Fourfold Division of Judah', *BASOR* 163 (1961), p. 12; Y. Aharoni *et al.*, *Investigations at Lachish: The Sanctuary and the Residency (Lachish V)* (Tel Aviv: Institute of Archaeology, 1975), pp. 17-18. (It should also be noted that some of the *lmlk* jar handles also bear private seal impressions; see most recently, Y. Garfinkel, '2 Chr 11:5-10: Fortified Cities List and the *lmlk* Stamps—Reply to Nadav Na'aman', *BASOR* 271 [August 1988], p. 71 and N. Na'aman, 'The Date of 2 Chronicles 11:5-10—A Reply to Y. Garfinkel', *BASOR* 271 [August 1988], pp. 75-76.)

close parallel to the morphology of both the four- and the two-winged emblems.

The Origin of the Solar Imagery

Before an interpretation can be offered concerning the possible religious significance of the emblems on the jar handles, it is important to establish the identity and provenance of both the two- and the four-winged emblems.

The identity of the four-winged emblem has never been in dispute and the two-winged only rarely (but see the qualification later in this discussion). The four-winged emblem is a variation of the two-winged Egyptian sun beetle, Chepri, who each morning was thought to bring forth the sun in a manner akin to the way in which new life appeared to emerge from the dung ball that the *Scarabaeus sacer* pushed along between its front legs.[1]

It is now generally agreed that the two-winged emblem is a winged sun disk, although it was for a time variously interpreted in light of some seal impressions as either a 'flying scroll'[2] or something like a bird.[3]

The origin of the imagery on the emblems has been studied at length by both Tushingham and Welten who basically agree in their understanding that both symbols, though originally derived from Egypt, are thoroughly akin to Syro-Palestinian exemplars of the two- and the four-winged emblems.[4]

1. Not surprisingly, the name Chepri is derived from Egyptian *ḫpr*, 'come into being, become, change'. On the identification of the four-winged emblem, see further Welten, *Königs-Stempel*, p. 10. On the beetle and its connection with the sun in Egyptian thought, see R. Giveon, 'Skarabäus', *LÄ* 5 (1984), pp. 968-70; J. Assmann, 'Chepre', *LÄ* 1 (1972), pp. 934-40.

2. See, for example, D. Diringer, 'The Royal Jar-Handle Stamps of Ancient Judah', *BA* 12 (1949), p. 74. The interpretation harks back to a time when the two-winged emblem was dated to the reign of Josiah, whose reforms were linked with the discovery of a law book or scroll (2 Kgs 22.8-13).

3. This option is discussed later in this study.

4. Tushingham, 'Royal Israelite Seal (Part One)', pp. 75-76; *idem*, 'Royal Israelite Seal (Part Two)', pp. 26-33; Welten, *Königs-Stempel*, pp. 11-16, 19-30.

The Origin of the Solar Emblems Reconsidered

To evaluate, Welten and Tushingham are almost certainly correct that the manner in which the emblems are depicted show the artisan's indebtedness to the Syro-Palestinian realm. It does not follow from this, however, that the imagery had necessarily lost whatever significance it had had in Egypt, but only that the artisan followed the style of a native of Syria-Palestine (in all probability Judah). Rather, as the following discussion of both the two- and the four-winged emblems will attempt to demonstrate, the provenance for the imagery on the royal Judaean jar handles is linked with Egypt much more directly than either Tushingham or Welten supposed.

a. Emblems of the North and South Respectively?

A logical starting point is with the curious presence of two varying emblems on the same type of royal jar handles. The traditional explanation is that the symbols are the emblems of the northern and southern kingdoms, although opinions have varied regarding which emblem represents which kingdom.[1] Though reasonable, the explanation, however, is no more than an attempt to account for the presence of two emblems on the jars. As noted in the previous discussion of the debate between Tushingham and Millard, the concept that the four-winged emblem was the royal emblem of the northern kingdom has very little evidence in its favour.[2] The issue is now further complicated by the contemporaneity of the jar handles.[3]

1. According to Yadin, the four-winged emblem was the symbol of the southern kingdom ('Ancient Judaean Weights and the Date of the Samaria Ostraca', *Scripta Hierosolymitana* 8 [1961], p. 14). To Tushingham, however, the four-winged emblem was the symbol of the northern domain. This emblem was used together with the two-winged emblem (to Tushingham the royal emblem of the south and, before it, of the United Monarchy) to convey hopes of a newly-founded united kingdom under Josiah. Although the handles are now known to date to the time of Hezekiah, Tushingham still maintains that the four- and the two-winged emblems were the emblems of the northern and southern kingdoms respectively (oral communication).

2. See the discussion in the previous section, 'A Solar Symbol for the Royal Israelite Seal?' If Tushingham's view were correct that the two-winged emblem was the symbol of the United Monarchy, one would ideally expect to find this emblem in the northern kingdom at an early period, particularly in royal contexts.

3. What is the likelihood that two emblems for the same kingdom would coexist and that a third, the rosette, would appear less than a century thereafter? On this

An alternative explanation which accords at least as well with the presence of two emblems on otherwise identical royal jars is that the emblems are in some way alternative expressions of essentially the same idea. Indeed, the equivalency of these two emblems is clearly attested in the ancient Near East, and to find it one needs to go no further than to Edfu in Egypt where the god Horus of Beḥdet (also known as Horus of Edfu), well known for his association with royalty, is attested as both winged sun disk and flying scarab beetle. Thus, in one of the concluding aetiological sections of the first section of the Horus myth, 'The Legend of the Winged Disk',[1] we read,

> Now as for the Winged Disk which is on the shrines of all the gods and goddesses of Upper and Lower Egypt, and on their chapels likewise, it is Horus of Beḥdet... As for the Winged Beetle which is on the shrines of all the gods and goddesses of Upper and Lower Egypt, he is Horus of Beḥdet, great god, lord of heaven, who overthrows [A]popis and the enemies and foes and the evil council in their ways. The living and the dead [12,8] are inscribed with his name, as is done for his father Rē'-Ḥarakhte to this day.[2]

Moreover, in the same myth, Horus of Edfu is called 'Lord of Mesen,

issue, see the subsection, 'The Royal Emblem of the Kingdom of Judah and the Problem of the Rosette: A Hypothesis', offered later in this section.

1. Although the earliest record of this myth dates to the Ptolemaic period, there is very little doubt that many of the traditions reflected in the myth date to a much earlier period. For example, Professor D.B. Redford, who dates many of the possible historical allusions in the myth to as late as the end of the Persian Period, does not think it unreasonable to suppose that the tradition of Horus as winged sun disk and flying scarab would have been known in the eighth century BCE (oral communication). On the date of the traditions behind the myth, see further, J.G. Griffiths, 'The Interpretation of the Horus-Myth of Edfu', *JEA* 44 (1958), pp. 75-85; *idem*, 'Horusmythe', *LÄ* 3 (1977), pp. 55-56; H.W. Fairman (ed.), *The Triumph of Horus* (London: B.T. Batsford, 1974), pp. 33-35. For the text of the myth of Horus, see E. Chassinat, *Le temple d'Edfou* (8 vols.; Cairo: L'institut français d'archéologie orientale, 1934–1978), VI, pp. 108-36, 60-90, 213-23; 13. pls. 518-35, 494-514, 576-84. For translations or discussions see, for example: H.W. Fairman, 'The Myth of Horus at Edfu—I', *JEA* 21 (1935), pp. 26-36; *idem* (ed.), *Triumph of Horus*; A.M. Blackman and H.W. Fairman, 'The Myth of Horus at Edfu—II', *JEA* 28 (1942), pp. 32-38; *JEA* 29 (1943), pp. 2-36; *JEA* 30 (1944), pp. 5-22; A.H. Gardiner, 'Horus the Beḥdetite', *JEA* 30 (1944), pp. 23-60; J.G. Griffiths, 'Horusmythe', *LÄ* 3 (1977), pp. 54-59.

2. Fairman, 'Horus at Edfu—I', pp. 35-36.

the noble winged scarab, who protects the two lands, the great god, pre-eminent one of Sile'.[1] Here Horus the winged scarab is associated aetiologically with the town of Sile which is at the far northeastern border of Egypt and which was in the late eighth century and at other times the starting place for the caravan route from Egypt to Palestine.[2]

A direct connection between the imagery on the royal jar handles and these Egyptian mythological notions can hardly be judged surprising in view of the relationship between Egypt and Judah in the late eighth century BCE. Once during the reign of Sargon II, Hezekiah was invited to join in a Philistine coalition with the twenty-fifth Egyptian (Ethiopian) dynasty against Assyria, and once during the reign of Sennacherib prior to 701 BCE, Hezekiah formed an alliance with this dynasty.[3] Thus, at the time of Hezekiah's preparation for the campaign of Sennacherib, the occasion which gave rise to the production of the *lmlk* jar handles, Hezekiah was allied with Egypt.

b. *The Two-Winged Emblem*
The interpretation offered here accounts also for a number of unique features associated with both jar handle emblems. Concerning the two-winged emblem, although certain that it is a winged sun disk, Lapp, Tushingham and Welten have difficulty finding parallels for the protrusion which extends vertically above the disk and which is similar to the equally peculiar striated tail-like extension below the disk.[4]

1. The translation is that of D.B. Redford, *Pharaonic King-Lists, Annals and Day-Books: A Contribution to the Study of the Egyptian Sense of History* (Mississauga, Ontario; Benben Publications, 1986), p. 280.

2. For a brief discussion of the aetiological relationship between the myth and cult traditions at Sile, see Redford, *Pharaonic King-Lists*, p. 280. On the location of Sile and its historical role as a place of access to Palestine, see F. Gomaà, 'Sile', *LÄ* 5 (1984), pp. 945-47. On the association of the winged scarab with Sile, see J. Vandier, 'Iousâas et (Hathor)-Nébet-Hétépet', *Revue d'Egyptologie* 17 (1965), pp. 169-76. (I am indebted to D.B. Redford for mentioning the possible connection between the four-winged emblems on the jar handles and the predominance of the winged scarab at Sile and for directing me to the work of Vandier.)

3. See further, J. Bright, *A History of Israel* (Philadelphia: Westminster Press, 3rd edn, 1981), pp. 281-82, 284-86.

4. P.W. Lapp, 'Late Royal Seals from Judah', *BASOR* 158 (1960), p. 12; Tushingham, 'Royal Israelite Seal (Part Two)', p. 26; Welten, *Königs-Stempel*, p. 30.

According to the interpretation offered here, however, the extensions above and below the disk, though now crudely fashioned and somewhat standardized, were understood at least originally to be the upper body and tail respectively of Horus of Edfu, the falcon-headed god who took the form of the winged sun disk. Indeed, were it not for the disk at the centre of some of the two-winged insignia, the emblem would be judged as a bird and not a sun disk, as a survey of the uninitiated observer will confirm. Nor has the bird-like appearance of the emblem gone unnoticed by archaeologists as well. For example, C.C. McCown, writing long ago, made the following judgment:

> The head... is a bird with a beak, usually turned left with a top-knot on the right... The head above and the tail below the central circle are so distinct in several examples that there can be no doubt as to the intention of the artist. The Palestinian seal-maker must have thought he was making a bird of some kind, although his original inspiration may have been Assyrian.[1]

Although more recent samples that underscore the crude nature of the emblem render McCown's identification of such details as a 'beak'[2] and a 'knot' dubious, the bird-like appearance of this winged sun disk is nonetheless unmistakable.[3] It appears from the evidence at present,

1.   C.C. McCown, *Tell en-Naṣbeh: Volume 1* (Berkeley, CA: The American Schools of Oriental Research, 1947), p. 156; cf. pl. 56.1-9. Lapp, however ('Seals from Judah', p. 12 n. 8), regards the attempt to see in McCown's 'bird with a flat head and beak to the left' as anything but a development based on the winged disk dubious, but his judgment is made on the assumption that the disk, evident on other impressions, necessarily precludes the possibility that the emblem is a 'bird'. Despite these reservations, however, Lapp nonetheless admits that 'there do not appear to be close affinities to the upturned wings and the *bird's* head' ('Seals from Judah', p. 12 [emphasis mine]).

2.   It is just possible that some of the heads do show a beak; for examples, see Y. Aharoni, *Excavations at Ramat Rahel: Seasons 1959 and 1960* (Rome: Centro di studi semitici, 1962), pl. 29.11 and G. Barkay, 'Northern and Western Jerusalem in the End of the Iron Age' (Unpublished PhD dissertation, Tel-Aviv University, 1985), II, p. 194, fig. 161.

3.   Tushingham ('Royal Israelite Seal [Part Two]', pp. 27-29), objects that 'nowhere is the winged sun disk depicted with a bird's head'. In response, the following may be noted. (1) It is not too much to allow the artisan this degree of 'innovation' (on which see point 4 below). (2) That the two-winged emblem is unique in combining features characteristic of both falcon and sun disk simply confirms the judgment that the artisan is alluding to a mythic idea which cannot be

then, that the two-winged emblem is a local (probably Judaean) rendition of the tradition of Horus of Beḥdet, the falcon-headed winged disk known for his identity with both the sun god and the king.[1]

Also in favour of the notion that the two-winged disk represented a falcon is a Phoenician seal published by W.A. Ward (see fig. 4). On this Phoenician seal, dated to no earlier than the eighth century BCE, there is a bird that bears unmistakably Egyptian motifs and which Ward identifies as a 'falcon'.[2] The bird's head and tail are crudely fashioned in a manner strikingly reminiscent of the 'head' and 'tail' on the two-winged emblem of the royal Judaean jar handles. Further, as is the case with many of the bird-like emblems on the jar handles, both the head and the tail on the Phoenician seal are striated. Furthermore, the 'body' of this bird is hollowed out in disk-like fashion as if to foreshadow the innovative transition from winged falcon to winged sun-disk-and-falcon.[3] The significance of the seal for

other than the Egyptian notion, or a Judaean variation thereof, of the falcon god Horus as winged sun disk. (3) There is no preferable explanation of which I am aware for what appears to be a head and for what is certainly a tail on the disk. (4) Regarding the so-called lack of a precedent, it must be emphasized that the Judaean artisan is making precisely the same logical connection that gave rise to the imagery of the winged sun disk in the first place, namely the artistic amalgamation of the notions of Horus as both falcon and sun (for which see Gardiner, 'Horus the Beḥdetite', p. 49).

1.   That the emblem represents a bird as well as a disk explains why the wings on the jar-handle emblem extend upwards in bird-like fashion like few (if any) other winged sun disks outside of Anatolia. For examples of the bird-like nature of the wings, see most conveniently, the two-winged examples drawn by Welten (*Königs-Stempel*, pp. 37-44). Both Welten (Königs-Stempel, p. 30) and Tushingham ('Royal Israelite Seal [Part Two]', pp. 27-29) refer to the upwards extension of wings on sun disks, but only in the Hittite realm. A preferable parallel, however, is many examples of Egyptian *birds* with upturned wings.

2.   W.A. Ward, 'Three Phoenician Seals of the Early First Millennium B.C.', *JEA* 53 (1967), pp. 69-74.

3.   Although circular, the 'body' of the falcon on the Phoenician seal cannot be interpreted as a sun disk because, although almost imperceptible, small legs protrude from the disk-like body. Moreover, although unlike the wings on the jar handles, the wings on the seal extend downwards, Ward nonetheless judged that 'the wings bend downwards to fit the curved space at the top of the design' (Ward, 'Three Phoenician Seals', p. 74). (For Egyptian birds with upturned wings on Syro-Phoenician seals see, for example, McCown, *Tell en-Naṣbeh*, pl. 54.1, 56; E. Porada [ed.], *The*

our purpose is this: the head and tail on this *falcon* resemble more closely the head and tail on the jar handle emblems than any of the parallel extensions above and below a *sun disk* that have been cited to date.[1]

c. *The Four-Winged Sun Beetle*

Turning now to the four-winged scarab, the place to begin is with the most peculiar feature, namely the head. Two things are noteworthy in particular. First, so far as I could determine, virtually all of the extant Syro-Phoenician four-winged scarabs have a round head, whereas the head of the scarab on the jar handles is relatively square shaped, remarkably similar in fact to the shape of the head on the two-winged emblems (for typical examples, see figs. 2 and 3).[2]

At least two explanations are possible. First, in view of the similarity in shape between the heads on the four- and the two-winged emblems, it is reasonable to ask whether the heads on the four-winged emblems are those of a falcon as they were shown to be in the case of heads on the two-winged emblems. Indeed, some scarabs do have the head of a bird, as is clear both from the Phoenician Palestrina bowl which combines Egyptian and Phoenician elements[3] and, more significantly, from the myth of Horus of Edfu.[4] Note, for example, what is said of Horus of Edfu as the winged scarab in the section of the Legend of the Winged Disk that immediately follows the description of Horus as the winged beetle:

Collection of the Pierpont Morgan Library [Corpus of Ancient Near Eastern Seals in North American Collections, vol. 1; The Bollingen Series 14; n.p.: Pantheon Books, 1948], pl. 151, no. 996E.)

1. For the winged disks referred to by Tushingham and/or Welten, see Mallowan, *Nimrud and its Remains*, II, figs. 395-97, or *ANEP*, nos. 281, 630. The *lmlk* jar handles lack completely the voluted 'flaring' of the feather-like plumage characteristic of these winged sun disks.

2. Note, for example, Y. Aharoni, *Excavations at Ramat Rahel: Seasons 1961 and 1962* (Rome: Centro di studi semitici, 1964), pl. 38.6, 11; *idem, Seasons 1959 and 1960*, pl. 29.8, 11.

3. In addition to the bibliography offered by Welten, *Königs-Stempel*, p. 14 n.12, see Harden, *Phoenicians*, pp. 179-80.

4. See also F.L. Griffith, 'Oxford Excavations in Nubia', *Liverpool Annals of Archaeology and Anthropology* 10 (1923), pl. 57.5 (cf. comment, p. 136).

The king shall act (?) on the day on which trouble and strife occur. A winged beetle in writing shall be made on his breast when he sees trouble, just as Rē'-Harakhte did [when he saw] the trouble of the son of Rē', its face being that of a falcon, <its> lips those of a vulture, and its body that of a beetle.[1]

The similar shape of the heads on both the four- and two-winged emblems on the *lmlk* jar handles thus fits perfectly with the notion that both emblems represent Horus of Edfu; this god, whether in the form of a winged beetle or a winged disk, had the head of a falcon.

Secondly, a typical head of the four-winged emblem on the Judaean jar handles bears a striking resemblance to one of the rare cases mentioned by Welten in which four-winged scarabs are attested outside of the Syro-Palestinian cultural realm, namely, in Nubia (see, for example, fig. 5). Significantly, Welten judged the parallels to be 'compelling' (*überzeugend*) and suggested that consideration should be given to the possibility that there was contact between the two realms in which these four-winged emblems occur.[2]

In light of what has become known about the date of the jar handles since the time of Welten's work, the possibility of historical contact between the four-winged emblems of Nubia and the four-winged emblems on the jar handles is very real indeed. The Nubian scarabs come from two late eighth-century BCE tombs which belonged to the wife of Piankhi, ruler of the twenty-fifth (Ethiopian) dynasty, who had extensive political dealings with Hezekiah. Even more striking than the contemporaneity of the scarabs and the historical ties between their owners is the context of the Nubian scarabs. The four-winged scarabs with 'flared' heads occur on amulets, and on many are found also both a two-winged sun disk and a rosette. Thus, the same three emblems that occur on the *lmlk* jar handles—four-winged scarab, winged sun disk and rosette—are attested on the Nubian amulets of the late eighth century (see, for example, fig. 6).

---

1. Fairman, 'Horus at Edfu—I', p. 36.
2. Welten, *Königs-Stempel*, pp. 15-16. On the scarabs in question, see, for example, D. Dunham, *El Kurru* (The Royal Cemeteries of Kush, vol. 1; Cambridge, MA; Harvard University Press for the Museum of Fine Arts, 1950), pls. 49A.1256/1257, 1260-69; 53A.1056, 1058, 1064, 1101; 55A.997-98.

The Significance of the Solar Imagery

Because the two-winged sun disk and the winged scarab are both common and widespread motifs, under normal circumstances very little could be said about any possible significance or meaning of either of these emblems. In the present case, however, the range of possible connotations for the jar handle emblems is limited by a number of morphological factors which point towards Egypt and by the apparent equivalency of the two emblems which points quite unambiguously towards a specific awareness of the mythic tradition of Horus of Edfu as both winged sun disk and flying scarab. Even in this specific case, however, caution is nonetheless warranted because it is difficult to know precisely how the mythic tradition was understood or what factors, if any, might have influenced the tradition as its emblems made their way towards adoption as the royal insignia of the kingdom of Judah.

In view of this need for caution, the place to begin is with an understanding of the general significance that each of these emblems had within Egypt. First is the classic statement of Sir Alan Gardiner regarding the significance of the winged disk:

> The evidence thus all goes to show the Winged Disk and name of King
> are so inextricably interconnected and blended that we cannot but regard
> the symbol as an image of the king himself, though simultaneously also of
> Rē' and of Horus, all three united into a trinity of solar and kingly
> dominion.[1]

Secondly, two major connotations are associated with the beetle *Scarabaeus sacer*. As a symbol of the deity, the scarab beetle is either Chepri, the god of the morning sun who daily emerges anew from his nightly trek through the netherworld and makes his ascent to heaven, or the sun god in general (that is, in all three of its phases: morning [Chepri], day [Re], and night [Atum/Osiris]). Moreover, in view of its links with Chepri, the scarab beetle can also signify solar resurrection and related concepts like the cyclical nature of life, birth without previous generation, change and the presence of life after death and thus 'deathlessness'.[2]

To evaluate from this general perspective, it is possible that neither

---

1. Gardiner, 'Horus the Behdetite', p. 51.
2. J. Assmann, 'Chepri', *LÄ* 1 (1972), pp. 934-40; *idem*, 'Sonnengott', *LÄ* 5 (1984), pp. 1087-94; Giveon, 'Skarabäus', pp. 968-69.

the two- nor the four-winged emblem on the *lmlk* jar handles conveyed a solar understanding of king or deity, as indeed some have argued.[1] To its credit, this evaluation reckons seriously with the possibility that many of the original connotations of an emblem were lost or altered through time and transference of cultures.[2] Nevertheless, though possible, it may be questioned whether it is likely that *two* rather specific emblems of deity as sun which occur in the same royal context have lost all solar connotations vis-à-vis king or deity. In any case, the view that the jar handle emblems are completely devoid of solar signification is clearly a minimalist's perspective.

As argued earlier, however, the occurrence of both the two- and the four-winged emblem on jars of identical function suggests that the significance to be attached to these symbols may be understood further in light of their role in the Horus myth where the winged scarab occurs as a variant of the two-winged sun disk. For this reason, it is worth noting important aspects of this mythic tradition.

Regarding the character of the falcon god Horus of Edfu, he is clearly a combative deity (*Kampfgott*), particularly where Seth and other enemies of Re are involved. He is a deity closely linked with the king (who is in fact said to be the image of Horus of Edfu on earth).[3] In addition, Horus of Edfu is inextricably linked with the sun god, mainly in its Heliopolitan form Re-Harachte. This link can take the form of being identified with Re or being the son, image or Ba of the sun god.[4]

Regarding the exploits of Horus of Edfu, the dominant impression

---

1. For example, Alan Millard makes the following remarks about the four-winged emblem (when it was commonly assigned to the reign of Josiah): 'Perhaps no more could be read into the four-winged scarab than an adaptation of the Egyptian symbol of renewal of life, hence "good luck," related, maybe, to the hopes of the Davidic dynasty' ('Israelite Royal Seal?', p. 8). It should be recognized, however, that the Egyptian symbol denotes not renewal of life in general but, quite specifically, *solar* renewal/resurrection. Moreover, in the case of the royal Judaean jar handles, it would presumably have to be a coincidence that as separate motifs both the four- and the two-winged emblem originally had solar connotations.

2. Compare for example the discussion of Barnett with respect to possible local influences on Egyptian motifs (*Nimrud Ivories*, pp. 56, 62, 137-53).

3. W. Barta, 'Horus von Edfu', *LÄ* 3 (1977), p. 34.

4. Barta, 'Horus von Edfu', p. 34. Horus of Edfu is also attested occasionally as the moon, that is, Re's representative at night ('Horus von Edfu', p. 34).

left by the Horus myth is that, as 'Winged Disk', he is a relentless
champion in battle against the foes of his father Re-Harachte.
Typically, then, Horus of Beḥdet is described fighting enemies (most
notably Seth) or manifestations of the enemy such as crocodiles and
hippopotami, often from the bark of the sun god Re. The combative
exploits of Horus of Edfu are such that in the Horus myth his name
becomes virtually synonymous with the protection of Upper and
Lower Egypt against the enemies of Re. For this reason the winged
disk (and flying scarab) can be found on shrines throughout Egypt, as
a means of honouring Horus of Beḥdet whose name is 'a warrant
against any future threat'.[1]

To evaluate from this more specific perspective, the problem of not
knowing which aspects of the Egyptian tradition might have been lost
or altered as they made their way to the royal house of Judah remains.
A minimalist's perspective here would be that, as representations of
Horus of Edfu, the four- and the two-winged royal emblems of the
kingdom of Judah symbolized no more than the protective power of
the king of Judah, a heroic warrior against the political enemies of
God (a meaning that is certainly apropos in view of the military
context of the jar handles themselves). On the other hand, a perspective that takes rather more full advantage of the mythic tradition and
assumes far less dilution of several Egyptian themes would be that, in
addition to the symbolic significance just noted, the following
connotations are also implied by the Judaean rendition of Horus of
Edfu in two forms of the sun god: the notion of the king as the son of
the deity (perhaps as the deity himself), and, since Horus of Edfu and
his father Re are both sun gods, the notion of the deity (in the case of
Judah, clearly Yahweh) as sun god.

Which of these perspectives (or one in between) is more likely is
difficult to say. All that can be stated with certainty is that the jar
handle emblems are for the Syro-Palestinian realm an apparently rare
and rather specific rendition of the two alternative means of representing the god Horus of Edfu. Moreover, it is reasonable to suppose
from the royal context of the jar handles that the Judaean understanding of these emblems probably included an awareness of Horus
of Edfu's close affinity with the king, the most predominant aspect of

1.   Griffiths, 'Horusmythe', pp. 54-55. See also Fairman, 'Horus at Edfu—I',
pp. 26-36.

which (and the most flattering for royalty) was the heroic fighting of
Horus of Edfu, the king figure, against the enemies of his father, the
sun god Re. Moreover, that Horus of Edfu is portrayed in two different ways specifically as a sun god on the jar handles may be judged
reasonably either to place emphasis on the solar character of the god
(that is, Yahweh) or to recall the legendary function of these emblems
as symbols of protection in the name of the king-god Horus of Edfu.

Beyond this one can only speculate. For example, it is perhaps
difficult to imagine that the king of Judah would have been able to
identify himself with these specific emblems of Horus of Beḥdet as
king, sun and son of the sun god Re, if neither the king nor the deity
were in some sense at least marginally associated with the sun, but
such is perhaps possible if the notion of the emblems as protective
symbols on shrines was an early part of the tradition known by the
royal house of Judah.

To conclude by applying the question of significance to solar
Yahwism, the following notions are possible but by no means certain
in the case of Horus of Edfu on the royal emblem of the kingdom of
Judah: (1) that the king was identified with the deity; (2) that the king
was identified with the sun; and (3) that Yahweh was identified with
the sun. Thus, the jar handles do not prove but are certainly consonant
with the notion that Yahweh, like both Horus of Edfu and Re, was in
some sense linked with the sun.

How does this evidence relate to the other archaeological evidence
examined thus far? That the emblems on the jar handles imply a
possible association between Yahweh and the sun is certainly
consistent with what has been seen in the cases of the Taanach cult
stand and the Hazor sun horse, both of which may also reflect the
outlook of royal Yahwistic solarism. Moreover, to relate the evidence
of the jar handles to the biblical material, although it is clearly difficult to reconcile the imagery on the royal jar handles with traditional
views concerning the religious outlook of Hezekiah, suffice it to say at
present that, as will be argued in the next chapter, there is a considerable amount of evidence in DH for the notion that Hezekiah, along
with other royal figures prior to the reign of Josiah, was indeed a
solar Yahwist.[1]

1. In any case, it does not necessarily follow from the dating of the jar handles
to the reign of Hezekiah that the emblems themselves originate with this king. With

The Royal Emblem of the Kingdom of Judah and the Problem of the Rosette: A Hypothesis

To this point little has been said about the significance of the rosette, which at about the time of Josiah appears to have replaced the four- and two-winged emblems as symbols of the kingdom of Judah (see pl. 2). Concerning the rosette in general, although perhaps solar in origin,[1] this emblem was nonetheless used so widely that in most contexts it is not possible to assign any 'significance' to the emblem. In the present peculiar case of occurrence as a royal emblem, however, the rosette does have a discernible significance on the basis of the following hypothesis which attempts to resolve several difficulties associated with the apparent occurrence of no less than three different royal emblems on the *lmlk* jar handles.

A number of problems and considerations warrant the formulation of a new hypothesis to the effect that the rosette was only one part of a *composite* royal emblem which consisted of the four-winged scarab, two-winged disk, and rosette. First, as noted earlier, Millard has argued convincingly that most of the royal seals of Israel's neighbours were inscribed, except in cases in which the emblem itself was 'unmistakably regal'[2] which the rosette obviously is not. Clearly there must have been something peculiar to the context of the rosette on the royal jar handles that helped to denote it as the royal emblem of the kingdom of Judah.[3] Secondly, in light of what is now known about

which ruler they originated is impossible to know, but evidence at present seems to suggest that the innovation was quite recent. So far as I am aware, the rarer of the two emblems, the four-winged scarab, is not attested in Judah or the Transjordan prior to the late eighth century BCE (although this is perhaps an accident of discovery). Moreover, though somewhat standardized, the emblems still show clear signs of their distinctive Egyptian origin and association with Horus of Edfu. Finally, what is in all probability a connection between the four-winged emblem and the twenty-fifth Ethiopian dynasty suggests that the emblems originated with Hezekiah, known for his ties with that dynasty.

1.   See, for example, Goodenough, *Jewish Symbols*, VII, pp. 175-98 and the editorial addition of W.F. Albright to p. 51 n. 21 of the article of I. Mendelsohn, 'Guilds in Ancient Mesopotamia', *BASOR* 80 (1940), pp. 17-21.

2.   Millard, 'Israelite Royal Seal?', pp. 6-8.

3.   Clearly that the emblem was on a jar with the same style as the previous royal jars helped to indicate that this jar with the rosette emblem was royal Judaean, but this does not resolve the difficulty of how in other contexts the rosette impression would alone denote the kingdom of Judah.

the contemporaneity of the four- and the two-winged emblems, how could there have been two alternative royal emblems for the kingdom of Judah in existence at the same time? Even if one emblem were the symbol of the northern kingdom and the other the sign of the southern realm (a notion for which there is very little evidence), how could it have been practical to have two royal emblems? Moreover, how could a third emblem, the rosette—far from a royal emblem in itself—replace the two traditional emblems and denote the same kingdom a century or so later?

In my judgment these difficulties and questions point to the hypothesis intimated above: the three emblems attested on the *lmlk* jar handles were not royal emblems in themselves, but were each part of a composite royal emblem that consisted of a four-winged scarab, a two-winged sun disk, and a rosette.

In support of the hypothesis, it is worth recalling the Nubian amulets attested from royal tombs associated with the twenty-fifth Ethiopian dynasty with which Hezekiah had direct connections. These amulets bear four-winged emblems strikingly similar to the four-winged emblems on the *lmlk* jar handles. Significantly, in addition to the four-winged emblem, these same amulets also bear a two-winged sun disk *and* a rosette (see, for example, fig. 6). Concerning the rosette itself, to judge from the Nubian parallels, it played a relatively minor role as a decorated form of the sun disk that the four-winged beetle clasped between both its fore- and hind-legs.[1] Moreover, based on these several points of analogy with the Nubian material, a tentative reconstruction of the royal insignia of the kingdom of Judah in the late eighth century BCE is possible (see fig. 7).

In light of the present hypothesis, the situation leading to three jar handle impressions may be reconstructed tentatively as follows. Though evidently well suited to the tastes of the king(s) of Judah, the royal solar insignia was rather too complex in design to be impressed on narrow surfaces such as the jar handles. To alleviate the difficulty, only part of the composite was chosen to represent the kingdom of Judah. Moreover, in order for this simpler emblem not to be mistaken for something other than the royal composite which it signified, not one but two of the more distinctive motifs of the composite emblem were chosen alternatively and, to remove all doubt, the two emblems

---

1. Dunham, *El-Kurru*, pls. 53A.1101; 55A.997-98; cf. pl. 49A.1260-69.

were similarly inscribed *lmlk*, 'of the king', on the jar handles. Later when it came time to publish a new issue of royal jars, the practice of selecting only one motif from the composite emblem had become a tradition well known from the days of Hezekiah. Since, to judge from the Nubian parallels, there was only one motif left with which to represent the composite, the rosette was chosen. In view of people's familiarity both with the royal emblem and with the shape of the royal jars which had been issued previously (and which in some cases were still being used), there was no real danger of so common a motif being mistaken for the royal emblem, and so it was left uninscribed.

To reflect briefly on the relevance of the hypothesis for the earlier discussion of a possible significance to the emblems, the rosette brings to three the total number of solar symbols on the *lmlk* jar handles (on which basis it perhaps becomes more difficult to imagine that that insignia as a whole was completely devoid of solar connotations). Since the rosette was introduced as a royal emblem at the same time as the other emblems, however, Josiah can by no means be implicated by the presence of this 'solar' symbol on the jar handles.[1] In all three cases, then, the issue of reference to solar elements within the cult must be addressed on the basis of further evidence pertaining to the reign of Hezekiah, considered fully in Chapter 3.

Horse Figurines with 'Sun Disks'

One of the more common artefacts found in eighth- to seventh-century strata in ancient Palestine are fairly small and simply fashioned terracotta figurines of horses which often bear riders. These horse figurines are frequently found with other figurines as well, most notably nude female figurines, animals and various pieces of furniture.[2] Although some scholars have expressed the opinion that

---

1. The rosette by itself is not a strong solar symbol and was in any case probably the only remaining motif available to Josiah with which to represent the royal emblem of the kingdom of Judah on the royal jar handles.

2. The most comprehensive analysis of these animal and female figurines to date is the dissertation of T.A. Holland, 'A Typological and Archaeological Study of Human and Animal Representations during the Iron Age' (2 vols.; unpublished PhD dissertation, The University of Oxford, 1975).

these objects are merely toys[1] or trinkets,[2] most scholars today agree that the objects served a cultic purpose.[3] These horse figurines are relevant for the present study because one of the more common cultic interpretations of the horse figurines is that some bear sun disks and are thus associated with sun worship.[4]

Description and the Case for Sun Disks

Although the view that these figurines were connected with sun worship was proffered as early as 1935,[5] it was revived in 1967, when Dame Kathleen Kenyon discovered horse figurines during the last two weeks of her excavations of the Ophel in Jerusalem.[6] While completing

---

1. For example, W.F. Albright, *The Excavations of Tell Beit Mirsim. III. The Iron Age* (AASOR, 21-22; New Haven: ASOR, 1943), p. 142.

2. For example, H.G. May, *Material Remains of the Megiddo Cult* (OIP, 26; Chicago: University of Chicago Press, 1935), p. 28.

3. A notable exception is Professor Y. Shiloh and many members of his team (personal communication) who found these animal figurines all over various Iron Age levels within their excavations at the City of David. However, several factors such as the occurrence of these figurines elsewhere in places which served only a cultic purpose, the occurrence of horse figurines with female 'fertility' figurines (hardly toys), and the strong possibility that many of these figurines were broken intentionally suggest that these figurines did in fact serve a religious purpose, likely at the level of 'popular religion'.

4. See, for example, J.B. Pritchard, *The Water System of Gibeon* (Museum Monographs; Philadelphia: The University Museum, University of Pennsylvania, 1961), pp. 17-19; and Crowfoot, Crowfoot and Kenyon, *Objects from Samaria*, p. 78.

5. May, *Megiddo Cult*, p. 24.

6. Information on the cave and the find in general can be gleaned from the following works: K.M. Kenyon, 'Excavations in Jerusalem, 1962', *PEQ* 96 (1964), pp. 8-10; *idem, Jerusalem: Excavating 3000 Years of History* (New Aspects in Antiquity; n.p.: Thames and Hudson, 1967), pp. 57, 63-66; *idem*, 'Excavations in Jerusalem: 1967', *PEQ* 100 (1968), pp. 107-109, pls. 33-36; *idem, Royal Cities of the Old Testament* (New York: Schocken Books, 1971), pp. 114-22; *idem, Digging up Jerusalem* (London: E. Benn, 1974), pp. 135-43 and pls. 52-61; T.A. Holland, 'A Study of Palestinian Iron Age Baked Clay Figurines, with Special Reference to Jerusalem: Cave 1', *Levant* 9 (1977), pp. 121-55, esp. 149-57. Note, however, that Kenyon's cultic interpretation of the area outside the cave (made on the basis, for example, of roof supports which she mistakenly identified as *maṣṣēbôt*) needs to be revised in light of the conclusion of Professor Shiloh and others who show this area to be a residential area outside the city gate (personal communication). See further,

the excavation of Square A 26 on the eastern slope of the Ophel, Kenyon[1] happened upon a cave with which were associated some thirteen hundred objects, 429 of which were registered as 'human or animal figurines'.[2] Concerning the horse figurines, Kenyon says, 'A very interesting feature is that several of the horses have a disk on the forehead between the ears'.[3] Assuming that the disks are sun disks, and apparently thinking of 2 Kgs 23.11, Kenyon elaborates as follows: 'It seems a perfectly reasonable assumption that horses with a sun disk on the forehead are miniature models of the Horses of the Sun'.[4]

In his detailed analysis of Iron Age animal and human figurines from Palestine, T.A. Holland upholds as 'probable' Kenyon's interpretation of these forms as sun disks.[5] Moreover, according to Holland, there are four clear cases of horse figurines with disks from Kenyon's Cave 1 at Jerusalem, and an additional two which have not been recognized as such previously: one from Tomb 106 at Lachish, and the other from Stratum 5A at Hazor. In view of the fact that these 'disks' present the interpreter with an apparently objective criterion with which to identify the cultic significance of these horse figurines as solar, each of Holland's six cases will be considered in detail, beginning with a description.

Case 1: Horse Head Fragment, Jerusalem Cave 1.[6] This fragment, roughly four centimetres high and two centimetres wide, was found inside Cave 1. On the top of the head is what Holland describes as a

Y. Shiloh, 'Iron Age Sanctuaries and Cult Elements in Palestine', in F.M. Cross (ed.), *Symposia Celebrating the Seventy-Fifth Anniversary of the American Schools of Oriental Research (1900–1975)* (Zion Research Foundation, vols. 1-2; Cambridge, MA: ASOR, 1979), p. 147 n. 3; L.E. Stager, 'The Archaeology of the East Slope of Jerusalem and the Terraces of the Kidron', *JNES* 41 (1982), pp. 111-21.

1.　The cave was actually discovered by the square's supervisor, Donald B. Redford.

2.　Kenyon, *Digging up Jerusalem*, p. 140.

3.　Kenyon, *Digging up Jerusalem*, p. 141.

4.　Kenyon, *Digging up Jerusalem*, p. 142.

5.　Holland, 'Typological and Archaeological Study'. (See also his article, 'A Study'.)

6.　This figurine is categorized by Holland ('A Study', p. 141) as type D.IV.d.1. (I decided not to offer a drawing of this figurine because the drawing upon which it would have been based is quite crude; in any case, the 'disk' does not resemble a sun disk.)

'flatish disc-shaped decoration applied between the ears on top of a barrel-shaped muzzle'.[1]

Case 2: Neck and Shoulder Fragment, Near Jerusalem Cave 1.[2] This fragment is clearly identifiable as a horse in spite of its broken head. It was found in Trench I of Square A 25. Holland categorizes it as a type with disk because it bears on the back of the neck a piece of clay like that which seems to support a disk on figurines with intact heads.[3]

Case 3: Riderless Horse with Disk, Jerusalem Cave 1 (see pls. 3 and 4).[4] This horse, 13.5 centimetres high and fourteen centimetres long, was found inside Cave 1. The horse bears no rider and no trappings. On its head is a piece of clay shaped like a solid cornucopia the inside curl of which rests on the horse's head between its ears such that the flared end faces ahead. Assuming that the cornucopia-shaped piece is a sun disk, the extension behind the ears and following the crest of the mane is explained as holding the disk in place.[5]

Case 4: Horse with Incised Disk and Rider, Jerusalem Cave 1 (see fig. 8).[6] This horse, 12.5 centimetres long and (originally) approximately 11.5 centimetres high, was found in the wash at the entrance of the cave. Holland's description is worth citing:

> The Type D. X. b.1 horse from Jerusalem has three applied strips of clay on top of its muzzle situated on a longitudinal axis, pierced nostrils and an upright 'solar' disc between the ears which is incised with small holes. The rider is not permanently attached to the horse, but it was found with

1. Holland, 'A Study', p. 141; cf. p. 138, fig. 7.20.
2. Holland ('A Study', p. 150) classified this fragment as type D.IV.d.2. For Holland's drawing of the figurine, see *idem*, 'Typological and Archaeological Study', II, fig. 28.2. Again no drawing is offered because only the neck of the horse (which includes a small notch for a 'disk') is preserved.
3. Holland, 'A Study', p. 150.
4. Holland ('A Study', p. 141) categorizes this figurine as type D.IV.d.3. For the published photo (the same in each case), see Kenyon, 'Jerusalem 1967', pl. 36A; *idem, Digging up Jerusalem*, pl. 61.
5. Holland, 'A Study', p. 150.
6. Holland ('A Study', p. 141) calls this type D.X.b.1. One photo has been published both in Kenyon, 'Jerusalem 1967', pl. 26A, and in *idem, Digging Up Jerusalem*, pl. 60. For a different photo, see 'The Mystery of the Horses of the Sun at the Temple Entrance', *BARev* 4 (1978), p. 9.

the horse in Square A XXVI, Cave 1 in a 7th century pottery context and is similar to the ware of that pottery. The rider fits the back of the horse nicely. The rider also appears to be carrying a shield on his left side which may add weight to the theory that the horse with disc between the ears has some cultic significance with regards to the horses and chariots of the sun in the Jerusalem temple.[1]

Case 5: Horse with Seated Rider, Lachish Tomb 106 (see fig. 9).[2] This horse, about fourteen centimetres high and roughly twelve centimetres long, was found in Tomb 106, dated by Tufnell to roughly between 670 and 580 BCE.[3] The now headless horseman rides bareback with arms reaching to points below the horse's ears. On top of the horse's head and reaching down the back of the neck is a piece of clay described by Holland as an 'upraised disc between the ears of which is perhaps a "solar" symbol'.[4]

Case 6: Head and Neck Fragment with 'Disk' and Bridle Pieces, Hazor (see fig. 10).[5] This fragment, 6.5 centimetres high and 6 centimetres wide, was found on a floor of the courtyard between the Main Citadel and Northern Buildings in locus 3054a of Area B at Hazor.[6] The horse was assigned to Stratum 5A which dates roughly between 745 and 732 BCE. Holland considers the 'plain disc between its ears' as 'typologically akin' to the first three horse figurines listed above.[7]

Several archaeologists since the time of Holland's work have continued to see a connection between these and other horse figurines and the sun.[8]

1. Holland, 'Typological and Archaeological Study', I, p. 239.
2. Holland ('A Study', p. 150) categorizes this figurine as Type D.IX.e.2. For a photo, see Tufnell, *Lachish III*, II, pl. 27.2.
3. Tufnell, *Lachish III*, I, p. 179.
4. Holland, 'Typological and Archaeological Study', I, p. 238. Holland in fact regards this type of figurine as 'almost identical to the Cave 1 Type D.X.b.1 (i.e. figurine four, fig. 8, in this book) except that the Cave 1 disc has stabbed incisions covering its surface and the Lachish disc does not' ('A Study', p. 150).
5. Holland ('A Study', p. 150) categorizes this type as J.VII.c.26. For the drawing and photo in the excavation report, see respectively pls. 103.9 and 163.12, 13 in Yadin *et al.*, *Hazor II*.
6. For a photo of the general area, see Yadin *et al.*, *Hazor II*, pl. 17.1.
7. Holland, 'A Study', p. 150.
8. See, for example, E. Mazar, '"Cows of Bashan"', pp. 151-52.

Evaluation

In my judgment it is doubtful that the 'sun disks' allegedly found on the heads of these figurines can be used to support a connection between these horse figurines and an Iron Age sun cult in Palestine.

First, as Holland himself affirms, the heads of many Iron Age animal figurines bear all kinds of odd-shaped pieces of clay, the vast majority of which bear no resemblance whatsoever to 'sun disks'.[1] In light of this it is my opinion that the 'disk' in case 1 is not a sun disk but a 'blob' akin to other clay pieces found on the heads of horse figurines. Moreover, although the horse in case 3 (pls. 3-4) is more impressive, when considered within the context of other animal figurines, the so-called sun disk is still difficult to distinguish from clay pieces found on other horse figurines.

Secondly, several incongruities between these horse figurines and 2 Kgs 23.11 make it unlikely that there is a direct correspondence between these figurines and the sun cult described in this verse with reference to the Jerusalem temple. For example, unlike many of the horse figurines, the horses at the temple clearly bore no riders because they formed a team with which to draw a chariot. Further, if the horse figurines were models of the phenomenon represented at the temple of Jerusalem, one would expect also that there would be a considerable number of model chariots as well, but these seem to be relatively rare.[2] Moreover, some of the riders on the horse figurines

1. Holland ('A Study', pp. 149-50) states, 'The major problem in evaluating the horses with discs is of a typological nature. Where does one draw the line between identifying specific examples of the horse with the disc and how positive should we be in actually identifying the disc with the symbol of the sun?' This difficulty in fact led Holland to make what he openly admits is a rather arbitrary distinction between two types of clay pieces on the heads of these animals, a 'sun disc' type and a 'forelock' type, the latter of which is a somewhat 'catch-all' term for various sorts of shapes which Holland justifiably felt uncomfortable identifying as sun disks. (See, for example, pls. 5 and 8, and Holland, 'A Study', fig. 8.1; *idem*, 'Archaeological and Typological Study', II, figs. 29.1, 3, 6; 32.2; 33.2, 3; 46.7.)

2. The number of figurines of chariots found in cultic contexts is far less than the number of figurines of horses and riders. Although J.W. McKay (*Religion in Judah*, p. 33) argues for extensive archaeological evidence for chariots associated with sun worship, his discussion cannot be regarded as a fully satisfactory treatment of the archaeological data. For example, McKay cites as possible votive offerings associated with a solar cult three models of chariots from tenth-century 'Gerar'. However, according to R. Amiran and G.W. van Beek ('Jemmeh, Tell', *EAEHL* 2

bore shields which, contrary to Holland, does not seem conducive to
the notion of a connection with sun horses which, presumably, drew
riderless the chariot of the sun god.[1] In short, the correspondence
between living horses that drew wooden chariots near the entrance to
the temple and small clay horse(-and-rider) figurines found in a wide
variety of contexts, both cultic and non cultic, is far from readily
apparent.

Thirdly, the so-called disks on these horse figurines can be
accounted for more plausibly by considering them within the context
of other horse figurines (especially those from Cyprus) than by
relating them to the sun and its cult within ancient Israel. In fact,
consideration of this context welcomes an alternative explanation for
the disks that consists of three parts. (1) Numerous parallels suggest
that it was often common practice to exaggerate the shape of the mane
by making it rise high on the horse's neck (see, for example, pls. 6–8;
cf. figs. 9–10).[2] Moreover, when the prominent manes on many of
these horses extend to a point between or in front of the ears, the
front part of the mane often ends abruptly, thereby giving the manes a

[1976], pp. 545-49) this place should be assigned a different name (Tell Jemmeh,
ancient Yurza), and a different date (Iron II) should be assigned to the relevant finds.
Moreover, McKay understands two photos of the same chariot to be two separate
chariots (for which, see Sir F. Petrie, *Gerar* [London: British School of
Archaeology in Egypt, 1928], pls. 39.12, 14). Finally, there is no indication from
Petrie that these chariots were found in a cultic context (*Gerar*, p. 18), and the
chariots from Anau with which Petrie compares these chariots are considered in the
excavation report on Anau to be 'playthings' (R. Pumpelly [ed.], *Explorations in
Turkestan: Carnegie Institute of Washington Publication No. 73, Volume 1*
[Washington, DC: Carnegie Institute of Washington, 1902], pp. 171-72, pls. 47.9-
11). Regarding a partially restored chariot from Ugarit with possible solar motif and
two riders, one of whom is perhaps the sun god, if these riders belong to the chariot
(they were found several metres away from the chariot), neither is likely to be the
solar deity, for the riders are male and the solar deity *špš* is female at Ugarit.

1.   Holland, 'Typological and Archaeological Study', I, p. 239. Surely the
shield, which is attested on other mounted horsemen even if it is not present on the
one Holland mentions, and which is attested on other figurines clearly having
nothing to do with 2 Kgs 23.11, suggests a martial significance for these figurines.

2.   The phenomenon may either be cases of exaggeration or examples of the
practice of cropping the hair on the neck, the equine equivalent to our brush cut. It is
thus not surprising to find that Tufnell interpreted the horse with 'disk' from Lachish
(case 5 [fig.9]) as simply a horse with 'mane' (Tufnell, *Lachish III*, II, pl. 27.2).

'disk'-like appearance when viewed from the front (see especially pl. 6; cf. figs. 9–10). (2) Since the arms of the clay riders on many of these horse figurines often extended forward to a point at or below the horse's ears (thereby blocking a view of all but the uppermost part of the mane), the artisan often chose to portray only the uppermost part of the mane (see for example, pl. 8; cf. pl. 7 and fig. 9). In the cases then of an unfinished figurine with no rider (plausibly case 3 [pls. 3 and 4]) or of a horse with a broken rider (case 4 [fig. 8]), the mane thus gives the appearance of a disk-like object between the ears with a long 'disk support' extending behind the ears.[1] (3) Because the 'disk' in cases 4, 5 and 6 occur in association with other clay pieces on the head which are clearly part of the horse's headgear, it is possible that the 'disks' on these horses are also part of this gear. At the very least, an interpretation which attempts to account for this 'disk' without possible reference to other clay pieces found on the heads of many of these animals is open to question.

Finally and most significantly, parallel horse figurines of similar date from Cyprus also bear cone-shaped protrusions on their heads, but neither the shape of the protrusions nor the context in which these horse figurines were found suggest a connection of any kind with a sun cult (for the Cypriote figurines in question see, for example, fig. 11).[2] Clearly, then, the finding of horse figurines so near the Jerusalem temple must be interpreted in light of the context of the

1.   Thus what Holland refers to as a 'disk support' is probably the crest of the mane. (If a disk support were needed, the horse's ears probably would have been used; cf. the disk between the horns of the bull Apis [*ANEP*, fig. 570].)

2.   See, for example, E. Gjerstad *et al.*, *The Swedish Cyprus Expedition* (4 vols.; Stockholm: The Swedish Cyprus Expedition, 1934–56), II.2, pl. 17.1.7. Scholars have occasionally drawn attention in the past to a close similarity between Cypriote figurines of the Cypro-Archaic period and figurines from the same period in Palestine. Thus Holland ('A Study', p. 149) noted a Cypriote or Phoenician influence in the case of the more elaborate 'Horses with Incised Trappings' from Samaria. Similarly Gjerstad *et al.* (*Swedish Cyprus Expedition*, IV.2.323) argue that a clay horse and rider from Beth Shemesh Tomb 8 (dated to the sixth century BCE) is either an imitation of a Cypriote form or an item imported from Cyprus. Further, in her discussion of case 5 above (fig. 9), O. Tufnell (*Lachish III*, II, pl. 27.2) compares this horse and rider with a similar figurine from Tomb 8 at Amathus in Cyprus (for a photo of which see Gjerstad *et al.*, *Swedish Cyprus Expedition*, II.2, pl. 14.1.67). For the photo on which fig. 11 is based, see A.C. Brown and W.W. Catling, *Ancient Cyprus* (Oxford: Ashmolean Museum, 1975), p. 53.

archaeology of Cyprus and Palestine in general and not 2 Kgs 23.11 in particular.

To summarize, the presence of so-called sun disks on the heads of some Palestinian Iron Age horse figurines cannot be used as direct evidence for linking these horses to sun worship as reflected in the Jerusalem temple for the following reasons: (1) the problem of the presence of various shapes (some of which are mere 'blobs') on the heads of many horses; (2) incongruities between the horse(-and-rider) figurines and the riderless horses described in 2 Kgs 23.11; (3) the likelihood that the 'disks' are to be understood with reference to one or more of the following: (a) prominent manes; (b) abbreviated manes (upper part only shown); (c) flat, round, disk-like endings to manes; and (d) trappings;[1] and (4) the presence of close parallels from Cyprus.

The Solar Orientation[2] of Cultic Structures

Archaeologists often suggest on the basis of the apparently solar-specific alignment of a cultic structure that it was built by a sun cult.[3] In the case of ancient Israel, some scholars of the past have similarly

---

1.   To be sure, it might still be that the horse figurines are related to a sun cult despite the unlikelihood that the horses actually bear sun disks, but the evidence for a link with a sun cult must now be judged slim. Moreover, in light of the purpose of the present preliminary study which is to examine relatively *unambiguous* evidence for sun worship in Ancient Israel, the many horse figurines from Iron Age levels in Syria-Palestine are omitted from consideration. In any case, should further research prove that the horses relevant to an indigenous sun cult in Ancient Israel, the main thesis of this book would probably only be supported.

2.   No attempt will be made here to explore the range of possible explanations for the orientation of cultic structures beyond the option of orientation toward the sun. (For a brief survey of various explanations, see, for example, T.A. Busink, *Der Tempel von Jerusalem, von Salomo bis Herodes* [2 vols.; Leiden: Brill, 1970, 1980], II, pp. 652-56; B. Diebner, 'Die Orientierung des Jerusalemer Tempels und die "Sacred Direction" der frühchristlichen Kirchen', *ZDPV* 87 [1971], pp. 153-66.) Also, for the purposes of the hypothesis explored in this section, the direction of orientation is defined by a line extending from the centre of the cult niche/Holy of Holies (or the presumed location thereof) along the central axis of the structure towards the wall opposite the cult niche/Holy of Holies and usually containing the main entrance to the structure.

3.   Stonehenge is an obvious example.

judged the eastward orientation of such structures as the temple of Solomon and the 'Solar Shrine' at Lachish to imply the presence of solar elements within the cult.[1] Although few scholars today are inclined to interpret the orientation of the temple of Solomon with reference to a solar cult, the eastward orientation of this and a few other Yahwistic structures is nonetheless unmistakable[2] and should thus not be overlooked in a study of possible solar elements in Israelite religion. Though dubious of the solar significance of the orientation of Solomon's temple, Van Dyke Parunak nonetheless underscores the possible relevance of orientation as follows:

> Numerous cultic structures, located outside of Jerusalem, have been excavated recently. May not their devotees have belonged to the same unorthodox groups who at times gained control even of the temple precincts (2 Kings 21.2-5; 23.5, 6)? While they could not change the orientation of the Solomonic temple, they might well align their own structures to point to the astronomical objects of their worship. It would be a simple and interesting part of the excavation and publication of such cultic remains to survey and compute possible astronomical alignments.[3]

In the analysis that follows, the relevant mathematical equations set forth originally by H. Van Dyke Parunak[4] are applied in such a way as to provide a close approximation (estimated to be within a few degrees of accuracy) of the position of the sun relative to a specified cult centre.[5] Moreover, the position of the sun is indicated not only for significant days within the solar calendar (as Parunak has done for the temple of Jerusalem), but for seven-day intervals throughout the

---

1. See, for example, the works of Hollis and Starkey discussed later in this section.

2. The eastward orientation of the Jerusalem temple is well known. Yahwistic shrines that face eastwards are also attested at Arad, Lachish and, by the inference of some, Beer-sheba (on which see later in this discussion). Z. Herzog, A.F. Rainey and S. Moshkovitz ('The Stratigraphy at Beer-sheba and the Location of the Sanctuary', *BASOR* 225 [1977], p. 56) in fact claim that one'of the criteria for cultic architecture is 'orientation to the sunrise'.

3. H. Van Dyke Parunak, 'Was Solomon's Temple Aligned to the Sun?', *PEQ* 110 (1978), pp. 29.

4. Parunak, 'Solomon's Temple', pp. 30-31.

5. I am greatly indebted to Dr D. Staley, applied mathematician at Carleton University, Ottawa, for his help with the mathematical results offered in this section of the book.

entire year, thus allowing for the possibility that solar elements may have become an important part of other festival days within the calendar. The calculations of alignments found in the appendices and the discussions of each cultic structure noted below are based on the results of these computations.[1]

The Temple of Solomon

Despite a recent claim to the contrary, it is doubtful that there are any archaeological remains on the temple mount that can be used to calculate the position of either the first or the second temple.[2] Any discussion of the orientation of the Solomonic temple must therefore be based upon other factors such as biblical data and the orientation of other cultic structures, considered below.[3]

1.	The fourth and fifth equations used by Parunak ('Solomon's Temple', p. 30) were used in this study to determine the values B (an intermediate angle for calculation purposes) and H (the angle of the sun above the horizon) respectively.

It should be emphasized that the calculations offered here are only close approximations. As Van Dyke Parunak notes ('Solomon's Temple', p. 31 nn. 10, 11) the exact determination of solar alignment would require on-site measurements with a transit and consideration of minor varying factors such as 'parallax, atmospheric refraction, and diameter of the heavenly body'. Further, published reports do not always specify whether the reported angle of a structure relates to true or magnetic north. Not surprisingly, measurements of the angle of the same cultic structure can vary by a few degrees depending on the excavation report consulted. In most cases, however, the cultic structures are so far from being aligned to the sun that more precise measurements are not required. In the exceptional cases it is possible in light of the data presently available to determine only whether or not solar alignment seems likely.

2.	The arguments adduced by A.S. Kaufman ('Where the Ancient Temple of Jerusalem Stood', *BARev* 9.2 [March–April 1983], pp. 40-59) have not been generally accepted by professional archaeologists. In any case the orientation offered by Kaufman ('Ancient Temple', p. 55) of 83.8 degrees would place the sun at about ten degrees below the (flat) horizon on the days of equinoxes and at an angle of 39.16 degrees during the summer solstice. In other words, even assuming the validity of Kaufman's calculations, the temple would not have been aligned to the sun; cf. Appendix H.

3.	A discussion of the orientation of the Solomonic temple, known to face eastwards on textual grounds, is reserved for an excursus at the end of this section, following the examination of the orientation of other religious structures. The matter is also considered in a section in Chapter 3 which considers biblical evidence.

Aharoni's Eastward-Facing Temples

Y. Aharoni argues for the presence of eastward-facing shrines at Arad, Lachish and Beer-sheba. Each of these cultic structures is examined in turn.

a. *The Iron Age Temple at Arad*

Although the Yahwistic shrine at Arad underwent several changes during its short history, it is clear that the position of the cult niche relative to the doorway that leads from the broadroom to the courtyard remained the same throughout the life of the shrine.[1] Appendix A gives a close approximation of the days of the year (numbered in the left-hand column and beginning arbitrarily with day 'zero' as the day of the winter solstice) on which the sun shone along an axis leading through the doorway of the broadroom and into the Holy of Holies. On the days of equinox, days 91 and 273,[2] the angle of the sun relative to the horizon was virtually zero, indicating that, unless obstructed, the sun would have shone directly into the Holy of Holies at sunrise on these two days.

Under normal circumstances it might be reasonable to judge from this orientation that the sanctuary at Arad was intentionally aligned to the sun. In the case of this shrine, however, the situation is complicated by the presence to the east of the fortress wall which would have prevented the sun from entering the Holy of Holies at sunrise.[3] Does

---

1. On the shrine at Arad, see Y. Aharoni, 'Arad: Its Inscriptions and Temple', *BA* 31 (1968), pp. 2-32; Z. Herzog *et al.*, 'The Israelite Fortress at Arad', *BASOR* 254 (1984), pp. 1-34; Z. Herzog, M. Aharoni and A.F. Rainey, 'Arad: An Ancient Israelite Fortress with a Temple to Yahweh', *BARev* 13 (1987), pp. 16-35; D. Ussishkin, 'The Date of the Judaean Shrine at Arad', *IEJ* 38 (1988), pp. 142-57. According to Ussishkin, the shrine was built in the late eighth or early seventh centuries BCE and was destroyed in the sixth century ('Date of the Judaean Shrine', p. 155).

2. The days of equinox are those on which the angle of the sun relative to the horizon is virtually zero. Conversely, the days on which this angle is greatest, days 0 and 182, denote respectively the winter and summer solstices.

3. For example, if the height of the eastern wall was 5.4 m, the building east of the temple 2.9 m, or the eastern wall of the temple courtyard 2 m, the sun would reach the floor at the back of the Holy of Holies only at an angle above 6.5 degrees. The upper limit, of course, would be set by the height of the roof over the niche and broad-room; for example, if the roof was 1.8 m high, the maximum angle at which the sun would reach the back of the Holy of Holies would be 18 degrees.

this mean that the alignment of the temple to the sun was coincidental or that a cult with solar elements (including presumably a solar understanding of Yahweh) had to compromise to meet the need for a fortress wall?

The issue still remains clouded when taken one step further. On the one hand, it may be significant that the Holy of Holies was located at the base of the western wall, the first possible place within the fortress where direct sunlight would fall on the morning of the spring and autumnal equinoxes. Was a sun cult thus doing its best to compensate for the eastern wall? On the other hand, however, it could be that the alignment of the shrine simply corresponds to the generally east-west alignment of the fortress as whole, in which case no solar inference should necessarily be drawn from the orientation. (Moreover, the doorway of the broadroom which lies in front of the Holy of Holies does not appear to be located precisely opposite to the centre of the Holy of Holies.) Thus, whether the alignment of the Arad shrine to the equinoxes is intentional and reflective of solar elements within the cult, or coincidental and thus irrelevant to the cult, cannot be determined with certainty. On the basis of the evidence at present, however, the latter option seems more likely.

b. *Two Temples at Lachish*

Word of a 'Solar Shrine' at Lachish first came as a result of excavations conducted by J.L. Starkey in 1935. Starkey uncovered a rectangular structure of approximately 17 by 27 m which he identified as 'the sanctuary of a building dedicated to one of the later intrusive cults introduced during the Persian regime'.[1] Starkey elaborates as follows: 'The eastern orientation of the building and the position of the libation altar on the open axis line suggest a solar cult'.[2]

---

1. Tufnell, *Lachish III*, I, p. 141.

2. Tufnell, *Lachish III*, I, p. 141. According to the publisher of the final excavation report, O. Tufnell (*Lachish III*, I, p. 141), Starkey was also drawn to this conclusion because the sanctuary at the west end of the structure was two metres higher than the courtyard, as if to prevent the storerooms on the east side of the temple from blocking a good view of the rising sun. Further, Tufnell interpreted the images of a large hand and a man with arms raised skyward, found on an incense altar in the temple, as 'symbols of the solar cult' (*Lachish III*, I, pp. 61, 384; II, pl. 42.8, 9). However, these additional factors have been interpreted satisfactorily on alternative grounds in the report on the sanctuary by Aharoni (*Lachish V*, pp. 9, 44-46).

When in 1966 and 1968 Aharoni re-examined sacral structures at Lachish, he judged them somewhat differently. He interpreted the 'Solar Shrine' not as the product of an intrusive cult, but as the work of Yahweh worshippers.[1] Accordingly, Aharoni renamed the structure 'Temple 106', noting that the Yahwistic Arad and Solomonic temples (which he implicitly assumed could not be solar cult structures) were also oriented to the east.[2] Finally, Aharoni noted that to the southeast of Temple 106, which he dated to the Hellenistic Period, lay its immediate predecessor from the Persian Period, another eastward-facing Yahwistic temple known simply as 'Building 10'. Since, in light of the purpose of this book, we cannot presume with Aharoni that the Yahwistic character of a shrine necessarily precludes it from being solar, it is worth reconsidering the suggestive orientation of these structures at Lachish.

The 'Solar Shrine'. Judging the orientation of this shrine to be based on a line drawn from the back of the Holy of Holies through the centre of the doorways of both the adyton and broadroom of the IA–IB structure, the temple was not aligned to allow the sun to enter the temple at sunrise on either the days of equinox or the days of solstice, as Appendix C makes clear. Thus, the most important criterion of Starkey for judging the temple to be solar has been shown to be lacking on these fairly objective grounds.

Building 10. During the course of research on this structure, I consulted Professor J.S. Holladay, Jr, who informs me that the similarities adduced by Aharoni between Temple 106 and Building 10 are not at all striking and that the latter is much more likely to be a farmstead than a 'temple'.[3] The orientation of this structure is

1. Aharoni, *Lachish V*, pp. 9, 44-46.
2. Aharoni, *Lachish V*, pp. 1-2.
3. Oral communication. For Aharoni's argument that Building 106 is a temple, see *Lachish V*, pp. 9-10. In response to Aharoni's claim in support of the sacral identity of the structure—that a limestone incense stand or altar was assigned by mistake to the Solar Shrine and not to Building 10—Holladay notes that similar objects have been found in *houses* elsewhere, such as at Beer-sheba. For secular parallels to Building 10 which are superior to the sacral parallels adduced by Aharoni, Holladay refers to structures of Persian/Hellenistic date in the area of the old citadel at Hazor.

therefore probably not relevant for the purposes of the present study.[1]

c. The Temples at Beer-sheba

According to Aharoni and his colleagues who have published
excavation reports on Beer-sheba since his death, Beer-sheba also
bears testimony to at least one east-west facing temple.

Tel Beer-sheba was excavated between 1969 and 1974 under the
direction of Yohanan Aharoni who was seeking corroborative
evidence for his theory that Judaean border sites such as Beer-sheba
would have Jewish temples as at Arad.[2] Although no Iron Age temple
was discovered at Beer-sheba, Aharoni's theory received considerable
support in 1973 from the discovery of a dismantled four-horned altar
in the walls of a pillared building of Stratum 2. Since the blocks
formed part of a wall built in Stratum 2, this horned altar, some 63
inches high, predates the time of the construction of Stratum 2.[3]
Naturally the discovery of a massive altar from the Israelite period
led to the conclusion that there must have been a sanctuary at this time
in Beer-sheba and speculations thus arose concerning its location.
Although more than one location has been mentioned, the most
compelling is that suggested by Aharoni, namely, that the temple once
stood underneath Building 32, excavated by A.F. Rainey and dubbed
the 'Basement House'.[4]

---

1. To judge from a diagram offered by Aharoni (*Lachish V*, fig. 3), the
orientation of this structure is approximately 103.5 degrees which means that its
alignment is probably not significant with respect to the sun in any case.

2. Works relevant for the following discussion are as follows: Y. Aharoni,
'The Horned Altar of Beer-sheba', *BA* 35 (1974), pp. 2-5; *idem*, 'Excavations at
Tel Beer-sheba. Preliminary Report of the Fifth and Sixth Seasons, 1973–1974', *TA*
2 (1975), pp. 146-68; *idem*, 'Tel Beersheba', *EAEHL* 1 (1975), pp. 160-68; *idem*
(ed.), *Beer-sheba I: Excavations at Tel Beer-sheba, 1969–1971 Seasons* (PIA, 2; Tel
Aviv: Institute of Archaeology, 1973); Y. Yadin, 'Beer-sheba: The High Place
Destroyed by King Josiah', *BASOR* 222 (1976), pp. 1-17; Z. Herzog,
A.F. Rainey and S. Moshkovitz, 'The Stratigraphy at Beer-sheba and the Location
of the Sanctuary', *BASOR* 225 (1977), pp. 49-58; A.F. Rainey, 'Beer-sheba',
ISBE 1 (1979), pp. 448-51.

3. Herzog, Rainey and Moshkovitz, 'Stratigraphy at Beer-sheba', pp. 57-58.
J.S. Holladay, Jr ('Religion in Israel', p. 256) suggests that the altar may be
associated with chalices found in Stratum 5 at the northeast corner of the tel, in which
case the altar would date to as early as the late tenth or early ninth centuries BCE.

4. Soon after the discovery, Y. Yadin ('Beer-sheba: The High Place') dated the

The 'Basement House'. As Appendix D makes clear, the orientation of the foundations of this building, under which the temple is thought to have stood, suggests strongly that, if this indeed is where the temple once stood, it was probably aligned in such a way as to greet the first rays of morning on the vernal and autumnal equinoxes. However, because we are dealing with a mere hole in the ground and not a temple, it is important to assess the arguments adduced by the Tel Aviv school in favour of the notion that this was the site of an Israelite temple destroyed by Hezekiah.

First, this building is unique in so far as the excavator was aware in that the foundation trenches were dug all the way down to bedrock, thereby completely obliterating all traces of the previously existing structure(s). Since there is no structural reason for doing this, Z. Herzog, A.F. Rainey, S. Moshkovitz and Y. Aharoni offer the following cultic explanation: just as the horned altar was dismantled block by block during the cultic reforms of Hezekiah, so too all traces of this sanctuary were obliterated when it was similarly dismantled block by block.[1]

Secondly, Building 32 is the only structure at Beer-sheba oriented east-west. This is relevant in view of the following claim of Herzog, Rainey and Moshkovitz:

> Cultic buildings of the Israelite period regularly were oriented towards the sunrise (that is, east-west), such as the biblical tabernacle and the temples of Solomon and Ezekiel as well as the Israelite cult building at Arad and the Hellenistic buildings at Lachish and Beer-sheba. All three of these latter structures, discovered in excavations, have a similar plan with a courtyard on the east... Is it really conceivable that such a beautiful monument [the horned altar] could have stood anywhere except in a spacious courtyard fronting on a cultic building facing east?[2]

altar to the seventh century and associated it with Building 430, which he suggested was a cult centre in view of the presence of a drain and staircase leading up to the supposed original location of the altar. This view, however, has been effectively refuted by Herzog, Rainey and Moshkovitz, 'The Stratigraphy at Beer-sheba', pp. 53-56.

1. Aharoni, 'Fifth and Sixth Seasons', p. 162. Aharoni (p. 163) suggests that the harsher treatment of the sanctuary at Beer-sheba relative to that at Arad is because Beer-sheba can be 'singled out' as the Judaean equivalent of Bethel in Israel (cf. Amos 5.5; 8.14).

2. Herzog, Rainey and Moshkovitz, 'Stratigraphy at Beer-sheba', p. 53.

Thirdly, the size occupied by Building 32 is about the same as that occupied by the Arad (Iron Age) temple.[1]

Fourthly, Building 32 is located at the top of the ascent and on the main road from the city gate and is thus an ideal location for a building of religious significance.

Fifthly, in view of the ideal location of the site and Aharoni's searches elsewhere on the tel, 'actually no other place is left'.[2]

Sixthly, Herzog, Rainey and Moshkovitz identify traces of a chalk floor underneath the courtyard of Building 32 with the floor of the courtyard of the previously existing Stratum 3 religious structure.[3] In view of this and the evidence just cited, these scholars offer the following interpretation: 'We believe that the altar once stood in the courtyard here and that Hezekiah gave the order to remove both the altar and all traces of the building when Stratum II was built'.[4]

Finally, to Aharoni the discovery of a temple of Hellenistic date near this 'basement house' (that is, Building 32) and crossing its court-yard, 'is the strongest argument regarding the preservation of the sanctified traditions at this spot as common at other venerated places'.[5]

To evaluate, Aharoni, Rainey and others make a good case for believing that prior to the time of Stratum 2 there was an eastward-facing Judaean temple on the site later occupied by Building 32. Moreover, as Appendix D makes clear, if the temple was located in the place of the cleared area and similarly oriented, the temple would have come at least close to greeting the morning sun on equinoctial days. Nevertheless, all of the evidence in favour of this location

1. Aharoni, 'Fifth and Sixth Seasons', p. 163; Herzog, Rainey, and Moshkovitz, 'Stratigraphy at Beer-sheba', p. 57. Building 32 occupies a space of about twelve by seventeen metres. The measurement is based on the size of the final phase of the Arad temple. As noted earlier, the dimensions of the Building 10 at Lachish are irrelevant since it is probably not a temple.

2. Aharoni, 'Fifth and Sixth Seasons', p. 163.

3. Herzog, Rainey and Moshkovitz, 'Stratigraphy of Beer-sheba', p. 58. (Apparently not all of the remnants of the Stratum 3 building were obliterated underneath the courtyard of Building 32.)

4. Herzog, Rainey and Moshkovitz, 'Stratigraphy of Beer-sheba', p. 58.

5. Aharoni, 'Fifth and Sixth Seasons', p. 163. He mentions further the prob-able presence in this area of a 'high place' dating to the Persian and early Hellenistic periods and concludes that 'in spite of this latter temple's pagan and cosmopolitan nature [that is, the Hellenistic temple's], it preserved the ancient cult tradition of the site' ('Fifth and Sixth Seasons', p. 165).

(including orientation not west but east) is indirect; besides, there are other possible locations for the sanctuary as well as other possible dates for the four-horned altar (that is, well before Stratum 2).[1] In short, though tantalizing, the cleared area under Building 32 is an insufficient basis upon which to build or test any theory regarding the nature of Yahwistic temples.

The Hellenistic Temple. This structure, in part overlying Building 32, consists of a broadroom of 4 by 12 m with a courtyard to the east of some 11 by 18 m. Several factors help to identify the structure as a temple, among which are a similarity between what was left of the plan of the structure evident at Beer-sheba and that of the temple at Arad,[2] the discovery in the courtyard area of an incense altar some 60 cm high, an iron incense shovel, a base (roughly 2 m square) for an altar of burnt offering, and several *favissae* containing many (often Egyptian) votive objects. Rainey claims that the first phase of this temple began no earlier than about 125 BCE and the second lasted until 95–90 BCE.[3] Significantly, Rainey further adds that 'the central axis was turned north of east, to line up with the summer solstice'.[4]

As Appendix E makes clear, although Rainey was close in his estimation that the temple was aligned to the summer solstice,[5] the sun would have fallen upon the adyton of the temple when the angle of the sun was approximately 6.5 degrees above the level of the horizon, considerably later than sunrise.[6]

1. Note, for example, the alternative location for the altar proposed by Holladay and mentioned earlier in this discussion.
2. Unfortunately the floor plan of the southwestern part of the structure including the area where the Holy of Holies is thought to have stood is no longer preserved.
3. Rainey, 'Beer-sheba', p. 450.
4. Rainey, 'Beer-sheba', p. 450.
5. The time of the summer solstice is indicated on the chart as the time at which the angle of the sun relative to the equator was 23.81 degrees, day 182 in the left-hand column.
6. The adyton is no longer preserved. The calculations were made on the basis of a line drawn on a diagram parallel to the north wall (still preserved) and at the point were it is probable that the adyton was located. If the sanctuary were aligned to the summer solstice, it would be at an angle of approximately 63.5 degrees relative to true north, approximately 2.5 degrees less than its present position. However, if the eastern wall was two metres high, the sun would have to be at approximately this angle before reaching the adyton in any case. It is difficult to believe, however, that

Yahwistic Temples outside of Judah
Several Yahwistic religious structures are known to have existed
outside of Judah in post-exilic times. It is important to examine the
orientation of these structures in order to determine whether any of
them suggest alignment to the sun.

a. *Elephantine*
Although there are no known archaeological remains of this
sanctuary, it is perhaps appropriate to offer here the results of
calculations based on the little that can be gleaned from the archives of
Elephantine concerning the orientation of the sanctuary. If B. Porten
is correct in his judgment that the temple faced north of east, towards
Jerusalem, the angle of the structure would be approximately 18.5
degrees, in which case direct sunlight never entered the temple.[1]

b. *Leontopolis/Tell el-Yehudiyeh*
In 1906 W.M. Flinders Petrie claimed to have found at Tell el-
Yehudiyeh in the Egyptian nome of Heliopolis remains of the Jewish
sanctuary built by Onias.[2] Although there is considerable doubt that
Petrie's identification of these remains is correct,[3] there is no harm in
analyzing the orientation of the structure discovered by Petrie, especially in view of the recent claim by Hayward that the temple of Onias
referred to by Josephus is a Zadokite reconstruction of the restored
temple of Jerusalem and a structure in which solar symbolism played
an important role.[4] The orientation of this structure to some 12.5

this is the reason for the displaced orientation, for it would have been far simpler to
compensate for the presence of the wall by locating the doorway along the central
axis of the temple.
    1.   B. Porten, 'The Structure and Orientation of the Jewish Temple at
Elephantine—A Revised Plan of the Jewish District', *JAOS* 81 (1961), pp. 38-42;
idem, Archives from Elephantine (Berkeley: University of California Press, 1968),
p. 110, fig. 5.
    2.   See W.M. Flinders Petrie, *Hyksos and Israelite Cities* (London: Office of
School of Archaeology, University College, 1906), pp. 23-24, pls. 22-24. For
another description of the temple and its discovery, see *idem, Egypt and Israel*
(London: SPCK, 1911), pp. 102-103, figs. 47-48.
    3.   Note, for example, the words of R. de Vaux on p. 205 of his two-page
'Post-Scriptum' following the article of M. Delcor, 'Le temple d'Onias en Egypte',
RB 75 (1968), pp. 188-203.
    4.   See R. Hayward, 'The Jewish Temple at Leontopolis: A Reconsideration',

degrees west of north precludes the possibility that this structure was aligned to the sun.

c. *Mt Gerizim/Tell er-Rās*
An estimation of the orientation of Building B, excavated by R.J. Bull in 1966 and 1968 and judged by him to be the remains of the Samaritan temple, reveals that this structure, aligned about 14.8 degrees east of north, clearly never had direct sunlight running parallel with its axis.[1]

d. *Qaṣr el-'Abd*
The orientation of the temple of the Tobiad Hyrcanus at 'Arāq el-Amīr is about nineteen degrees west of north. It is therefore not aligned towards the sun.[2]

JJS 33 (=Yadin Festschrift) (1982), pp. 429-43. Hayward argues, for example ('Jewish Temple', pp. 434-37, 440), that the adaptation of the seven-branched menorah signifying the planets in relation to the sun to a single brilliant light described in terms of a divine epiphany denotes Yahweh as the divine sun who, according to Isa. 60.19-21, replaces the sun as the source of light in the restored Jerusalem. See the section on Zadokites in the next chapter for further discussion of Hayward's notion. (I am indebted to P.R. Davies for drawing the article of Hayward to my attention.)

1. For details concerning the excavations, see, for example, R.J. Bull, 'The Excavations of Tell er-Ras on Mt. Gerizim', *BA* 31 (1968), pp. 58-72; *idem*, 'Er-Ras, Tell (Mount Gerizim)', *EAEHL* 4 (1978), pp. 1015-22; R.J. Bull and E.F. Campbell, 'The Sixth Campaign at Balâṭah (Shechem)', *BASOR* 190 (1968), pp. 4-19. For a brief general discussion, see also V. Fritz, *Tempel und Zelt* (WMANT, 47; Neukirchen–Vluyn: Neukirchener Verlag, 1977), pp. 79-81. The estimation of orientation offered here is based on the assumption that the directional arrow in the diagram offered by R.J. Bull ('Er-Ras, Tell', p. 1021) points to true north, as is confirmed later by Bull ('A Tripartite Sundial from Tell Er Râs on Mt. Gerizim', *BASOR* 219 [1975], p. 36). If this structure is correctly identified by Bull (which it may not be; see R.T. Anderson, 'The Elusive Samaritan Temple', *BA* 54.2 [June 1991], pp. 106-107) and if Josephus (*Ant.* 11.8) is correct in associating the construction of the temple with the expelled Zadokite priesthood from Jerusalem, then it appears that at least in this case Zadokites had no concern to align temples with the sun.

2. The calculation is based on the diagram offered by P.W. Lapp ('The Second and Third Campaigns at 'Arâq el-Emîr', *BASOR* 171 [1963], p. 22, fig. 7). Even if Lapp did not record true but magnetic north as 'north', the temple would not be aligned with the sun. For a general discussion, see Fritz, *Tempel*, pp. 87-91.

Other Religious Structures

Calculations made on the following additional cultic structures gave no suggestion of alignment on solar grounds: the 'Stelae Temple' of Hazor Area C;[1] the 'temples' of Hazor Area H (Strata 3, 2, 1B and 1A);[2] the 'High Place' at Tel Dan;[3] the temple at Tell Ta'yinat;[4] and Cult Room 49 at Lachish (Stratum 5).[5]

1.   The presence of a crescent with disk in the central stele in this shrine dating to the Late Bronze II–III period raises the question of the possible significance of the shrine's eastward orientation. Assuming the axis to extend from the back of the shrine following a line parallel to the southern and northern walls and extending through the inner doorway of the shrine, neither a calculation based on the assumption that the diagram offered by Yadin (*Head of all those Kingdoms*, fig. 16) records true north nor that it records magnetic north suggests that the level IA shrine was aligned with respect to the rising sun on solstices or equinoxes. (This is strongly suggested also by the indirect access to the shrine.)

2.   Yadin, *Head of all those Kingdoms*, figs. 18-21. (Cf. M. Ottosson, *Temples and Cult Places in Palestine* [Boreas, 12; Uppsala: n.p., 1980], pp. 28, 31.)

3.   At no point during the year does the sun shine directly in line with the high place at Dan at an angle below 32 degrees, meaning that alignment, towards the sun at mid morning, is not likely to be intentional. (Even if Biran's directional arrow points to magnetic north, the minimum angle of the sun in the horizon relative to the axis of the high place does not go below 32 degrees.) For the diagram of the site on which the calculation was based, see A. Biran, 'Two Discoveries at Tel Dan', *IEJ* 30 (1980), fig. 1. For a description of this cultic complex, see *idem*, 'Tel Dan Five Years Later', *BA* 43 (1980), pp. 175-76.

4.   This temple is of interest in the present context because of its close similarity with the plan of the Solomonic temple. (See, for example, E.G. Wright, 'Solomon's Temple Resurrected', *BA* 4 [1941], pp. 20-21. For a balanced recent appraisal, see J. Quellette, 'Temple of Solomon', *IDBSup*, p. 872.) The orientation of this national Syrian temple of the eighth century BCE can be determined on the basis of plans offered in the excavation report (R.C. Haines, *Excavations in the Plain of Antioch II* [OIP, 95; Chicago: University of Chicago Press, 1971], II, pls. 93, 103) to be approximately 83.5 degrees. As Appendix F shows, on the days of equinox the angle of the sun is about 8 degrees below the horizon. Even allowing for a margin of error of a few degrees, it is doubtful that the temple was aligned to greet the morning sun on the days of equinox or at any other time. (Thankfully, Haines [*Excavations*, pl. 93] distinguishes between true and magnetic north.)

5.   Assuming the orientation of this Yahwistic shrine of the tenth century BCE to be along a line drawn from perpendicular to the back of the wall outward through the presumed sight of the door, the direction is approximately 43.5 degrees. (The calculation was based on the plan of the sanctuary offered by Aharoni, *Lachish V*, pl. 60. On the problems with identifying the doorway, see *Lachish V*, p. 26.)

Summary

Except in the cases of the Iron Age sanctuaries at Arad and Beer-sheba, there is no reason to believe that the orientation of any of the temples discussed above reflects a concern for alignment to the sun on any significant days within the solar year. Concerning the exceptions, the alignment to the equinoctial sun of the sanctuary at Arad is probably not suggestive of solar elements within the cult and the alignment of the sanctuary at Beer-sheba is *in toto* a theoretical construct upon which no weight of evidence can be placed.

In addition to this summary, a few additional notes may be added that are relevant to some of these cultic structures. First, it is worth emphasizing that there is no indication that Yahwistic cultic architecture in the post-exilic period was influenced by considerations of solar alignment. Secondly, unlike the archaeological indications from the north in the tenth century BCE studied earlier in this chapter, Cult Room 49 at Lachish provides no artefactual indication of the presence of solar elements within Yahwism. Perhaps, then, solar elements in the tenth century BCE were sporadic or confined to the north (or both), or, more likely, these elements were present only in spheres under the influence of royal religion.

The 'Solar' Orientation of the Temple of Solomon[1]

As noted earlier, there are no confirmed archaeological remains with which to determine the precise orientation of the temple of Solomon. The task of assessment thus involves consideration of indirect evidence, which includes the following: (1) the biblical evidence (for which see Chapter 3); (2) the results of calculations conducted on the structures just examined (for the application of which see later in this section); and (3) the results of calculations conducted on various theoretical points of reference for the Solomonic temple that have

---

Neither orientation nor contents suggest solar elements within the variety of Yahwism represented by this shrine.

1.   For recent discussions of the orientation of the Solomonic temple which deal with the possibility of alignment on solar grounds, see, for example, Busink, *Der Tempel*, I, pp. 252-56; Diebner, 'Die Orientierung', pp. 157-59; Ottosson, *Temples and Cult Places*, pp. 115-18; L.A. Snijders, 'L'orientation du temple de Jérusalem', *OTS* 14 (1965), pp. 214-34, *passim*; Fritz, *Tempel*, p. 68; and Stähli, *Solare Elemente*, p. 15 n. 66.

been proposed in the history of scholarship[1] (for which see immediately below).

In the early part of this century two slightly different views concerning the 'solar' orientation of the Solomonic temple arose. First was the view of C.V.L. Charlier, according to whom the temple was aligned so that on the two equinoctial days of the year (estimated by him to be the first day of the first month and the tenth day of the seventh month) the sun rose over the Mount of Olives and shone through the eastern gate and into the Holy of Holies.[2] The second view was put forth by A.F. von Gall, according to whom the Solomonic temple was not aligned with respect to the equinoxes, but as a result of the answer Yahweh gave to Solomon when this king sought an oracle from him in light of one of the two eclipses that occurred during his reign, namely, the one on 22 May 948 BCE (cf. 1 Kgs 8.53 [LXX]). Thus, the central axis of the temple was aligned so that on the day of eclipse the rising sun would shine into the Holy of Holies from the crest of the Mount of Olives.[3] Since these views were built upon by Morgenstern[4] and Hollis[5] in the thirties, they will be evaluated in conjunction with the construals offered by these later scholars.

In his study 'The Gates of Righteousness' J. Morgenstern notes in detail many of the cosmic and even solar traditions associated with the

1. See, for example, W.C. Graham and H.G. May, *Culture and Conscience: An Archaeological Study of the New Religious Past in Ancient Palestine* (Chicago, IL: The University of Chicago Press, 1936), pp. 237-38; T.H. Gaster, *Thespis* (New York: Gordian, 2nd edn, 1975), p. 67; Fritz, *Tempel*, p. 68.

2. C.V.L. Charlier, 'Ein astronomischer Beitrag zur Exegese des Alten Testaments', *ZDMG* 58 (1904), pp. 386-94.

3. A.F. von Gall, 'Ein neues astronomisch zu erschließendes Datum der ältesten israelitischen Geschichte', in K. Marti (ed.), *K. Budde zum siebzigsten Geburtstag am 13 April 1920* (BZAW, 34; Giessen: Töpelmann, 1920), pp. 52-60.

4. J. Morgenstern, 'The Gates of Righteousness', *HUCA* 6 (1929), pp. 1-31.

5. F.J. Hollis, 'The Sun-Cult and the Temple at Jerusalem', in S.H. Hooke (ed.), *Myth and Ritual* (London: Oxford University Press, 1933), pp. 87-110; *idem*, *The Archaeology of Herod's Temple* (London: J.M. Dent and Sons, 1934), pp. 132-39.

It should be noted that H.G. May also did much to popularize the notion of a solar cult associated with the temple, but since his arguments are mostly literary and thus contribute nothing to the mathematical plausibility of solar orientation, they are not discussed in the present context. (See, for example, H.G. May, 'Some Aspects of Solar Worship at Jerusalem', *ZAW* 55 [1937], pp. 269-81.)

gate at the east of the temple area, known in ancient times as the eastern gate and still known today as the 'Golden' Gate.[1] Morgenstern adapts the talmudic tradition that associates the gate with the two days of solstice by associating it rather with the two days of equinox, thereby bringing the tradition into conformity with the work of Charlier and with what seems to be far more plausible on astronomical grounds (alignment of the gate to the solstice is clearly impossible).[2] Morgenstern thus hypothesizes that the temple was aligned so that the sun would rise over the Mount of Olives on the vernal and autumnal equinoctial days (the latter of which is to be associated with a New Year festival) and shine through the eastern gate into the Holy of Holies. The hypothesis thus attempts to explain in solar terms a considerable amount of biblical tradition, including the coming and leaving of the glory of Yahweh through the eastern gate.[3]

To evaluate, the mathematical reassessment offered H. Van Dyke Parunak is absolutely correct: a line drawn from the supposed site of the temple (the Sacred Rock on the temple mount) to the eastern gate (the Golden Gate) shows that the sun could not have shone into the Holy of Holies at this angle (calculated by Parunak to be 58.2 degrees[4]), as Appendix G confirms. The arguments, at least when based upon the points of reference chosen by Charlier and Morgenstern, are thus to be doubted.

Turning to consider the two studies of F.J. Hollis on 'solar orientation', they reflect an indebtedness to the view originally proposed by von Gall and overlap somewhat with the views of both Morgenstern and Charlier.[5] Hollis adduces four possible lines of evidence for a solar orientation of the Solomonic temple. (1) A line drawn from the centre of the Sacred Rock of the temple mount to the summit of the Mount of Olives passes at right angles to the line of the eastern retaining wall (that is, along the presumed axis of the Solomonic temple) which indicates that this line of view from the Holy of Holies to the summit of the Mount of Olives was sacred.[6] (2) Following von

1. Morgenstern, 'Gates of Righteousness', pp. 1-31.
2. Morgenstern, 'Gates of Righteousness', pp. 16-19.
3. Morgenstern, 'Gates of Righteousness', pp. 31-37.
4. Parunak, 'Solomon's Temple', pp. 31-33.
5. Hollis, 'Sun-Cult'; *idem, Herod's Temple*.
6. Hollis, 'Sun-Cult', pp. 100-102; *idem, Herod's Temple*, pp. 133, 136. Further, according to Hollis ('Sun-Cult', pp. 92, 94; *idem, Herod's Temple*,

Gall, the solar eclipse of 948 BCE resulted both in the oracle of 1 Kgs 8.12-13 (cf. LXX v. 53) and in the construction of the temple itself.[1] (3) The temple was built in the territory of the tribe of Benjamin who, to judge from an alternative form of the name which possibly means 'worshippers of the sun', were perhaps members of a sun cult.[2] (4) The temple was aligned to the sun as it rose over the Mount of Olives on the two days of equinox.[3] Moreover, Hollis adds that the eastern line of the temple platform (assumed to be at right angles to the post-exilic temple) is aligned some five degrees southwards relative to the line of the retaining wall (assumed to be at right angles to the Solomonic temple), a fact which likely reflects an intentional displacement of the orientation of the post-exilic temple away from its former offensive solar orientation.[4]

To evaluate, all four of Hollis's points are seemingly untenable. The first point suffers from a major difficulty noted also by Parunak, namely, that the top of the Mount of Olives is a long ridge with no clearly identifiable summit.[5] Hollis's 'summit' is thus somewhat arbitrary. Regarding the second point, the date of the solar eclipse

---

p. 133), Mishnaic traditions about the sacrifice of a red heifer on the Mount of Olives whence the priest is said to be able to see into the temple gives further evidence of both the significance and the sanctity of this line of view.

1.   Hollis, 'Sun-Cult', pp. 90-91; *idem, Herod's Temple*, pp. 138-39. Cf. von Gall, 'Ein neues astronomisch zu erschließendes Datum', pp. 57-59.

2.   Hollis, 'Sun-Cult', pp. 87-88; *idem, Herod's Temple*, p. 137. Hollis suggests that the alternate name for Benjamin offered in Gen. 35.18, *ben-'ônî* is perhaps not 'son of my sorrow', but 'people of On' (On being the 'ancient name of the city called by the Greeks "Heliopolis", that is, the city of the Sun-god' [*idem*, 'Sun-Cult', pp. 87-88]) and thus 'sun-worshippers' (*idem, Herod's Temple*, p. 137).

3.   Hollis, 'Sun-Cult', p. 104; *idem, Herod's Temple*, p. 133.

4.   Hollis, 'Sun-Cult', pp. 107-108, 110.

5.   Parunak, 'Solomon's Temple', p. 31 n. 12. That the summit is flat is mentioned by Hollis, but only in passing (Hollis, 'Sun-Cult', p. 92). If this line so important to Hollis pointed to a specifically discernible 'summit' on the Mount of Olives, the significance he accords to this line would perhaps be justified. But since there is no such point, and since this line is at a different angle than that required to line up with the sun at early morning on the days of equinox, it is difficult to see that this line has any significance whatever, in spite of Hollis's reference to the claim in the Mishnah that the temple entrance could be seen during the time of the sacrifice of a red heifer on the Mount of Olives.

(948 BCE) is too late to have been of any influence on the construction of the temple, as Petrie noted long ago.[1] The third point is based on a very unlikely interpretation of the alternate name for Benjamin, *ben-'ônî*, as 'worshippers of the sun'.[2] Regarding the fourth point, Parunak is correct that the angle of Hollis's sacred line, nearly 84 degrees east of true north, does not indicate alignment of the temple to the equinoxes.[3] Further, although Hollis seems to imply that, in order to compensate for the presence of the Mount of Olives, the angle of true alignment to the equinoxes would be to the north of east (and thus not far from the actual reckoning), the angle needed to align the temple with the sun on equinoctial sunrises would in fact be a few degrees *south* of east when an obstacle[4] such as the Mount of Olives lies to the east of the religious structure.[5] Thus, because the

1. W.M. Flinders Petrie, 'Supposed Sun Worship at Jerusalem', *Syro-Egypt* 3 (1938), p. 11; cf. Bright, *History of Israel*, p. 218.

2. The final *yod* on *'ônî* has to be ignored with Hollis's construal. Further, the rendition of the name as 'son of my sorrow', makes perfect sense and is welcomed by the context. See further BDB, p. 122; W.F. Albright, 'Review of *Myth and Ritual*, edited by S.H. Hooke', *JPOS* 14 (1934), p. 155.

3. See Appendix H and Parunak, 'Solomon's Temple', pp. 31-33. Hollis's seeming awareness of this issue and his attempt to deal with it are reflected in the following statements (Hollis, *Herod's Temple*, p. 133): 'Now this line [that is, the line of vision from the Sacred Rock at right angles to the line of the retaining wall] is 5 degrees north of the true east and west line. . . so that if in ancient times occasion of the sacrifice on the Sacred Rock, and the time of sacrifice was at the moment when the sun's disk appeared over the summit of the Mount of Olives, the sun would have had to rise north of east, viz. about one degree north of the line from the Rock to the summit. That is to say, the sacrifice would have taken place 15 days before the true equinox, a date early in September, which might well have been observed in that climate as the yearly feast of thanksgiving for the harvest.' In other words, Hollis admits that his alignment is correct only for a time roughly two weeks before the equinox. (This may be confirmed by reference to day 259 in Appendix H, two weeks before the equinoctial day 273 and at which time the sun would be just less than 2 degrees over the horizon when it shone into the Holy of Holies, assuming a flat horizon eastwards.) Moreover, in view of the presence of the Mount of Olives to the east of the temple mount, the sun would not shine into the Holy of Holies until a time closer to day 252, *more* than two weeks before the equinox.

4. Assuming a flat horizon to the east of the temple platform, the angle for alignment to the equinoctial sunrise would of course be 90 degrees. (See Appendix I on which is plotted the position of the sun at this hypothetical angle.)

5. See the earlier discussion of the Arad temple in which an analogous case was

crest of the Mount of Olives is some 60 m higher than the temple
mount and about 1050 m away (thus blocking the view of the sun
while it ascended almost 4 degrees), Hollis's angle is actually some 8
degrees[1] north of the orientation expected if the Solomonic temple
were aligned to meet the sun as it first appeared over the Mount of
Olives on the two days of equinox. For Hollis's angle to be significant,
it must reflect an event just prior to the equinox, such as the
commencement of the Feast of Booths, a point which Hollis himself
admits.[2]

Although my evaluation of earlier scholarship sympathetic to the
notion of the solar orientation of the Solomonic temple has been
largely negative to this point, three factors temper this negative
climate at least to a certain extent. First, it must be remembered that
the evidence examined in this section merely calls into question the
solar significance of the points of alignment chosen by Morgenstern
and Hollis, little more than arbitrary points to be sure, and not the
theoretical possibility of solar alignment. Secondly, it has to be
admitted that from the standpoint of astronomy, temple architecture,
or even topography[3] it is theoretically possible for the sun to have
shone through the eastern gate of the Temple and into the Holy of
Holies on a significant occasion within the year such as a time of

noted with respect to the eastern wall of the fortress.

1. In fact, on the basis of Parunak's recalculation of the angle offered by Hollis
(Parunak, 'Solomon's Temple', pp. 29, 32), Hollis's angle of alignment is roughly
9 degrees off the line required for the equinox.

2. Hollis, *Herod's Temple*, p. 133.

3. This merely involves that assumption that the biblical description of the
temple gives a fairly accurate portrayal of the dimensions of the temple. For example,
if the dimensions of the temple (specifically the length of the structure and the height
of the doors in each section of the temple) were those which Busink suggests (*Der
Tempel*, I, p. 167), the sun would have been able to shine into the Holy of Holies at
an angle between roughly 3.5 and 13 degrees, the lower limit being defined by the
height of the crest of the Mount of Olives (roughly 800 m above sea level and thus
60 m higher than the temple mount), and the upper limit being defined by the height
of the doors of the temple (for which see Busink, *Der Tempel*, I, p. 167). Moreover, calculations conducted for this study but not recorded here confirm Parunak's
judgment that the temple would have to be aligned at 61 degrees and 119 degrees to
line up directly with the summer and winter solstices respectively. (Again the angle
would be about 3.5 degrees greater in each case if the Mount of Olives is made the
practical horizon; cf. Parunak, 'Solomon's Temple', pp. 32-33.)

equinox.[1] (The issue whether solar orientation seems not just theoretically possible but likely is of course the remaining question; whereas examination of archaeological data has offered no clear analogue, examination of the biblical material will offer strong support for the influence of solar elements at the time of the construction of the temple, but not necessarily support for an effect of these elements on the alignment of the temple.) Thirdly, in light of evidence considered in Chapter 3 for the Feast of Booths as a locus for solar Yahwism, it is worth noting in passing that there is a correspondence between the time of the Feast of Booths and the time during which Hollis's 'sacred line' (that is, his theorized axis of the temple) would be of significance for a solar cult. (It of course remains uncertain whether Hollis's line reflects the real axis of the temple.)

In sum, although no firm judgment can be made concerning the orientation of the temple without consideration of biblical evidence,[2]

1.   For example, if the temple were aligned at an angle of 90 or 93 degrees (depending on whether the temple was aligned to a theoretically flat horizon or to the summit of the Mount of Olives) the sun would have shone into the Holy of Holies when it rose over the horizon on the two equinoctial days.

2.   The need for caution until the biblical evidence is considered may be illustrated by reference to one example. Ezek. 8.16 describes a climactic abomination in which a group of priests are prostrating themselves before the sun at a point between the porch of the temple and the altar of burnt offerings. Assuming that this eastward-facing temple was aligned at 90 degrees (or a little more to compensate for the height of the Mount of Olives) then, at least according to the date for this event given by Greenberg (cf. Ezek. 8.1), these men were prostrating themselves toward the sun in the temple area during one of the two fortnightly periods during the whole year when the sun shone directly inside the temple into the Holy of Holies. (On the date of 19 September 596 BCE given by M. Greenberg, see his *Ezekiel 1–20* [AB, 22; Garden City, NY: Doubleday, 1983], p. 166 and the discussion of Ezek. 8.16 offered in Chapter 3.)

Moreover, although Busink argues that the location of the men between the porch and altar of burnt offerings in Ezek. 8.16 is suggestive (*Der Tempel*, II, p. 652) that the temple was not well suited to a solar cult, this assumes that what took place at the altar of burnt offerings merely compensated for some inherent inadequacy in the temple itself as a solar facility. It could equally be the case, however, that the altar of burnt offerings was simply part of a comprehensive solar cult establishment that might have included the temple itself, an alternative that can be supported by a considerable amount of biblical evidence (see Chapter 3). Moreover, regarding Busink's argument that the location of the worshippers behind the altar of Ahaz suggests that the sun was already quite high in the sky, this is a minor point which I strongly

the indirect archaeological evidence of the orientation of analogous structures offers little or no reason to believe that the temple of Solomon was intentionally aligned to the sun as a reflection of cultic practice. While orientation to the sun is not always characteristic of sun temples, the lack of clear orientation to the sun on the part of any Yahwistic cultic structure attested provides no firm indication of the presence of solar elements within the cult.

A Royal Stamp with Bull and Disk

The discovery at Ramat Raḥel, just south of Jerusalem, of seal impressions that depict a bull between the horns of which is a sun disk possibly provides further evidence for sun worship in ancient Israel.[1] According to G. Ahlström, the common association of Yahweh and the bull, and the location of the seal in a royal palace of Judah means in fact that the bull with the sun disk is Yahweh.[2] The matter clearly merits further study.

The context in which the impressions were found is as follows. Each of the five years in which Y. Aharoni excavated at Ramat Raḥel (1954, 1959–1962) brought to light one seal impression with bull and sun disk, except for the 1960 season which yielded three.[3] These seven seal impressions, discovered in conjunction with anepigraphic impressions that bear mostly lions and rosettes as well as epigraphic impressions that include those of the Yehud variety, were found in dump pits and fills in the area of the destroyed Stratum 5-A Citadel, which dates to the end of the Iron Age.[4] There is a consensus that

suspect is irrelevant in view of the scale of the altar relative to the angle of the sun and the distance of the worshippers away from the altar.

1. This solar interpretation was first suggested to the excavator, Y. Aharoni, by L. Rahmani (Aharoni, *Seasons 1959 and 1960*, p. 10 n. 29).

2. G.W. Ahlström, 'An Archaeological Picture of Iron Age Religions', *StudOr* 55 (1984), p. 130.

3. For a discussion of these finds and diagrams or photos, see the following reports: Y. Aharoni, 'Excavations at Ramath Raḥel, 1954: Preliminary Report', *IEJ* 6 (1956), p. 147; *idem, Seasons 1959 and 1960*, p. 10, fig. 9.11; p. 34, pl. 30.8; *idem, Seasons 1961 and 1962*, p. 22, pl. 21.9; pp. 45-46, pl. 21.8.

4. Y. Aharoni, 'Ramat Raḥel', *EAEHL* 4 (1978), p. 1007. In this respect Ahlström's claim that the impressions were found in the area of the palace is somewhat misleading.

these seal impressions belong to the Persian Period,[1] and within that period it is reasonable to suppose that they belong between the end of the sixth and the latter part of the fifth centuries BCE.[2] Moreover, because they were found with inscribed seal impressions belonging to officials within the administration of Judah, the animal impressions are also assumed to have belonged to these officials.[3]

Ephraim Stern's important work on the origin of the imagery on these seal impressions provides an important clue to understanding the possible significance of the bull with the sun disk. According to Stern, the seal impressions with bull and disk are typologically akin to two types of lion impressions that were found in the same context at Ramat Raḥel (as well as to other types of animal impressions that have been found elsewhere).[4] Moreover, these two types of lion impressions appear to be crude imitations of Achaemenid motifs, similar to those attested in royal archives from both Persepolis and Ur.[5] Thus, on the basis of these two considerations, it is reasonable to suppose that the seal impressions with bull and sun disk are also imitations of Achaemenid motifs, although it must be admitted that the parallels which Stern adduces between the bull impressions from Judah and those from Ur are less striking than the parallels which he notes between the lions from Judah and those from the Achaemenid realm.[6]

To evaluate, in view of the typological relationship just noted, no

1. For a summary of various views, see E. Stern, *Material Culture of the Land of the Bible in the Persian Period 538–332 BC* (Warminster, England: Aris & Phillips, 1982 [Hebrew, 1973]), pp. 209-10.

2. Stern, *Material Culture*, pp. 209-11.

3. E. Stern, 'Seal-Impressions in the Achaemenid Style in the Province of Judah', *BASOR* 202 (1971), p. 14.

4. Stern, *Material Culture*, pp. 209-11.

5. Stern, *Material Culture*, pp. 209-11. See also, *idem*, 'Seal-Impressions', p. 10.

6. The parallel between the bull impressions is less than striking because the Achaemenian example is a bull with a lunar crescent over its croup (for which see L. Legrain, *Seal Cylinders* [Ur Excavations, 10; London: Oxford University Press, 1951], p. 51, pl. 41.790), whereas the Judaean example is a bull with a sun disk between its horns. Sun disks attested on the Achaemenian examples are shown as a winged sun disk (the symbol of the supreme deity Ahura-mazda), or as a rosette with a circle in it comfortingly like another impression found at Ramat Raḥel (for which see Stern, *Material Culture*, fig. 344). On the discovery of the collection from Ur, see Legrain, *Seal Cylinders*, pp. ix-x, 47.

more significance should be attributed to these impressions than to the
other animal impressions that also appear to have been borrowed
from royal archives of the Achaemenid realm. Further, according to
Stern, these animal impressions likely date to a time prior to the
attainment of Judaean autonomy from Samaria and they appear also to
have been replaced by seal impressions of the Yehud variety, devoid
of such imagery.[1] All of these factors thus suggest that the use by a
royal Judaean official (or officials) of a seal impression of a bull with
a sun disk should be regarded as not necessarily indicative of the
presence of solar elements within the religious outlook of royal
officials of Judah in the Persian Period.

Yahwistic Personal Names from Epigraphic Sources

Personal names attested on Hebrew inscriptions might be expected to
provide insight into the relationship between sun worship and
Yahwism. J. Tigay's recent compilation of Israelite personal names
from both epigraphic onomastic and non-onomastic inscriptional
sources provides a convenient source from which to extract Israelite
personal names containing possible solar elements.[2] These names,
listed in Appendix J, are evaluated below.

To evaluate, the names *'wryhw*, *'ryhw* and *'ryw* are roughly akin to
the biblical names Uriah and Uriyahu and, like them, mean 'Yahweh
is (my) light'. Although Yahweh is clearly associated with a luminous
body here, there is no way of knowing on the basis of the name alone
whether Yahweh was associated with the sun (or some other light) in
reality, as Stähli claims, or only figuratively, as Noth suggests.[3] In
either case, that the element 'light' (*'[w]r*) occurs (albeit rarely) in

---

1.   Stern, *Material Culture*, p. 213.

2.   Tigay, *No Other Gods*. Following Tigay, names with the ambiguous element
'l, 'god (or perhaps El)', are excluded from the study. Tigay judges that there is
virtually no evidence from either epigraphic onomastic evidence or non-onomastic
inscriptional evidence to suggest that Shemesh was worshipped by Judahites as a
deity *independent from Yahweh*, at least from the eighth century BCE to the end of
the southern kingdom, and probably from as early as the time of the United
Monarchy or even the period of the Judges (emphasis mine).

3.   Stähli, *Solare Elemente*, pp. 40-41; M. Noth, *Die israelitischen Personennamen im Rahmen der gemeinsemitischen Namengebung* (BWANT, 3.10; Stuttgart:
Kohlhammer, 1928), p. 167.

non-Israelite personal names with the names of deities not known to have solar associations makes it advisable not to assume solar implications in the case of these Yahwistic names.[1] The same must be said in the case of Neriyahu (*nryhw*), 'My lamp is Yahweh'; though suggestive, the first element occurs frequently in non-Israelite personal names with theophoric elements that have no known association with the sun.[2]

Turning finally to Yehozarah (*yhwzrḥ*), 'Yahweh has shone forth', although it might be that Yahweh is understood to shine forth in a purely figurative sense, that this is so in the present case is perhaps doubtful. First, apart from cases in which the verb describes the action of Yahweh or his glory (*kābôd*), the verb *zrḥ*, 'rise, shine forth', is used almost exclusively of the action of the sun.[3] Thus,

1. Noth (*Die israelitischen Personennamen*, p. 168) considered personal names with *'ûr* to be evidently 'genuinely Israelite'. He compares (p. 169) the (figurative) link between the deity and light in Isa. 10.17 and Ps. 27.1, which seems entirely plausible. Non-Israelite cases attest to the use of the element with known astral bodies (for example, the Amorite personal name *Ú-ri-e-ra-aḫ* from Mari in which 'light' occurs with the name of the moon god, Yariḫ) as well as with deities with no clear astral link (for example, *Mlkm'wr* in the Ammonite Baalis seal from Tell el-Umeiri, or *U-ri-adu* attested in the Alalakh tablets). (On these names, see respectively, H.B. Huffmon, *Amorite Personal Names in the Mari Texts* [Baltimore, MD: The Johns Hopkins University Press, 1965], pp. 169-70; Younker, 'Baalis Seal', pp. 173-80; and Huffmon, *Amorite Personal Names*, p. 170.)

2. In addition to the examples cited by Noth (*Personennamen*, pp. 167-68), see Huffmon, *Amorite Personal Names*, p. 243; and F. Gröndahl, *Die Personennamen der Texte aus Ugarit* (Studia Pohl, 1; Rome: Pontifical Biblical Institute, 1967), pp. 165-66.

3. Exceptions to usage of *zrḥ* with reference to the sun or Yahweh and his glory are 2 Chron. 26.19 where it is used of an 'outbreak' of leprosy, and Ps. 112.4 where it is not clear whether the light (*'ôr*) said to shine forth refers to sunlight. That the verb should be understood as referring to the shining or breaking forth of the sun in the Israelite personal names with Yahwistic elements is further supported by Deut. 33.2 and Isa. 60.1-2 which have Yahweh and his glory (respectively) as the subject of the verb and which in fact elaborate upon the solar imagery strongly implied by *zrḥ*, 'shine forth'. (It could be that the usage of poetic imagery in passages like these provided the inspiration for the application of solar imagery in the personal names. However, that *zārah*, 'shine', was perhaps not used merely metaphorically at least in the case of Deut. 33.2 is argued in the next chapter.) On the usage of this verb with respect to both Yahweh and the sun, see also F. Schnutenhaus, 'Das Kommen und Erscheinen Gottes im Alten Testament', *ZAW* 76 (1964), p. 9; Stähli, *Solare*

although it might be that biblical passages referring to the shining forth of Yahweh are themselves to be understood figuratively, there can be little doubt that the 'figure' in question is that of the appearance of Yahweh as the sun. Secondly, unlike *'wr/'yr* and *nr, zrḥ*, 'shine forth', is not as widely attested in non-Israelite personal names[1] as one might expect if Noth were right that the use of the verb is merely figurative, reflecting the widespread belief in the ancient Near East that the sun's light at dawn denoted luck and blessing.[2] Moreover, in addition to Yehozarah, the name Sheharya (*šḥryh*), 'Yahweh is dawn', is equally explicit in its association of Yahweh with the sun and is also rarely associated with clearly identifiable non-solar deities outside of Israel. The name is attested both in the Bible and in hypocoristic form in several late-Judahite Hebrew bullae.[3] Thus, though far from proving the case, all of this tends to suggest that the solar element in such names as Yehozarah and Sheharya refers not to a general figurative notion also common outside of Israel, but to a perception of Yahweh as 'solar' within ancient Israel.[4]

Elemente, pp. 40-41. (Schnutenhaus notes that the verb is used of the sun twelve out of eighteen times in the Old Testament.)

1.   Comparable forms are the South Arabian *drḥ'l* (cited by Noth, *Personennamen*, p. 184 n.1) and Akkadian *Za-ar-ḫilu* (for which see K.L. Tallqvist, *Assyrian Personal Names* [Leipzig: August, 1914], p. 247), but it is not clear whether the deity referred to is solar.

2.   Interestingly, the only evidence that Noth (*Personennamen*, pp. 167, 184) cites in favour of the existence of this figurative understanding of light by the people of the 'ancient orient' is biblical.

3.   For the biblical case, see 1 Chron. 8.26. There is in 1 Chron. 7.10 also an Ahishahar (*'ᵃḥîšāhar*), but the referent is uncertain. On the Hebrew bullae in question, see N. Avigad, *Hebrew Bullae from the Time of Jeremiah* (Jerusalem: IES, 1986), nos. 22-26, 95, 112 and 113 (partially reconstructed), which refer to at least four individuals whose names may be judged in all probability to be Yahwistic in view of the clear predominance of Yahwistic theophoric elements elsewhere in the hoard. Moreover, although it may be reading too much into a subtle distinction, these personal names with the element *šḥr* emphasize not the shining forth of Yahweh with its implicit notion of light which might lend itself to being understood figuratively, but the 'dawn' as a whole.

4.   As noted, the names might have been inspired by motifs evident in the Bible in which Yahweh is described with reference to the use of words like *zrḥ*, 'rise'. However, in the case of the two biblical passages in which Yahweh is the subject of *zrḥ*, Deut. 33.2 and Isa. 60.1, evidence is presented in the next chapter which suggests that the language of Yahweh 'rising' here may be more than simply metaphorical.

To conclude, evidence about Israelite religion that is based upon personal names alone is tenuous and uncertain at best. The little insight that can be gleaned from these names, however, suggests that whereas some names linking Yahweh with light are perhaps best interpreted as common figures associating the deity with light in general, others are perhaps best understood as references to the actual shining forth of Yahweh as the sun. Fortunately, however, the case for solar Yahwism rests on more than the modest amount of evidence that can be gleaned from these personal names.[1]

Conclusion

A lengthy conclusion awaits consideration also of biblical evidence. Suffice it to note here that the evidence of this chapter has been mixed with respect to the issue of the presence of solar elements in ancient Israelite religion. Thus, whereas some artefacts traditionally understood to shed light on possible solar elements have proven to be not so clear, other artefacts, some of which have not received a great deal of attention, have not only provided evidence for solar elements within ancient Israelite religion, but have suggested a close association between Yahweh and the sun. This association can be identified with royal circles from as early as the reign of Solomon and quite possibly included the reign of Hezekiah.

It remains now to consider the biblical material which must be allowed to tell its own story of solar elements in ancient Israel.

---

1.   For more on personal names, see the discussion at the beginning of Chapter 3.

Chapter 3

BIBLICAL EVIDENCE

It remains now to be determined what the biblical material indicates about sun worship in ancient Israel, and what this material may be judged to say in light of the archaeological evidence examined in the previous chapter.

A brief word is in order concerning the approach adopted in this chapter. First, because of the problem of determining whether references to God as light or sun in poetic material is reflective of the use of merely figurative language or a solar understanding of Yahweh, the major focus of this chapter is on narrative material, particularly the so-called Deuteronomistic History (DH). (Poetic material is nonetheless considered when clearly relevant.) Secondly, rather than offering a detailed reconstruction of the history and development of solar elements within Yahwism, it seems prudent at this early stage in the history of the discussion to focus on the nature of the relationship between the cult of Yahweh and the sun and on identifying some of the parameters within which solar elements existed in ancient Israel. Thirdly and finally, the order in which topics and passages are presented in this chapter has been determined on the basis of logic and their contribution to the overall argument, with consideration given where possible to presenting passages in the order in which they occur in the Hebrew Bible.

Personal Names

Suggestions about the extent to which solar elements in personal names may reflect an understanding of Yahweh as sun have already been offered in the penultimate section of the previous chapter. In light of that discussion, the following biblical names possibly (but by no means certainly) reflect an understanding of Yahweh as sun:

šᵉharyâ, 'Dawn is Yah', (a Benjaminite mentioned in 1 Chron. 8.26); *zᵉrahyâ*, 'Yah has shone forth', (a man of Issachar referred to in 1 Chron. 5.32, 6.36, Ezra 7.4, and the head of a family of returned exiles in Ezra 8.4); *yizrahyâ*, 'Yah will shine forth', (a man of Issachar noted in 1 Chron. 7.3, and a name mentioned also in Neh. 12.42); and probably the non-theophoric *zerah* (a Levite referred to in 1 Chron. 6.6; cf. 6.26).[1] These names have a wider range in date than the extrabiblical names considered earlier and, like those names which by chance were predominant between the eighth and seventh centuries BCE, they very plausibly constitute evidence for a solar understanding of Yahweh. Nevertheless these names alone cannot be used as evidence for the identification of Yahweh with the sun.

There are also a few non-theophoric names which possibly reflect solar elements within Yahwism. The most famous of these is the Danite *šimšôn*, 'Samson', a name attested in extrabiblical material as well.[2] That the name is derived from the root *šmš*, 'sun', is certain. The *-ôn* ending here is often thought to be diminutive,[3] yielding a sense 'Little Sun', or 'Sun's Child', but it could also be abstract.[4]

---

1.   Other names of less certain relevance include the following: *yā'îr*, used of (1) a son of Manasseh (Num. 32.41; Deut. 3.14; Josh. 13.30; 1 Kgs 4.13; 1 Chron. 2.22, 23), (2) a judge in Gilead (Judg. 10.3, 4, 5), and (3) the father of Mordecai (Esth. 5.2); *'ûrî*, the name of (1) a prince of Judah (Exod. 31.2; 35.30; 38.22; 1 Chron. 2.20; 2 Chron. 1.5), (2) a porter (Ezra 10.24), and (3) the father of an officer of Solomon (1 Kgs 4.19); *'ûrîyâ*, used of (1) a Hittite (?) (2 Sam. 11.3-4; 23.39), (2) a priest in the time of Ahaz (Isa. 8.2; 2 Kgs 16.10-11), and (3) a priest in the time of Nehemiah (Ezra 8.33; Neh. 3.4, 21; 8.4); and *'ûrîyāhû*, a prophet slain by Jeremiah (Jer. 26.20).

2.   Noth, *Personennamen*, p. 223 n. 4; C.F. Kraft, 'Samson', *IDB*, IV, p. 198; BDB, p. 1039. Closely related to *šimšôn* is also the biblical (but foreign) name *šimšay*, the official of the Persian province 'Beyond the River' who with Rehum opposed Jews in their attempts to rebuild Jerusalem (Ezra 4.8, 9, 17, 23). Finally, *šamšᵉray*, the name of a member of the tribe of Benjamin and the first born son of Jehoram (1 Chron. 8.26), might be a combination of the names *šimšay* and *šamray* (KB, p. 995).

3.   J.L. Crenshaw, *Samson: A Secret Betrayed, a Vow Ignored* (Macon, GA: Mercer University Press, 1978), p. 15.

4.   See, for example, S. Moscati (ed.), *An Introduction to the Comparative Grammar of the Semitic Languages: Phonology and Morphology* (Wiesbaden: Otto Harrassowitz, 1980), p. 82.

Other suggested meanings include 'solar', 'sunny', or 'sun's man'.[1] Interestingly, that the solar character of Samson's name was of some importance is suggested by evidence for a connection between the biblical story in Judges 13–16 and an underlying solar myth. Crenshaw summarizes the evidence as follows:

> Evidence of a solar myth within the Samson narrative has been found in many of the episodes themselves. A Mithraic plaque depicting a lion with a bee in its mouth raises the possibility that a solar myth about the proper month for locating honey (when the sun stands in the sign of Leo) lies behind the incident in which Samson slew a lion and subsequently found honey in its carcass. Similarly, certain rituals involving foxes existed in Roman solar worship. Ovid explained the ritual associated with the month Ceres as a result of a misfortune when a young boy captured a fox that had broken into a hen house, wrapped it in straw, and set it on fire, only to watch in horror as the fox escaped and ran through local grainfields. In addition, partridges and asses were integral to solar worship in the ancient world, and stories exist of miraculous water sources provided by the sun god.
>
> The seven locks of Samson's hair represented the sun's rays, and his blinding recalled the sun as a one-eyed God. Samson's death pointed to the similar fate of the sun, which pulls down the western pillars, upon which the heavenly vault stands, and brings darkness to all. Likewise, Samson's hiding in a rocky crag symbolized the sun's retreat behind dark clouds; just as Samson burst forth from hiding and destroyed his foes, so the sun's devastating power emerged from a violent storm. Furthermore, when Delilah's web pointed to winter's icy grip on the weakened sun, Samson's casting off the web and pin to free his hair pointed to the rays of the sun melting frozen nature. Delilah's name, connoting flirtation, suggested a relation to Ishtar, sacred to solar worship.[2] Finally, a favorite epithet of the sun god Shamash, Judge, was said to be reflected in the clan name Dan, which comes from the root meaning 'to judge'.[3]

Crenshaw, however, finds reason to doubt the theory of an underlying solar myth in the overstatement of the case by some and in the

1.	Kraft, 'Samson', p. 198.

2.	Kraft ('Samson', p. 200) notes a variation on the significance of the role of Delilah. Assuming that the name *dlylh* perhaps functioned as a pun on the Hebrew word for night, *lylh*, Kraft mentions a possible correspondence between night bringing an end to a sunny day of importance agriculturally, and Delilah cutting Samson's hair, symbolic of the rays of the sun.

3.	Crenshaw, *Samson*, pp. 15-16.

unsettling fact that striking parallels can also be drawn between Samson and Heracles or Enkidu in the Epic of Gilgamesh.[1]

To evaluate, dubiety in the case of *some* claims for the presence of allusions to solar mythology in the Samson cycle[2] does not mean that *all* of the parallels are contrived. In any case, since the possible solar allusions apply to Samson as sun and not to Yahweh as sun, and since this material, popular in nature, is not well suited to scrutiny for historical information on the cult of Yahweh at this period, we must be content to note simply the following: (1) as Kraft observes, 'whether or not Samson is to be regarded as originally the hero of a sun myth...the connection of his name with the sun is indubitable';[3] (2) assuming for the moment that Yahweh and the sun were related at an early period and in the general vicinity of Samson (to be established a little later in this study), and recalling Samson's role as a judge of the God of Israel, it is possible that the deity to whom Samson's name alludes was understood to have been Yahweh. On the basis of evidence at present, however, this is obviously only a possibility.

Place Names

Various place names with solar elements and found in the Bible are discussed briefly below.

There are four places referred to in the Bible as Beth-shemesh. As La Sor has noted, the anarthrous genitive after the construct *bêt* is suggestive that *šemeš* refers here to the name of the sun deity rather than simply to the sun.[4]

The first and best known Beth-shemesh is the one located on a level

---

1. For the particular correspondences, see Crenshaw, 'Samson', p. 17. Additional correspondences between the legends of Heracles and Judg. 13.16-22 have been adduced recently by O. Margalit ('More Samson Legends', *VT* 36 [1986], pp. 397-405).

2. An example of excess in this regard is E.G.H. Kraeling's reconstruction of an aspect of a solar cult at Hebron on the basis of the story of Samson carrying the gates of Gaza to Hebron, itself supposedly a demythologized tale of Shamash's nightly entry into his chamber to cohabit with his consort ('The Early Cult of Hebron and Judg. 16.1-3', *AJSL* 41 [1925], pp. 174-78).

3. Kraft, 'Samson', p. 198.

4. W.S. La Sor, 'Beth-shemesh', *ISBE*, I, pp. 478-79.

ridge in the Valley of Sorek, at Tell el-Rumeileh in the northeastern
Shephelah, some 20 kilometres west of Jerusalem. According to 1 Kgs
14.11 it lay in Judah, but if the city is the same as *ʿîr šemeš*
mentioned in Josh. 19.41, it originally fell within the territory of Dan.
This town is probably the Beth-shemesh referred to in the Egyptian
execration texts, in which case the name of the town, suggestive of the
presence of a temple to a Canaanite solar deity, dates at least to the
eighteenth or nineteenth centuries BCE, long before Israelite
occupation.[1] Designated as a levitical city in Josh. 21.16, Beth-
shemesh was under strong Philistine influence if not control at the
time when the ark made its way to Beth-shemesh on the border
between Philistia and Judah.[2] Apart from possible indirect witnesses
such as the Samson cycle and place names with solar elements in the
general vicinity, there is no strong indication on the basis of literary
evidence to assume that there were solar elements within the cult at
Beth-shemesh in the biblical period.

'The waters of En-shemesh' and 'En-shemesh'[3] are mentioned
respectively in Josh. 15.7 and 18.17 as marking the northern border
of Judah and the southern border of Benjamin. It is almost certainly to
be identified with the spring Ain el-Ḥod, 'Spring of the Apostles',[4] just
to the east of Bethany, the last spring on the road from Jerusalem to
the Jordan Valley.[5] The name is apparently not attested outside of
Josh. 15.7, 18.17.

Timnath-ḥeres, probably 'portion of the sun',[6] is a town in the hill
country of Ephraim and commonly identified with Khirbet Tibnah,[7]

---

1. See *ANET*, p. 328 n. 8. This observation comes from M.S. Smith, Review
of H.-P. Stähli, *Solare Elemente im Jahweglauben des Alten Testaments*, *JBL* 106
(1987), p. 514.

2. See La Sor, 'Beth-shemesh', p. 478, and G.E. Wright, 'Beth-shemesh',
EAEHL, I, p. 252.

3. On the unlikelihood of there being a distinction between the two, see
Z. Kallai, *Historical Geography of the Bible* (Jerusalem: Magnes; Leiden: Brill,
1986), p. 121 n. 48; R.G. Boling and G.E. Wright, *Joshua* (AB, 6; Garden City,
NY: Doubleday, 1982), pp. 362-63.

4. Aharoni, *Land of the Bible*, p. 255.

5. V.R. Gold, 'En-shemesh', *IDB*, II, p. 106.

6. Judg. 2.9. The reading *seraḥ* is attested in the Peshitta and the Vulgate.

7. For example, Aharoni, *Land of the Bible*, p. 442; A. van Selms, 'Timnath-
serah', *ISBE*, IV, p. 856.

some 24 kilometers southwest of Shechem. Although it lay on the border of Ephraim and Dan, it belonged to neither. Timnath-ḥeres was chosen by Joshua as his inheritance, a place in which he would settle and which he would fortify.[1] Interesting in light of what will be observed later in this chapter about a tradition elsewhere in DH that links Joshua with a solar understanding of Yahweh,[2] although the town is called Timnath-seraḥ in Josh. 19.50[3] and 24.30,[4] this place name is usually regarded as a later variant caused either by a conscious attempt to rid the chosen town of Joshua of the implication of sun worship inherent in the name Timnath-ḥeres or by a scribal error in which *sr̯ḥ* was mistaken for *ḥrs*.[5] The theological explanation for the textual corruption seems more plausible than scribal error since the latter would have involved the transposition of more than one consonant.[6] The name is not attested before the Israelite period.

Har-ḥeres, 'mountain of the sun', is mentioned together with Aijalon and Shaalbim in Judg. 1.35 as a place from which the tribe of Dan failed to expel the Amorites. Some identify Har-ḥeres with the best known Beth-shemesh/Ir-shemesh;[7] others regard it as the name of an area in the southwestern part of the hill country of Ephraim, near

1. Josh. 19.49-50.

2. See the discussion of Josh. 10.12-14.

3. In addition to Judg. 2.9, LXX[B] and the Old Latin witness to Timnath-ḥeres.

4. The options here are as follows: MT, *ḥrs*; LXX, *shr*; some manuscripts of the Vulgate (cf. Judg. 2.9), *ḥrs*.

5. See, for example, Boling and Wright, *Joshua*, p. 469; W.L. Reed, 'Timnath-heres', *IDB*, IV, p. 650.

6. Theological sensitivity to the perceived meaning of the name and its relationship to Joshua is attested in rabbinic tradition which explained the name of the town in light of the standing-still of the sun in Josh. 10.13 and which claimed that there was an emblem of the sun on Joshua's tomb (Reed, 'Timnath-heres', p. 650). (More likely than scribal error is the suggestion of Boling and Wright [*Joshua*, p. 469] that Timnath-serah has been altered to the popular etymology, 'portion remaining', but even so the original form is still Timnath-ḥeres, 'portion of the sun'.)

7. Aharoni, *Land of the Bible*, p. 236; J.B. Pritchard (ed.), *The Harper Atlas of the Bible* (Toronto: Fitzhenry & Whiteside, 1987), p. 227. F. Weddle notes ('Heres', *ISBE*, II, p. 684) that the mention of Ir-shemesh with Aijalon and Shaalabbin (cf. Shaalbim in Judg. 1.35) offers some support for the identification of Har-ḥeres with Ir-shemesh/Beth-shemesh.

the vale of Aijalon.[1] This name with its solar element is not attested before the Israelite period.[2]

Also mentioned in Judges is what appears to be a place called 'Ascent of Ḥeres [i.e. Sun]',[3] a place in Transjordan from which Gideon turned back from pursuing the Midianites. Although the KJV translated *ma'ᵃlê heḥāres*, 'before the sun was up', *ma'ᵃlê* here probably refers to a geographical 'pass' or 'ascent'.[4] The exact location is unknown. As Gray notes, however, the locality was 'familiar to the inhabitants of Succoth [and, I would add, probably Penuel[5] as well], and indicative of local tradition'.[6] Although later in this study it will be suggested that the local solar tradition that underlies the name is probably reflected in Gen. 32.23-33 [22-32], this is all that can be gleaned about the site in light of the evidence at present.[7]

In summary, several biblical place names,[8] predominantly in the area of the tribes of Dan, Benjamin and Ephraim, are suggestive of the presence of a solar cult. Among place names in the Transjordan possibly dating to the time of Israelite presence, 'The Ascent of Heres' is suggestive of a local tradition concerning the sun. Perhaps significantly, except for Beth-shemesh, there is no evidence that any of the names cited here necessarily predate the time of Israelite influence.

1. For example, Kallai, *Historical Geography*, p. 108. Weddle ('Heres', p. 684) cites as possibilities Bain Harasheh, northeast of Aijalon and Bit Nibid, mentioned in the Amarna Letters (EA 290), the latter of which Aharoni (*Land of the Bible*, p. 174) suggests refers to Beth-ḥoron.

2. Unless one presumes an association with Bit Nibid.

3. Judg. 8.13. Aquila and Symmachus reflect *mlm'lh hhrym*, 'from up in the mountains'.

4. Weddle, 'Heres'. Cf. virtually all recent English translations.

5. Judg. 8.17.

6. J. Gray, *Joshua, Judges and Ruth* (NCB; Greenwood, NC: Attic Press, 1967), p. 239.

7. Later in this chapter (specifically, point 9 in the section, 'An Autumnal Festival as a Locus for Solar Yahwism?', pp. 248-55) it will be observed that Succoth and Penuel also appear to reflect a tradition concerning (Yahweh and) the sun (cf. Gen. 32.23-33 [22-32]).

8. For the place name *'îr haḥeres*, 'city of the sun', in Isa. 19.18, see the discussion of Isa. 1–39 later in this chapter.

The Expressions 'Yahweh of Hosts' and 'Host of Heaven'

The expressions 'Yahweh of Hosts' and 'Host of Heaven' occur frequently in the Hebrew Bible. The relevance of the latter expression, though involving more than the sun, is obvious; that of the former is perhaps less obvious, but will become clear.

The Epithet 'Yahweh of Hosts'
The problem of the meaning and significance of the expression 'Yahweh of Hosts' is so complex that only a brief summary of various kinds of approaches to the problem can be offered here.[1] At the risk of oversimplification, three basic approaches may be distinguished: (1) contextual (focusing most often on the use of the expression in various contexts, the most important of which is its original 'life setting')[2]; (2) lexical (focusing in particular on the etymology of *ṣᵉbā'ôt*, 'armies, host', and the meaning of its root in this and other contexts); and (3) syntactical (focusing on peculiarities[3] and what these might imply about the meaning of *yhwh ṣᵉbā'ôt* or a more original expanded version thereof).

Only a brief evaluation of these approaches is necessary in order to lay the groundwork for the present discussion, the primary purpose of which is to offer a new possible meaning of 'Yahweh of Hosts'. First, regarding the contextual approach mentioned above, a significant majority of scholars are almost certainly correct that it is extremely

1. For a fairly comprehensive review of scholarship up to 1972, see R. Schmitt, *Zelt und Lade* (Gütersloh: Gütersloher Verlagshaus, 1972), pp. 145-59. For basic overviews, see, for example, A.S. van der Woude, '*ṣābā*' *THAT*, II, pp. 498-507; B.W. Anderson, 'Hosts, Host of Heaven', *IDB*, II, pp. 654-56; *idem*, 'Lord of Hosts', *IDB*, III, p. 151; T. Mettinger, 'YHWH SABAOTH—The Heavenly King on the Cherubim Throne', in T. Ishida (ed.), *Studies in the Period of David and Solomon* (Winona Lake, IN: Eisenbrauns, 1982), pp. 109-11, 127; *idem, In Search of God*, pp. 154-57.
2. For a similar summary of approaches which includes references to most of the important bibliography and which is itself an example of the third kind of approach, see Mettinger, 'YHWH SABAOTH', pp. 109-11.
3. That is, on the assumption that the two words are in a construct relationship, the determination of YHWH (no longer without clear precedent in light of the similar expressions 'Yahweh of Samaria' and 'Yahweh of Teman', attested at Kuntillet 'Ajrûd) and the indetermination of 'hosts'.

difficult to divorce on traditio-historical grounds the epithet 'Yahweh of Hosts' from the phrase with which it occurs very frequently, 'who sits enthroned upon the cherubim', and they appear also to be correct that 'Yahweh of Hosts' can be traced back to traditions associated with the sanctuary at Shiloh which made their way to Jerusalem and which are evident in temple and Zion theology.[1] Secondly, regarding the lexical meaning of $s^e b\bar{a}'\hat{o}t$, there is little reason to doubt the extremely well-attested meaning, 'armies, horde', in which case the reference is to armies (either celestial or earthly). And thirdly, regarding syntactical factors, the noun could be one of the following (the exact meaning of which depends on lexical considerations): (1) a concrete noun in the genitive after the construct (for example 'Yahweh of Hosts'); (2) a concrete noun in apposition to *yhwh* (for example 'Yahweh who is Sebaoth'); (3) an adjectival genitive (for example 'Yahweh militant'); or (4) an intensive abstract plural (for example, following Eissfeldt,[2] 'Yahweh the Sebaoth-like/Almighty').[3] In the third case of syntax, the matter is particularly difficult and is best left open.

In my judgment a new interpretation of Yahweh of Hosts merits careful consideration, namely that the epithet strongly implies a solar dimension to the character of Yahweh. Inspired in part by new evidence based on the Taanach cult stand, this interpretation will be put forth as a hypothesis to the effect that 'Yahweh of Hosts' perhaps originally conveyed (and continued to convey at least to some) a solar understanding of Yahweh, whether through its designation of him as the most important of all astral bodies or through one of several other possible connotations.

A number of factors support this hypothesis. To begin, as just implied, a solar interpretation of the epithet is suggested by the iconography of the Taanach cult stand which, as may be recalled, places in juxtaposition imagery of Yahweh as 'solar' in character (tier one) with parallel imagery of the invisible god who resides among the cherubim (tier three) (cf. pls. 1d and 1c). In other words, the cult

---

1. See, for example, Mettinger 'YHWH SABAOTH', pp. 111-38; *idem, In Search of God*, pp. 148-49; F.M. Cross, Jr, *Canaanite Myth and Hebrew Epic* (Cambridge, MA: Harvard University Press, 1973), p. 69.

2. O. Eissfeldt, 'Jahwe Zebaoth', in R. Sellheim and F. Maass (eds.), *Kleine Schriften* (Tübingen: J.C.B. Mohr, 1966), III, pp. 103-23.

3. Eissfeldt's interpretation ('Jahwe Zebaoth', pp. 110-13) is based on the understanding that the root meaning of $s\bar{a}b\bar{a}'$ is 'mass', 'weight', 'power'.

stand portrays not simply Yahweh, but 'Yahweh of Hosts, who dwells among the cherubim'.

Further direct association of some kind between Yahweh and the celestial bodies is clearly implied by perhaps the most common interpretation of the epithet, namely, 'Yahweh of heavenly armies'. Significantly, not only does the present 'solar' interpretation do justice to the common meaning of $ṣ^eḇā'ôt$ (i.e. 'armies'), but it also offers an obvious reason for the clear avoidance of this expression by some biblical writers such as Ezekiel: the expression leaves a dangerous amount of room for possibly justifying the worship of the Heavenly Host by Yahwists.[1]

Perhaps more significantly, however, there is another 'danger' associated with the use of the expression that is at least as obvious as the one just noted: the expression leaves room for identifying Yahweh with the most prominent of celestial bodies, namely, the sun. In other words, the widespread 'theological' understanding of Yahweh as the head of the astral bodies could have given rise quite naturally to a 'literal' association between Yahweh and the sun.[2] Of course this interpretation assumes that the meaning of $ṣ^eḇā'ôt$ with which Yahweh is linked is 'heavenly bodies' which is clearly possible but by no means certain.

Several other interpretations are no less amenable to the hypothesis of a solar understanding for the expression *yhwh ṣ^eḇā'ôt*. For example, following Eissfeldt's lead that the noun $ṣ^eḇā'ôt$ is an intensive abstract plural, a rendition much closer to the common meaning of the root than Eissfeldt's Yahweh 'Almighty' is Yahweh the 'Host-like' or Yahweh, 'Host *par excellence*', on which interpretation the epithet

---

1. The explanation dates back to the time when scholars were certain that the worship of the Host of Heaven was obligatory under Assyrian overlordship (a view somewhat revived by Spieckermann [on which see later]). The danger of worshipping the Heavenly Host explains why in the DH, so the argument goes, normally the expression is avoided, except in cases where the expression was unavoidable (apparently for historical reasons).

2. That the logic of the primacy of the sun was apparent in ancient Israel may be inferred from the placement of the sun at the head of Deuteronomistic expressions like 'the sun, the moon, the stars, the whole host of heaven' (Deut. 4.19; cf. Deut. 17.3; 2 Kgs 17.3; Jer. 8.2). Note also that in 1 Kgs 22.19 Yahweh is clearly head of the Host of Heaven. (I thank M.S. Smith for pointing out the possible relevancy of these two points for the present argument.)

(and with it the deity) could also be solar. Nor can a 'solar' connotation be excluded by following Mettinger who opines that the epithet 'contains a reference to the [heavenly] hosts around God's throne... [and] could well be an adjectival, descriptive genitive'.[1] Although Mettinger does not venture to translate *ṣᵉbāʾôt* (which he associates with attestations elsewhere in Scripture of a Yahwistic 'host' [singular] of heaven), possibilities like 'host-like', or 'celestial Yahweh' cannot be far from the adjectival, descriptive-genitive meaning for this root suggested by Mettinger.

To return to the matter of the selective usage of the expression by some biblical writers, an 'acid test' for any interpretation of the meaning of the epithet has traditionally been its ability to account for the complete avoidance of the term in Ezekiel. In light of the hypothesis, it is worth noting that Ezekiel is well known for his scathing condemnation of what Zimmerli refers to as a possible case of 'a solar interpretation of Yahweh' (Ezek. 8.16).[2]

Is there any additional evidence that suggests a solar understanding for the expression *yhwh ṣᵉbāʾôt*? Several things may be noted. First, Mettinger has drawn attention to what he calls a 'Canaanite formation that deserves to be mentioned as an interesting analogue', namely *ᵈšamaš līmīma*, 'Sun of thousands', in a tablet from el-Amarna (EA 205.6). Like Yahweh in 'Yahweh of Hosts' (and elsewhere), Shamash occurs here with determination. Moreover, even apart from the additional possible correspondence that I am suggesting between the two deities and their respective hordes, *ᵈšamaš līmīma*, 'Sun of thousands', is the closest parallel of which I am aware in either the Canaanite or Mesopotamian realms to the biblical expression *yhwh ṣᵉbāʾôt*, 'Yahweh of Hosts'.

Second is Psalm 80, one of only eight psalms in which the words *yhwh ṣᵉbāʾôt* are now attested, and, because of some peculiar features, well known as a promising source of information on the early significance of the epithet. In the second verse [v. 1] of this poem we read:

> *yōšēb hakkᵉrûbîm hôpîʿâ*
> He who dwells among the cherubim, shine forth![3]

1.	Mettinger, *In Search of God*, p. 135.
2.	See the discussion of Ezek. 8.16 by Zimmerli, *Ezekiel I*, p. 244.
3.	As argued by O. Loretz, 'Ugaritische und hebräische Lexikographie', *UF* 12 (1980), pp. 279-86, *hôpîʿâ*, 'shine forth', is not to be compared with Ugaritic *ypʿ*,

In light of the possibility that this poetic language is not merely figurative but genuinely reflective of the character of the deity who dwells among the cherubim, it is interesting to observe also the refrain which appears three times (with slight variations) in this same psalm:

> *yhwh 'elōhîm ṣebā'ôt hašî bēnû*
> *hā'ēr pānêkā wen iwwāšē'â*

> Yahweh, God of Hosts, restore us,
> Let your face shine, that we may be delivered.[1]

Moreover, vv. 15a-b [14a-b], commonly considered to be a variation of the refrain cited immediately above, uses in the second colon completely different language of Yahweh, but language no less amenable to a solar interpretation:

> *'elōhîm ṣebā'ôt šûb-nā'*
> O God of hosts, turn, Look down from heaven and see;

Even if one argues that the language of the 'shining forth' of the 'face' of God is merely figurative in the refrain (see, however, later in this chapter where sun and face of God are equated in the Old Testament),[2] a number of peculiar features suggest that the psalm probably preserves a genuine tradition about the character of Yahweh of Hosts. First, as noted, it is one of only eight psalms in the whole Psalter in which the expression 'Yahweh of Hosts' occurs.[3] Secondly,

'rise up'. The traditional understanding of *hôpî'â* as 'shine forth' appears to be correct (cf. also v. 15 [14] and the comment concerning it).

1. Ps. 80.20 [19]. In v. 4 [3] the divine name is simply 'God', in v. 8 [7] 'God of Hosts'.

2. Suffice it to note here that although the notion of seeing the face of the deity is clearly an expression for divine favour, it does not follow from this that the expression is always devoid of solar connotations. (As I attempt to show later in this chapter [pp. 239-42], a solar character to the notion of 'seeing the face of God' is clearly attested in Gen. 32.23-33 [22-32].)

3. As Mettinger notes, the psalms in which the epithet remains (Pss. 24.10; 46.8, 12 [7, 11]; 48.9 [8]; 59.6 [5]; 69.7 [6]; 80.5, 8, 15, 20 [4, 7, 14, 19]; 84.2, 4, 9, 13 [1, 3, 8, 12]; 89.9 [8]) are mostly Hymns of Zion (Mettinger, 'YHWH SABAOTH', p. 138 n. 23). The distribution of the expression fits nicely with the view advocated in this book, namely that, like the expression Yahweh of Hosts, 'solar Yahweh worship' was particularly at home within the context of royal Jerusalemite theology.

Yahweh is referred to as *ṣᵉbā'ôt* more frequently in this psalm than in any other. Thirdly, here alone in the Psalms the epithet occurs together with its early counterpart *yōšēb hakkᵉrūbîm*. Fourthly, whereas all of the other psalms in which *yhwh ṣᵉbā'ôt* occurs are clearly Hymns of Zion (suggestive of the relevance this epithet had within the context of the theology of the Jerusalem temple), a number of factors suggest that this is a rare case of a psalm from the north, dating to within a few years of the fall of the northern kingdom, as Eissfeldt and others have argued.[1] There are good reasons, then, for believing that, as H.-J. Kraus puts it, 'important clues are given in Psalm 80 for the search for the origin of the epithet in terms of tradition history and the cult'.[2]

Finally, H.-P. Stähli has already drawn attention to the use of solar allusions in Jewish incantations and prayers of a much later period. Among them is the prayer of a young woman which begins as follows: 'Hail Helios, thou God in the heavens, your name is almighty...'[3] In

---

It is perhaps relevant to observe in passing that the expression *yhwh ṣᵉbā'ôt* occurs in the two psalms in which solar imagery is perhaps most evident, Ps. 84 in which Yahweh is called *šmš*, 'sun', and Ps. 89, and in both cases the epithet lies within the immediate context of that solar imagery. The epithet occurs also in Ps. 24, judged later in this study to presuppose a solar understanding of Yahweh. In the case of Ps. 84, the epithet 'Yahweh of Hosts' occurs in v. 13 [12], the verse that immediately precedes the reference to Yahweh as 'sun' and it occurs also in v. 2 [1] (cf. v. 9 [8]). In the case of Ps. 89 the epithet (including *'ᵉlōhê*, 'God of') occurs in v. 9 [8], immediately after the solar imagery in vv. 6-8 [5-7]. Moreover, with the probable exception of Ps. 80, these psalms are all Zion Hymns.

1.   On the northern provenance, note, for example, the mention of Israel and Joseph (v. 2 [1]) and the tribes of Ephraim, Benjamin and Manasseh; cf. Dahood, *Psalms II* (AB, 17; Garden City, NY: Doubleday, 1968), p. 255. The exceptional nature of the psalm has been noted, for example, by van der Woude (*'ṣābā'*', p. 499) and W. Kessler ('Aus welchem Gründen wird die Bezeichnung "Jahwe Zebaoth" in der späteren Zeit gemieden?', *Wissenschaftliche Zeitschrift der Martin-Luther Universität, Halle* 7/3 [1957–58], p. 767 n. 6) who adds, 'a psalm from the sanctuary at Shilo?' Even if the psalm is another Psalm of Zion, it is still relevant for the meaning of Yahweh of Hosts and comes from a context no less suggestive of the possible presence of solar elements within Yahwism (that is, royal religion linked with the temple).

2.   H.-J. Kraus, *Theology of the Psalms* (trans. K. Crim; Minneapolis: Augsburg, 1986 [1979]), p. 18. (It should not be inferred from the citation of Kraus here that he believes that the psalm implies a solar character for Yahweh of Hosts.)

3.   Stähli, *Solare Elemente*, p. 4 (citing Goodenough).

addition, Stähli refers to a brief incantation which calls upon one referred to as 'Helios on the cherubim'.[1]

In sum, several lines of evidence and more than one possible interpretation point in a similar direction, toward *yhwh ṣᵉbā'ôt* as a solar epithet for Yahweh. To be sure, the expression may have had varying connotations through time, but a solar nuance appears to be relevant to early contexts within which the expression functioned and was perhaps its original connotation. At any rate, given the complexity of the issue, the present interpretation must be included within a more comprehensive framework before any firm judgment can be made about a possibly solar understanding of Yahweh within the tradition streams within which the epithet is attested.

The Expression 'Host of Heaven'
A full study of the expression *ṣᵉbā' haššāmayim*, 'Host of Heaven', a comprehensive term that obviously included more entities than the sun, would extend beyond the scope of this chapter. It is nonetheless deserving of mention both here and later in this chapter (see the section 'Tensions Suggestive of a Yahwistic Host of Heaven') because of the clear association made in Deuteronomistic literature between the worship of 'the sun' on the one hand and the worship of 'the moon, stars and all the Host of Heaven' on the other hand. More specifically, because it will be argued later in this chapter that references to the worship of the sun in Deuteronomistic literature are references primarily to a Yahwistic phenomenon, it is important to note that a reasonably good similar case can also be made for regarding the worship of the 'Host of Heaven' as a Yahwistic phenomenon.

At first glance, the claim that the worship of the Host of Heaven was a Yahwistic phenomenon seems to run counter to the implication of DH itself that this cultic practice belonged to peoples such as the Amorites whom the Israelites supplanted upon entry into the land of Canaan.[2] This view, however, must be taken to represent only part of the picture because an equally clear picture emerges from DH that the

---

1. Stähli, *Solare Elemente*, p. 4.
2. The expression Host of Heaven occurs in the following passages: Deut. 4.19; 17.3; 1 Kgs 22.19 (= 2 Chron. 18.18); 2 Kgs 17.16; 21.3, 5 (= 2 Chron. 33.3, 5); 23.4, 5; Isa. 34.4; Jer. 8.2; 19.13; 33.22; Dan. 8.10; Neh. 9.6; Zeph. 1.5.

worship of the Host of Heaven was a Yahwistic phenomenon.[1] How are these apparently different perspectives to be explained? One tack might be to follow the lead of Olyan who has dealt with a similar tension in DH concerning the worship of asherah (or Asherah). He suggests that Deuteronomistic theology for polemical purposes *falsely* attributed to the cult of Baal ('Canaanite') a genuinely Yahwistic cult symbol.[2] In my judgment, however, the tension at least in the case of the Host of Heaven may be understood in light of two factors which consider more seriously the complex portrait and integrity of DH. First, the number of Deuteronomistic passages which imply a link with foreign peoples or gods are surprisingly few and even these (Deut. 4.19, 17.3 and 2 Kgs 17.16) seem compatible with a Yahwistic understanding of the Host of Heaven.[3] Secondly, the apparent implication of DH that the worship of the Host of Heaven belonged in the category of the worship of 'other gods' may be a theological judgment; as an idolatrous act involving the worship of an object, it was tantamount to the worship of other gods. And thirdly, there may have been little difference between the Israelite worship of the sun, moon and Heavenly Host and the practice of outside groups, apart from the name of the deity invoked. At any rate, although the claim that solar and astral worship was characteristic of other nations should not be dismissed outright—at least according to recent thought, the roots of early Israel were, after all, 'Canaanite'—the worship of the Host of Heaven including the sun refers in Deuteronomistic literature primarily to a Yahwistic phenomenon.

1.   For example, 1 Kgs 22.19; cf. Zeph. 1.5 in which the worship of Yahweh is condemned (!) in the same breath as the worship of the Host of Heaven. See further my discussion of Zeph. 1.5 and the section, 'The Accounts of the Reign of Ahaz, Hezekiah, Manasseh and Josiah' (especially the subsection, 'Tensions Suggestive of a Yahwistic Host of Heaven'), pp. 164-83.

2.   Olyan, *Asherah and the Cult of Yahweh*, pp. 1-22.

3.   See most conveniently my discussion of Deut. 4.19 and 17.3. In the case of 2 Kgs 17.16, among the 'foreign' entities are 'two calves' and a sacred post ('asherah'), both of which are commonly understood to have been Yahwistic. Baal is referred to with the article in this verse (though elsewhere as well) which perhaps implies reference to something other than the Canaanite deity. As I attempt to show later on, it is probably no mistake that 2 Kgs 21.3b, 5; 23.5, 12 (cf. 21.5) are ambiguous with respect to the question whether the Host of Heaven is 'idolatrous' or 'Yahwistic' (since, when the Host is worshipped, the latter in effect becomes the former).

There is a second tension in DH concerning the Host of Heaven. When is the worship of the Host of Heaven legitimate and when is it not? The basis for my reasoning will become evident as the book progresses; suffice it to say for now that DH is concerned not so much with the worship of Yahweh as a member of the Host of Heaven (2 Kgs 22.19) as it is with the reverse phenomenon, namely with *the worship of an object as Yahweh* (that is the sun) or objects as members of his Heavenly Host (that is the stars). In other words, the issue is not syncretism but iconism. Part of the reason why the centralization of the cult was so important to Deuteronomistic thinking, then, was that it was a helpful means (though not an infallible one) of controlling Israel's iconism (for example the making of a bronze serpent or an asherah). In the case of the worship of the sun, moon, stars and Host of Heaven, however, Israel was particularly susceptible to iconism; not being human artefacts, the sun and other astral bodies as objects of worship lay outside the limitations of the second commandment.[1] To say that Hezekiah was an iconoclast whose aniconism did not yet extend to the realm of the sun and other bodies made by Yahweh, as did the aniconism of Josiah and a Josianic redaction of DH, would be jumping too far ahead. Suffice it to note at present that a careful study of DH and Chronicles provides important clues to the nature and development of solar Yahwism.

Sun Worship in the Deuteronomistic History and Chronicles

Consideration of sun worship in the DH and Chronicles points to a fascinating chapter in the history of Israelite religion.

The material in DH and Chronicles is presented under three separate headings, the first of which concerns Deuteronomy and the references therein to the worship of the sun, moon, stars and the Host of Heaven, the second of which examines relevant material in DH and Chronicles in light of the theory that there was a Gibeonite sun cult, and the last of which concerns the worship of the sun and the Host of Heaven during the reigns of Hezekiah through Josiah.

---

1. Not surprisingly, Deut. 4.19 seeks to address this loophole, as will be demonstrated.

Deuteronomy
To be considered here are the two passages in Deuteronomy in which
the worship of the sun is mentioned specifically, Deut. 4.19 and 17.3.

a. *Deuteronomy 4.19*
I begin by citing this passage within the context of its unit,
vv. 15-20:[1]

> Be very careful for your own sakes, since you did not see any form when
> the Lord spoke to you at Horeb out of the midst of the fire, lest you act
> corruptly and make for yourselves an image in the form of any figure: the
> likeness of a male or female, the likeness of any land animal, the likeness
> of any winged bird which flies through the skies, the likeness of anything
> that creeps on the ground, the likeness of any fish which is in the waters
> under the earth. And [beware] lest you lift up your eyes toward heaven
> and when you see the sun, and the moon and the stars, all the Host of
> Heaven, you be led astray and worship them and serve them, things
> which the Lord your God has allotted to all the peoples under all the
> heavens. But you the Lord took and he brought you out from the iron
> furnace, from Egypt, to be a people of his own possession, as today.

This passage is central to the purpose of Deut. 4.1-40 which functions
as an extended commentary on the second commandment. The point
of the present passage is not only (or perhaps not even primarily) to
list those things that the Israelites must not worship (although such a
list is provided), but rather to demonstrate that the worship of the
Lord alone—without the aid of any object—is incumbent upon Israel.
Two primary reasons are offered in vv. 8-18: (1) by receiving the law
and enjoying a close relationship with Yahweh, Israel has 'favoured-
nation' status; and (2) when Yahweh appeared at Mount Horeb, he
took no visible 'form', but appeared from skyward-reaching fire as a
mere shapeless voice amidst darkness, cloud and gloom.

A number of implications can be drawn which are relevant to the
relationship between Yahweh and the sun. First, the text presupposes
a setting in which astral bodies including the sun were worshipped
by Israelites.[2] Secondly, the passage is perhaps surprisingly

---

1.   The division made here follows JPSV. For other breakdowns, see, for
example, R.D. Nelson, *The Double Redaction of the Deuteronomistic History*
(JSOTS, 18; Sheffield: JSOT Press, 1981), p. 92; A.D.H. Mayes, 'Deuteronomy 4
and the Literary Criticism of Deuteronomy', *JBL* 100 (1981), p. 25.

2.   Presumably, the further refinement of the prohibition of idolatry as applying

concessionary; the worship of astral deities by others peoples was acceptable—albeit for them. Thirdly, if the opinion of many is correct that the passage is exilic,[1] this would suggest that the closing of an important loophole in the second commandment to exclude the worship of objects not made by people but by Yahweh himself (that is, the Host of Heaven, including the fiery sun) was the inspiration of an exilic editor. Fourthly and perhaps most significantly, that the prohibitions are based upon the rationale that Israel did not see *Yahweh* appear in any form at Horeb clearly implies that at least some of the images against which the passage preaches were understood to be images of Yahweh. As Mayes puts it, 'The reference to the revelation at Horeb and the absence of any "form" there (vv. 12, 15-16), implies that images of Yahweh are then included in the prohibition of vv. 15-18'.[2] Thus, although the sun, moon, stars and Host of Heaven are distinct from the made items referred to in vv. 15-18, the fact that the writer mentions them in this context implies that they too were forms identified or associated with Yahweh. In offering a comprehensive[3] ban on the worship by Israelites of anything other than Yahweh or, probably preferable in light of the context, of Yahweh in any 'form', the passage is concerned to omit all possible loopholes, one of which was clearly the worship of the sun, probably as Yahweh himself.

to the sun, moon, stars and all the host of heaven would be given only if there was a need for it.

1. See, for example, Mayes ('Deuteronomy 4', pp. 32-35) who regards vv. 1-40 as a unity and who assigns the passage to the second Deuteronomist. Although the setting in vv. 28-31 could perhaps be other than exilic (see, for example, J.A. Thompson, *Deuteronomy* [TOTC, 5; Leicester, Inter-Varsity Press, 1974], pp. 107-108), it is preferable to regard the present passage—probably a unit with vv. 28-31—as exilic at least in its setting.

2. Mayes, 'Deuteronomy 4', p. 26 n. 12.

3. As Mayes has noted ('Deuteronomy 4', p. 29 n. 24), the order is in fact the reverse of the list of all created objects assigned to realms in Genesis 1, except for the 'things which creep upon the earth', which is slightly out of order.

b. *Deuteronomy 17.3*

The Deuteronomistic phrase referring to the worship of the sun, moon and Host of Heaven[1] occurs also in Deut. 17.3, which in its context is as follows (based on MT):

> If there is found in your midst, in any of your towns, which the Lord your God is giving you, a man or a woman who does what is evil in the sight of the Lord your God, by transgressing His covenant, and has gone and served other gods and worshipped them, or the sun or the moon or any of the heavenly host, which I have not commanded, and if it is told you... then you shall bring out that man or that woman who has done this evil deed, to your gates, *that is*, the man or woman, and you shall stone them to death (NASB).

This passage clearly associates the worship of the sun, moon and Host of Heaven with the worship of *'elōhîm 'ªḥērîm*, 'other gods'. I have already suggested a way of resolving an apparent tension between this passage and others which suggest that the worship of these astral bodies was a Yahwistic phenomenon.[2] Even without this explanation, the problem of reconciling this verse with the *Yahwistic* veneration of the Host of Heaven could be resolved quite easily by observing that, from a grammatical standpoint, the phrase 'and the sun or the moon or any of the Host of Heaven, which I have not commanded' is clearly 'awkwardly related to the previous words',[3] and thus arguably secondary.[4] There is no reason to believe, then, that the view represented in this (late?) witness is necessarily typical of an earlier Deuteronomistic outlook. Regardless of the date of v. 19, the statement, 'something which I never commanded', probably betrays an awareness that there

---

1. The form of expression differs slightly from that found in Deut. 4.19. The biggest difference lies in the omission in 17.3 of the reference to the stars, nonetheless included in the comprehensive phrase *kol ṣ^ebā' haššāmayim*, 'any of the Host of Heaven'.

2. See the previous section, 'The Expression "Host of Heaven"'.

3. Mayes, *Deuteronomy*, p. 266.

4. This is the view, for example, of G. von Rad, *Deuteronomy* (trans. D. Barton; OTL; Philadelphia: Westminster Press, 1966 [German, 1964]), p. 117. Moreover, if the phrase regarding sun, moon and Host of Heaven were original to the statement concerning the worship of *other gods*, there would be no need for the reference to the worship of the sun, moon and Host of Heaven as that 'which I have not commanded' (a statement which is itself awkward [though not unique] in view of the change to the first person).

were some who felt that the worship of the sun and other members of the Host of Heaven was a legitimate *Yahwistic* practice.[1]

Passages Relevant to the Influence of a Gibeonite Sun Cult
Much of the material relevant to the worship of the sun in DH and Chronicles may be examined in light of a theory with which I had very little sympathy in its original form, but which, in light of the reformulation offered here, I regard to be an important key to discerning the role of the sun within the cult of early Israel. Before a reformulation can be offered, however, the theory as originally formulated will be rehearsed briefly.

a. *Introduction*
The modern theory of the presence of a sun cult at Gibeon began in 1958 when J. Heller[2] offered a striking new interpretation of the account of the arrest of the sun in Josh. 10.12-13. According to Heller, the original form of the address to the sun and moon was a command by Joshua that the sun god whose cult place was 'in' Gibeon and the moon god whose cult place was 'in' Aijalon be 'silenced', that is, be kept from offering favourable oracles.[3]

The interpretation offered by Heller presupposes the presence of a sun cult at Gibeon and a moon cult at Aijalon. In favour of the latter proposition, Heller argued that *'ayyālôn*, 'Ayyalon', was probably related to *'ayyāl*, 'fallow-deer', and that the deer was a sacred beast of the moon god, and the deer-cow a beast ridden by Artemis.[4] Heller conceded, however, that neither the excavations nor the literary evidence (with the exception Josh. 10 in which the activity of the sun had to be in agreement with the character of the locality) were of much help in illuminating a sun cult at Gibeon.

In an article that appeared in 1960, J. Dus sought to bolster the evidence adduced by Heller in favour of a sun cult at Gibeon.[5] To

---

1. On the idolatrous context of *lō' ṣiwwîtî*, 'I have not commanded', see J. L'Hour, 'Une législation criminelle dans le Deutéronome', *Bib* 44 (1963), p. 14 n. 4.
2. J. Heller, 'Der Name *Eva* ', *ArOr* 26 (1958), pp. 653-55.
3. Heller, 'Der Name *Eva* ', p. 654.
4. Heller, 'Der Name *Eva* ', p. 654.
5. J. Dus, 'Gibeon—Eine Kultstätte des *šmš* und die Stadt des benjaminitischen Schicksals', *VT* 10 (1960), pp. 353-74.

Heller's evidence Dus added several arguments. The names of three Israelite place names which contain solar elements attest to the familiarity of the Israelites with this Canaanite deity.[1] Three cases in which it is implied that *šemeš* occurs without the article (which suggests the proper name of a deity) pertain to[2] Gibeon. 1 Kgs 8.53 (LXX), the temple dedication speech, is Solomon's public account of the orders he received from Yahweh to build the temple, orders which he must have received during the visit to Gibeon in 1 Kings 3 (which in its present form, however, makes no mention of orders to build the temple). When 'properly' understood in accordance with Dus's reconstruction, 1 Kgs 8.53 (LXX) originally equated *šemeš*, 'Sun' with Yahweh, which Dus considers to be striking testimony independent of Joshua 10 to the presence of a pre-Israelite sun cult at Gibeon.[3] Moreover, Dus outlines an important connection between solar Gibeon and Solomon's plans to build the temple:

> That Solomon had founded the Jerusalem Temple as a sun temple under Egyptian and Tyrian influence has always been upheld in recent times. Solomon must have found it opportune that Gibeon, the city which in premonarchic times had been included into the tribe of Benjamin and in reality passed for Israelite, had in his time worshipped Yahweh as a sun-god. To be sure, the temple that Solomon proposed to build had to stand in Jerusalem. Nevertheless, in order to establish a connection with the sun tradition of the city near to Jerusalem, Solomon went to Gibeon to receive

1.   Dus, 'Gibeon', p. 353. He refers to Beth-shemesh, En-shemesh and Ir-shemesh. As noted earlier, Ir-shemesh is perhaps the same as Beth-shemesh which is also attested at a time earlier than the Israelite presence. In any case, none are *necessarily* indicative of an Israelite preoccupation with a solar deity.

2.   Dus ('Gibeon', p. 353) refers to Josh. 10.12, 1 Kgs 8.53 (LXX) and Num. 25.4. The first passage is the only one with a clear link with Gibeon; the second probably originally mentioned the Book of Jashar (cf. Josh. 10.13); and the third concerns the worship of Baal-Peor at Shittim and in its present form contains the article.

3.   Dus, 'Gibeon', pp. 363-64. According to Dus ('Gibeon', p. 364), the names 'Sun' and 'Yahweh' have replaced the names of the deities who were the original revealers of this oracle which, prior to its adaptation for Yahwistic purposes, was originally used by the speaker of a speech on the occasion of the founding of the *šmš*, 'Sun', temple at Gibeon. The theoretical reconstruction of the setting is not convincing, but is, as will be shown, an equation of Yahweh with the sun is nonetheless an important feature of the poetic fragment. (See further my treatment of 1 Kgs 8.12.)

there the order to build the temple. It was the Yahweh worshipped at Gibeon who ordered Solomon to build him a temple, and who wished, so Solomon thought, to be worshipped at Jerusalem as in Gibeon, namely as a solar deity named *šmš*.[1]

Moreover, that Yahweh was worshipped as *šmš* (as he was at Gibeon) in the Jerusalem temple gains further support from 2 Kgs 23.11 which describes Josiah's removal from the temple of horses and chariots dedicated to the sun, and from such passages as Ezek. 8.16 and Pss. 84.12 [11] and 72.5.[2]

The final piece of evidence adduced by Dus for the worship of *šmš* by the Gibeonites comes from the combined testimony of Num. 25.4 and 2 Sam. 21.6. The former passage narrates the sin of the Israelites with the Baal-of-Peor and contains the phrase *hôqaʿ ʾôtām layhwh neged haššemeš*, 'dislocate them for YHWH in the presence of the sun', which, according to Dus, was originally a Canaanite expression into which Yahweh has been interjected and which denoted a kind of sacrificial rite peculiar to the worship of *šmš* by the Canaanites.[3] Turning to the latter passage (that is, 2 Sam. 21 which describes a rite used by the Gibeonites to avenge the carnage of Saul), Dus notes that it contains the only other reference to *hôqîaʿ*. Since this verb when used in Num. 25.4 clearly refers to an action involving the sun, and since when used in 2 Sam. 21.6 it is translated in the LXX by the word *exēliasōmen*, a denominative verb based upon *hēlios*, 'sun', the occurrence of the verb in the latter passage, set at Gibeon, suggests the presence of a solar cult there. In other words, in light of the presence of a solar rite underlying the use of *hôqîaʿ* in Num. 25.4, 2 Sam. 21.6 points to Gibeon as a cult place of *šmš* and highlights further the practice at Gibeon of worshipping Yahweh according to the former manner of worshipping *šmš*.[4]

To evaluate briefly,[5] although Heller has offered a genuinely compelling case for the possible prehistory of Josh. 10.12-13 lying in

1. Dus, 'Gibeon', p. 366 (my translation).
2. Dus, 'Gibeon', pp. 366-67.
3. Dus, 'Gibeon', p. 369.
4. Dus concludes this on the basis of the valid understanding that this apparently Canaanite rite is construed in 2 Sam. 21 as being Yahwistic or at least acceptable to Yahweh.
5. A more detailed evaluation will be offered in the sections dealing with the passages discussed by Heller and Dus.

an old curse of silence against the Sun in Gibeon and the Moon in
Aijalon vale, this interpretation is not without difficulties.[1] Dus's highly
imaginative reconstruction of 1 Kgs 8.12 and its alleged setting in life
can hardly be judged convincing as a means of establishing either the
presence of a sun cult at Gibeon or a direct association between 'Sun'
and Yahweh. However, as Heller himself was to acknowledge in a
popular update of his earlier study, written after the article of Dus,[2]
the use of the verb *exēliazein* to render the *hiphil* of *yq'* in 2 Samuel
21 is striking and possibly suggestive of the presence of a solar cult at
Gibeon. Moreover, although none of the arguments demonstrate a sun
cult at Gibeon conclusively, some adduced particularly by Dus[3] and
many of the passages considered by both Dus and Heller are certainly
worthy of re-examination in light of the possibility that among them is
still to be found an important clue which would tip the scales either in
favour of or against their interpretation. As will be noted in the
course of the discussion of Josh. 10.12-14, considered below, a first
clue can be found in the Deuteronomistic framing of the account of
the sun standing still at Gibeon.

b. *Joshua 10.12-14*

In my judgment Josh. 10.12-14 provides important testimony to DH's
understanding of the relationship between Yahweh and the sun at an
early period. The passage in question is as follows:

> 12 Then Joshua spoke to the Lord[4] on the day the Lord gave the
> Amorites[5] over to the Israelites; he said in the presence of Israel:

---

1. See later in this discussion.
2. J. Heller, 'Die schweigende Sonne', *Communio Viatorum* 9 (1966),
pp. 75-76.
3. For example, Dus might have added to his evidence for the knowledge of a
solar deity in the area the place names Timnath-heres and Har-heres, neither far from
Gibeon, though neither provide evidence that the sun cult to which they allude was
necessarily associated with Yahwism.
4. Here and in the case of its first occurrence in v. 14, 'Lord' should perhaps
be read 'God', following the LXX.
5. Between *hā'emōrî*, 'the Amorite', and *lipnê benê yiśrā'ēl*, 'before the
Israelites', the LXX reads, 'into the hand of Israel, when he defeated them in Gibeon
and they were defeated'. Whether or not the reading is correct (which it probably is)
is not relevant within the context of this study.

'O sun in Gibeon cease,
And moon in the valley of Aijalon!'
13 And the sun ceased and the moon stood still
Until a nation defeated its foes.[1]

Is this not written in the Book of Jashar? The sun stayed at mid-heaven and did not hurry to set for a whole day. 14 There has not been a day like it before or since, when the Lord listened to the voice of a man; for the Lord fought for Israel.

The general meaning of the passage has always been clear: the text cites a poem from a different context and understands it as the statement which gave rise to Yahweh's miraculous halting of the sun which allowed the Israelites extended daylight with which to defeat their foes.

When examined in detail, however, the passage poses a number of problems. Among these difficulties, the best studied is the original setting of the poetic fragment (and here the original settings proposed by Dus,[2] Holladay[3] and Miller[4] are particularly noteworthy). For the present purposes, however, it is important to focus on an additional difficulty over which virtually every commentator has also justifiably stumbled. The problem is this: whereas the Deuteronomistic narrative framework introduces what one clearly expects to be Joshua's speech to Yahweh, in its place is a poetic fragment in which an outcry is made to '*Sun*' (*šemeš*).

The apparent omission of the words of Yahweh is certainly problematic. For one thing, as Boling notes, the point of the whole story focuses on what Yahweh did in response to his being addressed by Joshua.[5] For another, the substitution poses a religious problem, put in the following way by Holladay:

---

1. The phrase '*ad yiqqōm gôy 'ōyᵉbāyw* might also be read, 'until he had executed vengeance against the nation of his enemies', following the suggestion of Patrick Miller (*The Divine Warrior in Early Israel* [Cambridge, MA: Harvard University Press, 1973], p. 128) that a *min* preposition has dropped off of *gôy* and that the subject of *yiqqōm* was either Yahweh (so Miller) or Joshua.

2. Dus, 'Gibeon—Eine Kultstätte des *šmš*', pp. 353-74. See the previous section which discusses the early proposal of Dus and Heller.

3. J.S. Holladay, Jr, 'The Day(s) the *Moon* Stood Still', *JBL* 87 (1968), pp. 166-78.

4. Miller, *Divine Warrior*, pp. 125-27.

5. Boling and Wright, *Joshua*, p. 282.

It must be admitted that the phenomena portrayed in this fragment of poetry, when taken at face value, do not fit readily into what we have reconstructed... of the history of the religion of Israel (would the leader of the Hosts of Israel pray to Shemesh or *Yārēah*?)[1]

To be sure, there are ways around the problem apart from assuming that Joshua's address to 'sun-in-Gibeon' was in fact his speech to 'Yahweh (-in-Gibeon)', as I believe, but none of these alternatives are particularly compelling. For example, in his important work on the divine warrior in ancient Israel, P.D. Miller accounts for the difficulty by regarding the poem in its original context to have been the words of Yahweh to Sun and Moon who were members of his heavenly entourage.[2] However, although this is a very plausible *original setting* for the poetic fragment, it is nonetheless highly unlikely that the poetic fragment can be taken within its *present setting* still to denote the words of Yahweh to the sun, as Miller maintains.[3] The reasons for this are several. First, in v. 12 of the MT the line introducing the poetic fragment clearly states, *'āz yᵉdabbēr yᵉhôšuaʿ layhwh*, 'then Joshua spoke to Yahweh'.[4] Secondly, in v. 14 the significance of the event according to the narrator is that 'there has not been a day like that neither before nor since when Yahweh listened to the voice of a man'. Thirdly, the question must be asked: Why would the narrator frame the story around the hearkened-to words of a man to Yahweh, but include instead, contrary to his own expressed purpose, the words of Yahweh to sun and moon?

As noted earlier, my own opinion is that the Deuteronomistic framing of the poetic fragment must be taken to clearly imply a one-to-one correspondence between Yahweh and *šemeš bᵉgibʿôn*, 'Shemesh-in-Gibeon'. A number of considerations support this interpretation. First and most importantly, as Holladay has implied in part already, this is how the passage appears to read when taken at face value. This is evident in v. 12 in which Joshua who addresses only

1. Holladay, 'Day(s) the *Moon* Stood Still', p. 167.
2. Miller, *Divine Warrior*, pp. 125-27. Miller draws support for this possible understanding by referring to Judg. 5.20 and Hab. 3.11.
3. Miller, *Divine Warrior*, pp. 125-27.
4. As noted, the LXX reads *'ᵉlōhîm*, 'God', here and in the first instance in v. 14. According to my interpretation 'God' is secondary and arose as a theological reaction in response to the MT's identification between *yhwh*, 'Yahweh', and the sun in vv. 12 and 14.

'Sun' and 'Moon' is said to have spoken nonetheless to Yahweh[1] and
also in vv. 13b-14. In the latter case of vv. 13b-14, equation between
Yahweh and the sun is apparent because its assumption is the only
means of resolving two difficulties otherwise posed by these verses.
First, only on the assumption that Yahweh-in-Gibeon is the sun can
one take seriously the claim that it was unusual for 'Yahweh' to listen
to the voice of a man (which Yahweh regularly does with Joshua and
others in DH). Secondly, only on the assumption that Yahweh was the
sun at Gibeon can one account for the way in which Yahweh's
listening to the voice of a man is implied by its placement in v. 14b
(that is, after the halt of the sun) as a phenomenon equal to or even
greater than the sun's miraculous arrest in mid-heaven. In other
words, only by equating the sun's halting with Yahweh's hearing the
voice of a man can the latter be interpreted as a miracle on a par with
the stoppage of the sun in mid-heaven.

If the present interpretation is correct, two things about Josh.
10.12-14 seem clear. First, there is new reason to uphold the claim of
the narrator that Yahweh indeed listened to the voice of a man in a
way in which he had never done before: 'Thus did Yahweh fight for
the armies of Israel'. And secondly, there is no basis upon which to
complain of the narrator (or the history of the transmission of the
text) that the all-important words of Joshua to Yahweh have been
omitted and in its place an obscure poetic fragment inserted that is

1.   It might be argued that the reference to 'Moon' as well as 'Sun' is problematic for my thesis that Yahweh is identified with the latter here. The following may be
noted in response. First, I do not deny that the poetic fragment with reference also to
moon might originally have come from a different setting, as the text itself claims by
referring to the Book of Jashar. Secondly, regardless of its origin, the fragment was
chosen for its reference to both 'sun' and 'Gibeon' and not necessarily for its
(perhaps incidental) reference also to moon. Thirdly, 'moon' is in poetic parallelism
with 'sun' and thus probably functions as a simple bi-form or close equivalent of
sun. Fourthly, and perhaps most significantly, that no particular emphasis should be
placed upon moon is supported by the context of vv. 13-14 in which significance is
assigned exclusively to the activity of the sun in response to Joshua's having
addressed it (as Yahweh). And finally, even if one assumes significance to the reference to moon for the story beyond its occurrence in the poetic fragment, this would
still occasion little difficulty since the moon probably functioned as a nocturnal
counterpart to the sun as representative of the deity (here Yahweh), something for
which there is precedent elsewhere in the ancient Near East (as in the case of Horus
of Edfu, for example).

largely irrelevant to the present context. More importantly, Josh. 10.12-14 provides important new evidence for the notion of a sun cult at Gibeon that was evidently Yahwistic in character.

In light of the presence of fresh evidence for a Yahwistic sun cult at Gibeon, it is worth re-examining one of the more promising lines of evidence adduced earlier by Dus and Heller, namely 2 Sam. 21.1-14 and Num. 25.4.

c. *2 Samuel 21.1-14*

By way of background, this passage which lies in the so-called Appendix to 2 Samuel[1] tells the story of how the Gibeonites, with David's permission, got revenge for Saul's crime, of trying to root out the Gibeonites. Their vengeance came through the performing of an obscure rite in which seven members of Saul's family were killed at the start of the barley harvest in a manner expressed by the rare verb *hôqîa'*, 'to hang, impale' (or the like). They were subsequently left exposed on a hill, and guarded from birds and wild beasts by Rizpah (the daughter of Saul's concubine) until it rained, perhaps a period of months.

To begin the comparison between this rite and the one found in Num. 25.4,[2] the latter passage reads as follows (in context):

> Israel yoked itself to Baal-of-Peor, and the anger of the Lord was against Israel. And the Lord said unto Moses, 'Take all the leaders of the people and *hôqa'* them to Yahweh before the sun, that the fierce anger of the Lord against Israel be turned back'. And Moses said unto the judges of Israel, 'Each man slay the men of his who have yoked themselves to Baal-of-Peor'.

---

1.   Whether or not this passage was part of the DH is debated: Blenkinsopp, for example (*Gibeon and Israel*, p. 89), regards it as 'almost certainly absent from the Deuteronomist historical work', whereas P.K. McCarter, Jr (*II Samuel* [AB, 9; New York: Doubleday, 1984], p. 16) regards the passage as having been 'originally connected to passages in the succession narrative'. On the role of 2 Sam. 20.23– 24.25, see further McCarter, *II Samuel*, pp. 16-19 and the discussion later in this study.

2.   Note, for example, Blenkinsopp (*Gibeon and Israel*, p. 48): 'We may admit that there are at least some striking points of resemblance between the two narratives'. Cf. also McCarter, *II Samuel*, p. 442, and R. Polzin, 'HWQ' and Covenantal Institutions in Early Israel', *HTR* 62 (1969), pp. 229-31.

Relevant here is the way in which the rite is described vis-à-vis the sun: *wᵉhôqa' 'ôtām layhwh neged haššemeš*, 'and impale them to Yahweh before the sun'. On the basis of the expression *neged haššemeš*, it is often noted that an important aspect of this ritual was that it took place 'before the sun', which either alludes to an ancient rite done before the sun but taken over into a Yahwistic rite (so Dus) or, more straightforwardly, to a rite done 'in public'.

Turning to 2 Sam. 21.6, according to the textual witness of Aquila and Symmachus which the vast majority of commentators and several translations follow,[1] the text reads, *wᵉhôqaʿᵃnûm layhwh bᵉgibʿôn bᵉhar yhwh*, 'so that we may crucify them to Yahweh-in-Gibeon on the mountain of Yahweh'.[2] The parallel, now bolstered by Josh. 10.12-14 in which Yahweh is addressed as 'sun-in-Gibeon', is that the rite was the same in both Num. 25.4 and in 2 Sam. 21.6: whereas in the former passage the rite is made 'to Yahweh before the sun', in the latter it is made 'to Yahweh-in-Gibeon'. Because in the latter case impalement to Yahweh-in-Gibeon is impalement also before the sun, the rite is identical in both Num. 25.4 and in 2 Sam. 21.6. Moreover, the same equivalency can be inferred by further comparison between Num. 25.4, in which occurs the expression *hwqʿ* + *neged haššemeš*, 'impale...in the presence of the sun', and 2 Sam. 21.9, in which occurs the expression *hwqʿ* + *lipnê yhwh*, 'impale...in the presence of Yahweh'.[3]

To evaluate, the parallels in phraseology between Num. 25.4 and

---

1. See, for example, Blenkinsopp, *Gibeon and Israel*, p. 93; McCarter, *II Samuel*, p. 438; H.W. Hertzberg, *I and II Samuel* (OTL; Philadelphia: Westminster Press, 1964), p. 380; de Vaux, *Ancient Israel*, p. 306; RSV, JB.

2. The translation is McCarter's (*II Samuel*, p. 436). The unlikely reading of the MT is, *wᵉhôqaʿᵃnûm layhwh bᵉgibʿat šā'ûl bᵉhîr yhwh*, 'hang them up before the Lord, at Gibeah of Saul, the chosen of the Lord'.

3. The sentence in 2 Sam. 21.9 reads: *wayyittᵉnēm bᵉyad haggibʿōnîm wayyōqîʿûm bāhār lipnê yhwh*, 'and he gave them into the hand of the Gibeonites and they impaled them on the mountain, in the presence of Yahweh'.

On the basis of the occurrence of *har yhwh* 'mountain of Yahweh', as a name for Gibeon in 2 Sam. 21.6 (LXX) and the apparent identification of Yahweh with the sun at Gibeon, could it be that the enigmatic place name *har ḥeres*, 'mountain of the sun', according to Kallai located somewhere in the area of the southwestern part of Benjamin and near Aijalon, is Gibeon? (Interestingly, in both the case of Har-ḥeres and Gibeon, there is mention of an Amorite population at the site, and the imposition upon that population of forced labour; cf. Judg. 1.35 and Josh. 9.21-27; 10.12.)

2 Sam. 21.6, 9 are not sufficient in themselves to warrant the conclusion that the Yahweh-in-Gibeon was solar—after all, little is known of this rite apart from these two passages and the suggestion of equivalency is admittedly informed by the notion of Yahweh as sun—but these parallels can be used as supplementary evidence, essentially confirming the judgment made in light of the apparently clear witness of Josh. 10.12-14 that at Gibeon, the sun and Yahweh were one.[1] In other words, based upon a combination of factors, it is logical to suppose an equation between *šemeš bᵉgibʿôn*, 'Sun-in-Gibeon' (Josh. 10.12) and *yhwh bᵉgibʿôn*, 'Yahweh-in-Gibeon' (2 Sam. 21.6).

d. *Gibeon*

At this point it may be asked: Is the interpretation that Yahweh of Gibeon was solar in character consistent with what is known elsewhere in biblical literature about Gibeon and the theology of the sanctuary at Gibeon?

At the outset it must be admitted that relatively little is known about the high place at Gibeon and the nature of the Yahweh cult there. Although this makes any judgment about the cult of Yahweh at Gibeon tentative, two factors provide some basis for regarding the theology of the high place at Gibeon to have been viewed suspiciously by biblical writers. First, as Blenkinsopp has noted, there is a strange silence in the MT concerning Gibeon and its high place during the period of Judges and Saul; after all, according to 1 Kgs 3.4, which there is no reason to doubt, Gibeon was during this period 'the most important high place' of Yahweh.[2] And secondly, as Blenkinsopp also argues, since this silence occurs at a time when 'we would expect this "great city" and "great high place" to have played a significant role in the political and religious history of Israel', the silence itself is suspicious, perhaps reflecting a Jerusalemite attempt to 'play down' the significance of Gibeon.[3]

---

1. To return to Heller and Dus, this study suggests that in terms of their basic thesis of a Yahwistic sun cult at Gibeon they made up in intuition for what they lacked in evidence at the time.

2. Cf. 1 Kgs 3.4, in which Gibeon is referred to as *habbāmâ haggᵉdôlâ*, rendered by the NEB, 'the chief hill-shrine' and NIV, 'the most important high place'. There is no reason to doubt the historical reliability of the reference.

3. Blenkinsopp, *Gibeon and Israel*, pp. 65-83. Blenkinsopp notes the same silence about the ark, a matter to be discussed shortly.

In addition to these general factors, passages in both DH (including for practical purposes the Appendix to 2 Samuel) and Chronicles support the view that key cultic elements associated with Gibeonite Yahwism were controversial and played down. As will be argued, on the one hand both DH and the Chronicler betray an awareness of significant input from Gibeon, an awareness which they seem almost obliged to acknowledge (no doubt because of the historical reality of Jerusalem's indebtedness to Gibeon and also, probably and notably, because of the abiding influence of those sympathetic with Gibeonite Yahwism). On the other hand, however, DH and the Chronicler (or later editors) each suppress different aspects of Jerusalem's indebtedness to the Yahwistic (solar) cult centre at Gibeon. What each chooses to reveal or suppress will become clear as the various passages that mention Gibeon are considered. By reconsidering what each suppresses or divulges a picture emerges which does not prove, but which is nonetheless perfectly consistent with, the notion that Gibeonite Yahwism was controversial in terms of cult and theology.

2 Chronicles 1.3-5. This passage, based on 1 Kgs 3.3-5, but with additional comments concerning the tabernacle, ark and bronze altar, reads as follows:

> And Solomon, and all the assembly with him, went to the high place at Gibeon; for the tent of meeting of God, which Moses the servant of the Lord had made in the wilderness, was there. (But David had brought up the ark of God from Kiriath-jearim to the place that David had pitched a tent for it in Jerusalem.) Moreover the bronze altar that Bezalel the son of Uri, son of Hur, had made, was there before the tabernacle of the Lord. And Solomon and the assembly sought the Lord. And Solomon went up there to the bronze altar before the Lord, which was at the tent of meeting, and offered a thousand burnt offerings upon it (RSV).

Of particular interest is the claim that the tabernacle and bronze altar were located at Gibeon, a claim mentioned elsewhere only in 1 Chron. 16.39-40 (which refers to a division of labour between Asaphites who minister at the ark and Zadokites who minister at the tabernacle) and 21.29 (which explains that prior to the divinely ordained choice for a new cultic centre revealed to David, the tabernacle and bronze altar had been at Gibeon). Significantly, Joshua–Kings nowhere claims that the altar of burnt offering or tabernacle were situated at Gibeon.

The location of these cultic items at Gibeon has traditionally been regarded as fictitious, but this assessment should not be adopted uncritically. The three main reasons for not taking the testimony of Chronicles seriously are as follows. (1) Nowhere else in the Old Testament is there mention of 'what by all rights ought to be a most important item'.[1] (2) The division of labour in 1 Chronicles 16 between Asaphites who minister at the ark and Zadokites who minister at the tabernacle appears artificial in light of 1 Chron. 6.31-48 where no such division is specified.[2] (3) A clear motive for this addition by the Chronicler can be found in his desire to provide justification for Solomon's visit to a high place and to bring his actions into line with Lev. 17.8-9 which legislates that even a *gēr*, 'sojourner', cannot offer sacrifices or burnt offerings at a place other than where the tent of meeting is located.[3]

To evaluate the arguments in reverse order, there is no doubt that the third argument is compelling. As Williamson notes, 'it is certainly the case that these features would have made the tradition attractive to the Chronicler'.[4] Regarding the second argument, however, although the reference to the tabernacle and bronze altar might be judged simply a secondary addition in 2 Chron. 1.3b-6, it is very difficult to make the same claim about their reference in 1 Chron. 16.39-40 where 'the division of Levites between ministry before the ark and somewhere else, on which the whole of this chapter is based, presupposes the inclusion of this and the following verse for its explanation', as Williamson has noted.[5] Moreover, the same argument

---

1.   R.L. Braun, *1 Chronicles* (WBC, 14; Waco, TX: Word Books, 1986), pp. 193-94; cf. H.G.M. Williamson, *1 and 2 Chronicles* (NCB; Grand Rapids: Eerdmans, 1982), pp. 130-31.

2.   See, for example, Blenkinsopp, *Gibeon and Israel*, p. 102.

3.   Blenkinsopp, *Gibeon and Israel*, p. 102.

4.   Williamson, *Chronicles*, p. 131.

5.   Williamson, *Chronicles*, p. 131. Williamson adds the following five arguments in favour of the presence of a genuine tradition behind the reference to the tabernacle at Gibeon: (1) the absence of the reference to tabernacle and ark in the parallel account in 1 Kgs 3.3b is not necessarily significant because 'the Kings' account is as polemical against the legitimacy of Solomon's worship at Gibeon as the Chronicler is towards it'; (2) the tension between the division of labour in 1 Chron 16.39-40 and 1 Chron. 6.31-48, by no means irreconcilable, might be accounted for by assuming 'that the Chronicler was here working under the compulsion of inherited tradition'; (3) 2 Sam. 7.6 implies an ongoing regard for a tent sanctuary, a regard for which there is some evidence (though more problematic) also prior

can be adduced with even greater force in the case of the mention of tabernacle and altar in Gibeon in 1 Chron. 21.29–22.1, where the Chronicler's lengthy justification for David's innovative decision to build his own altar at the threshing floor of Araunah presupposes the existence of the traditional altar (and with it the tabernacle) at Gibeon. Thus, although the explanation that the Chronicler added the reference to this cultic apparatus to justify Solomon's visit seems entirely plausible when 2 Chron. 1.3-5 is considered alone, it cannot account for the same information provided in 1 Chron. 16.39-40 and in 21.29–22.1. There are good reasons, then, for believing that the Chronicler's repeated claims that the bronze altar and tabernacle were at Gibeon rest on an earlier tradition.

There remains, however, the first argument, namely, the absence of any reference in Samuel or Kings to what one would indeed expect to be a noteworthy item if it was historical. But this view does not reckon sufficiently with the possibility that the DH may have had some reason for suppressing a genuine tradition that has been preserved in Chronicles. Moreover, as further comparison of Samuel–Kings and Chronicles reveals, material relevant to the location of key cultic items has indeed been suppressed in the DH which the Chronicler locates at Gibeon.

Traditions of the Altar of Burnt Offering Missing in Kings but Evident in Chronicles. As might be judged from what has been noted already, there cannot be found in 2 Samuel 24 (the account of David's relocation of the site of the altar to Araunah's threshing floor) any mention of the presence of the altar of burnt offering or tabernacle at Gibeon, as could be found in the parallel passage in 1 Chron. 21.29. There is little reason to believe that the Chronicler simply invented this tradition. Rather, in associating this incident etiologically with the

to the time of the temple; and (4) Josh. 9.27 refers to a sanctuary 'most naturally understood as referring to an altar at Gibeon'; and (5) Görg has argued that the tent mentioned in 1 Kgs 1.39 cannot refer to the temporary one erected by David for the ark, but to the one which may have been at Gibeon. (Both Görg and Hertzberg favour the notion that the tradition is early, based upon the identity or proximity of Gibeon and Nob.) Although there are problems with some of these arguments (particularly the fifth one; cf. Blenkinsopp, *Gibeon and Israel*, p. 95), their cumulative effect legitimates Williamson's claim that the issue of whether or not the Chronicler was working with an earlier tradition 'must be left open'.

choice of the location of the altar of burnt offering at Araunah's
threshing floor *as opposed to Gibeon*, the Chronicler is preserving a
tradition which has been intentionally suppressed in Samuel and
Kings.

Considering the account in Chronicles, immediately after the
Chronicler refers to the threshing floor of Araunah as a replacement
for the site of the altar at Gibeon, there is in the very next verse
(1 Chron. 22.2) the description of the role which the *gērîm* (among
whom, of course, were most notably the Gibeonites) had in the
construction of the new temple. The verse can be understood to function, then, as a concession to the Gibeonite Yahwists who, in light of
the extended etiology offered in 1 Chronicles 21, had no choice[1] but
to accept the legitimacy of a new cult place.

Turning to the account in 2 Samuel 24, even without the parallel
passage in Chronicles referring to the altar of burnt offering at
Gibeon, connections with Gibeon can still be seen in 2 Samuel 24
through its clear affinity with 2 Sam. 21.1-14 which concerns the
revenge of the Gibeonites against the house of Saul. This link between
2 Samuel 24 and 21 is evident in the following ways: (1) through the
role of 2 Samuel 24 forming with 2 Sam. 21.1-14 a narrative
'parenthesis' around the lists of 21.13-22 and 23.8-39 (which in turn
form a parenthesis around the poems in 22.1-51 and 23.1-7); (2)
through the word 'again' in 2 Sam. 24.1 which forms a clear link with
21.1-14; and (3) through virtually identical endings in both 21.14c
and 24.25b, namely, 'and God/Yahweh heeded supplication for the
land'. Moreover, although the purpose of the placement of 2 Samuel
24 (or for that matter the whole Appendix) is not fully understood,
there can be little doubt that the chapter functions as an etiology
justifying the future Solomonic altar of burnt offering and its new
location at the site of the threshing floor of Araunah. This being the

---

1.   The narrative leaves no room for debate about the legitimacy of the new cultic
site at Araunah's threshing floor as opposed to Gibeon; there is a direct order from a
sword-bearing angel addressing David himself (known in light of the tandem
2 Sam. 21 to have no a priori opposition to Gibeonite theology) to build an altar of
burnt offering in this new location. Confirmation of divine approval of this site is
clearly indicated by the presence of 'fire from heaven upon the altar of burnt
offering'. Immediately afterwards, at the Lord's command, the angel who is said
specifically to have prevented David from going to Gibeon (vv. 27, 30) puts away
his sword.

case, is it too much to go one step further and state that the etiology
sought to justify the use of a new place of sacrifice (with altar) on the
site of the future Solomonic temple *as opposed* to the use of the old
place of sacrifice (with altar) at Gibeon? Surely not, especially in light
of the following considerations: (1) the Gibeonite context of 2 Samuel
24 vis-à-vis 21.1-14; (2) 1 Chron. 21.29–22.1 in which this
explanation for the etiology is explicitly stated; (3) the acknowledge-
ment in DH of the inaugural visit of Solomon to Gibeon (1 Kgs 3.3-4)
which says of Gibeon, 'that was the great high place' and which goes
so far as to mention 'that altar' at Gibeon upon which 'Solomon used
to offer a thousand burnt offerings'[1]; (4) 1 Kgs 9.1-2 which reads,
'When Solomon had finished building the house of the Lord and the
king's house and all that Solomon desired to build, the Lord appeared
to Solomon as second time, *as he had appeared to him at Gibeon*'.[2]

One final argument can be adduced by reference to 2 Chron. 4.1:

> wayya῾aś mizbaḥ n^eḥōšet ῾eśrîm ᾽ammâ ᾽orkô w^e῾eśrîm ᾽ammâ roḥbô
> w^e῾eśer ᾽ammôt qômātô
>
> And he [Solomon] made a bronze altar with ten cubits its length, ten
> cubits its breadth and ten cubits its height.

Surprisingly, there is no reference to the construction of the bronze
altar by Solomon in Kings comparable to that just cited from
Chronicles in spite of the fact that Kings otherwise contains a rather
comprehensive list of the descriptions of temple furnishings.[3] Moreover, commentators are virtually unanimous in their opinion that,
although for some reason no longer preserved in Kings, 2 Chron. 4.1
is original to it. Note, for example, the words of Williamson:

> The altar of bronze appears accidentally to have been lost from the
> description of the building in 1 Kg., though later references both in Kg.
> and Chron. show that it originally stood in both books... The way in
> which the measurements are listed does not conform to the Chronicler's
> own style, and so it is likely to reflect the influence of his *Vorlage*.[4]

In light of what has just been argued, there is of course a clear
theological explanation for the 'accidental' lack of mention of the

---

1. 1 Kgs 3.4.
2. RSV (emphasis mine).
3. I am indebted to S.D. Walters for drawing this omission to my attention.
4. Williamson, *Chronicles*, p. 210.

bronze altar in Kings: the bronze altar was a piece of cultic apparatus, the Gibeonite origin of which was controversial. Could the controversy have lain in the fact that the bronze altar reflected (perhaps quite literally) the solar nature of the cult of Yahweh at Gibeon?

A further omission from the fairly comprehensive description of furnishings in Kings (the absence of which, however, can also be accounted for by homoioteleuton) is the description of the building of the platform for the bronze altar which the Chronicler claimed came from Gibeon:

> Solomon had made a bronze platform five cubits long, five cubits wide, and three cubits high, and had set it in the court; he stood upon it. Then he knelt upon his knees in the presence of all the assembly of Israel, and spread forth his hands toward heaven... (2 Chron. 6.13, RSV).

Again it is clear that this verse does not originate with Chronicles but with Kings (or at least a form of Kings not identical with the MT but upon which the Chronicler's account was based).[1] This can be supported on two counts: (1) as with 2 Chron. 4.1, the description is not characteristic of Chronicles but Kings, and (2) 1 Kgs 8.54 indicates that Solomon rose from having knelt before the altar, which perhaps presupposes a knowledge of this verse by the writer of 1 Kgs 8.54.[2]

Summary and Evaluation. To summarize, both DH[3] and the Chronicler in their own ways appear to be conceding Jerusalem's clear indebtedness to the old cultic establishment at Gibeon, while at the same time maintaining a distance from specific (presumably sensitive) aspects of that indebtedness, such as the altar of burnt offering. Thus, for example, regarding Gibeon in general, the Chronicler does not include the accounts of David 'seeking the Lord' (probably at the Gibeonite sanctuary), and conceding to a somewhat dubious ritual in which members of Saul's family are hung out before Yahweh-in-Gibeon (that is, the sun), but mentions on the other hand

---

1.   Williamson, *Chronicles*, p. 218.

2.   One could only judge in light of the present form of Kings that Solomon would have been standing before the altar (cf. 1 Kgs 8.22).

3.   What is said here about the Deuteronomic historical work clearly applies also to the Appendix to 2 Sam. The relationship between the work and the Appendix are beyond the scope of this study.

the original presence at Gibeon of the tabernacle and altar of burnt offering. Conversely, the writer(s) of the Appendix to 2 Samuel mention(s) David's concession to the Gibeonites vis-à-vis Saul (plausibly in order to gain favour with a pro-Gibeonite element), but decline(s) to complete the details of the etiology in 2 Samuel 24 by stating, as did the Chronicler, that David was compelled to choose as a cult site the obscure threshing floor of Araunah *over against the sanctuary at Gibeon*. Regarding the altar about which there seems clearly to have been some controversy, neither the Chronicler nor DH are willing to state outrightly that Solomon brought the bronze altar from Gibeon.[1] Thus, although willing to note the presence of a bronze altar at Gibeon, the Chronicler claimed that Solomon built another altar. DH on the other hand (and here we must speak of a later hand that apparently removed from Kings the references to Solomon's construction of the bronze altar and its platform) adopted a middle-of-the-road position, neither explicitly stating that there was an altar of burnt offering with tabernacle at Gibeon,[2] nor claiming that Solomon built a new one. This non-committal position, a brilliant case of theological tact, leaves the reader with *two* possibilities for the origin of the altar of burnt offering: the huge altar at Gibeon mentioned only in passing in 1 Kgs 3.5, and the altar built by David at Araunah's threshing floor mentioned in 2 Samuel 24![3]

Clearly none of what has been said about Gibeon in this section specifically supports the notion that Yahweh-of-Gibeon was solar in character. It does indicate, however, that some form of religious controversy lay behind Gibeon's contribution to the cultic apparatus at Jerusalem. In light of what has been argued thus far and what will be argued further, I suggest that a solar understanding of

1. As will be noted, there is a parallel here between ambiguity about the origin of the altar of burnt offerings and that of the ark which Blenkinsopp (*Gibeon and Israel*) feels was at Gibeon, but which in any case could be transferred to Jerusalem only after residing passively at the obscure town of Kiriath-jearim (a Gibeonite town nonetheless!) for some twenty years.

2. Cf. 1 Kgs 3.5, however.

3. To its credit, the explanation offered here appropriately underscores the importance of what is the last verse in Samuel (MT). Moreover, S.D. Walters has drawn my attention to the comment in the LXX at 2 Sam. 24.25 that Solomon increased the size of the altar which David built at the threshing floor of Araunah, which perhaps alludes to the controversial nature of the altar.

Yahweh-of-Gibeon is most likely the theologically sensitive issue around which the biblical writers are dodging.

Before moving on, it is worth noting in passing a few additional considerations which offer further support for the notion of solar elements within Gibeonite Yahwism. First, and very generally, because the biblical material indicates a high degree of continuity between the high place at Gibeon and the temple of Jerusalem (a continuity that included even the transference of key pieces of cultic paraphernalia from one place to the other), it is only reasonable to assume at least some measure of continuity between the theology of the two sanctuaries, especially when a case can be made on independent grounds for the presence of solar elements at both Gibeon and Jerusalem. Second, it deserves a quick note that the altar of burnt offering was constructed with bronze. Of course, bronze on an altar does not itself suggest a solar cult (a bronze altar is mentioned, for example, in the Yehaumilk inscription).[1] Nevertheless, if Gibeon was a Yahwistic solar cult centre, that the altar literally gleamed with the radiance of the sun would not have gone unnoticed. Thirdly and finally, it is well worth noting where Ezekiel locates the climactic abomination of sun worship to which he refers in Ezek. 8.16:

> And He brought me to the inner court of the House of the Lord, and there at the entrance of the temple of the Lord between the porch and the altar, there were about twenty five men with their backs to the temple of the Lord and their faces to the east, and they were worshipping eastwards, to the sun.

According to Ezekiel, the practice of facing eastwards in worship of the sun took place in the middle of the court, between the entrance to the temple and the altar of burnt offering/bronze altar.[2] This is the

---

1. *KAI* 10.4; cf. J.C.L. Gibson, *Syrian Semitic Inscriptions*. III. *Phoenician Inscriptions* (Oxford: Clarendon Press, 1982), pp. 93-96.

2. The situation is somewhat complicated by Ahaz's introduction of a new 'great' altar which took the place of the bronze altar (2 Kgs 16.10-16). If the new altar introduced by Ahaz (presumably the one to which Ezek. 8.16 refers) signals a significant change in cultic practice, then we are not justified in assuming continuity between what took place before this altar in Ezekiel's day and what cultic practices might have taken place before the bronze altar in Solomon's time. Fortunately, however, there is little chance of a significant break in cultic practice in spite of the introduction of Ahaz's altar, for the following reasons. (1) The same priest, Uriah, was in charge of the new altar (cf. G.H. Jones, *1 and 2 Kings* [NCB; Grand

same zone consecrated by Solomon in 1 Kgs 8.64 and which, as Greenberg has noted, is ranked in *m. Kel.* 1.9 as second only to the sanctuary itself in degrees of sanctity.[1] Perhaps then, like the high place at Gibeon from which it came, the altar of burnt offering was associated with the worship of Yahweh as the sun. This would account for the later purging from Kings of references to the altar of burnt offering which are still preserved in Chronicles.

e. *The Ark*
There are at least three reasons for considering the ark and ark narratives: (1) consideration of Gibeon would otherwise be incomplete; (2) a possible connection between the ark and solar Yahwism may be inferred through the clear association of the ark with the expression 'Yahweh of Hosts'; and (3) Psalm 24, clearly connected with the procession of the ark, is considered later in this chapter to reflect the

Rapids: Eerdmans, 1984], II, p. 538). (2) The account in 2 Kings gives no indication that the cultic practice at the altar was other than Yahwistic (in fact, as J. Gray notes [*I and 2 Kings* (OTL; Philadelphia: Westminster Press, 2nd edn, 1970), p. 636], the description of sacrifice at the new altar 'is a *locus classicus* for sacrifice in the Temple'). (3) The bronze altar, clearly portable, was not discarded in spite of the fact that Ahaz was desperate for valuable metal with which to pay off the king of Assyria (vv. 17-18), but placed next to the new altar (as if to suggest continuity of practice) for the king's ongoing private use. (4) Spieckermann's criticisms of the thesis of McKay and Cogan notwithstanding, there is no reason to believe that Ahaz's vassalage to Tiglath-Pileser which looms large in the context, carried with it an obligation on the part of Ahaz to worship an Assyrian deity (see most conveniently, Jones, *1 and 2 Kings*, II, p. 538).

What was the purpose of the change of altars if it was not to reflect a cultic innovation? Although the choice of an altar from the city in which Ahaz expressed vassalage to Tiglath-Pileser may have been politically advantageous, an important reason for the change was no doubt that a larger altar was needed. In favour of this suggestion are the following observations. (1) The bronze altar, probably built originally for the cult place at Gibeon, was from the outset too small for its role within the Jerusalem cult (1 Kgs 8.64). (2) A tradition reflecting a problem with the small size of the altar is preserved in the LXX of 2 Sam. 24.25 which states that Solomon had to add on to the altar built originally by David. (3) In the speech of Ahaz which explains his cultic innovation, the new altar is referred to as 'the large altar' (*hammizbēaḥ haggādôl*)which is set in clear contrast with 'the bronze altar' (*mizbaḥ hannᵉḥōšet*) which Ahaz deemed suitable for his own private use (v. 15).

1. Greenberg, *Ezekiel 1–20*, p. 171.

outlook of solar Yahwism. A brief highlighting of several issues relevant to the ark is in order.

Concerning the ark and Gibeon, Blenkinsopp has noted a parallel between the obscurity surrounding Gibeon and that surrounding the ark from prior to the reign of Saul to well into the reign of David.[1] If a primary location of the ark prior to its transference to Jerusalem was Gibeon, as Blenkinsopp argues,[2] or even included it,[3] then the

---

1. Blenkinsopp, *Gibeon and Israel*, pp. 65-83. To Blenkinsopp, the ark narratives in their present form are the result of a redactional effort from the perspective of the Jerusalem sanctuary which for both political and religious reasons sought to play down Gibeon as a major cult centre which must have rivalled Jerusalem.

2. Blenkinsopp (*Gibeon and Israel*, pp. 65-83) is almost certainly correct that the present form of the narrative concerning the ark and the Gibeonite cities (including Beth-shemesh) fails to give the full picture of both the residency of the ark and the role of Gibeon during this period; it is extremely difficult to fit all of the events into the twenty-year period (probably a Deuteronomistic generalization in any case) mentioned in 1 Sam. 7.2. Moreover, although there is no reason to doubt the testimony of 1 Sam. 7.2 that the ark spent *some* time in Kiriath-jearim (see the following note), the abbreviated time span and clearly selective mention of places of residency for the ark leave ample room for Blenkinsopp's well-founded supposition that it was not in the interests of the Jerusalem sanctuary to mention Gibeon as a place for the residency of the ark.

Blenkinsopp's theory that the location of the ark, mentioned in 1 Sam. 7.1 and 2 Sam. 6.3 as being at *bêt 'ᵃbînādāb baggibʿâ*, 'the house of Abinadab on the "hill"', is Gibeon in these passages is compelling on two counts: (1) Gibeon, a levitical city, is a logical place for the Levite Abinadab; and (2) there is clearly confusion elsewhere between *gibʿôn*, 'Gibeon', and *gibʿâ*, 'Gibeah' (or simply 'hill' which even without the confusion might remind one of the prominent Nebi Samwil nearby Gibeon and probably associated with it). (For cases of confusion in the second case, see Blenkinsopp, *Gibeon and Israel*, pp. 2-3.) Moreover, it is striking in light of the argument offered earlier for the presence of intentional ambiguity in deference to both those opposed to and in favour of Gibeonite Yahwism that 2 Sam. 6, clearly written from the outlook of the Jerusalem sanctuary, does not use the term Kiriath-jearim attested in 1 Sam. 7.2, but the (intentionally) ambiguous *bêt 'ᵃbînādāb baggibʿâ*, which could be understood *either* as Gibeon *or* Kiriath-jearim.

3. Even if Blenkinsopp (*Gibeon and Israel*, p. 53) is correct in his judgment that 1 Sam. 7.2-19, the only passage specifically mentioning the obscure Kiriath-jearim, is 'a late composition and generally untrustworthy as a historical source for the period', there is still the testimony in 1 Sam. 6.21, from a different source, which refers to the men of Beth-shemesh saying to the residents of Kiriath-jearim, 'come down and take it up to you'. (Blenkinsopp's explanation [*Gibeon and Israel*, p. 78]

same theological concern might lie behind the obscurity concerning both Gibeon and the ark (i.e. Gibeonite solar Yahwism).

Some have assigned solar significance to the narrative of the journey of the ark to Beth-shemesh in 1 Samuel 6. For example, H.-P. Stähli sees in the coming of the ark to Beth-shemesh in 1 Sam. 6.7-18 an example of the taking over of a sun-cult centre by Yahweh, and in the judgment of God against the few who scornfully looked upon the ark in the sequel to this account in 6.19–7.1 a case of the opposition to the Yahweh cult by those who clung to the traditional sun cult at Beth-shemesh.[1] As Stähli himself notes, however, this interpretation arose at a time when the two accounts were assumed to be a unit which is no longer thought to be the case.[2] Moreover, Stähli pleads ignorance concerning how the details of this interpretation might be worked out.[3] His interpretation is thus not convincing. In light of what has been argued concerning the presence of solar elements in the Gibeonite realm, however, Blenkinsopp's general impression concerning the account of the ark's sojourn at nearby Beth-shemesh is worth noting:

> What we detect behind the confused traditions preserved in I Sam. vi.14-21 is a definite stage of the ark's history, though one of unknown duration, comparable to the equally obscure period which followed after the ark was taken over by the inhabitants of Kiriath-jearim. Religious ideas and practices which must have been suspect from the Israelite viewpoint are attested for both Dan and Beth-shemesh on the one hand and Benjamin and the Gibeonite cities on the other. For the former we have the idol in the house of Micah (Judges xvii-xviii), the Samson cycle of stories, place-names with -ŠMŠ and the tradition behind I Sam. vi. 18b-19; for the latter, the $p^e s \hat{\imath} l \hat{\imath} m$ of Judges iii. 19, the crime of the men of Gibeah

that 'the request addressed to the people of Kiriath-jearim to "take it up to you" could refer to them *qua* Gibeonites' is not convincing.)

1. Stähli, *Solare Elemente*, pp. 16-17.
2. Stähli, *Solare Elemente*, p. 17.
3. Stähli, *Solare Elemente*, p. 17. A more promising approach might be to interpret the ark's almost magnetic attraction to 'Beth-shemesh' as the writer's subtle way of denoting an affinity between the ark and a (Yahwistic) solar cult. (Beth-shemesh is the obvious 'place' [v. 2] of the ark, the ark's 'own land' [v. 9], and the milch cows when released take the ark straight for Beth-shemesh, not turning to the right or left.) The attraction of the ark to Beth-shemesh, however, probably has more to do with location of Beth-shemesh just within 'Israelite' territory than with it being a 'solar' site.

(Judges xix), the ritual immolation of the Saulites (2 Sam. xxi.1-14) and other indirect indications.[1]

Several other factors are relevant to the possibility that the ark was linked with solar aspects within the cult. For example, it is perhaps significant that, immediately upon returning from the high place at Gibeon, 'Solomon stood before the ark of the covenant of the Lord, and offered up burnt offerings and peace offerings...' (1 Kgs. 3.15). Further, 1 Kgs 8.53 LXX (8.12 MT), which refers to *šemeš* and *yhwh* in a way that clearly implies a historical association between the two, occurs in MT within the context of the transference of the ark to Jerusalem, as will be noted later in this study.[2] Moreover, as will also be argued later in this chapter, Psalm 24, an ark-procession psalm, seems quite clearly to presuppose a solar understanding of *yhwh ṣᵉbā'ôt*.[3]

To evaluate, no line of evidence examined in this section is particularly compelling, but the combined weight of various lines of evidence (including the meaning of 'Yahweh of Hosts' examined earlier, and 1 Kgs 8.12 and Ps. 24, yet to be examined) permits us to suggest that a historical affinity between the ark and a solar understanding of Yahweh is clearly possible.

f. *Zadokites as Mediators of Solarized Yahwism? A Hypothesis*

It has been argued thus far that solar elements made their way into royal Jerusalemite theology via Gibeon and quite possibly also via the traditions of 'Yahweh of Hosts' and the ark. Moreover, since it will be argued further that solar elements within Yahwism continued to characterize royal Jerusalemite theology throughout most of the period of the monarchy, it is important to consider the following question: Who was responsible for carrying and promoting solar

1.   Blenkinsopp, *Gibeon and Israel*, p. 76. It is noteworthy that his reference to *hā'eben haggᵉdôlâ*, 'the great stone' (1 Sam. 6.15, 18), obviously an object of significance for the cult of Yahweh at Beth-shemesh, is reminiscent of 'the great stone' found at Gibeon (2 Sam. 20.8).

2.   See the discussion later in this chapter.

3.   Possibly relevant also is 1 Chron. 28.18 which mentions 'the plan for the golden chariot that spread forth their wings and covered the ark of the covenant of the Lord'. The verse is problematic, but at least one scholar has suggested a connection between the chariot referred to in this verse and the sun chariot mentioned in 2 Kgs 23.11 (McKay, *Religion in Judah*, pp. 34-35).

Yahwism within the royal Jerusalemite establishment?

Apart from the obvious influence of the kings themselves, the most logical candidates are the Zadokites, who controlled the priesthood in Jerusalem from the time of Solomon to the exile and during the period of the second temple until 171 BCE.[1] Though not plentiful, there is some evidence for linking the Zadokites with solar aspects of Yahwism.

For one thing, among the options for Zadok's place of origin are Gibeon and Hebron, the former claimed by the Chronicler and the latter argued for most notably by Cross.[2] Although the latter option enjoys more favour at present, consideration of the former, Gibeon, repays attention.

First, the merits of Cross's argument notwithstanding, the evidence adduced earlier in this study in favour of the tradition in Chronicles concerning the presence of the altar (and tabernacle) at Gibeon lends some credence to that aspect of the same tradition which claims that the Zadokites presided over the high place at Gibeon. The relevant account of the Chronicler, 1 Chron. 16.39-40, is as follows:

> And he [David] left Zadok the priest and his brethren the priests before the tabernacle of the Lord in the high place that was at Gibeon, to offer burnt offerings to the Lord upon the altar of burnt offering continually morning and evening, according to all that is written in the law of the Lord which he commanded Israel.[3]

The virtual neglect of the Gibeonite ministry of Zadok in recent scholarship is probably due in large measure to the view challenged earlier, namely that the Chronicler simply 'fabricated' the claim in order to justify Solomon's visit to Gibeon. It seems more likely, however, that the DH avoided the Zadokites' involvement with ministry at the theologically suspect altar and tabernacle of Gibeon.[4] The explicit

---

1. E.g. F.F. Bruce, 'Zadok', *NBD*, p. 1272.

2. Cross, *Canaanite Myth*, pp. 195-215.

3. RSV. See also the earlier treatment of this passage, 1 Chron. 21.29–22.1, and 2 Chron. 1.3-5.

4. As we have seen, however, although the notion of a fabricated tradition suits extremely well with 2 Chron. 1.3-5 and to some extent 1 Chron. 6.31-48, it creates tension in light of 1 Chron. 16.39-40, difficulty in light of 1 Chron. 21.29–22.1, and it does not reckon with the curious omission of reference to the (Gibeonite) origin of the bronze altar in Kings. Also relevant is the evidence in support of the

claim of the Chronicler that the Zadokite priesthood ministered at the altar at Gibeon should thus be taken seriously, or at the very least be considered alongside a prevailing opinion that Zadok was associated with Hebron.[1]

Other factors suggest Zadokite links with solar Yahwism. First, as Robert Hayward has argued recently, there is some evidence that solar symbolism played an important role within the temple of Leontopolis, founded by the Zadokite priest Onias.[2] For example, there is the claim in Josephus that the temple at Leontopolis was furnished with a single 'lamp wrought of gold, which shed a brilliant light', a clear variation of the seven-branched menorah typical of the Jerusalem temple.[3] Since, according to Josephus, Philo and rabbinic writings, 'the *menorah* represents the planets in relation to the sun, the latter represented by the central lamp-candlestick', Hayward argues that in the case of the single lamp from Leontopolis, 'the overwhelming probability is that it represented the sun', a point which can be supported further from the golden colour of the lamp and from the language of divine epiphany behind the expression used by Josephus to

legitimacy of the tradition in 1 Chron. 16.39 noted by Williamson, *Chronicles*, pp. 130-31. Of further significance is the way in which several arguments made with respect to Kiriath-jearim indirectly support an association with Gibeon as well (for example, W.R. Arnold, *Ephod and Ark* [HTS, 3; Cambridge, MA: Harvard University Press, 1917], pp. 61-62; R.W. Corney, 'Zadok the Priest', *IDB*, IV, p. 928). The most notable example of this is an argument of Blenkinsopp, who finds a striking correspondence between the Chronicler's claim that Zadok had an Aaronide genealogy (about which he is dubious, but which has been well defended more recently by Cross [*Canaanite Myth*, pp. 211-15]) and the presence of Aaronide names among the priests of 'Kiriath-jearim' or rather, as he argues, Gibeon, a levitical city unlike Kiriath-jearim (Blenkinsopp, *Gibeon and Israel*, pp. 79-83, 100-105, 132 n. 72).

1.   For traditional arguments in favour of a Gibeonite origin of Zadok, see, for example, Arnold, *Ephod*, pp. 61-62; Corney, 'Zadok', p. 928. On the question of the origin of Zadok in general, see in addition to the works of Corney ('Zadok') and Cross (*Canaanite Myth*, pp. 208-15), de Vaux, *Ancient Israel*, pp. 372-76; M.D. Rehm, 'Zadok the Priest', *IDBSup*, pp. 976-77 and the bibliographies cited there and in Blenkinsopp, *Gibeon and Israel*, p. 139 n. 30.

2.   Hayward, 'Leontopolis', pp. 429-43.

3.   *War* 7.429-30. The translation, that of H. St J. Thackeray (*Josephus III: The Jewish War, Books IV-VII* [LCL; London: Heinemann, 1957], p. 625), is of the Greek *luchnon chrusoun epiphainonta selas*.

describe the lamp.[1] In light of this evidence, additional evidence associating the description of the temple with apocalyptic notions of the role of the sun, and still further evidence associating Onias's mission with the statement in Isa. 19.18 concerning the founding of a temple in the 'city of the sun/righteousness', Hayward concludes that the lamp was symbolic 'both as the renewed sun and as suggesting a manifestation of God'.[2] To be sure, Hayward does not see behind this symbolism a Zadokite understanding of Yahweh as sun in the sense that I am suggesting, but the claim that solar symbolism was characteristic of this Zadokite temple is entirely consistent with my hypothesis of possible Zadokite links with solar Yahwism at a later period.

Secondly, as Hayward and others have noted, the presence of solar imagery with respect to the deity is also suggested by some data concerning the Essenes at Qumran. For example, it appears that the Qumran community adhered to a solar calendar at least somewhat akin to that found in the book of Jubilees.[3] More importantly, direct evidence of a solar understanding of Yahweh is evident in Josephus, who offers the following description of an aspect of worship by the Essenes:

> Their piety towards the Deity takes a peculiar form. Before the sun is up they utter no word on mundane matters, but offer to him certain prayers, which have been handed down from their forefathers, as though entreating him to rise.[4]

What appears here to be an admission of sun worship by a Jewish sect has caused difficulty for some commentators. For example, Thackeray adds the following note to his translation in the Loeb Classical Library Series:

> How far the Essenes, with their affinities to Judaism, can be regarded as sun-*worshippers* is doubtful. But, un-Jewish as this custom seems, there was a time when even Jews at Jerusalem 'turned their backs on the

---

1. Hayward, 'Leontopolis', p. 435.

2. Hayward, 'Leontopolis', p. 440. For a discussion of the term 'city of the sun' in Isa. 19.18, see later in this chapter.

3. See, for example, S.J. de Vries, 'Calendar', *IDB*, I, p. 487; Smith, 'Helios in Palestine', p. 207.

4. *War* 2.128-29. The translation is that of H. St J. Thackeray (*Josephus II: The Jewish War, Books I-III* [LCL; London: Heinemann, 1956], pp. 371, 373).

Temple and their faces towards the east and worshipped the sun towards
the east' (Mishnah, *Sukkah*, v. 2-4; Ezek. viii. 16).[1]

It is indeed doubtful that even a Jewish sect would worship a deity
other than Yahweh, in which case it follows that they were praying
before the sun *as Yahweh*.[2] This interpretation can be supported by
reference to a passage later in the same work of Josephus in which he
offers the following rationale for the Essenes' custom of covering
their excrement, *hōs mē tas augas hubrizoien tou theou*, 'that they may
not offend the rays of the deity'.[3] That neither of these passages can be
accounted for adequately on grounds other than the assumption of
Morton Smith that 'Josephus's report thus seems to derive from an
equation of Yahweh with the Sun God, present in his rays',[4] has been
argued forcefully already by Smith,[5] making it unnecessary to
elaborate.[6]

As compelling as Smith's interpretation might be, however, it
cannot be assumed that these solar aspects of worship by the Essenes
are necessarily of relevance with respect to the Zadokite priesthood
because it can no longer be assumed that the Qumran community was
Zadokite.[7]

Another problem with a possible link between the Zadokites and
solar Yahwism in addition to uncertainty about the relevance of the
material from Qumran to Zadokites is as follows. If Zadokites were

1.   *Josephus II*, pp. 372-73 n. *a*. (The emphasis is Thackeray's.)
2.   The notion of Yahweh as the sun in this context is original to Smith, 'Helios
in Palestine', p. 203.
3.   *War* 2.148-49 (translation: Thackeray, *Josephus II*, pp. 371, 373).
4.   Smith, 'Helios in Palestine', p. 203. (I was first made aware of these
references through the work of Smith and make no claim to originality in interpreting
them as referring to Yahweh as the sun.)
5.   *Helios in Palestine*, pp. 202-203, 211-12 (nn. 24-46).
6.   In the case of the DSS, there is also, of course, the further evidence adduced
by Smith in favour of a solar interpretation of the significance of a gilded staircase
leading to the roof of the temple described in the Temple Scroll (*Helios in Palestine*,
pp. 199-202).
7.   See P.R. Davies, *Behind the Essenes: History and Ideology in the Dead Sea
Scrolls* (BJS, 94; Atlanta: Scholars Press, 1987), pp. 51-72. Davies is open,
however, to the possibility of a short-lived '"Zadokite" infiltration' which might have
involved a return from Leontopolis, a judgment made on the basis of the 'tantalising'
'connections between this Temple and its site on the one hand, and Qumran on the
other...' (*Behind the Essenes*, pp. 71-72).

sympathetic with solar Yahwism, why does the book of Ezekiel, written from a Zadokite perspective, condemn solar Yahwism[1] and yet defend the exclusive right of Zadokites to perform priestly functions on the grounds that they alone were innocent of apostasy during the period of the monarchy? The answer to the question must await a study of Ezekiel to follow shortly, but suffice it to say here that the problem can be resolved in one of several ways.

h. *1 Kings 8.12 (LXX v. 53)*

This poetic fragment, almost certainly ancient and perhaps originally part or all of a dedicatory inscription[2] of the Jerusalem temple, mentions both Yahweh and the sun (cf. LXX). The text, as commonly reconstructed with reference to attestation in the LXX (1 Kgs 8.53) is as follows:[3]

> '*z 'mr šlmh*
> *šmš hkyn bšmym*
> *yhwh[4] 'mr lškn b'rpl*
> *bnh bnyty byt zbl lk*
> *mkwn lšbtk 'wlmym*
> *hl' hy' ktwbh bspr hyšr[5]*

Then Solomon said:
'Sun He placed in the heavens,
But Yahweh himself has decided to dwell in thick cloud;

1. See the discussion of Ezek. 8.16 offered later in this chapter.
2. Long, *1 Kings*, pp. 97-98.
3. I follow here the vast majority of scholars in seeing the LXX as preserving a more original form of the poem.
4. It is preferable to regard Yahweh as the first word in the second stichos of the first bicolon on textual and contextual grounds. Thus, whereas *yhwh* is normally placed in the first stichos, this is suggested neither by LXX *Hēlion egnōrisen* [Lucian *estēken*] *en ouranō Kurios eipe tou katoiken en gnophō* which implies the Hebrew *šmš hkyn bšmym*, nor by the MT of 8.12 which at least in its present form reads *yhwh 'mr lškn b'rpl* (cf. 2 Chron. 6.1b which reads similarly and suggests that the more original form preserved in the LXX had been expunged by the time of the Chronicler). Even if the more traditional rendering is correct (that is, 'Yahweh has set the sun in the heavens / But He has decided to dwell in thick darkness'), the interpretation of the poem offered here is not affected.
5. The reading *yšr* is a slight emendation of the Hebrew behind the Greek *ōdēs*, 'song' (Hebrew *šîr*); cf. Josh. 10.13 and 2 Sam. 1.18 which make reference to *spr yšr*.

Surely I have built an exalted house for You,
A place for You to dwell in forever.'

Lo, is this not written in the Book of Jashar?[1]

This obscure passage has been interpreted variously. For example, Würthwein interprets the clear contrast in the first bicolon between Yahweh and the sun as a distinction between Yahweh and storm-cloud imagery associated with Baal. A difficulty with this view, however, is that reference in the first stichos to *šemeš*, 'Sun', as placed in the heavens, is quite specific and thus seems not to refer to storm imagery in general.[2] The same point may be made in the case of Jones who regards the contrast between Yahweh and the sun here to denote the distinction between Yahweh and creation (to which Yahweh is superior).[3] Moreover, although 'sun' might represent something more general as these commentators suggest, the role of the message within the context of the dedication of the temple remains a difficulty for these interpretations.

The challenge of relating the fragment to its context is indeed real, as may be illustrated by the view of O. Loretz, according to whom the location of the poetic fragment in two contexts—8.12-13 in the MT and 8.53 in the LXX—suggests that the poetic fragment in its present fragmentary form is virtually meaningless and has no relationship to the context beyond its being a fragment of a Canaanite temple-dedication speech.[4] Whilst possible, a view which regards the given context(s) of a passage as merely accidental must be embraced only as a last resort.

Although attempts thus far to account for the poetic fragment with

1. See the previous note.
2. E. Würthwein, *Das Erste Buch der Könige* (ATD; Göttingen: Vandenhoeck & Ruprecht, 1977), pp. 88-89.
3. Jones, *Kings*, I, p. 196.
4. O. Loretz, 'Der Torso eines kanaanäisch-israelitischen Tempelweihspruches in 1 Kg 8,12-13', *UF* 6 (1974), pp. 478-80. A distinctive feature of Loretz's interpretation is his rejection on metric grounds of the originality of the stichos preserved in the LXX of 8.53. As will be seen, however, the problem posed by the metre in no way warrants the omission of the line preserved in the LXX. Moreover, Loretz offers no explanation for how the obscure LXX tradition would have arisen if it was not original (which it seems to be in light of the LXX's citation of the source from which the poetic fragment came). On the problem of the fragment's two locations, see later in this discussion.

reference to a solar cult have proven to be similarly problematic,[1] the thesis advocated in the present study provides a way in which the text can be understood both in terms of its specific reference to Sun and in terms of its contexts in LXX and MT.

To begin, it is reasonable to assume with the vast majority of scholars that the LXX's reference to this poetic material as being written *en bibliō tēs ōdēs*, 'in the Book of the Song (Hebrew *haššîr*)', should be emended slightly to 'in the Book of Jashar (Hebrew *hayyāšār*)', citations from the latter being attested elsewhere in the DH, such as Josh. 10.12-14.[2] In support of this slight adjustment and against the interpretation of Würthwein and Jones, it may be added that the 'other' poetic fragment from the Book of Jashar, Josh. 10.12b-13a, makes equally specific reference to *šmš*, 'Sun'. Moreover, unlike the more obscure witness of LXX to 1 Kgs 8.12, the poem in Joshua benefits from a Deuteronomistic interpretation according to which Yahweh is to be identified with *šmš* in the Book of Jashar.

That we are probably justified in applying this Deuteronomistic interpretation in the case also of the Jashar poem in 1 Kings 8 can be supported on two additional counts: (1) 'Sun' and 'Yahweh' are placed in poetic parallelism within the poem itself;[3] and (2) the relationship between Yahweh and Sun suggested here seems to go a long way toward accounting for the expungement of the first stichos mentioning

1. According to H.G. May ('Aspects of Solar Worship at Jerusalem', pp. 269-70) the MT reflects the original text which identifies 'Yahweh' with Baal the sun god (cf. *z^{e}būl*, 'Zebul', short for Baal-Zebul) and the LXX reflects a later attempt to dissociate Yahweh from this sun cult. To May, the statement that Yahweh has purposed to dwell in thick darkness signalled at the autumnal equinox (on which occasion this dedication was allegedly made) that the Lord as sun god was going below the equator. Correspondingly, the statement concerning the shrine of Zebul indicates that Yahweh has a permanent shrine to which it is hoped that he will return and to which appeals to him can be made in the meantime ('Aspects of Solar Worship', p. 270).

2. The LXX's *ouk idou autē gegraptai en bibliō tēs ōdēs* is in all respects equivalent to *h^{a}lō' hî' k^{e}tûbâ 'al sēper hay(y)āšār* in the MT of Josh. 10.13 except that the reflex of *tēs ōdēs* is *haš(š)îr*, 'The Song'. The difference can be accounted for by assuming that the initial *y* in *yāšār*, 'Jashar', has been omitted, perhaps by haplography in view of the similarity in appearance between *h* and *y* in the Hebrew script.

3. In Josh. 10, the poem itself does not mention Yahweh except by reference to sun. In both the case of Josh. 10.12 and 1 Kgs 8.53, *šemeš* occurs without the article.

'Sun' from MT and perhaps also for the placement of the fuller form of the poem in LXX in a different context. Moreover, on what grounds other than religio-historical is it possible to account for the reference to Sun here?

The view that the poetic fragment alludes to the kind of religio-historical relationship between Yahweh and the sun that I have been arguing for makes it possible to understand the role of the poetic fragment within its context, namely a speech of Solomon commemorating the founding of the temple of Jerusalem against the background of the transference of the cult from Gibeon. Before considering further aspects of the context of 1 Kings 8, however, it is worth digressing to consider briefly what the poetic fragment implies about the nature of the relationship between Yahweh and the sun.

The Significance of God Setting the Sun in the Heavens. 1 Kgs 8.53 (LXX) and other passages such as Ps. 19.5-6, Psalm 104 and Gen. 1.14-19 imply or state that Yahweh (or God) placed the sun in the heavens. At first it would appear that statements like this indicate that no direct relationship can exist between God and the sun. This is true of course but only if strong emphasis is placed upon the word 'direct' for, as may be illustrated by reference to Egypt, solar deities are typically considered to be distinct from the sun itself.

The Egyptian material shows clearly that the sun god Re was by no means *directly* associated or identified with the physical sun.[1] The sun was only one way of denoting Re (other ways, for example, were as a ram-headed human or as a falcon).[2] Moreover, except during (and just prior to) the reign of Amenophis IV at which time the sun god was actually—and peculiarly and heretically—equated with the physical form of the sun, a clear distinction was always maintained between Re and the sun.[3] The relationship between the sun and Re was

1. This point is argued at length by D.B. Redford, 'The Sun-Disc in Akhenaten's Program: Its Worship and Antecedents, I', *JARCE* 13 (1976), pp. 47-61; *idem,* 'The Sun-Disc in Akhenaten's Program: Its Worship and Antecedents, II', *JARCE* 17 (1980), pp. 21-38. A summary of these articles appears in Redford's book, *Akhenaten: The Heretic King* (Princeton, NJ: Princeton University Press, 1984), pp. 169-80.

2. See, for example, J. Černý, *Ancient Egyptian Religion* (London: Hutchison's University Library, 1952), pp. 39-66 *passim.*

3. Redford, 'Sun-disc in Akhenaten's Program, I', pp. 46-51.

such that the former was a mere manifestation of Re or the vehicle in which he (and others) rode. Common references which illustrate the distinction between the sun-god and the sun itself include 'Re who is in his disk', 'the lord of the disk', and 'Re and his disk', the latter of which indicates possession as well as distinction.[1] In view of references such as these and other evidence from the Coffin Texts, Redford thus concludes, 'Re is never confused with his Disc; the two are separate entities'.[2] As a manifestation of the deity, the sun is a 'solar icon'.[3] Moreover, even in cases in which the sun disk is, to use Redford's words again, 'an individualized "Power," a hierophany in its own right', and thus showing its potential for consideration as a separate deity, the visible disk is still easily distinguishable from the sun god in these texts and elsewhere (with the exception of the cult of Aten and its antecedents).[4]

It follows from this (or at least it is not a far step from it) that *biblical passages such as 1 Kgs 8.12 which distinguish between Yahweh and the sun do not necessarily imply that there was no relationship between the God of Israel and sun, nor do they imply that Yahweh could not have been understood in solar terms.* Moreover, in the particular case of 1 Kgs 8.12 (LXX v. 53) some kind of relationship between Yahweh and the sun is virtually assured, for without such a relationship there would be no need to compose and preserve a poetic passage in which 'Sun' and 'Yahweh' (along with their respective abodes) are juxtaposed.[5]

1. Redford, 'Akhenaten's Program', p. 48. The sun was also known as the 'eye' of Re.

2. Redford, 'Akhenaten's Program', p. 48.

3. Redford, *Heretic King*, p. 170.

4. Redford, 'Akhenaten's Program, I', p. 48. Redford formulates the following rule in such cases: 'In Egyptian religion, deities are distinct from merely potential hierophanies by the complete subordination of the latter to the former as non-personalized agents through whom the gods work. As soon as the Egyptian feels that the potency with which a religious object is imbued emanates from the object itself and not as a god behind the scenes, he treats it as a "Power", and automatically thinks of it as having the attributes of a person.'

5. To be sure, the Egyptians do not use the language of the deity 'setting' the sun in the heavens (they refer rather to the sun god generating the solar disk from himself), but we are dealing here with a Hebrew notion which in all probability underwent a development of its own. In either case, however, that the deity creates the sun and is distinct from it can as much be used as an argument *for* a solar

In the case of 1 Kgs 8.12 as preserved in the LXX[1] (and, it will be argued, in the cases also of Ps. 19.5-6, Psalm 104 and Gen. 1.14-19; cf. vv. 3-5) *the idea that Yahweh (God) placed the sun in the heavens should probably not be understood as a polemic against a 'foreign' solar deity*; rather, these passages probably reflect a theological outlook that presupposes both continuity and discontinuity between the God of Israel and the physical form 'sun'. Whereas the continuity involved the sun as a manifestation representative of certain aspects of Yahweh's character, the discontinuity involved a clear distinction between Yahweh and that which he had created and set in the heavens.

To consider the poetic bicolon restored in 1 Kgs 8.12 in light of its context, the passage does not necessarily convey a radical distinction between the theology of the high place at Gibeon and the temple at Jerusalem. The extent to which the latter differed from the former is difficult to determine given the paucity of detailed evidence with respect to Gibeon. On the basis of Josh. 10.12-14, it would appear that the link between Yahweh and the physical sun was relatively more direct at Gibeon (perhaps something not all that different from the cult of Aten?). In any case, we can be sure that any form of solar Yahwism, Gibeonite or otherwise, in which there was a direct and simplistic equation between Yahweh and the physical form of the sun was being rejected in 1 Kgs 8.12 and it would not have survived as a viable understanding of God in ancient Israel.

h. *1 Kings 8.12 within the Context of 1 Kings 8*
Further insight into DH's understanding of the poetic fragment in 1 Kings 8 may be gained by considering the poetic piece in light of its narrative context. From this consideration of context two things will be surmised: (1) that there is an apparent correspondence between the glory of Yahweh in the narrative and the 'Sun' of the poetic fragment (both of which are set in contrast with Yahweh's residency in cloud and darkness), and (2) that there is a further correspondence between

character for the deity as it can be *against* a solar nature for the god.
1.   The option that the poetic piece makes an important statement about the nature of the relationship between Yahweh and the sun rather than denying such a relationship allows for consistency in theology between the fragments preserved in Josh. 10.12-14 and 1 Kgs 8.53 (LXX) (or at least consistency in the Deuteronomic understanding of that theology).

the double location of God (in heaven or in the temple?) in both the narrative and the poetic fragment. In this second case the tension in the poetic fragment between 'Sun' in heaven and Yahweh in the temple is played out in the prayer that surrounds it through a concern about the direction one should properly face in prayer, whether in the direction of God in heaven (Yahweh-in-Gibeon, alias Sun) or in the direction of the temple (the Deuteronomistic alternative). Solomon's prayer for God in heaven to hear prayers now offered in the direction of the temple, then, is an attempt to redirect the focus of attention away from the sun in the heavens toward his alternative manifestation in 'glory' and 'name' in the temple. Solomon's prayer is thus transitional. Praying with traditional posture towards the God of Gibeon (i.e. with hands extended skyward), Solomon asks Yahweh's blessing upon those who from henceforth would redirect their prayers towards the temple.

The context relevant to the first case (a context relevant also to the case for a solar understanding of the ark, discussed earlier) is the following:

> 6 Then the priests brought the ark of the covenant of the Lord to its place, to the inner sanctuary of the house, to the Holy of Holies, under the wings of the cherubim... 10 And when the priests came out from the holy place, a cloud filled the house of the Lord, 11 so that the priests were not able to stay ministering because of the cloud, for the glory of the Lord filled the House of the Lord. 12 Then Solomon said:
>
> > 'Sun He set in the heavens,
> > But Yahweh has chosen to dwell in thick cloud.
> > Surely I have built an exalted house for You,
> > A place for You to dwell in forever'.

By restoring the full form of the poem to what was probably its original context, a clear motive can be discerned for the rearrangement of this passage in both the MT and LXX, namely an apparent association between the 'glory of the Lord' of the narrative and the 'Sun' of the poetic fragment, an association which is evident through Solomon's citation of the poetic fragment in this context (cf. LXX) and through the contrast of 'glory' and 'Sun' alike with 'cloud'/'thick cloud'.[1] For the purposes of the thesis of this book, it is important to

---

1. The latter term, *ʿᵃrāpel*, is regularly used of the obscurity in which the deity chooses to dwell; cf. v. 11.

note that the link in this poetic passage clearly supports some form of association between Sun and Yahweh (for there is no need to dissociate elements that are distinct), and suggests further that, as manifestation, the 'glory' of Yahweh was perhaps the earthly counterpart to the radiance of the sun in heaven.[1]

In the second case noted above, namely the residency of God both in heaven and in the temple in poem and prayer alike, it is interesting to recall, for example, how the prayer of Solomon begins, while keeping in mind also the role of the altar as a piece of a Gibeonite cultic apparatus:

> 22 Then Solomon stood before the altar of the Lord in the presence of all the assembly of Israel, and spread forth his hands towards heaven...

Possible consciousness of an almost 'literal' residency in heaven of Yahweh to whom the prayer is directed is also evident in the conclusion to the prayer:

> 54 Now as Solomon finished offering all this prayer and supplication to the Lord, he arose from before the altar of the Lord, where he had knelt with hands outstretched toward heaven...[2]

The presence of the same tension in the narrative as was seen in the poetic fragment (that is, between the sun in the heavens and Yahweh in the temple) is even more apparent in the following:

> 27 But will God indeed dwell on the earth? Behold, heaven and the highest heaven cannot contain thee; how much less this house which I have built! 28 Yet have regard for the prayer of thy servant and to his supplication, O Lord my God, hearkening to the cry and to the prayer which thy servant prays before thee this day; 29 that thy eyes may be open

---

1.   A further point from the Egyptian material may be relevant to 1 Kgs 8, namely, the notion that although in a sense God resides in his temple, his true dwelling place is in heaven. Note, for example, the words of Redford: 'the use of *ḥry-ib*, ["who resides in", an expression used in reference to a deity worshipped away from its home] in preference to *m* ["in"] or some other locution, suggests that the Disc is not in any structure, nor in art is he depicted in a shrine; he is always above it, shining down upon it, in graphic illustration of the dictum, "heaven is thy temple"' (Redford, 'Akhenaten's Program, I', p. 55).

2.   The gesture of stretching forth the hands towards heaven has a parallel in the portrayals at Tell el-Amarna of worshippers in the time of Akhenaten either standing or kneeling and extending their hands upwards. See most conveniently the drawing in T.H. Gaster, 'Sun', *IDB*, IV, p. 464, fig. 91.

night and day toward this house, the place of which thou hast said, 'My
name shall be there', that thou mayest hearken to the prayer which thy
servant offers toward this place. 30 And hearken thou to the supplication
of thy servant and of thy people Israel, when they pray toward this place;
yea, hear thou in heaven thy dwelling place; and when thou hearest,
forgive (RSV).

A clear case can thus be made for seeing a correspondence between
Yahweh both in heaven and in the temple (narrative) and between
Yahweh as Sun in heaven and yet resident in the temple (poem).[1]

Finally, the following points are important in light of the further
claim that this correspondence reflects a historical tension between
worshippers who are accustomed to praying to Yahweh in heaven
(Sun from the perspective of the poetic fragment and of Gibeon) and
worshippers who are now being asked to pray in the direction of the
temple in which Yahweh has taken residency in glory.

1. Solomon in this prayer is clearly concerned about the direction
in which the worshipper is to pray,[2] namely 'towards this place [i.e.
the temple]', a concern for which there must have been some
historical reason.

2. A similar concern for the direction of prayer may be seen in the
case of Solomon himself, but his orientation during the course of the

---

1.   If correct, the correspondence appears to hold forth promise for understanding the classic problem of the relationship between the residency of Yahweh in
heaven and in the temple (a major problem of which has always been that, in spite of
the apparent contradiction, little tension may be detected between the two under-
standings of Yahweh's residency), but to pursue such would lie beyond the scope of
the present study. (On the issue, see, for example, W. Eichrodt, *Old Testament
Theology* [2 vols.; OTL; Philadelphia: Westminster Press, 1967], II, pp. 186-94.)

2.   Thus, something like the following occurs several times in the prayer: 'if
they... pray and make supplication to thee in this house, then hear thou in
heaven...' In the event of drought, they are to 'pray towards this place', (that is, the
temple) (v. 35); in the event of famine, plague or sickness, they are to 'pray towards
this house' (v. 38; cf. v. 42); in the event of battle taking them out of town (where
they can no longer see the temple), they are to pray 'toward the city which thou hast
chosen and the house which I have built' (v. 44); and even in the event that they are
sent into exile, they are to pray 'toward their land... the city... and the house which I
have built' (v. 48). (In the latter two cases, since the temple was not visible, the
worshipper was apparently to face the general direction of the temple [but under no
circumstances, we might add, was he/she to pray towards Yahweh (as the sun) in
heaven].)

prayer appears transitional, as if to signal a change from a posture of prayer towards (the sun in) heaven to a posture of prayer towards the temple. Thus, Solomon extends his hands 'towards heaven' (that is, to the God of heaven whom the Gibeonites and poem call 'Sun') to pray that God might hearken to the prayers of those who from henceforth are to direct their prayers towards the temple (that is, to Yahweh who now resides in 'glory' within the temple). This concern for orientation is real and may be seen not only in the passages cited earlier above, but in the curious statement of 8.14, 'Then the king turned about face', which immediately follows the poem in 8.12-13. Further, a correspondence between Solomon's prayer towards heaven and the people's towards the temple may be seen in the expression in 8.38, concerning the future worshipper at the newly founded temple 'stretching out his hands toward this house', a similar expression to that used of Solomon with respect to his posture relative to heaven.

3. As others have noted, there appear to be allusions to the Gibeonites in the poem.[1] For example, there is a parallel between the hypothetical situation in which 'heaven is shut up and there is no rain because they have sinned against thee' in vv. 35-36 and the situation of there being no rain due to Yahweh's anger for Saul's crime against the Gibeonites in 2 Sam. 21.1-14, a parallel which implies that the temple was to be regarded as a suitable focal point for prayer by the Gibeonites. Indeed, that the prayer of Solomon in 1 Kings 8 is directed with reference to Gibeonite sympathies gains clear support from 1 Kgs 9.1-3, which does not state simply that Yahweh appeared to Solomon at Jerusalem, but that 'the Lord appeared to him a second time, *as he had appeared to him at Gibeon*'.[2] Moreover, as if to confirm that the temple could indeed be a place of worship for

1.   On Gibeonite allusions in 1 Kgs 8, see further P.J. Kearney, 'The Role of the Gibeonites in the Deuteronomistic History', *CBQ* 35 (1973), pp. 13-14, who is nonetheless inclined to overstate the case. For example, although there are similarities between 1 Kgs 8.41-43 and descriptions of the Gibeonites, the latter are referred to as *gērîm*, 'sojourners', whereas 1 Kgs 8.41-43 uses the term *nokrîm*, 'foreigners'. (Also containing possible allusions to the Gibeonites are vv. 37-39 [cf. 2 Sam. 24] and vv. 41-43 [cf. Josh. 9].)

2.   Emphasis mine. Interestingly, as if to make the same point from a perspective more in sympathy with the new perspective of dissociation between Yahweh and the physical sun, the Chronicler notes that 'The Lord appeared to Solomon *at night* ' (2 Chron. 6.12 [emphasis mine]).

Gibeonites, the same Yahweh who appeared to Solomon at Gibeon says to Solomon (who has thus far prayed only in the direction of heaven) 'I have heard your prayer and your supplication, which you have made before *me* '.[1]

To summarize, Solomon's prayer in 1 Kings 8 provides clear evidence of the association of Yahweh with the sun and of the importance of Gibeon in perpetuating this theology. In this prayer, however, Solomon is consciously moving away from a one-to-one correspondence between Yahweh and the sun. In the poetic section this move is reflected in the statement that defines the sun as something which Yahweh (though still having solar characteristics) has set in the heavens, whereas in the prayer itself, this move is evident in the apparent 'phasing out' of the practice of praying to Yahweh as the sun in the heavens (the practice at Gibeon) in favour of the practice of orienting prayers in the direction of Yahweh as resident in his temple. Unfortunately, however, without further insight into the exact nature of solar Yahwism at Gibeon, it is impossible to tell to what extent Solomon's theology was a move away from or in keeping with Gibeonite theology. One thing seems to be clear nonetheless: despite the move away from Gibeonite Yahwism, Solomon's theology is still far from devoid of solar elements.

This interpretation will now be substantiated further by reference to Ezek. 8.16-18, which attests to the same tension between worshipping Yahweh in the direction of the temple or the sun (as Yahweh) in the direction of heaven.

i. *Ezekiel (especially 8.16-18)*
Although the present section seeks primarily to consider the solar rite described in Ezek. 8.16-18, other relevant passages in Ezekiel will be considered at the end of the discussion of 8.16-18.

Ezekiel 8.16-18. Perhaps the most explicit reference to sun worship in the Old Testament is Ezek. 8.16, which reads in its context as follows:

> And He brought me into the inner court of the House of the Lord, and there, at the entrance to the Temple of the Lord, between the porch and the altar, were about twenty-five[2] men, their backs to the Temple of the Lord

1. Emphasis mine.
2. Or, following some LXX manuscripts, 'twenty'.

and their faces toward the east, and they were worshipping[1] toward the east, the sun. 17 And He said to me, 'Have you seen, son of man? Is it no small matter for the House of Judah to be practicing the abominations which they have committed here, that they should fill the land with violence and provoke me to further anger? And here they are extending a vine branch to my[2] nose!' 18 'But I will deal in wrath; my eye will not spare, nor will I have compassion; and though they shout in my ears with a loud voice, I will not hear them'.

To state the context briefly, this passage forms part of a literary unit that consists of 8.1–11.25,[3] appropriately entitled by Greenberg 'The Defiled Temple and its Abandonment'.[4]

There are at least two striking features about this passage which have often been noted by interpreters. First, the literal translation offered above shows that the direction in which the worshippers face—with backs to the temple of Yahweh and facing towards the east[5]—appears to be of greater concern in the text than the worship of the sun (which follows the comment concerning direction). Note, for example, the comment offered by Zimmerli:

> He [Ezekiel] does not stress the fact that in such worship the sun appears as a second Lord beside Yahweh. Just as the first abomination consisted in the distance from the abode of Yahweh (v. 6), so he sees here the particular abomination which offended Yahweh in the infringement of the ordained direction of prayer and the turning of men's backs to the Lord who dwelt in the *hykl*.[6]

Though dependent upon the unity of vv. 16 and 17–18 which I have yet to substantiate (see shortly), a second striking feature can also be noted here, namely a tension concerning the relationship between Yahweh and the sun which supports their association; whereas the idolators bow to the sun and with backs turned to Yahweh in the

---

1. The reading *mšthwytm* in the MT is generally regarded as a scribal error for *mšthwym*; cf. *GKC*, p. 75 kk.

2. The MT has *'appām*, 'their nose', but this is one of the Tiqqune Sopherim. The original reading was clearly *'appay*, 'My [that is, God's] nose'.

3. See, for example, Zimmerli, *Ezekiel 1*, pp. 215-64; Greenberg, *Ezekiel 1–20*, pp. 164-206.

4. Zimmerli, *Ezekiel 1*, p. 164.

5. A similar concern with the direction faced, namely with 'eyes... turned toward the Lord', is reflected in the Mishnah (*m. Suk.* 5.4, which cites Ezek. 8.16).

6. Zimmerli, *Ezekiel 1*, p. 244.

temple, they are nonetheless said to be extending a branch to the nose of Yahweh.[1]

Significantly, the same two peculiarities evident in Ezek. 8.16—concern with the direction of prayer and confusion about the location of Yahweh in the temple or the sun—can be found in both 1 Kgs 8.12 (v. 53 LXX) and 1 Kgs 8.22-61. In the former of the Kings passages the tension was seen to be between the relationship between Yahweh and the sun ('Sun He set in the heavens, but Yahweh has said that he would dwell in thick darkness'), whereas in the latter the dominant preoccupation was with the direction of prayer, whether to God in heaven (that is, the sun) or to Yahweh in the temple.

Consideration of the contexts of both 1 Kings 8 and Ezek. 8.16 suggests that the similar preoccupation with orientation reflected in these passages is not coincidental. Whereas the setting of 1 Kgs 8.12, 22-61 was on the occasion of the dedication of the temple, at which time the glory of the Lord entered the temple (8.11), the setting of Ezek. 8.16 is the abomination that occasions the exact opposite of what took place in 1 Kings 8, namely, the departure of the glory of the Lord from the temple. Moreover, in Ezek. 9.2[2] judgment for the abominations described in Ezekiel 8, including the solar rite noted climactically in 8.16, begins at *hammizbēaḥ hannᵉḥōšet*, 'the bronze altar', the altar of burnt offering of fame from Gibeon and 1 Kings 8.[3] And further, Ezekiel 8 describes a group of executioners whose duty of destroying Jerusalem is reminiscent of the role of the executioner of Jerusalem in 2 Samuel 24/1 Chron. 21.1–22.1. The executioner's grisly mission, in Ezekiel carried out in light of the abomination committed before the altar of burnt offering, was originally stayed through David's act of building an altar of burnt offering, the divinely ordained alternative to that at Gibeon.[4]

---

1. On the unity of vv. 16 and 17 and the meaning of the latter, see later in this discussion.

2. It is widely acknowledged and apparent from the text that ch. 9 is closely related to 8 and a continuation from it. See, for example, Zimmerli, *Ezekiel 1*, p. 231.

3. See earlier in this chapter for a discussion of the relationship between this altar and that of Ahaz.

4. It is unlikely that the parallel is direct in the sense that the writer of the Ezekiel passage consciously alludes to the account of the founding of the altar at the threshing floor of Araunah. Behind them both, however, there seems to be a

In light of what appear to be clear correspondences between these passages, the following interpretation can be offered. First, there is every reason to believe that Zimmerli was correct in his tentative judgment that the passage reflects 'a solar understanding of Yahweh'.[1] Secondly, the practice reflected in Ezek. 8.16 which contributed greatly to the departure of the glory of Yahweh is effectively the reverse of that advocated in 1 Kings 8 which formed the theological basis for the entry of that glory. Moreover, that this alternative means of praying to Yahweh is attested at the time of the late pre-exilic period is an important witness to the apparent longevity of the tradition. And thirdly, the Deuteronomistic concern with orientation away from the sun reflected in both 1 Kings 8 and Ezek. 8.16, like the Deuteronomistic concern with bowing to the Host of Heaven (of which bowing to the sun is a part),[2] is not a concern over syncretism or even solar elements in Yahwism per se, but with iconism. In other words, DH and Ezek. 8.16-17 are probably not so much opposed to the worship of *Yahweh* as the sun, but with the worship of *the sun* (that is, a physical object) as Yahweh (or to other members of the Host of Heaven as members of his entourage).

Also relevant to both Ezek. 8.16 and possible solar rites associated with the temple of Solomon is the question of the date of the rite described in Ezek. 8.16. Although the issue of date is complex, some evidence points in the direction of further continuity between this passage and 1 Kings 8 and in the direction also of a possible (but by no means certain) solar alignment of the temple.

---

tradition, not clear in its details, of an association between the altar of burnt offering and the execution of Jerusalem through means of an angelic messenger or messengers (cf. 1 Chron. 21.15–22.1/2 Sam. 24.16–25; Ezek. 9.1-2). If the parallel exists, the record of 'seven' executioners in Ezek. 9.2 seems to be a development from the single messenger in Samuel/Chronicles. (It is interesting, in view of my claim that the altar of burnt offering/bronze altar had solar connotations, that many associate these seven executioners with seven planetary deities, among whom was perhaps the counterpart to Nebo, 'he who holds the scribe's stylus' [regarding which, see, for example, Zimmerli, *Ezekiel 1*, pp. 246-47, and Eichrodt, *Ezekiel*, p. 130 and the bibliography cited there].)

1. Zimmerli, *Ezekiel 1*, p. 244. See also the remainder of my discussion of Ezek. 8.16-18.

2. See my discussion earlier in the section 'The Expression "Host of Heaven"'.

Some scholars (notably Gaster,[1] Morgenstern[2] and more recently Brownlee[3]) have argued that the solar rite described in Ezek. 8.16 took place during the autumnal equinox. Although some of the arguments adduced by these scholars in favour of this date are not compelling,[4] three considerations possibly allude to a time roughly during the autumnal equinox.

The first is the date offered at the beginning of Ezekiel 8, the fifth day of the sixth month of the sixth year according to MT (roughly 18 September 592), exactly one month less according to LXX (that is, 18 August). It is perhaps significant that the date of MT, favoured by most scholars,[5] is at the time of the autumnal equinox, a time when unobstructed sunlight could have shone into the Holy of Holies if the temple was aligned at an angle of roughly 90 degrees.[6] It is not clear, however, that the date given in Ezek. 8.1, the date for the vision in the chapter as a whole, applies specifically to the solar rite since it clearly does not apply to the preceding abomination involving women weeping for Tammuz (known to have taken place in July).

Secondly, as Morgenstern and Fohrer have noted,[7] there is a tradition in the Mishnah that refers to this solar rite within the context of the Feast of Booths. Tractate *Suk.* 5.4 describes a ceremony in which

---

1. T.H. Gaster, 'Ezekiel and the Mysteries', *JBL* 60 (1941), pp. 289-310.

2. For example, Morgenstern, *Fire*, pp. 34, 53.

3. W.H. Brownlee, *Ezekiel 1–19* (WBC, 28; Waco, TX: Word Books, 1986), p. 128.

4. The arguments adduced by Gaster ('Ezekiel and the Mysteries') in favour of a date for this ritual during the autumnal equinox are not convincing. Gaster's case is based upon his interpretation of the Ugaritic myth of Shachar and Shalim, in which he finds parallels to all the rites described in Ezekiel 8. Gaster confidently assigns a date of the autumnal equinox to the Ugaritic rite (the season of which is much debated) and uses this as justification for finding subtle allusions to the autumnal equinox behind such words, for example, as $q\bar{e}s$, 'end', and $s^e fir\hat{a}$ (the meaning of which is uncertain) in the preceding chapter, Ezek. 7 (vv. 2 and 7 respectively), which is in a different block of material from 8.1–11.25.

5. On the varying dates given in 8.1 with rationales given for favouring the MT, see, for example, Zimmerli, *Ezekiel 1*, p. 216; Greenberg, *Ezekiel 1–20*, p. 166; J.W. Wevers, *Ezekiel* [NCB; London: Nelson, 1969], pp. 78-79.

6. The angle depends, for example, on whether one reckons with a theoretical flat horizon to the east or with the Mount of Olives. See the discussion in the previous chapter concerning the orientation of the Solomonic temple.

7. See especially Morgenstern, *Fire*, p. 34 n. 1.

two priests at the time of cock-crowing ceremoniously blast trumpets at appropriate places as they make their way from the upper gate to their final destination, the east gate.[1] The text continues as follows:

> Arrived there, they turned their faces towards the west and said, 'Our fathers who were in this place had their backs towards the Temple and their faces eastward, and they would prostrate themselves eastward towards the sun; but as for us, our eyes are towards Him (or "towards Yah")'.

Especially in light of the judgment that Ezek. 8.16 alludes to a solar *Yahwistic* rite, it must be asked what significance specific reference to this rite had within the context of the later celebration of the Feast of Booths unless the rite denounced here played some role within this same feast at an earlier period. Significantly, a setting at the Feast of Booths for the rite of Ezek. 8.16 corresponds perfectly with the time of the occasion of the dedication of the temple of Solomon in 1 Kings 8 with which Ezek. 8.16 has been shown to have clear parallels:

> So Solomon held the Feast at that time, and all Israel with him, a great assembly, from the entrance to Hamath to the Brook of Egypt, before the Lord our God, seven days.[2] On the eighth day he sent the people away; and they blessed the king and went to their homes...[3]

---

1. It is of interest that, whereas Ezek. 8.16 locates the solar rite in the sacred space near the altar, the Mishnah places it at the east gate. The influence of Ezek. 11.1 which mentions the presence at the east gate of 'twenty-five men' (cf. MT Ezek. 8.16) is possible here, but the tradition of the location could also be independent from 11.1. To complicate matters further, although many have claimed a connection between 8.16 and 11.1 on the basis of similarities between these passages, whether the connection between 8.16 and 11.1 has any basis in reality is by no means certain (in favour, for example, is Greenberg, *Ezekiel 1–20*, p. 186; against is Zimmerli, *Ezekiel 1*, p. 257; and somewhere in between are Wevers, *Ezekiel*, p. 92 and Eichrodt, *Ezekiel*, pp. 134-35). In any case, Jewish tradition is on the side of a connection. Moreover, although the vices of the leadership in 11.1 are distinctly social and thus difficult to reconcile with the cultic crimes of the twenty-five in 8.16, a curious interplay between cultic and social vices is similarly evident in chs. 8-9 and this seems to provide a basis for seeing a connection between 8.16 and 11.1.

2. LXX followed, for example, by the RSV. There is widespread agreement that the additional 'and seven days, fourteen days' of the MT was added in light of 2 Chron. 7.8-10 which assigns the ceremony of dedication to a period of seven days before the Feast of Tabernacles which in Chronicles concluded with the eighth day of solemn assembly (cf. Lev. 23.34-43).

3. 1 Kgs 8.65-66a.

There is no question that the 'Feast', though not named, was the Feast of Tabernacles[1] which of course coincided with the time of the autumnal equinox.[2] Several factors, then, point to the Feast of Booths and autumnal equinox as the time of the rite described in Ezek. 8.16, including a Mishnaic tradition, the time given for the dedication of the temple in both DH and Chronicles (though with minor variations) and, perhaps, Ezek. 8.1. This much seems clear.

Even it it were possible to establish the exact time[3] of the occasion

---

1. See 1 Kgs 8.2 which, as de Vaux argues, there is no reason to doubt (de Vaux, *Ancient Israel*, p. 498); cf. 2 Chron. 7.8-10, Lev. 23.34-43. On the Feast of Booths as a possible locus for solar Yahwism, see the section, 'An Autumnal Festival as a Locus for Solar Yahwism?', offered later in this chapter.

2. That the time of the Feast of Booths was perhaps significant to the occasion of the founding of the temple can be suggested from the observation that for some reason there was a delay of eleven months between the completion of the temple and its dedication (cf. 1 Kgs 6.38; 8.32).

3. Several factors prevent this. As Morgenstern admits (*Fire*, p. 34 n. 1), the Mishnah leaves it unclear whether the rite was practiced each morning during Sukkoth or whether it took place on one day. Moreover, even according to Morgenstern's own unique understanding that the festival of Asif, the predecessor to Sukkoth, took place between the third and the ninth day of the seventh month, the festival still does not coincide exactly with the equinox. Morgenstern's suggestion (*Fire*, pp. 34-35) that the problem with the timing can be attributed to the pro-Yahweh (that is, anti-sun) perspective from which the account in the Mishnah is written seems forced.

On a more balanced note, the confusion about the exact time of the dedication of the Temple in Kings and Chronicles precludes the possibility of certainty. Moreover, although it is clear that the timing of rituals such as the Feast of Tabernacles, set for between the fifteenth and the twenty-first of the seventh month, was set in light of a calendar conscious of solstices and equinoxes and took place roughly at the time of the autumnal equinox, too much remains unclear about the exact nature of the relationship between the major Feasts and the calendar in pre-exilic times to be sure about an exact reckoning in light of the equinox. To illustrate the difficulty, Clines questions the validity of the notion of an autumnal New Year in pre-exilic Israel (D.J.A. Clines, 'The Evidence for an Autumnal New Year in Pre-exilic Israel Reconsidered', *JBL* 93 (1974), pp. 22-40; *idem*, 'New Year', *IDBSup*, pp. 625-29). Or again, for example, de Vaux (*Ancient Israel*, pp. 190, 498) regards the times given for the Feast of Tabernacles at the beginning and end of the year in the two ancient calendars Exod. 23.14-17 and 34.18-23 respectively as indicative that the time of Ingathering varied from year to year, depending on when the crops matured. Further, he urges that *tᵉqûpâ*, 'revolution', in 34.22 not be equated with the later associations of this term with solstices and equinoxes. He nonetheless argues that a

when the direction one faced was evidently indicative of one's theology, uncertainties about the exact orientation of the temple and the question of the awkward presence of the Mount of Olives would still preclude the possibility of knowing whether or not, for example, the sun shone into the Holy of Holies at any given time during the year (a matter to which reconsideration will be given soon in the section on the orientation of the Temple).

Relevant both to a solar-Yahwistic interpretation of Ezek. 8.16 and to the question of a possible setting during the Feast of Booths is a final consideration from the context of Ezekiel 8. I refer to v. 17b in which the Lord says, $w^e hinn\bar{a}m$ $\check{s}\bar{o}l^e h\hat{i}m$ '*et* $hazz^e m\hat{o}r\hat{a}$ '*el* '*app\bar{a}m*, 'And here they are extending a vine branch to my[1] nose!' Consideration here is given to two possible interpretations of the verse[2], both of which are based on a common view that the practice should not be dissociated from the solar rite described in v. 16.[3]

knowledge of the Egyptian solar calendar of 365 days is not unknown in intertestamental literature (cf., for example, the witness of a solar calendar [364 days] at Qumran, in the book of *Jubilees* [6.23-32], and in *1 Enoch* [72]). In view of uncertainties relating to the time of both feast and ritual, as well as to the exact orientation of the temple, there is little point in pursuing further the complicated issue of the nature of the calendar in ancient Israel. (See further, however, the section, 'An Autumnal Festival as a Locus for Solar Yahwism?', at the end of this chapter.)

1. 'Their' is an intentional scribal emendation for 'my', one of the Tiqqune Sopherim.

2. For a summary of various interpretations, see already Stähli, *Solare Elemente*, pp. 47-49 n. 231.

3. There is some debate about whether or not Ezek. 8.17 describes a rite separate from the one involving sun worship mentioned in v. 16. Those who regard it as separate (for example, N. Sarna ['Ezekiel 8:17: A Fresh Examination', *HTR* 57 (1964), pp. 347-52], Greenberg [*Ezekiel 1–20*, p. 172]), and many with interpretations not dependent upon a solar interpretation [cf. Greenberg, *Ezekiel 1–20*, p. 173]) typically note the intervening general references in v. 17a to 'abominations' and social wrong doing, both of which might lead one to believe that the writer has moved on from referring to the rite described in v. 16. Those in favour of the association between vv. 17bβ and 16 (for example, Zimmerli, *Ezekiel 1*, p. 244, and those with interpretations consistent with the solar reference in v. 16) typically note that v. 17, a divine speech offering Yahweh's interpretation and comments, is analogous to similar divine elaborations found in vv. 6 and 12 (though not v. 15). The omission of *wyšbw lhk'ysny* in the LXX offers support for seeing at least v. 17bα as an addition. Finally, as Zimmerli notes (*Ezekiel 1*, p. 244), seeing in 17bβ an additional cultic act 'would immediately disturb the framework of four

Possibly relevant to the notion of Yahweh as the sun in Ezek. 8.16 is the view of Fohrer, according to whom Ezek 8.17 is a Canaanite counterpart to the well-known Egyptian practice of extending a bouquet to the nose of the deity as a means of bestowing upon the deity the wish of eternal life.[1] In stating this interpretation, however, Fohrer faces a tension between his understanding on the one hand that the worshippers are performing this gesture before the rising sun and his view on the other hand that they are performing this gesture before Yahweh.[2] This tension leads Zimmerli to reject the interpretation with the question: 'Is it likely…that Yahweh, of whom we have just been told that the "men" turn their backs on him, now suddenly takes the place of the rising sun and then says that "they stretch out the branch to *my* nose?"'[3] Regardless of whether or not the details of Fohrer's interpretation are correct, if Zimmerli's own suggestion of a solar understanding of Yahweh is taken seriously, the answer to the question would appear to be yes.

To be sure, the rite alluded to in Ezek. 8.17 is obscure and difficult to interpret. In my judgment, however, an explanation as plausible as

scenes'. (On the careful crafting of the section as a whole, see further Greenberg, *Ezekiel 1–20*, pp. 192-205).

In favour of a connection between vv. 16 and 17, the following can also be noted. (1) If v. 17 was separate from the abomination described in v. 16, one would expect it to merit elaboration commensurate with its role as the climactic abomination within the section as a whole. (On the other hand, assuming v. 16 is the final, climactic abomination, it cannot be judged surprising that this abomination merited an extended comment in which, as a prelude of the judgment to follow, final mention was made in v. 17bβ of a particularly offensive aspect of this ritual.) (2) To dissociate v. 17bβ from v. 16 is to be inconsistent with the broader context of the narrative material in which reversions back and forth from descriptions of ritual and social vices are quite characteristic (see for example 8.12 and 9.9 in which the same phrase, 'The Lord has forsaken the land, and the Lord does not see', functions in a ritual, then a social context). (3) As will be argued shortly, an explanation is possible for the enigmatic phrase referring to a branch to the nose which presupposes a ritual context involving sun worship and which can account at least to some degree for the social vices described not only in 17bα but also in ch. 9, clearly related to the preceding ch. 8.

1. G. Fohrer, *Ezechiel* (HAT, 13; Tübingen: Mohr, 1955), pp. 52-53; cf. A. de Buck, 'La fleur au front du grand-prêtre', *OTS* 9 (1951), pp. 18-29.

2. Fohrer, *Ezechiel*, pp. 52-53.

3. Zimmerli, *Ezekiel 1*, p. 244.

any offered to date arises from consideration of the rite also as possibly Yahwistic in origin. Particularly on the assumption of unity with 8.16,[1] the setting of 8.17 corresponds remarkably well with a rite described in the Mishnah in association with the Feast of Booths. In the tractate *Sukkah* in which the solar rite of Ezek. 8.16 is mentioned, reference is made in the same context to a practice in which pilgrims are required to collect various sorts of branches, palm, willow, myrtle, some of which were to be made into a festal plume, a *lulab*, which was waved daily during the singing of the Hallel (Pss. 113-18).[2] More specifically, daily during the ceremony of water libation a procession of priests walked around the altar waving branches, while the pilgrims themselves watched, waving their *lulabs* and joining in the chorus of Ps. 118.25 in which the pilgrims address Yahweh by saying, 'Save us, we beseech thee, O Lord!'[3]

The correspondences between this rite and Ezek. 8.16-17 are numerous: the presence in both contexts of priests,[4] reference to the extending of branches, location near the altar of burnt offering and probably also a setting at the Feast of Booths. Moreover, further correspondences arise upon examination of the context of Ezek. 8.17. I refer to what can be judged from Ezek. 8.18 about the setting of the preceding verse in which people are said to have extended a branch to the 'nose' of Yahweh:

> But I will deal in wrath; my eye will not spare, nor will I have compassion; and though they shout in my ears with a loud voice, I will not hear them.

Although the reference to shouting in the 'ears' of Yahweh could be hypothetical here, it could also be that the shouting was part of the same rite in which branches were held forth to the 'nose' of Yahweh. If so, one can surmise further that the shouting was done within the

---

1. See the discussion of the debate four notes earlier.
2. *M. Suk.* 3.1-4, 8-9; cf. for example, Rylaarsdam, 'Booths', p. 456. Cf. also *Jub.* 16.31.
3. *M. Suk.* 3.9, 4.5; cf. Rylaarsdam, 'Booths', p. 456, C.N. Hillyers, 'First Peter and the Feast of Tabernacles', *TynBul* 21 (1971), p. 48.
4. This is not specifically stated, but most interpreters judge the 'twenty' or 'twenty-five' referred to in 8.16 to be priests on the grounds of their number and/or, more importantly, on the basis of their location in the temple complex (that is, in an area in which only priests were likely to be found).

context specifically of an appeal for deliverance since, by refusing to hear the cries of the people, Yahweh here denies them mercy. This corresponds remarkably well, then, with the setting for the Feast of Booths described in tractate *Sukkah*, namely a setting in which a group of people who extend branches at an altar shout for deliverance and in which, earlier, reference is made to the solar rite of Ezek. 8.16. Moreover, although the Mishnaic tradition of branch waving is attested rather late, that in Lev. 23.40 branches of different kinds are referred to in the context of rejoicing before the Lord during the Feast of Booths rather than for constructing the booths themselves suggests a relatively early date for the celebrative waving of branches during the feast.[1] In light of these and other possible correspondences,[2] then, it is reasonable to suppose that the setting for Ezek. 8.17 is that part of the Feast of Booths in which branches were

1. That the book of *Jubilees* attributes the rite of branch waving to Abraham (*Jub.* 16.31) is also suggestive that the practice was considered early.

2. First, that the rite of branch-waving by the priests is done near the altar in both tractate *Sukkah* and Ezek. 8.17 helps to 'bridge' the gap between the location of the eastward-facing priesthood in 8.16 (near the altar) and the location for the reference to this rite in *m. Suk.* 5.4 (at the eastern gate). Secondly, underlying the interpretation offered here is the assumption that rites performed at the altar itself were performed for Yahweh as sun, a view which matches our understanding that the original altar of the first temple, perhaps originally at Gibeon, was a cult object of Yahweh as sun. In light of the possibility that the bronze altar was a solar cult apparatus which perhaps literally reflected the character of the god of the cult, sense can perhaps be made of the very curious statement in *m. Suk.* 4.5, 'Praise to you, O altar! Praise to you, O altar!' which directs praise to the altar as if to Yahweh himself and for which there is a variant expression, attributed to R. Eliezer, which makes the connection quite explicit: 'To Yah and to you, O altar! To Yah and to you, O altar. (My attention was drawn to this curious statement through the discussion of Tigay, 'Addenda' to *No Other Gods*.) Thirdly, immediately after the climactic shout at which time the branches were raised during the Feast of Booths, the following passage in which altar and God as light are brought together was read (Ps. 118.26-27):

> Blessed be he who enters in the name of the Lord!
> We bless you from the house of the Lord
> The Lord is God, and he has given us light.
> Bind the festal procession with branches,
> up to the horns of the altar! (RSV)

Finally, if not to this rite in which priests assemble at the altar waving branches, to what other rite could Ezek. 8.16-18 refer?

held upwards (to the 'nose' of Yahweh as it were) and that this was
part of the same solar occasion during which priests worshipped
Yahweh in the direction of the sun[1] rather than in the direction of the
temple. Thus, according to Ezek. 8.16-17, solar Yahwism was alive
and well within the context of the Jerusalem priesthood at the end of
the monarchy.

Other Passages in Ezekiel. Finally, to complete the discussion of
Ezekiel within the context of the present section primarily on 8.16-18,
what passages elsewhere in Ezekiel bear on the question of sun
worship in ancient Israel? First, although the glory of the Lord in
Ezekiel clearly has a life of its own (due at least in part to its association with the portable cherub-throne), it is nonetheless of interest
that such expressions as *nōgah kᵉbôd yhwh*, 'the brightness of the
glory of the Lord' (10.4) and *wᵉhā'āreṣ hē'îrâ mikkᵉbōdô*, 'and the
whole earth shone with his glory' (43.2) support the comparison
between the glory of the Lord and the sun argued for tentatively on
the basis of the placement of 1 Kgs 8.12 (cf. v. 53 LXX) in light of its
immediately preceding context (8.11).[2]

One observation on the well-known accounts of the departure of the
glory of the Lord to the east (10.18-19; 11.22-25) and its return from
the same direction (43.1-5) seems particularly relevant to the present
study. Whereas the glory of the Lord advances under its own earth-
illuminating power[3] when it moves from east to west, when it leaves
the temple (thereby necessitating travel from west to east) this glory
departs not under its own 'natural' power but with the aid of the
throne-chariot. This of course corresponds perfectly with the direction in which the sun moves naturally: from east to west but not vice-
versa. This is not to imply a simplistic and direct correspondence in

1.   According to later tradition, the branches were to be waved in the direction of
the four points of the compass, as well as upwards and downwards, symbolic in part
of the presence of God everywhere. Though the tradition is late and thus perhaps not
relevant, its concern with orientation is familiar and its rationale rooted in the location
of God might be a corrective to the theological implication of waving the branches
upwards (that is, toward God).

2.   Interestingly, in the former of these passages in Ezekiel, the language and
context is similar to that in 1 Kgs 8.11, and in the latter passage the occasion is the
return of the glory of the Lord from the east and through the east gate.

3.   This passage states that 'the whole earth shone with his glory'.

Ezekiel between the glory of the Lord (which can clearly go wherever it wishes) and the movement of the sun,[1] but to suggest rather that the notions of 'glory' and the 'sun' were probably related (for which we have seen some evidence already in 1 Kgs 8).

Finally, Ezek. 41.12 includes in the plan of the ideal temple an enormous 'building' of unspecified function to the west of the temple. Zimmerli speculates that the building 'has been constructed on theological grounds, as an element for blocking off the western side'.[2] Moreover, to Zimmerli the theological grounds for such are that 'its intention is to forbid all access to the area behind the temple, that is behind the back of the Lord of the holy of holies who is facing forward that is, eastwards'.[3] Whereas to Zimmerli the theological motive relates to the impossibility of 'approaching God on one's own initiative from behind',[4] it is also possible that there was in this case the same abominable temptation as reflected in Ezek. 8.16, namely the temptation to pray in the direction of the sun again, 'with backs to the temple' (only, in this case, bowing westward, towards the *setting* sun).

Another explanation for the building is that it is to be associated with a possible counterpart in the pre-exilic temple. The best candidate for this is the obscure 'parbar' of 1 Chron. 26.18, said to be on the west and to which two gate-keepers were assigned, along with four more on the road. According to some, the word *parbar*, 'colonnade' or the like, is the singular form of *parwārîm*, mentioned in 2 Kgs 23.11 as being a place from which the sun horses were removed by Josiah. Thus, Zimmerli says of the possible relevance of this to Ezek. 41.12,

> the unmistakable function of this building [greatly expanded in size] as a
> barrier makes it appear as not impossible that precisely at this spot an

1.   References to the entrance of the glory of the Lord through the north gate and its departure to the east rule out a direct correspondence. Moreover, whereas the arrival of the glory of the Lord perhaps had a natural reflex (perhaps the autumnal equinox), theological considerations alone account for its departure (on which see, for example, R.R. Wilson, 'Ezekiel', *HBD*, p. 668.) Also relevant to the issue are possible solar connotations for the cherubim upon which the glory rides and Ezekiel's avoidance of the expression *yhwh $s^eb\bar{a}'\hat{o}t$*.

2.   W. Zimmerli, *Ezekiel 2* (trans. J.D. Martin; Hermeneia; Philadelphia: Fortress Press, 1983 [German, 1969]), p. 380.

3.   *Ezekiel 2*, p. 380.

4.   *Ezekiel 2*, p. 381.

earlier misuse of the place, such as is discernible in 2 Kgs 23.11, had to be warded off as forcefully as possible. But all the discussions are here moving in the realm of supposition.[1]

Although a tantalizing suggestion, only the last sentence quoted here is certain.

Finally, consideration must be given to the problem noted earlier concerning the apparent incongruity between the view that solar elements within royal Jerusalemite theology were promoted by the Zadokite priesthood and the condemnation of solar Yahwism in Ezek. 8.16-18, clearly a Zadokite work. The problem may be accounted for in a few ways. First, although Ezekiel condemns those who worship in the direction of the sun in Ezek. 8.16, it is evident that some form of a solar understanding of Yahweh was perhaps presupposed nonetheless.[2] Perhaps Ezekiel's objection is not to solar Yahwism per se, but to an aspect which emphasizes the sun more as a locus for Yahweh's presence than the temple itself. And secondly, although a Zadokite, Ezekiel bears here, as elsewhere, the clear marks of Deuteronomistic influence. Note, for example, the following judgment of Robert R. Wilson:

> It is preferable to assume that Ezekiel was influenced by the Deuteronomic reform movement before he was exiled to Babylon. However, rather than becoming a total convert to the Deuteronomic position, he seems to have attempted to make his own personal synthesis of the Zadokite and Deuteronomic positions. This synthesis is reflected in his oracles.[3]

In short, Ezek. 8.16-18 which may reflect a blending of Deuteronomistic[4] and Zadokite concerns does not necessarily condemn solar Yahwism, but only an offensive aspect of it, namely, directing one's worship of Yahweh specifically towards the sun as opposed to the temple.

---

1. *Ezekiel 2*, p. 380.

2. This is evident, for example, in Ezekiel's reference in 8.17 to the idolators holding branches to the sun and yet to '*my* [Yahweh's] nose'. As just observed in the discussion of Ezekiel as a whole, the notion of the glory of the Lord probably had *some* relation to the sun, its radiance and, at times, its movement.

3. R.R. Wilson, *Prophecy and Society in Ancient Israel* (Philadelphia: Fortress Press, 1980), p. 284.

4. Note, for example, the similarities between 1 Kgs 8 and Ezek. 8.16-17 noted earlier in this chapter.

The Orientation of Solomon's Temple
The previous chapter considered in some detail the orientation of
Solomon's temple from the perspective of both archaeological
evidence and the history of scholarship. The purpose of this section is
to discuss biblical evidence relevant to the issue of orientation. As the
following points suggest when compared with evidence adduced
earlier, the biblical material permits a relatively positive attitude
towards the notion that Solomon's temple was intentionally aligned to
the sun, although certainty about this matter is far from attainable.

First, biblical evidence has been adduced in the present study to
suggest some kind of direct relationship between Yahweh and the sun
during the time of the founding of the temple in Jerusalem. More
specifically, far from being tangential to the issue of the construction
of the temple (including perhaps its alignment), an association of some
kind between the sun and the God of Israel appears to have been a
significant (and perhaps even central) part of the background to the
founding of the temple. Thus, for Solomon to have succeeded in trans-
ferring the most significant cult centre of the day from Gibeon to
Jerusalem, his stance must have been concessionary towards Gibeonite
Yahwism, a point which the Deuteronomistic rendition of the
founding of the temple makes clear in general and which the witness
of the LXX to the early poetic fragment 1 Kgs 8.12 appears to make
explicit in terms of linking 'Yahweh' with *šemeš*, 'Sun' (that is,
Yahweh-in-Gibeon; cf. Josh. 10.12-13). It does not follow from this
concessionary stance, however, that the temple was *necessarily* aligned
to the sun. On this point there is in fact ample room for uncertainty.
On the one hand we are told that the temple faced eastwards which
leaves open the possibility of alignment to the sun. But on the other
hand we are also told that the God who placed the physical sun in the
heavens (logically a deity with solar traits) had nonetheless decided to
dwell in the darkness of the temple adyton, which leaves open the
possibility that solar alignment was irrelevant to the cult. This latter
possibility, however, must be balanced by the further possibility of a
link between the radiant glory of the Lord entering the darkness of
the temple, and sunlight entering the temple.

Secondly, our examination of Ezek. 8.16 offers clear indication also
of a *Yahwistic* solar rite being performed by priests within the context
of the temple at least at a later period. Moreover, a number of
affinities between this passage and 1 Kings 8, which recounts the

occasion of the temple's initial dedication, are suggestive of continuity with the early history of the temple.

Thirdly, more than one line of evidence, including dates offered in the texts (a few of which are elusive however), suggests that the solar rite alluded to in these texts took place during the Feast of Booths which coincided with the harvest moon and the time of the autumnal equinox.[1] Indeed since the Feast of Booths coincides with the time of the harvest moon and autumnal equinox, this feast is ideally suited to a theology which understands the sun to be a symbol of Yahweh and the moon its symbolic nocturnal counterpart, since each night for more than a week the full moon of harvest appears precisely at the time of the setting of the sun, itself at the point of equinox.[2]

Fourthly, although not evidence in itself, the results of calculations of temple alignment considered in the previous chapter are worth reconsidering in light of a fairly fixed date at the Feast of Booths for both the solar rite in Ezek. 8.16 and in 1 Kings 8 (or even for only one of the two). To review briefly results of those calculations that are illustrative here, patterns were seen which suggest that, to be significant, solar alignment had to be in excess of 90 degrees in the case of an obstacle to the east, and which indicate also that significant solar alignment had to be less than 90 degrees for a given period prior to the autumnal equinox. Although the precise angle of the temple remains the critical unknown factor, it is nonetheless possible in light of a rough date to work the other way round by estimating what the angle of the temple would be if it were aligned to the sun relative to both the Mount of Olives and the Feast of Booths. Thus, for example, reckoning a date for the start of the Feast of Booths at a week or so prior to the autumnal equinox and a height for the Mount of Olives of some 64 m above the temple mount and roughly 1050 m away, the temple would have been aligned at 90 degrees for unobstructed light

---

1. See the discussion of the date of Ezek. 8.16 offered in the previous section and the section on the autumnal festival offered toward the end of this chapter. A timing with deference to both moon and sun is also possible, the former being suggested by the role of the moon as possible a night-time reflex of Yahweh as sun and by the coincidence of the Feast of Booths in the lunisolar calendar with the equinox in general and the full (harvest) moon in particular.

2. I am indebted to A. Wolters for the observation that the harvest moon appears precisely at the point of sunset and the possible relevance of this point to my thesis.

to have shone into the Holy of Holies during the Feast of Booths.[1] Similarly, the later the time of the feast relative to the equinox, the more in excess of 90 degrees the temple would have to be for the same effect of sunlight to occur. Of course the problem of the *precise* timing of the feast relative to the equinox, a problem not unrelated to uncertainties over the nature of the calendar, remains.

Fifthly, whereas the temple was completed in the eighth month, it was dedicated in the seventh month, at the Feast of Booths.[2] Whether the dedication preceded the completion of the temple by one month or followed it by eleven,[3] the discrepancy in time suggests that there must have been some significance to the dedication coinciding with the Feast of Booths.[4] It is thus possible that the autumnal equinox which accompanied the feast was perhaps essential to the auspicious occasion when the glory of the Lord entered the Holy of Holies and took its place with the ark beneath the cherubim.[5]

To evaluate, the biblical material offers important evidence that lends considerable weight to the possibility that the temple was aligned to the sun. On a more cautionary note, however, none of the factors mentioned above is in itself sufficient to prove or in some cases even to remove reasonable doubt that the temple of Solomon was aligned intentionally to the sun. In each case one might wish to have a clearer understanding of several factors (for example further clarity about the exact nature of the calendar in pre-exilic Israel).

When the biblical evidence is blended with the archaeological evidence examined earlier, the prospect of a resolution to the issue appears

1. This angle corresponds perfectly with several guesses based upon the best of indirect evidence, namely the angle of the sanctuary at Arad, the calculations of Hollis as corrected earlier in this study and at least a very literal rendition of the direction of the biblical witness to the orientation of the temple, 'to the east'.

2. Cf. 1 Kgs 6.38; 8.2. There is no reason to doubt either the date of completion or dedication, although the exact date of the latter has slight variations and is somewhat complex (cf. 1 Kgs 8.65; 2 Chron. 7.8-10; Lev. 23.34-43).

3. See, for example, de Vaux, *Ancient Israel*, pp. 498-99.

4. On the apparent link between the Feast of Booths and Temple dedication, see further Hillyers, 'Feast of Tabernacles', pp. 49, 52.

5. Other explanations for the apparent delay are of course possible, but none are so compelling as to preclude the interpretation offered here. For example, on the assumption that the dedication was delayed by eleven months, de Vaux (*Ancient Israel*, pp. 498-99) suggests that 'the delay could be explained by the fact that all the bronze furnishings were still being cast'.

dim. Whereas the archaeological evidence offered no analogue that
suggests solar alignment, the evidence is necessarily indirect.
Moreover, in light of the specific context for which the temple was
constructed (which appears to have been solar to no small extent) we
should perhaps not expect a clear Yahwistic analogue. While the
archaeological evidence does not favour a solar orientation for the
temple of Solomon, such orientation is certainly possible in light of
the biblical evidence—and is indeed more possible than has often been
recognized. Whether the temple was aligned to the sun as some form
of an expression of Yahweh remains uncertain.[1]

The Accounts of the Reigns of Ahaz, Hezekiah, Manasseh and Josiah
There is much in the accounts of the reigns of these kings that either
states or suggests that the cult of Yahweh was influenced by astral or
solar features. At times it is difficult to discern what may or may not
be relevant to solarized Yahwism (especially in the reign of Ahaz),[2]
but the items outlined below are clearly worthy of consideration.

1.   That other Yahwistic sanctuaries did not on the whole follow suit could be
accounted for in light of the fact that there was in the case of the Jerusalem temple the
need for a concessionary attitude toward the high place of Gibeon. The lack of
analogy nonetheless warrants the use of caution.
2.   For example, J. Morgenstern (*Fire*, pp. 33-35, 52-53) has suggested that
2 Chron. 28.24 and 29.6-7, mentioning Ahaz's closing of the Temple doors and
extinguishing of lamps, originally described two rites associated with the equinoctial
New Year's Day ritual, both done in preparation for the coming of the *kᵉbôd yhwh*,
'radiance of Yahweh', but there seems to be little evidence for this. If relevant to the
present discussion at all, these references to the closing of the Temple doors and the
cessation of the cult of Yahweh therein on the one hand (2 Chron. 28.24; 29.6-7)
and the adopting of a new larger altar of burnt offerings on the other (2 Kgs 16.10-
16) are perhaps suggestive that Ahaz was guilty of an imbalanced regard for Yahweh
as Sun in the heavens at the expense of Yahweh as resident in the Holy of Holies, a
point supported at first glance by the use in 2 Chron. 29.6 of the imagery of 'turning
the back' on Yahweh's Temple. It is best, however, not to take these passages into
consideration for the following reasons: (1) 2 Kgs 16.10-16 cannot easily be
reconciled with 2 Chron. 29 which makes it clear that the closing of the temple
meant that burnt offerings were no longer offered in the Temple court (2 Chron.
29.7; cf. v. 18); (2) the mention of 'turning the back' to the Temple in 2 Chron.
29.6, unlike Ezek. 8.16 or 1 Kgs 8, is not specifically the direction of prayer or
prostration, but a general figure of speech akin to Jer. 2.27, 32.33, occurring
moreover not in a description of the acts of Ahaz alone but in a general reference to
the behaviour of the 'fathers'.

a. *A Case for Hezekiah as a Solar Yahwist*
If what I have argued in the previous chapter regarding the royal jar handles is correct (or if on any other interpretations of the imagery on the handles are judged to have possible solar connotations vis-à-vis the God of Judah), they imply that Hezekiah perhaps had a solar understanding of Yahweh. Although this might seem unlikely in light of a traditional understanding of the biblical evidence, Deuteronomistic literature examined thus far leaves room for the possibility that solar elements belonged to the Yahwistic outlook of other key figures such as Joshua and Solomon. The following passages constitute a case then for Hezekiah as a 'solar Yahwist'.

2 Kings 20.8-11/Isaiah 38.7-8: A Sign on the Upper Chamber of Ahaz. First is the account of the sign of the healing of King Hezekiah in 2 Kgs 20. 8-11 and Isa. 38.7-8. According to the fuller account in 2 Kings, the penitent King Hezekiah requests a sign from Isaiah to confirm that he will not die from his illness after all.[1] The passages in 2 Kings and Isaiah read (respectively) as follows:

> 8 And Hezekiah said to Isaiah, 'What shall be a sign that the Lord will heal me, and that I shall go up to the house of the Lord on the third day?' 9 And Isaiah said, 'This is the sign to you from the Lord, that the Lord will do the thing that he has promised: shall the shadow go forward[2] ten steps, or go back ten steps?' 10 And Hezekiah answered, 'It is an easy thing for the shadow to lengthen ten steps; rather let the shadow go back ten steps'. 11 And Isaiah the prophet cried to the Lord; and he brought the shadow back ten steps by which (the sun)[3] had declined on the dial[4] of Ahaz. (2 Kgs 20.8-11)

1.   2 Kgs 20.8. Isa. 38.22 logically belongs before v. 7 (see, for example, R.E. Clements, *Isaiah 1–39* [NCB; Grand Rapids: Eerdmans, 1980], p. 293 and compare the position of 2 Kgs 20.8).
2.   The translation given here follows the Targum in understanding Isaiah to have posed a question to Hezekiah that involved two alternatives. This view, favoured by most commentators, is strongly suggested by the response of Hezekiah in v. 10.
3.   That the verb is feminine suggests that its subject is the sun and not the shadow (cf. Isa. 38.8); in either case the meaning is the same.
4.   Concerning the translation 'dial' here and in Isa. 38.8, the long-standing debate about whether *ma'ªlôt* should be rendered 'steps' on the basis of the word's meaning, or 'sun dial' on the basis of the context, has been resolved through the understanding that the steps of the upper chamber of Ahaz were themselves an integral part of the means by which time was kept. (See later in this discussion.)

> 7 This is the sign to you from the Lord, that the Lord will do this thing
> which he promised: 8 Behold, I will make to turn backwards by ten steps
> the shadow of the steps on which the sun descended on the steps of the
> upper chamber of[1] Ahaz. And the sun went backwards ten steps on the
> dial on which it had descended. (Isa. 38.7-8)

A comparison of these two renditions in the MT with the LXX and
1 QIsa[a] makes it clear that the text has suffered in transmission.[2] In
any case, the basic message of the story has always been clear (i.e. that
the prophet gave Isaiah a miraculous sign in which the direction of the
sun was reversed, resulting in the reversal of the sun/shadow on the
'steps' of a structure attributed to Ahaz).

Within the past thirty years two developments have brought the
original form of the sign into sharper focus. First, the reading of
1 QIsa[a] of *m'lwt 'lyt 'ḥz*, 'steps of the upper chamber of Ahaz', in
Isa. 38.8 has identified the place at which the miracle took place with
the *'ᵃliyyat 'āḥāz*, 'upper chamber of Ahaz', mentioned in 2 Kgs 23.12
(on which see later in this study). Secondly, due to this greater clarity
brought by the reading from 1 QIsa[a], it is now possible to identify the
method of time-keeping implied by the biblical data with that evident
from a model found in Egypt which also kept time by means of steps
(and which corresponds with the biblical data at many other points as
well).[3] These two developments have clarified that the *ma'ᵃlôt 'āḥāz*,

---

1.   Following 1 QIsa[a] in which *'lyt*, 'upper chamber', is placed between *m'lwt*
and *'ḥz*. See further S. Iwry, 'The Qumrân Isaiah and the End of the Dial of Ahaz',
BASOR 147 (1957), pp. 30-33.

2.   For an attempt at reconstructing the original form of the story, see Iwry,
'Qumrân Isaiah', pp. 32-33.

3.   For a picture of the shadow clock, see R.W. Sloley, 'Primitive Methods of
Measuring Time', *JEA* 17 (1931), pl. 17.2, 3, 4. The parallel between this shadow
clock and the shadow clock of the upper chamber of Ahaz was noted first by
Y. Yadin, 'The Dial of Ahaz', *EI* 5 (1958), pp. 91-96 (Hebrew). The shadow
clock, a block-shaped piece made of limestone about 15 inches in length, is in the
Cairo Museum. It consists of two flights of steps which are oriented back-to-back (as
if the two sides of an equilateral triangle had steps for lateral edges) and which before
converging lead onto a level platform. Walls opposite to the bottom of the steps and
at right angles to them form barriers, the shadow of which during the morning
descends one set of stairs when oriented eastward, and in the afternoon climbs the
opposite set of steps which face west. As Yadin notes ('The Dial of Ahaz'), this
phenomenon indeed offers a striking parallel to the biblical accounts in which the
shadow (or if examined in a different sense, the sun) descends and ascends the steps

'steps of Ahaz', doubled as a sun-dial and were an integral part of the architecture of the *ᵃliyyat 'āḥāz*, 'upper chamber of Ahaz'.[1]

Although clarity has been brought to the passage through the equating of the 'steps of Ahaz' with the 'upper chamber of Ahaz', a difficulty still remains. The problem concerns the correspondence between the reversal of the sun's direction and its function as a meaningful 'sign' to Hezekiah that Yahweh would cure him of his illness.[2] Moreover, although several suggestions have been made concerning the nature of the correspondence,[3] none are particularly compelling. The thesis of this study, however, effectively resolves the issue, for when one assumes a direct correspondence between the action of the sun and the action of Yahweh, the significance of the sun event as a sign to the ill Hezekiah is simple and self evident: the reversal of the direction of the sun indicated to Hezekiah the reversal of the direction of Yahweh concerning his illness.

In its favour, this interpretation corresponds perfectly with the significance which the narrative itself attributes to the sign, namely that it is a sign 'from Yahweh that Yahweh will do that which he promised'[4] (that is, to heal Hezekiah and not to allow him to die as

---

of the upper chamber of Ahaz. (On problems associated with archaeological parallels to the *ma ᵃlôt 'āḥāz* offered earlier by H. Lesêtre and E.J. Pilcher, see E. Stern, '*ma ᵃlôt 'āḥāz*', *EncMik* 8 [1968], p. 197 [Hebrew].)

1. For diagrams of the structure, see Yadin, 'Dial of Ahaz', pp. 95-96 (figs. 1-6) or, similarly, Stern, '*ma ᵃlôt 'āḥāz*', pp. 196-97.

2. As Gray notes especially in light of the other 'signs' in Isaiah, one expects there to be some kind of correspondence between the sign and that which it allegedly signifies (Gray, *I and II Kings*, p. 699).

3. According to Abarbanel (cited in M. Cogan and H. Tadmor, *II Kings* [AB, 11; Garden City, NY: Doubleday, 1988], p. 255), the travel of the sun 10 degrees and its reversal corresponded with the approach of Hezekiah towards death and the reversal of this pattern to Hezekiah's return to life and health for another fifteen years. Gray (*I and II Kings*, pp. 699-700) suggests that a more original form of the sign might have been relevant to v. 6 in which case the irreversibility of the shadow's course was a sign of 'God's abiding favour to the house of David'. On the other hand, if the sign was relevant to v. 1, the shadow's irreversibility would have applied to the certainty of his impending death, in which case Hezekiah's recovery might then account for the tradition of the shadow's reversal.

4. *mē'ēt yhwh 'ᵃšer ya ᵃśeh yhwh 'et haddābār hazzeh 'ᵃšer dibbēr* (Isa. 38.7; cf. 2 Kgs 20.8).

previously decreed). Moreover, it helps to explain several points of affinity often noted between this passage and Josh. 10.12-14.[1]

2 Kings 23.12: Altars on the Upper Chamber of Ahaz. The starting point for this line of evidence favouring solar elements in the Yahwism of Hezekiah is 2 Kgs 21.3-5 which reads as follows:

> 3 And again he [Manasseh] built the high places which Hezekiah his father had destroyed; and he erected altars for Baal and he made an asherah, as Ahab king of Israel had done. He worshipped the Host of Heaven and served them, 4 and he built altars in the house of the Lord where Yahweh had said, 'In Jerusalem I will set my name'. 5 And he built altars for all the Host of Heaven in the two courts of the House of the Lord.

Regardless of which critical assessment one follows in examining this passage,[2] an important point for the present argument remains unaffected. In reporting the negative cultic reforms of Manasseh nothing is held back; the account of the vices of Manasseh in the DH is climactic and relatively comprehensive. Moreover, the report pays particular attention to Manasseh's role in erecting altars.[3]

Turning now to 2 Kgs 23.12, part of the report of the reforms of Josiah, the passage reads as follows:

1. See, for example, Jones, *1 and 2 Kings*, II, p. 589; Gray, *I and II Kings*, p. 700.
2. One can perhaps do no better at present than to follow the assessment of H.-D. Hoffmann (*Reform und Reformen* [ATANT, 66; Zürich: Theologischer Verlag, 1980], pp. 157-67), according to whom v. 3 contains four *Kultnotizen* and vv. 4 and 5 a fifth and sixth respectively. Moreover, it is possible to understand the references to the introduction of cultic elements into the temple itself in vv. 4-5, and 7, each containing the election formula, as climaxes in which the various abominable practices have actually made their way into the Temple. In both cases there is before these passages (that is, vv. 3 and 7) a description without localization of an implicating mass of negative cultic elements. (In light of its final position and link with Ahab [cf. v. 3 and 1 Kgs 16.33], v. 7 is a crucial high point. In mentioning Ahab, there is an intentional link made between him who for his vices was associated with the fall of the northern kingdom and him who for similar vices will be judged responsible for the fall of the southern kingdom.) The report functions both as a negative foil for the reform report of Josiah and as the rationale for the fall of the southern kingdom, in effect a counterpart to 2 Kgs 17.
3. In vv. 3-5 there are mentioned altars (plural) for Baal, altars for either Baal or the host of heaven (v. 4; cf. 2 Kgs 23.4) in the Temple, and altars also for 'all the Host of Heaven' in both Temple courts.

And the altars which were upon the roof of upper[1] chamber of Ahaz
which the kings of Judah had made, and the altars which Manasseh made
in the two courts of the Temple, the king pulled down and smashed them
there,[2] and discarded their dust in the Kidron Valley.

A problem is posed by the reference to 'the altars which were upon
the roof of [the] upper chamber of Ahaz which the kings of Judah had
made'. Still on the upper chamber of Ahaz in the time of Josiah, these
altars were not put there by 'Manasseh' (mentioned specifically by
name in this verse, but with reference only to other altars), but rather
by the 'kings of Judah' (plural). Thus, by stating that altars on a
structure attributed to Ahaz existed through the reign of several kings
prior to Josiah, the passage implies at least tolerance on the part of
Hezekiah for these 'pagan' altars.

None of the traditional explanations for the awkwardness
occasioned by the presence of these altars in the time of Hezekiah are
particularly compelling. For example, many scholars imply that
Hezekiah took down the altars and Manasseh re-erected them, but in
view of the concern in DH to highlight the positive aspects of
Hezekiah's reign and the negative aspects of Manasseh's, this is an
inference based upon a most unlikely silence.

Another approach might appear to lie in the recognition that *'ᵃliyyat
'āḥāz*, 'upper chamber of Ahaz', in 2 Kgs 23.12 is a gloss. But even
before knowledge of the relevance of 1 QIsaᵃ, it was judged 'even so'
to be 'a worthy historical gloss',[3] and since then all doubt has been
removed.[4] Moreover, if the phrase is a gloss (which seems likely in

---

1. The article is omitted before 'upper chamber of Ahaz' as a crude means of
conveying a similar degree of awkwardness occasioned by the presence of the article
on the construct *gag*, 'roof'. (The point becomes important later in this study.)

2. Based upon the common emendation *wayyᵉraṣṣēm šām*. (The MT reads
wayyaroṣ miššām, 'he ran from there', which makes little sense in the context. See
further, Hoffmann, *Reform und Reformen*, p. 228 n. 26.)

3. J.A. Montgomery, *The Book of Kings* (ICC; Edinburgh: T. & T. Clark,
1951), p. 533. (Prior to the article of Iwry ['Qumrân Isaiah'], the reading *'ᵃliyyat* in
Isa. 38.8 in 1QIsaᵃ was overlooked.)

4. Even Hoffmann (who is inclined to doubt that genuine historical traditions
underlie much of the reform reports in DH) regards the reference to the altars of the
upper chamber of Ahaz in 23.12 as a worthy and precise piece of historical
information (*Reform und Reformen*, p. 249 n. 163). (To Hoffmann, one of the
reasons for its inclusion in the DH was in fact to underscore the reliability of the

view of the awkward presence of the article on the preceding construct *gag*, 'roof'), the tension becomes greater because the remaining original form of the text would then state that the altars were simply 'on the roof'—in this context almost certainly the roof of the temple itself.[1]

A few scholars have attempted to resolve the problem of the presence of idolatrous altars in the time of Hezekiah by arguing that the reference in 2 Kgs 23.12 to the erection of the altars by the 'kings of Judah' refers only to Manasseh and Amon.[2] While some warrant for this conclusion might be adduced from an attempt to harmonize strictly 2 Kgs 21.3 (which mentions the introduction of the Host of Heaven by Manasseh) with 2 Kgs 23.5 (which implies that the Host of Heaven were worshipped by priests appointed by the 'kings of Judah'), the suggestion is nonetheless highly unlikely for the following reasons. (1) According to 2 Kgs 21.21-22, the actions of Amon were virtually identical to those of Manasseh; it is thus quite improbable that the distinction made in v. 12 between the actions of 'Manasseh' and those of the 'kings of Judah' included in the latter case only Manasseh and Amon. (2) It would be surprising if so general an expression as the 'kings of Judah' implicated only the last two of sixteen kings of Judah. Surely the reference is at the very least to more than two in which case, in referring to a structure built by Ahaz, Hezekiah is almost certainly to be included.

Finally, it is relevant for my point about the seemingly telling

report by means of a precise statement [*Reform und Reformen*, p. 249].) Note also the opinion of Iwry who says, 'The new variant in 1 QIsa^a makes clear reference to the old palace of Ahaz, still standing at the time of Hezekiah and surviving, *with or without the altars on the roof*, into the time of Josiah' ('Qumrân Isaiah', p. 31 [emphasis mine]).

1. E. Kaufmann noted this with sufficient dismay to cause him to simply disregard the article and thus retain the gloss as original. To Kaufmann it is certain that Hezekiah, who removed the brazen serpent from the temple, would not have allowed altars on the roof of the temple. According to Kaufmann, Hezekiah nonetheless tolerated the presence of altars on the roof of the upper chamber of Ahaz because these were merely for private royal worship (presumably excluding the worship practices of Hezekiah himself). (I know of this work of Kaufmann only through reference to it by Iwry, 'Qumrân Isaiah', p. 31 n. 9.)

2. See, for example, Cogan, *Imperialism and Religion*, p. 87 n. 125 and others (by implication) who attribute to Manasseh this rite and that of dedication of the horses of the sun (also an act of the 'kings of Judah').

presence of these altars during the reign of Hezekiah to clarify that the altars were more likely for the Host of Heaven, including probably Yahweh as the sun, than for some other deity. Thus, although there is some precedent for El, Baal and Kemosh receiving offerings from on top of structures, the parallels cited in favour of such are quite general and there is no particular reason to believe that the passage in question alludes to any of these deities.[1] Moreover, there is no deity more likely to have received offerings from a roof-top structure than a member of the starry host such as the sun. McKay makes this point as follows:

> It has often been thought that the structure [that is, the roof-top altar of Ahaz] was erected for the worship of astral deities. This suggestion is entirely possible, for the roof-top was particularly suited to worship in the presence of the stars in Mesopotamia and to worship of the Host of Heaven in Palestine (Jer. 19.13; Zeph. 1.5), while the chamber itself was the scene of an extraordinary solar event (II Kings 20.8-11; Isa. 38.7-8)... The Nabataeans also appear to have used the roof-top as a place for erecting altars for the daily offering of libations and incense to the Sun.[2]

A few additional considerations favour the option that the altars were for the Host of Heaven including perhaps Yahweh as the sun. First, that DH here implicates Hezekiah with respect to these altars and nonetheless praises him elsewhere suggests that there must have been some kind of ambiguity about the validity of the altars. This ambiguity of course corresponds very well with that noted already in this study concerning the validity of Yahwistic regard for the Host of Heaven and for Yahweh as sun (probably as chief of the heavenly host). Secondly, the reference to the altars on the roof comes between the reference to the removal of solar-cult apparatus from the temple and the reference to altars made by Manasseh in the two courts of the temple (presumably for the Host of Heaven). It is reasonable to

---

1. For parallels in each case, see McKay, *Religion in Judah*, pp. 9-10, and on the option regarding the Host of Heaven, cf. *Religion in ʾJudah*, pp. 31-32. The parallels cited by McKay in the case of El and Baal (to whom Keret in the Ugaritic texts offered sacrifices from on top of a tower) are indeed general. Moreover, despite possible parallels, it is doubtful that a subtle allusion to the worship of Baal or Kemosh stands behind the reference to altars on the upper chamber of Ahaz, because explicit reference is made to Baal and Kemosh in a different context within the same reform report (respectively, 2 Kgs 23.5 and 13).

2. McKay, *Religion in Judah*, pp. 9-10.

assume from this context[1] then that the roof-top altars were for the Host of Heaven including presumably the sun as a manifestation of Yahweh.

To conclude, the textual evidence in favour of the notion that Hezekiah worshipped Yahweh as the sun is as follows: (1) the solar nature of the sign from Yahweh to Hezekiah (and intelligible to him), given on a built-in sun dial atop the roof of Ahaz's upper chamber, and (2) the presence during the reign of Hezekiah of altars to the Host of Heaven (or its chief member, the sun) on this same structure; having escaped his purge (but not Josiah's), the altars imply Hezekiah's sympathies with this aspect of Yahwism. When this evidence is combined with the archaeological evidence for Hezekiah's choice of a solar symbol as the royal emblem of his kingdom, it may be judged as distinctly possible that Hezekiah had a solar understanding of Yahweh (along with a regard for Yahweh's Host of Heaven).

b. *Tensions Suggestive of a Yahwistic Host of Heaven*
If the thesis of this book is correct that the worship of the sun and Host of Heaven was a Yahwistic phenomenon, it should be possible to detect points of tension within DH between the worship of the Host of Heaven (including the sun) as Yahwistic on the one hand and as idolatrous on the other hand. The following passages illustrate the clear presence of this tension (which can best be resolved by regarding the worship of the Host of Heaven as a Yahwistic phenomenon that came to be viewed with contempt within Deuteronomistic circles).

2 Kings 21.4. This verse has already been noted together with vv. 3 and 5 for its comprehensive listing of the various altars built by Manasseh. Here, however, the focus is on the altars mentioned in v. 4:

> And he [Manasseh] built altars in the house of the Lord concerning which
> the Lord had said, 'In Jerusalem I will place my name'.

There is a tension here concerning the one for whom the altars were made. On the one hand, the altars seem clearly to have been erected for the Host of Heaven; both the immediately preceding context which refers to Manasseh's worship of the Host of Heaven (v. 3) and the

---

1.   Although suggestive, this last point should not be pressed because of the individualistic nature of the listing of *Kultnotizen*.

following context which refers to 'altars to the Host of Heaven in the two courts of the Lord' (v. 5) leave virtually no room for doubt that DH wants the reader to identify the altars with the heavenly host.[1]

On the other hand, DH leaves a number of clues to the effect that the 'pagan' altars were Yahwistic nonetheless. The clues, three in number and derived from consideration of the verse within its broader context, are as follows. (1) There is no specific mention in v. 4 of the one for whom the altars were built, quite uncharacteristic for these reform reports.[2] (2) No reference is made to the removal of these altars by Josiah (or anyone else), virtually inconceivable if they were non-Yahwistic altars within the temple of Yahweh. (3) A point related to the previous one but viewed from a literary rather than a historical perspective, the lack of reference to Josiah's removal of these altars runs counter to a pattern according to which specific cultic reforms normally have a counterpart in the reform of another king.[3] Thus, although Hoffmann attempts to gloss over the exception here by including 21.4 in the clear reflex between the negative cult reform of Manasseh in 21.5 and the positive counter reform of Josiah in 23.12, neither 23.12 nor Hoffmann in his discussion of it makes any allusion at all to the 'negative' reform of Manasseh in 21.4. For some reason, then, what is traditionally regarded as a case of 'foreign' intrusion into the temple of Yahweh was ignored. The problem of course

1.   It should be noted that some wonder if 21.4 might refer to the implements of Baal. This judgment is made on the grounds that there is no reflex in the reign of Manasseh to the reference to implements belonging to Baal being removed from the temple. However, unless one insists on a clear counterpart specifically in the reign of Manasseh to that found in 23.4, there is no reason to expect this to be the case. Besides, can an altar be classed as a 'vessel'? In any case, it is clear that there is room for uncertainty about the one(s) for whom the altars were made, an ambiguity that I believe was intentional.

2.   That failure to divulge the name of the deity is not an insignificant technicality is not only suggested by the practice of DH elsewhere to specify the deity but perhaps also by the likelihood that, were the deity pagan, the same history would not pass up the opportunity to state such in the case of Manasseh, particularly in the highly offensive case of erecting altars in the temple itself.

3.   Since Hoffmann bases his understanding that the *Kultnotizen* are a literary device devoid of historical reference on the fact that they have clear reflexes in the descriptions of the reform reports of other kings, the absence of a reflex in the case of 21.4 speaks for the historical veracity of at least this *Kultnotiz* (a criterion Hoffmann himself uses for the historical veracity of 2 Kgs 23.11 for example).

disappears if the altars are Yahwistic but nonetheless 'idolatrous' from the Deuteronomistic perspective. As in the case of the solar-Yahwistic bronze altar in the time of Solomon, here, too, DH uses kid gloves with reference to the erection of an altar in the area of the temple concerning which the Lord has said, 'in Jerusalem I will place my name'.[1]

2 Kings 23.5. This verse offers additional support for the tension between the worship of the sun and other members of the Host of Heaven as idolatrous on the one hand and as Yahwistic on the other hand:

> 5 And he [Josiah] retired the idolatrous priests (*k^{e}mārîm*) whom the kings of Judah had dedicated to burn incense[2] at the high places in the towns of Judah and the environs of Jerusalem, those who burned incense to Baal, to the sun, and to the moon and to all the Host of Heaven.

Scholars are divided about whether the priests referred to here are Yahwistic as the Judaean setting suggests or 'idolatrous' as the force of the word *k^{e}mārîm*, 'idolatrous priests', suggests.[3] For the present purposes the ambiguity itself is as relevant as the debate,[4] into which one further option may be added: the priests who were worshipping Baal,[5] the sun, moon and stars were both Yahwistic and 'idolatrous'.

---

1.   In both cases, there is apostasy when the worship offered on these altars is directed to the heavens rather than to Yahweh of Hosts who resides in 'name/glory' in the temple.

2.   The MT reads *wayy^{e}qaṭṭēr*, 'and he burned incense'.

3.   Illustrative aspects of the debate are as follows. Many scholars regard it as doubtful that *k^{e}mārîm* is likely a reference to Yahwistic priests. On the basis of his own examination of the meaning of Akkadian *kumru kumritu*, Spieckermann (*Juda unter Assur*, pp. 85-86) argues that the word was a designation for priests collaborating with the Assyrians. In response, however, Würthwein (*Bücher der Könige*, p. 456) wonders if these priests, according to Spieckermann, based in Jerusalem (?), would have been present in Jerusalem even during a period of Assyrian decline. In responding further to Spieckermann, Würthwein also wonders if it is likely that these priests could have been installed by the kings of Judah and appointed to the high places, a point which which may be raised in response to those who regard the *k^{e}mārîm* as 'foreign priests'.

4.   A similar ambiguity has been noted by Hoffmann (*Reform und Reformen*, p. 214) with respect to the high places in v. 5: Are they Yahwistic or foreign?

5.   The relationship between Baal and Yahweh is beyond the scope of the present

2 Kings 23.12 (cf. 21.5). An element of the positive reform report of Josiah in 2 Kgs 23.12 reveals a similar tension when compared with its negative reflex in the reform of Manasseh, 2 Kgs 21.5. As Hoffmann has noted, the account in 23.12 of Josiah's removal of the altars from the two courts of the Lord erected by Manasseh is the same as the original report in 21.5 of the erection of these altars, with one exception: 23.12 fails to specify that the altars were for the Host of Heaven.[1] According to Hoffmann the reason for the omission of the purpose of the altars from 23.12 is that their purpose was self-evident in light of 21.5,[2] but this appears to apply only in the case of a very careful reader; this reflex of 21.5 in 23.12 occurs two chapters later and in a context in which no mention whatsoever is made of the Host of Heaven. Perhaps more plausible then is another explanation: as with the mention in the same immediate context of other items also being removed from the sensitive area of the temple complex itself, the writer is being intentionally ambiguous about the fact that they are Yahwistic.[3]

To summarize, the tensions reflected in all three passages noted above point in the same direction as other elements in this study, towards the conclusion that the worship of the Host of Heaven was a Yahwistic phenomenon which DH considered nonetheless to be an 'idolatrous' act. In seeking to understand why Deuteronomistic theology would interpret a Yahwistic practice as idol worship akin to the Amorites, it is important to emphasize that the mere notion of an association between Host of Heaven and Yahweh appears to be condemned no more outrightly prior to the reign of Josiah than the notion of some kind of association between Yahweh and the sun. In my judgment, Deuteronomistic theology's quarrel is not with the notion of Yahweh's entourage as the heavenly Host[4] or with Yahweh

discussion. I see no reason to doubt, however, that the relationship between Yahweh and Baal, like that between Yahweh and the sun, is closer than has traditionally been thought. (For a recent discussion, see Smith, *Early History of God*, pp. 41-79.)

1. Hoffmann, *Reform und Reformen*, p. 164.

2. Hoffmann, *Reform und Reformen*, p. 164.

3. Besides, by omitting reference to the Host of Heaven with respect to the altars of Manasseh in v. 12b, DH is covering tracks that lead straight to the Host of Heaven (or the chief member thereof) with reference to the altars on the roof of the upper chamber of Ahaz during the reign of Hezekiah in v. 12a.

4. Cf. 1 Kgs 22.19; Judg. 5.20.

himself as the sun, but with the practice of directing one's worship specifically toward these *objects* (at which time they become akin to the 'idols' of the nations whom Yahweh displaced from the land). The fact that these astral bodies were not made with human hands and thus fell outside the limits of the second commandment no doubt contributed to the widespread notion that the sun, moon and stars were legitimate symbols or tangible manifestations of Yahweh and his heavenly army (which DH does not oppose)—after all, was it not Yahweh himself who created these stellar objects which in times past had actually acted on Israel's behalf? In Deuteronomistic circles, however, the role of these objects as Yahwistic symbols or icons did not legitimate the *actual worship of these objects*.

2 Kings 23.11. This verse, the most explicit account in DH of the worship of the sun, merits close examination. The MT of 2 Kgs 23.11 is as follows:

> 11 And he removed[1] the horses which the kings of Judah had dedicated to the sun from the entrance[2] of the House of the Lord, by the chamber of Nathan-Melech the official, within the stoas, and the chariots of the sun he burned with fire.

Most of the relevant discussions arising from this passage centre on two issues: (1) the origin of the cult associated with the horses[3] and

---

1.   The verb *šbt* in the *hiphil* is often rendered in contexts of idolatry 'put an end to', but in most of these cases that which is done away with bears the prefix *min*. The present verse parallels closely Exod. 12.15 and Isa. 30.11, both of which provide clear support for translating *hišbît* here in the sense of 'remove'. (Cf. also 2 Kgs 23.5 where 'put an end to' would be harsh action in the case of the priests.)

2.   The vocalization of the MT, *mibbō'*, 'from entering', is virtually impossible in its present context. Could this vocalization have arisen from a variant tradition in which the singular referent was the sun? This is pure speculation, but such is perhaps suggested by the common use of the verb *bw'* in connection with the sun. Perhaps a variant had Josiah keeping the sun from either 'entering' the temple or from 'setting' at the temple (locative adverbial accusative) in the area of the *liškâ* in the *parwārîm* which some evidence suggests was located at the western side of the temple (concerning which, however, see later in this discussion). (See also the preceding note in which attention is drawn to the use of *min* with *šbt*.)

3.   The reference simply to 'horses' offers no reason to believe that they were other than literal horses; the same applies in the case of the chariot(s) which are said to have been burned (technically not possible in the case of clay chariots). Even if the

chariots of the sun, and (2) topographic uncertainties arising from the use of terms no longer well understood.

Concerning the first issue, there has arisen in the wake of the recent work of Spieckermann[1] a revival of the view that the horses and chariots of the sun reflect the imposition by Assyria of her own cult practices.[2]

To evaluate, although some aspects of official religion in Judah at the time of Assyrian domination might have been concessionary towards Assyrian practice (in light of Spieckermann's work, the matter deserves reconsideration), in light of evidence adduced thus far about a Yahwistic rite involving the use of horses and chariots of the sun, the cultic practice reflected in 2 Kgs 23.11 is far from a showcase example of the presence of Assyrian influence.[3] The Taanach cult stand provides warrant for suggesting that a *Yahwistic* rite involving horse and chariot was in vogue within the context of a temple from as early as the time of the founding of the temple itself, in which case its introduction into the temple obviously had nothing to do with the

clay horse figurines examined in the previous chapter were relevant to 2 Kgs 23.11, it would not follow from this that horses which these figurines model were themselves figurines. Moreover, though made of clay, the equid on the top tier of the Taanach cult stand appears to represent a live animal and not a figurine. (If the equid on the Taanach stand were a figure of a figure, it is doubtful that the latter would have been able to stand up. The animal is depicted as running freely outside the temple entrance.)

1. Spieckermann, *Juda unter Assur*, pp. 245-56. According to Spieckermann, the chariots mentioned in 2 Kgs 23.11 could have been linked originally either to a cult of Ashur or of Shamash. He is inclined to favour the former option.

2. Note, for example, Würthwein (*Die Bücher der Könige I*, p. 459) who unequivocally states that the cult apparatus was for Shamash. Note also Cogan and Tadmor, *II Kings*, p. 288.

3. Spieckermann, *Juda unter Assur*, pp. 107-109, 238, 245-56. Spieckermann draws particular attention to *KAR* 218, an oracle text occasioned by the giving over by a donor of a horse for the purpose of drawing the processional chariot of Marduk (*Juda unter Assur*, pp. 245-51). 2 Kgs 23.11 can thus be accounted for on the grounds that a horse was similarly given over to Shamash, something which Spieckermann regards as plausible on account of the growing importance in the seventh century BCE of Shamash as an oracular deity and iconographic evidence (including perhaps the horse figurines found by Kenyon) which associates the horse with the solar deity (*Juda unter Assur*, p. 251).

imposition of Assyrian cult practices upon Judah.[1] The Taanach cult stand with horse and sun located at the entrance to a Yahwistic shrine (together with a griffin, known to draw the chariot of the sun god) and Hazor horse figurine with a sun disk offer perfectly plausible native parallels to 2 Kgs 23.11 which are more direct than the Assyrian counterparts proposed by Spieckermann.[2] Moreover, if it is a reference to Shamash, then 'the sun' (*haššemeš*) should be anarthrous in 2 Kgs 23.11. Of course the article is easy to account for on the understanding that cultic practice was associated with 'the sun' which up to this time had functioned in royal Jerusalemite circles as a symbol of the deity for whom the temple was built, namely Yahweh.

The problem of the reference to the sun horses and chariot(s) being erected by 'the kings of Judah'[3] (plural) parallels the difficulty noted already in the discussion of altars. Unless the rite of the sun horses was introduced by Manasseh and Amon (already shown to be most unlikely), the problem arises as to why Hezekiah did not do away with the practice. The difficulty is considerable for those who would see here a practice concessionary to the Assyrians, for the rebellious Hezekiah would almost certainly have done away with such an official sign of subservience to Assyria.[4] If, however, one assumes that the practice reflects a form of Yahwism that was in accordance with royal

1. Moreover, although it might be that considerable development in the understanding of these solar cult features took place (to the extent that the cult as practiced in the time of Josiah might have fallen under strong Assyrian influence), the similarity between the portraits of this cultic phenomenon in the tenth and seventh centuries appears to offer little evidence for such development.

2. Neither is it relevant to discuss the often cited possible parallel between the chariot(s) mentioned in this verse and the Assyrian title of the sun god, *rākib narkabti*, 'rider of the chariot' (see, for example, Gray, *I and II Kings*, p. 736). The relevance of the reference has been called into question by McKay (*Religion in Judah*, p. 32) already on the grounds that the phenomenon of the deity riding simply a chariot is not unique to the sun god but is characteristic of most of the gods of Assyria.

3. On the unlikelihood of 'kings of Judah' referring only to Manasseh and Amon (so, for example, Cogan, *Imperialism and Religion*, p. 87 n. 125) see the earlier discussion of the 'kings of Judah' with reference to v. 12. It is again surprising that, in spite of the reference to the dedication of the horses by the 'kings' (plural, v. 11) as opposed to 'Manasseh' (singular, v. 12b), many scholars attribute the dedication of the horses to Manasseh.

4. Sarna, '*šemeš*', p. 188.

Jerusalemite theology and at least tolerated by Deuteronomistic theology prior to the time of Josiah, then there is no reason to expect its removal prior to Josiah's reform, as indeed the text strongly implies.[1]

Concerning the second matter of the terms for places referred to in 2 Kgs 23.11, it should be recalled at the outset that the possibility exists that at least in some cases the description of places within the temple reflects the situation of the post-exilic temple.[2] The phrase *'el liškat n^{e}tan-melek hassārîs '^{a}šer bapparwārîm*, 'at/near the chamber of Nathan-melech the chamberlain which was in the stoas', poses a number of problems. The word *sārîs* can mean a eunuch or chamberlain (usually chamberlains were eunuchs)[3] or an official, in which case it can refer to one of high rank[4] within the military or to one who performs menial tasks within the royal court.[5] In either case, some connection with the royal house (as opposed to the priesthood) is probable in the case of Nathan-melech. Unfortunately, the preposition *'el* makes it impossible to know whether the horses were kept 'at' the chamber of this official (which implies his involvement) or whether they were simply 'near' his chamber (in which case nothing can be inferred about his possible involvement).[6]

Also problematic is the biblical hapax legomenon *parwārîm*. Leaving aside for the moment the issue of the etymology of the word (which may not be relevant to usage in any case), there are two

1. As noted, the claim that Hezekiah might have eliminated the horses of the sun and Manasseh re-erected them is unlikely in light of DH which lauds Hezekiah for all worthy acts and which accuses Manasseh of a host of vices.

2. For example, the mention of two temple courts in v. 12 is often thought to be influenced by Ezekiel and the post-exilic temple.

3. F.F. Bruce, 'Chamberlain', *NBD*, p. 182.

4. Cf., for example, 2 Kgs 25.19.

5. Cf. 1 Kgs 22.9.

6. Though not to the present context, it is relevant to the general thesis of this book to note in passing that at a later period Judaism knew of two kinds of eunuchs: the *sārîs 'ādām* 'Eunuch of man', which indicated a man-made eunuch, and the *sārîs ḥammâ*, 'Eunuch of the sun', which denoted one born that way (*m. Zab.* 2.1). Although Marcus Jastrow (*A Dictionary of the Targumim, the Talmud Babli and Yerushalmi, and the Midrashic Literature* [Brooklyn, NY: Traditional Press, n.d.], p. 476) explains the second category as 'a eunuch from the time of seeing the sun', its counterpart 'Eunuch of man', appears to welcome the interpretation 'Eunuch of God' (that is, *ḥammâ*, 'sun') (emphasis mine).

possible affinities to *parwārîm* within Hebrew and with reference to temple architecture. The first is the singular word *parbār* found both in 1 Chron. 26.18 and in the Temple Scroll.[1] In both of these texts, *parbār* refers to a structure lying to the west of the temple. Moreover, if one assumes in the former case of 1 Chron. 26.18 an association with the structure mentioned in Ezek. 41.12, as is probable,[2] then in both texts the *parbār* refers more specifically to a large building lying immediately to the west of the *hêkāl* of the temple.[3]

The second possible affinity to *parwārîm* occurs in connection with another kind of structure mentioned in the Temple Scroll. In columns 42 and 37 the term is used to refer to structures along the inside of the walls of the outer courts and inner courts respectively. Yadin says the following concerning these *parwārîm*:

> The fullest treatment of the *prwr* is given in Col. XLII, where the outer court and its chambers and rooms are discussed. These structures, which adjoin the inner side of the outer court wall, have three storeys. Each storey has chambers, rooms and *prwrym* facing the center of the court. The *prwrym* are thus buildings that open towards the court, that is to say, stoas of a kind. They have stairhouses with spiral staircases, which allowed access to the upper storeys[4]... Col. XXXVII, which deals with the inner court, mentions an inner stoa near its outer wall. The tables and places for the animal sacrifices of the priests are found in this stoa.[5]

1. The word occurs also in line 3 of the bilingual Lydian-Aramaic funerary inscription, *KAI* 260. (Donner and Röllig translate the term 'vestibule' [*Vorraum*].)

2. See the discussion of Ezekiel earlier in this chapter and in Y. Yadin (ed.), *The Temple Scroll* (3 vols; Jerusalem: Israel Exploration Society, 1983 [Hebrew, 1977]), I, p. 236.

3. Yadin, *Temple Scroll*, I, p. 236. According to col. 35.8-15 of the Temple Scroll, the *parbār* lying to the west of the *hêkal* was for the sin offerings of the priests and the guilt offerings of the people. The area around the *parbār* (along with the areas around the *hêkal*, altar and laver) was to be 'holy of holies for ever'. The *parbār* was a building of free-standing columns and separated into two areas to separate the offerings of the priests from the people. (See Yadin, *Temple Scroll*, II, pp. 149-51.) One should expect quite naturally that the description of the temple of Ezekiel has influenced the Temple Scroll; see, for example, Yadin, *Temple Scroll*, I, p. 236.

4. Interestingly, in the lines which follow this account (that is, col. 42.10-17), the text makes it clear that there was access from the third storey onto the roof of the third storey and that on it booths were erected for the annual celebration of the Feast of Booths; cf. Yadin, *Temple Scroll*, II, pp. 179-80 and the further references cited there.

5. Yadin, *Temple Scroll*, I, p. 237.

To evaluate these two clues to the meaning of *parwārîm* in 2 Kgs 23.11, the latter option of an association with the stoas mentioned in connection with these inner and outer courts of the temple scroll should be favoured over a direct link with the western *parbār* referred to in both 1 Chron. 26.18 and the Temple Scroll. First, although it may be coincidental, only the singular form of the noun is used with reference to the *parbār* behind the temple.[1] Secondly, 'chambers' (*nškwt*) are found in association with both the *parwārîm* in the Temple Scroll and in 2 Kgs 23.11.[2] And thirdly and most importantly, it is extremely difficult to reconcile the western location of the *parbār* with that of the chamber and *parwārîm* near the entrance to the House of the Lord in 2 Kgs 23.11.[3]

Applying this judgment to 2 Kgs 23.11, which concerns the first temple (but which perhaps conveys some notions associated more closely with the second), since mention is made of priestly *liškôt*, 'chambers', which would no doubt have lain within the courtyard of the Solomonic temple,[4] it is logical to conclude that Nathan-melech had a chamber within the courtyard. This chamber was no doubt within the 'inner court' and not far from the entrance to the House of the Lord. Moreover, although there is no detailed description of the construction of the inner court of the first temple[5] ('inner' at least

---

1. The use of the noun in the singular in the Temple Scroll should not be taken as separate evidence in addition to the descriptions of a western building and *parbār* (both singular) in Ezek. 41.12 and 1 Chron. 26.18, both of which may have influenced the description in the Temple Scroll.

2. Again, however, influence from 2 Kgs 23.11 on the description of the chambers, rooms and stoas is probable.

3. Even if one follows the vocalization of *mb'* in the MT (which makes no sense) the chamber and stoas are still near a point of 'entering' the temple. Hoffmann's suggestion that *'el liškat n^etan melek b^eparwārîm* should not be understood as a place 'near' the entrance to the temple where the horses of the sun were, but the place 'to' which these horses were removed would alleviate the tension, but if this were the correct sense we should expect '"from" the entrance of the House of the Lord "to" the chamber of Nathan-melech' to be expressed by the combination of prepositions *min* and *'ad* respectively. (See, for example, *BDB*, p. 583 [§9.1]). The closest parallel involving the *hiphil* of *šbt* is Ps. 46.10a [9a], *mašbît milḥāmôt 'ad q^eṣēh hā'āreṣ*, 'He puts an end to wars to the end of the earth', which uses *'ad*.)

4. 1 Chron. 9.26-27, 33.

5. The only indication is 1 Kgs 6.36 according to which the inner court contained three rows of hewn stone and a single row of cedar beams.

relative to the 'great court' if not to an 'outer court', generally regarded to be a later retrojection),[1] the notion of chambers within the wall of the inner court is at least as early as the time of Ezekiel.[2] It is probably in such an area that the *parwārîm* were located, at least to judge from the Temple Scroll which locates such structures within a wall of an inner court.

A few more details are worth noting regarding the location of the horses of the sun. First, being near the entrance to the temple (or perhaps more technically correct, the entrance to the inner court of the temple), the horses perhaps stood to the east of the temple where they may have thus been associated with a Yahwistic solar ritual involving the rising sun.[3] Secondly, assuming that the reference in 2 Kgs 23.11 to the 'chamber' and 'stoas' had a signal that went beyond mere location, it is striking that in the Temple Scroll a characteristic usage of the pillars in the western *parbār* (the description of which Yadin did not wish to separate entirely from that of the 'stoas' in the inner court)[4] was for tying animals. If pillared (as Yadin assumes in the case of both the *parwārîm* west of the temple and within the court walls), the *parwārîm* in 2 Kgs 23.11 were probably places in which (live) horses were tethered. Were these animals also tied in preparation for sacrifice?[5]

Finally, that the plural form of the noun is found in the Temple Scroll only with reference to a description of multi-storeyed stoas is suggestive perhaps of some connection between the horses dedicated to the sun in 2 Kgs 23.11 and rites possibly associated with the (multi-storeyed?) *parwārîm*.[6]

1. For discussions, see T.W. Davies, 'Temple', *HDB*, IV, pp. 695, 702; S. Westerholm, 'Temple', *ISBE*, IV, p. 762.

2. Davies, 'Temple', p. 704, fig. 5.

3. Might this explain the naming of an eastern gate of the temple the 'Horse Gate'? Cf. Jer. 31.40, Neh. 3.28. For possible implications, see Morgenstern, 'Gates of Righteousness', pp. 19-21, n. 42.

4. Yadin, *Temple Scroll*, I, p. 235.

5. This would seem more likely if Nathan-melech were a priest; his ties with the royal court as a (military?) official/chamberlain suggest another function.

6. The 'chambers' within the temple itself were clearly multi-storeyed and contained stairways which perhaps provided access to the roof of the temple itself.

c. *The Worship of the Sun and Heavenly Host during the Reigns of Hezekiah and Josiah*

There can be no doubt that the reforms of Josiah were far more extensive in their purging of solar and astral elements from the cult of Yahweh than those of any of his predecessors, including Hezekiah. But was his opposition to solar and astral Yahwism complete, or was it limited only to certain practices related to the notion of Yahweh as sun and his entourage as Host of Heaven? The present evidence offers little support for the former. Rather, the actions of Josiah are similar to those of Hezekiah; both defined apostasy primarily in terms of iconism, and the iconoclasm of both extended even to ancient *Yahwistic* icons such as the bronze serpent and the asherah. However, whereas Josiah's aniconic bent included objection to the worship of objects which Yahweh himself had made (that is, the sun, moon and stars), Hezekiah's evidently did not go this far, reaching its climax rather with the smashing of a Yahwistic icon made by a human (no less than Moses himself!)[1] In the interests of writing both a credible history and a partisan theological document in which opposition to the worship of the Host of Heaven is made clear, DH is content to live with a tension between points at which Hezekiah's worship of the Host of Heaven (including the sun as Yahweh) can be readily inferred[2] on the one hand and its own positive assessment of Hezekiah on the other hand.[3]

At the level of the final form of the text a relatively more consistent picture nonetheless emerges, one of opposition not so much to the sun or Host of Heaven as symbols of Yahweh and his entourage, but rather of opposition to the actual worship of these objects.

---

1. 2 Kgs 18.4.

2. The report of Hezekiah's reforms include no mention of opposition to the worship of the Host of Heaven. In telling of reforms carried out by Josiah, 2 Kgs 23.5, 11-12 tell equally of reforms not carried out by Hezekiah. (See also the passages discussed earlier in this section.)

3. The problem arises why Hezekiah received a positive report despite his apparent sympathy with the worship of Yahweh and his Host as sun and stars. The solution extends beyond the scope of this discussion but includes no doubt probability of an earlier form of the DH dating to the time of Hezekiah and development in Deuteronomistic theology.

Sun Worship in the Prophets

There are numerous passage in the latter prophets which allude to the
sun in such a way as to raise the issue of its relationship with
Yahwism. The major passages will be examined.

Isaiah 1–39

The possibility of a relationship between the prophet Isaiah and solar
Yahwism has already been raised indirectly with reference to royal
Jerusalemite theology in general and with Isa. 38.7-8/2 Kgs 20.8-11 in
particular. Moreover, there is little within the corpus of Isaiah 1–39
that appears to be inconsistent with a notion that solar dimensions
formed a part of the royal theological perspective of the prophet. In
view of this only two passages will be considered: Isa. 2.7 which,
according to at least one scholar, condemns a solar cult involving
horses and chariots; and Isa. 19.18 which, as will be argued, dubs a
city of Yahweh worshippers 'city of the sun'.

Beginning with Isa. 2.7, G. Pettinato has argued that the horses and
chariots referred to within the following context are cultic, associated
most likely with a solar cult to which the prophet is opposed:[1]

> 6 For thou hast rejected thy people,
> the house of Jacob,
> because they are full of diviners from the east
> and of soothsayers like the Philistines,
> and they strike hands with foreigners.
> 7 Their land is filled with silver and gold,
> and there is no end to their treasures;
> their land is filled with horses,
> and there is no end to their chariots.
> 8 Their land is filled with idols;
> they bow to the work of their hands,
> to what their own hands have made. (RSV)

It is not clear how to interpret the reference to horses and chariots in
v. 7. Although the general context is one of idolatry, the immediately
preceding context which refers to silver, gold and *'ōṣᵉrôt* ('treasures',
'storehouses' or the like) suggests to most commentators that the

---

1. G. Pettinato, 'Is. 2,7 e il culto del sole in Giuda nel sec. VIII av. Cr.',
OrAnt 4 (1965), pp. 1-30.

horses and chariots must refer here to caravans bearing the afore-
mentioned wealth.[1]

Pettinato circumvents the apparently awkward presence of a reference to material wealth within a context of idolatry by noting that
'silver' and 'gold' might refer here to the material from which idols
were often made[2] and the horses and chariots to a solar cult. In
support of a solar interpretation for the horses and chariots, Pettinato
cites 2 Kgs 23.11, figurines of horses and chariots found in archaeological contexts, and Mic. 5.9-14 which similarly refers to horses
and chariots in a judgment against idolatry:

> 9 I will destroy the horses in your midst
> And wreck your chariots.
> 10 I will destroy the cities of your land
> And demolish all your fortresses.
> 11 I will destroy the sorcery you practice,
> And you shall have no more soothsayers.
> 12 I will destroy your idols
> And the sacred pillars in your midst;
> And no more shall you bow down
> To the work of your hands.
> 13 I will tear down the sacred posts in your midst
> And destroy your cities.
> 14 In anger and wrath
> Will I wreak retribution
> On the nations that have not obeyed. (JPSV)

To evaluate this passage (and here too, for the sake of convenience,
this passage from Micah), Pettinato's case is worthy of more attention
than it has often received.[3] It nonetheless rivals other more plausible
interpretations. In the case of Mic. 5.9, for example, a majority of
scholars interpret the horse and chariots as military[4] and receive

---

1. See, for example, Clements, *Isaiah 1–39*, p. 44. In light of the context,
Clements considers the merchandise to include idolatrous items.

2. Pettinato ('Is. 2, 7', pp. 23-24) mentions, for example, Exod. 20.23, Deut.
7.25, 29.16-17, Isa. 46.6, Jer. 10.3-4, Ezek. 16.17, Hos. 8.4, all of which clearly
support his case.

3. One is hard pressed to find mention of the article of Pettinato in most English
commentaries.

4. See, for example, J.L. Mays, *Micah* (OTL; Philadelphia: Westminster Press,
1976), pp. 124, 126; L.C. Allen, *The Books of Joel, Obadiah, Jonah and Micah*
(NICOT; Grand Rapids: Eerdmans, 1976), p. 357.

support from the context of the following verse mentioning the destruction of cities and fortresses. In the case of Isa. 2.7, its virtues notwithstanding, Pettinato's argument is weakest at the point of his attempt to deal with the term '*ōṣᵉrôt*, 'treasures' for which his alternative 'jewellery box' or the like, in which the idols of silver and gold were perhaps stored, does not seem likely.[1] These considerations make it highly uncertain that the horses and chariots of v. 7 refer to the apparatus of a solar cult. Thus, although the problem of the relationship of Isa. 2.7 to its context remains, this single verse cannot be used as a clear case against possible sympathies with royal Jerusalemite solar Yahwism on the part of Isaiah.

Turning now to Isa. 19.18 which seemingly supports the notion of solar Yahwism, though perhaps at a later period,[2] the passage reads as follows in the RSV.

> In that day there will be five cities in the land of Egypt which speak the language of Canaan and swear allegiance to the Lord of hosts. One of these will be called the City of the Sun.

Two aspects of this verse are relevant for the present purposes[3]: a textual problem relating to the name of the Egyptian city of Yahweh-worshippers, and the meaning of that name within the context of this

---

1. Pettinato, 'Is. 2,7', pp. 24-25. In support of his meaning '*scrigno*', Pettinato cites Deut. 32.34, archaeological evidence from synagogues (including the one at Beth Alpha) in which a box contains the law, and from Beth-shan in which items including three gods were found in a model of a similar kind of box. However, the word '*ōṣᵉrôt* occurs in 2 Kgs 20.13 (= Isa. 39.2) and refers there to 'storehouses' in which were kept silver and gold, clearly material wealth.

2. The passage is generally regarded as late on the grounds that it seems conscious of the establishment of Jewish colonies in the period of the diaspora (most notably Leontopolis in the nome of Heliopolis and where the Zadokite priest Onias erected a temple). For an evaluation critical of this interpretation, however, see later in this section.

3. A case for the relevance of this verse vis-à-vis solar Yahwism has been made already by Stähli (*Solare Elemente*, p. 45), who nonetheless follows a very different line of argumentation from that chosen here. Stähli uses both the variant readings 'city of righteousness' (LXX) and 'city of the sun' (MT [*sic*. according to most MSS]) as evidence in support of a connection between Hebrew 'righteousness' and Yahweh on the one hand and Egyptian 'Maat' and Re on the other hand. To Stähli, a solar affinity of Hebrew *ṣedeq*, 'righteousness (as world order)', can be deduced here by the LXX's rendition of MT 'sun' as 'righteousness', the latter of which is a term used in MT of Isa. 1.26 to describe Jerusalem, the 'city of righteousness'.

passage. These difficulties may be combined and examined under four possible options for the original form of the name of the city: (1) that the name was 'city of destruction'; (2) that the name was 'city of righteousness'; (3) that the name was 'City of the Sun' in the sense that it referred to Heliopolis; and (4) that the name was 'city of the sun' in the sense that it was a general designation that aptly characterized the new city of Yahweh of Hosts. I intend to argue in favour of the fourth option which has been noted by others in the past but which has not been embraced because of the problem of reconciling the name chosen for the city of Yahweh, 'city of the sun', with the character of Yahweh worship itself. The merits and shortcomings of each option are noted briefly.

Although attested by the M T , Syriac, Targum, Aquila and Theodotion, the reading *'îr haheres*, 'city of destruction', makes no sense in the present context of future gains and widespread salvation[1] and is an excellent candidate as a pejorative substitute for an earlier reading.[2] This reading may be safely overlooked as virtually all modern commentators and not a few translation committees have done.

The textual witness for 'city of righteousness', the LXX, is weak here but the reading suits the context. Elsewhere in Isaiah Jerusalem itself is called the 'city of righteousness',[3] and from this comparison the prophecy might be judged to predict the establishment of an 'Egyptian Jerusalem'.[4] If this was the original reading, that the

1.   The only way to make sense of the reference in context is to take *heres* to denote 'destruction' (of pagan altars and the like) (so, for example, F. Delitzsch, *Isaiah* [repr.; Grand Rapids: Eerdmans, n.d.], p. 364), but there is nothing in the context to warrant such an interpretation. The witness of a few MSS to *'îr herem*, 'city devoted (to destruction)' can also be dismissed on these contextual grounds; cf. G.B. Gray, *The Book of Isaiah I–XXVII* (ICC; Edinburgh: T. & T. Clarke, 1912), pp. 335-36.

2.   For example, Gray (*Isaiah*, I–XXVII, p. 336) notes that since it is clear from Josephus that these verses were understood to refer to the temple at Leontopolis and also clear that Palestinian Jews were opposed to the temple, it is likely that 'destruction' reflects this negative attitude towards the temple. (On Josephus, Leontopolis and the relevant passages in Isaiah, see Hayward, 'Leontopolis', pp. 438-41.)

3   Isa. 1.26.

4.   Another point cited in favour of 'city of righteousness' was that it was perhaps *originally* a reference to the Jewish temple at Leontopolis. But, as J.N. Oswalt (*The Book of Isaiah, Chapters 1–39* [NICOT; Grand Rapids: Eerdmans, 1986], p. 378) notes, 'the development of the temple at Leontopolis is so

Jerusalem of Egypt was at a later stage emended to 'city of the sun' might suggest that this redactor had a solar understanding of the character of Jerusalem,[1] but neither this nor the originality of 'city of righteousness' is certain.

In favour of the reading *'îr haheres*, 'city of the sun', are some manuscripts of the MT, Targum (which combines this reading with 'city of destruction'[2]), Jerome,[3] Symmachus[4] and also 1 QIsa[a]. The combined character of these witnesses is strong, accounting for its current popularity. Problems arise, however, with a common deduction based on this reading, namely that 'city of the sun' here refers to Heliopolis. Among the difficulties with this deduction are the following. (1) Only here is Heliopolis referred to in this way; elsewhere in the Old Testament it is called 'Beth-shemesh',[5] 'On'[6] or 'Aven',[7] the latter two of which are Hebrew renditions of Egyptian Heliopolis. (2) A specific place name, whether Heliopolis or another, does not seem likely in this passage;[8] more specifically, it does not make sense in this predictive context for there to be an announcement that a place 'will be called' by a name by which it has been known since Early Dynastic times.[9]

late that there is no time for the whole process to have taken place and for the *heres* to have ended up already in 1 QIsa[a] by 100 BC'. In other words, 'city of righteousness' as a reference to the temple at Leontopolis properly belongs to the history of the interpretation of the passage.

1.	If 'sun' were a mere geographical term designating the land of the sun, Egypt, or the city of the sun, Heliopolis (or even Leontopolis), there would be no reason for emending the text further to 'destruction', especially in this unoffensive context of a bold triumph of the worship of Yahweh over that of Re.

2.	The Targum reads *qrt'byt šmš d'tyd' lmhrb*, 'city of Beth-shemesh which is about to be destroyed'.

3.	The text here reads *civitas solas*.

4.	(*Polis*) *hēliou*.

5.	Jer. 43.13. Targum 'Beth-shemesh' suggests perhaps identification with Heliopolis; if so, it is an interpretation of the text nonetheless.

6.	Gen. 41.45, 50; 46.20.

7.	Ezek. 30.17.

8.	Gray (*Isaiah I–XXVII*, p. 334) makes a similar point: 'It must not be merely the actual name of some city, insignificant in the context and serving merely to identify the city intended'.

9.	There is no apparent significance for what might be argued to be an intentional variation of the name Heliopolis.

In my judgment the reading 'city of the sun' is most likely the original form of the name, but the interpretation that it is a known place name should be rejected. A more plausible alternative in light of the context is that the name is a new name that aptly characterizes the nature of that city as a place in which Yahweh of Hosts would be worshipped. Although logical, the interpretation poses a problem for a traditional understanding of the character of that Yahwistic city. A case in point is the following discussion by G.B. Gray:

> If... we suppose that *'yr hhrs* means, indeed, *city of the sun*, but was not used here as a mere translation of the Egyptian name of the nome, what quality of the city was it intended to express? Certainly not that it was to be a city distinguished by the worship of the sun! Yet this would be the obvious force of the phrase (cp. *'yr* YHWH, 60:14). Unless some more suitable meaning can be discovered... this interpretation must be dismissed.[1]

The difficulty that led Gray to reject this interpretation, namely that a place of Yahweh worship is not likely to be described in solar terms, is of course easy to reconcile with the thesis of this book. Moreover, even apart from the evidence adduced in this study in favour of the presence of solar Yahwism, a number of factors lend additional force to the textual reading 'city of the sun' with its face-value solar connotation. (1) The context of the parallel with 'city of Yahweh' in Isa. 60.14 suggests that the title is used in 19.18 to describe the condition of a restored city in which Yahweh will be worshipped. (2) The most plausible alternative, *'îr haṣṣedeq*, is attested only in the LXX, which is quite free and it tends to paraphrase in Isaiah. (3) As the most controversial of all readings, 'city of the sun' accounts best for the numerous textual variants, many of which appear to have arisen from theological considerations. (4) As an original reading, *ḥeres*, 'sun', accounts for the presence later of what seem to be two opposite evaluations: 'righteousness' and 'destruction'. In sum, the best candidate for the original reading of Isa. 19.18 is 'city of the sun', the prophet's way of describing a city that would be characterized by the worship of 'Yahweh of Hosts'.

Finally, the implications of the interpretation may be summarized briefly. First, since the place is to be called 'city of the sun' on the day in which linguistic and religious gains will be made in that city by

1. Gray, *Isaiah I–XXVII*, p. 336.

worshippers of Yahweh,[1] it is logical to conclude with Gray that 'the name must be of favourable import'.[2] Secondly, presumably *haḥeres*, 'the sun', was an apt description of the deity who was worshipped there (that is, *yhwh ṣᵉbā'ôt*). Moreover, that 'sun' would be used of the deity in this context might suggest that the worship of Yahweh as sun was prevalent among worshippers of Yahweh in Egypt (similar forms of integration are attested at Elephantine for example). Finally, as might be expected, the usage of the expression was almost certainly controversial, resulting in a negative reaction evident in the MT (which rendered the place 'city of destruction') and what in the LXX (which rendered the town 'city of righteousness') may be understood variously as a toning down of the explicitly solar reference, as an expression of outright favour towards it, or as an identification of it with either Jerusalem (cf. Isa. 1.26) or a specific place in Egypt such as Leontopolis—or a combination of one or more of these options. Finally, that the passage cannot be dated with certainty leaves room for what can only be speculation concerning the date of the reference to 'city of the sun', which nonetheless might be earlier than is often supposed.[3]

---

1. It is not completely clear whether these worshippers are Egyptian proselytes or Jews.

2. Gray, *Isaiah I-XXVII*, p. 334.

3. Each of the five statements in vv. 16-25 beginning with 'in that day' are difficult to date and v. 18 alone is almost impossible to date. Though perhaps originating from within an oppressed minority within Egypt with apocalyptic expectations, as some suggest, vv. 16-25 seem quite unlikely as describing the actual setting of the diaspora community. The impression given by these verses is not of scattered Jewish elements within Egypt, but of Egypt living in dread of a Judah that has the upper hand, having made remarkable inroads into Egypt. Thus, the entire population of these cities speak Hebrew (less likely Aramaic) (v. 18); Egypt will cry to Yahweh for help and receive a saviour who will bring deliverance (v. 20); and the Egyptians, having received a revelation, will themselves worship Yahweh (v. 21). In fact, then, the passage describes a setting fulfilled at no time, and if produced by an oppressed minority within Egypt, this minority could have existed at any time from the time of Solomon onwards, including the eighth century. (On Jewish elements in Egypt at various times, see conveniently Watts, *Isaiah 1-33*, p. 259.) Thus, although the verse cannot be dated, as a designation of a centre of Yahwism, the phrase 'city of the sun' would not be surprising in the late eighth century.

Isaiah 40–66

Some scholars such as J. Morgenstern and H.-P. Stähli have argued for the presence of solar elements in one or more passages within Isaiah 40–66.[1] The most explicit usage of solar language with reference to Yahweh in this corpus is Isa. 60.1-3.[2] Addressed to Jerusalem, the passage reads as follows:

> 1 Arise, shine, for your light has dawned,
> And the glory of the Lord has shone upon you;
> 2 For, lo, darkness[3] will cover the earth,
> Thick cloud the peoples;
> But upon you Yahweh will shine,
> His glory will be seen over you.
> 3 And the nations shall walk to your light
> And kings to the brightness of your shining.

That Yahweh and his glory are described with the imagery of the sun in this poetic passage is unmistakable.[4]

The passage has been interpreted variously by advocates of solar Yahwism. Thus, according to H.-P. Stähli, this passage is a poetic example of what Schnutenhaus argued in the case of theophoric personal names, namely an instance of Yahweh replacing the sun god as the subject of the verb *zāraḥ*, 'shine'.[5] Moreover, although

---

1. For example, Morgenstern ('Biblical Theophanies [Part 2]', p. 47) states regarding Isa. 66.15 in which there is mention of a chariot and reference to the deity being accompanied by fire, 'It is not at all improbable that at the bottom of the prophet's figure lies the conscious picture of a sun-god coming from the east in his bright chariot, accompanied by fire and other similar phenomena'. On Stähli's contribution, see later in this section.

2. The passage is commonly regarded as having come from an early post-exilic prophet whose choice of phraseology here and elsewhere in the chapter shows direct indebtedness to so-called Second Isaiah (for example, G. Fohrer, *Das Buch Jesaja*. III. *Kapitel 40–66* [Zürich: Zwingli Verlag, 1964], pp. 226-27) and whose eschatological notions of Zion find similar expression in Isa. 2.2-4 (on which see further, G. von Rad, 'The City on the Hill', in *The Problem of the Hexateuch and Other Essays* [London: SCM Press, 1984], pp. 232-42).

3. Following most commentators, I consider the article on *ḥōšek*, 'darkness', in MT to be due to dittography (cf. the preceding *hinnê*, 'lo').

4. This is suggested by the use of the verb *bw'* together with *zrḥ* (used most commonly with reference to the sun), translated respectively, for example, by JPSV as 'shine' and 'dawned'; cf. also vv. 19-20.

5. Stähli, *Solare Elemente*, p. 40.

Schnutenhaus did not conclude that a solar understanding of Yahweh is implied by this substitution, Stähli makes this conclusion, citing Ps. 84.12 [11] in which Yahweh is called 'sun'. To Stähli, then, the passage is a clear case of 'Yahweh as sun'.[1]

To evaluate, because the language of Yahweh as sun in Isa. 60.1-3 is poetic and thus perhaps merely figurative, this passage cannot be used convincingly as evidence in a case for solar Yahwism. Moreover, as others have noted, this passage should not be considered without reference to Isa. 58.8, 10 which also employs solar language but with no clear indication there either that the language is more than merely figurative:[2]

> 8 Then shall your light burst forth as the dawn,
> Your healing spring up quickly;
> Your righteousness shall go before you,
> The glory of the Lord shall be your rear guard.
> 9 Then, when you call, Yahweh will answer;
> When you cry, he will say, 'Here I am'
> If you banish from your midst the yoke,
> Pointing the finger and speaking evil,
> 10 If you pour yourself out for the hungry
> And satisfy the life of the afflicted,
> Then your light will shine in the darkness
> And your gloom be as noon-time.

This is not to suggest, however, that the language of Yahweh as sun is not striking in Isa. 60.1-3; it clearly is. Nevertheless, the extent to which this solar language *may* be suggestive of a solar understanding of Yahweh depends entirely on the extent to which a case can be made on other grounds for a concrete understanding of Yahweh as sun within the cult. Thus, because I believe that a fairly solid case can be made on other grounds, I am inclined to think that the poetic imagery is probably particularly appropriate in this context. As evidence in itself for an understanding of Yahweh as sun, however, Isa. 60.1-3 is best not included, at least not without some indication of its relevance beyond the use of poetic 'solar' language for Yahweh.

---

1. Stähli, *Solare Elemente*, pp. 40-42. On this verse and its (uncertain) contribution to a solar understanding of Yahweh, see the discussion of Psalms later in this chapter.

2. In an early study Morgenstern acknowledged with respect to Isa. 58.8 that 'the thought is highly figurative' ('Biblical Theophanies [Part 2]', p. 47).

Such further indication of the relevance of Isa. 60.1-3 to solar Yahwism is offered by J. Morgenstern, according to whom the proper setting of the passage is the equinoctial New Year's Day of the solar calendar, inaugurated at the time of Solomon.[1] According to Morgenstern, that *zārah*, '"to rise (like the sun)"', is used with reference to the *kᵉbôd yhwh*, '"radiance of Yahweh"', can only mean an equinoctial setting for v. 1. Further, Morgenstern avers that on this occasion the (solar) 'glory' (*kābôd*) entered the temple court through the eastern gate at dawn, and made its way through the temple doors, down the axis of the temple, and into the Holy of Holies, thereby signifying the coming of Yahweh to reside in his temple for another year.[2] Moreover, in view of the fact that the temple had lain in ruins for years, the setting of this passage was 'the coming of the Light, of "the radiance of Yahweh," upon the very New Year's Day upon which...the second Temple was dedicated, the New Year's Day of 516 BCE. This much is certain'.[3]

Regarding Morgenstern's case for an equinoctial setting for this passage, there is some circularity in his argument and not a little that fails to carry conviction on other grounds as well.[4] In view of the

1. J. Morgenstern, 'Two Prophecies from 520–516 BC', *HUCA* 22 (1949), pp. 365-431, esp. pp. 383-400. For Morgenstern's early understanding of this passage in light of his extensive study of the usage of the expression *kᵉbôd yhwh*, see his 'Biblical Theophanies', *ZA* 28 (1914), pp. 5-60.

2. Morgenstern, 'Two Prophecies', p. 388; cf. *idem*, 'The Gates of Righteousness', *HUCA* 6 (1929), pp. 1-37. A problem with this view of course is that the fleeting moment at which time the sun allegedly enters the Holy of Holies is not a particularly apt sign of Yahweh's decision to reside in the Temple for a whole year. The criticism, however, is not sufficiently weighty to rule out the theory in general with which I have some sympathy, though based upon evidence discussed elsewhere in this book.

3. Morgenstern, 'Two Prophecies', p. 390.

4. Morgenstern's attempt to demonstrate from the context a setting on the occasion of the autumnal equinox must be judged unsuccessful. For example, he tries to elucidate the possible relevance of Isa. 60.2 first in light of Hag. 1.7-8 (which he places after Hag. 1.9-11 and assigns on dubious grounds also to have a setting at the autumnal equinox) ('Two Prophecies', pp. 390-91), secondly on political grounds (pp. 391-92), and thirdly on spiritual grounds (p. 392). Moreover, he makes no mention of v. 4 until the end of his discussion at which time he somewhat arbitrarily assigns it alone in Isaiah 60 A (vv. 1-7) to a later Isaiah 60 B (vv. 7-22) ('Two Prophecies', p. 400 n. 70). Further, as von Rad notes ('City on

former of these difficulties, an equinoctial setting will probably carry
weight only for those who accept his understanding of what transpired
on that occasion.

Although Morgenstern's own case for an equinoctial setting may be
judged inadequate, other scholars have used different evidence to
arrive at a similar conclusion, namely that the setting of Isa. 60.1-3 is
the Feast of Booths. Thus, for example, Volz argues that although
'light' is often used elsewhere of salvation (*Heil*), it is associated in
this song specifically with the New Year festival, the Feast of Booths,
and in particular with its first ceremonial act which involved celebration with light.[1] Or again, for example, von Rad argues that Isaiah 60
is related to several passages, most notably Isa. 2.2-4[2] to which he
assigns a setting at the Feast of Booths,[3] and Zechariah 14 to which the
passage itself assigns the same setting (cf. v. 16).[4] Moreover, perhaps
of some help in determining whether the imagery of light in Isaiah 60
has a reflex in the cult, although no reference is made to light in Isa.
2.2-4 with which our passage is akin, appended to the Isaiah passage
and probably related to it is the summons to Israel: 'Come, O house of
Jacob, let us walk in the light of the Lord'.[5]

To evaluate, because of the possibility that solar language in Isa.
60.1-3 is merely figurative in this poetic context, the passage should
not be considered as solid evidence for solar Yahwism in ancient
Israel. The passage is nonetheless suggestive, particularly in view of a

the Hill', p. 237), it seems clear from v. 13 that the temple has yet to be rebuilt.
Finally and more generally, Morgenstern's discussion does not give sufficient
attention to the eschatological dimensions of the passage.

1. P. Volz, *Jesaja II* (KAT; Leipzig: A. Deichertsche Verlagsbuchhandlung,
1932), p. 244. Volz's evidence is admittedly slim. He points specifically to the
correspondence between the reference to light and the initial rite in the ceremony
involving light, and to that between the feast as a time of looking to a new year and
the theme of creation in v. 2. He also cites Amos 5.18 which mentions the Day of
the Lord (which he understands to refer to the Feast of Booths) as, contrary to
expectation, a day of darkness and not light.

2. Von Rad, 'City on the Hill', p. 237.

3. Von Rad, 'City on the Hill', pp. 234-35.

4. Von Rad, 'City on the Hill', p. 241. On Zech. 14, see later in this chapter.

5. As von Rad notes ('City on the Hill', p. 242 n. 18), the verse was probably
appended to compensate for the lack of mention of a role for Israel in the
eschatological event. Whatever the reason may have been, an appeal to Israelite
pilgrims to walk in the 'light of the Lord' in this setting is certainly striking.

possible setting at the Feast of Booths and in view of evidence adduced elsewhere for relatively concrete indications of a link between Yahweh and the sun within the context of the royal Jerusalem establishment.[1]

Also relevant to the question of Yahweh and the sun in Isaiah 40–66 is another passage in Isaiah 60 that mentions the sun as well as moon:

> 19 No longer shall the sun be for you a light by day,
> Nor the brightness of the moon [by night][2] give light for you;
> For Yahweh shall be for you an eternal light,
> Your God shall be your splendour.
> 20 No longer shall your sun set,
> Nor your moon retract;
> For Yahweh will be an eternal light for you,
> And your days of mourning shall be completed.

According to Stähli, this passage is a case in which the sun has been subordinated to the cult of Yahweh.[3] It may be questioned, however, whether the claim of 'subordination' is appropriate in the same context which, according to Stähli, contains a case of 'Yahweh as sun' (that is, Isa. 60.1-3). To be sure, however, a problem is posed by the apparent discontinuity between Yahweh and the sun evident in Yahweh's replacement of sun here and the portrait of continuity (even if merely figurative) implied in Isa. 60.1-3. If Stähli's explanation of Isa. 60.19-20 is not accepted, the issue remains how to account for the apparent discontinuity between Yahweh and the sun in this passage.

At first, this passage and others in which Yahweh replaces the sun and moon do appear to pose a problem for my thesis that Yahweh and the sun were closely associated or even identified. The problem, however, is more apparent than real as the following points demonstrate. First, the notion itself that Yahweh will 'fill in' for the sun in Isa. 60.19-20 presupposes what it at first appears to deny, namely that there must have been some kind of continuity between the sun and Yahweh. Secondly, although Yahweh and the sun are spoken of as separate entities, this does nothing to discredit the notion of possible

---

1. As Fohrer points out in his discussion of Isa. 60, however, though indebted to the language of second Isaiah, trito-Isaiah often develops this language according to his own outlook.
2. So LXX, 1 QIsa[a], and Targum.
3. Stähli, *Solare Elemente*, pp. 17-23, esp. pp. 22-23.

continuity for, as we have seen already, solar cults normally distinguish between their sun god and the physical form of the sun itself. Thirdly, that some form of continuity between the sun and Yahweh underlies the imagery in Isa. 60.19-20 may be implied through the use of solar imagery for Yahweh earlier in this same context (Isa. 60.1-3) and also, for example, in Isa. 30.26, a passage akin to 60.9-12 and one in which the healing action of Yahweh is equated with a 'sublime sun':

> And the light of the sun shall become sevenfold, like the light of the seven days, when the Lord binds up his people's wounds and heals the injuries it has suffered.

Fourthly, it is important to consider the eschatological context of passages in which Yahweh replaces the sun. It is of course in the very nature of these passages to describe the end time as far superior to what can be experienced in the present, which is bound by the limitations and realities of the natural order. In the case of the sun as a symbol of Yahweh in ancient Israel, it was no doubt a constant frustration that so meaningful an icon was nonetheless limited by natural phenomena such as its apparent disappearance and replacement by the moon at night. Far from being inconsistent with the notion that Yahweh was understood in solar terms, then, passages that point to a future day in which Yahweh will replace the sun simply look forward to a time when the limitations of the sun as a symbol of Yahweh will be replaced by the appearance of Yahweh himself as a kind of 'sublime sun'.

The significance of this eschatological dimension for the understanding of Yahweh as sun in Isaiah 60 illustrates the continuity that is to be seen between the different portraits of Yahweh as sun in the chapter. Both passages point to the end time which is new and improved. In the former passage (Isa. 60.1-3) emphasis falls primarily upon Zion which in an improved condition becomes a gathering place for the wealth of the nations and which shines with radiant light, light which is a reflection of the Lord who, as the sun, 'dawns' and shines upon the city. In the latter passage (Isa. 60.19-20) emphasis clearly falls upon the Lord himself, and that which is new and improved is thus related to God as light. In the new and improved eschaton the natural limitations of the sun, which shines only in the day and which has the moon 'fill in' at night, will be replaced by God himself, whose radiant and glorious light will shine eternally. In sum then, Yahweh as sun in Isa. 60.1-3 shines upon Zion whose glory reflects the light of Yahweh, and in vv. 19-20 Yahweh, sun sublime, shines not just for a time but for eternity.[1]

Jeremiah
Specific mention of sun worship is limited to one passage in Jeremiah, 8.1-3.[2] The passage, a judgment oracle and one of several passages appended to the Temple Sermon, 7.1-5,[3] reads as follows:

> 1 At that time, says the Lord, they will bring out the bones of the kings of Judah and the bones of its princes and the bones of the priests and the bones of the prophets and the bones of the residents from their graves. 2 And they shall spread them before the sun and the moon and all the Host of Heaven which they have loved and which they have served and which they have gone after and which they have pursued and which they have worshipped; they shall not be gathered or buried but be as dung on the face of the ground. 3 Death will be chosen over life from the remnant remaining from this evil family in all the places (remaining)[4] where I have cast them, says the Lord of Hosts.

The first issue concerns the date of the passage. Though assigned to the exilic period by Holladay and others, the passage is perhaps best dated to the end of the monarchy, as Bright and Wilson have argued.[5]

---

1. Compare also Zech. 14.6c-7 in which the notion of eternal day is in complete harmony with the understanding of Yahweh as sun in Zech. 14.3-6b.

2. An indirect reference to sun worship is Jer. 19.13 which mentions the worship of the Host of Heaven, but which adds little new information to the discussion.

Another possible indirect reference to the sun deity in Jeremiah has been suggested by M. Dahood ('La Regina del Cielo in Geremia', *RivB* 8 [1960], pp. 166-68). Dahood argues that the queen of heaven, mentioned several times in Jeremiah (7.18, 44.17-19, 25), should be identified with the sun goddess Shapash, but this seems unlikely in view of the clear identification of Akkadian *šarrat šamē*, 'queen of heaven', and Ishtar. (See further, W.L. Holladay *Jeremiah 1* [Hermeneia; Philadelphia: Fortress Press, 1986], pp. 254-55 and the bibliography cited there.)

3. See, for example, T.W. Overholt, 'Jeremiah', in J.L. Mays (ed.), *Harper's Bible Commentary* (San Francisco: Harper & Row, 1988), p. 615; E.W. Nicholson, *Preaching to the Exiles* (Oxford: Basil Blackwell, 1970), p. 68.

4. The word is lacking in LXX and Syriac and should probably be regarded as a case of dittography.

5. J. Bright (*Jeremiah* [AB, 21; New York: Doubleday, 1965], p. 59) dates the

In favour of their claim, if Holladay's impressive case in support of Keunen's judgment that ch. 19 is a narrative rendition of 7.30-34 is correct and that this narrative rendition is associated with Baruch,[1] then 8.1-3 must have been appended to 7.30-34 at an early period, since its position after 7.30-34 is presupposed in 19.13. Moreover, although Holladay's point that the reference here to the triad 'sun, moon and stars' is found elsewhere only in passages suspected of being exilic insertions into their surrounding material[2] is legitimate, passages like Ezek. 8.16-18, which point to the presence of solar Yahwism at a late date, suggest that the 'hard-line' prohibition of Jer. 8.1-3 is better dated to the late pre-exilic period when a particularly pungent Deuteronomistic theology was in vogue.[3]

Secondly, in light of the inference of some that this passage refers to idolatrous elements that are foreign to Israel,[4] it is worth underscoring the clear presence of Deuteronomistic elements in these verses.[5] Jer. 8.1-3 thus does not offer an outlook on sun worship independent of Deuteronomistic theology and is an example of the abhorrence which this theology had for worship that is directed towards (even Yahwistic heavenly) objects.

Thirdly, regarding the similarity between Jeremiah and Josiah with respect to solar Yahwism, the reconstruction of Wilson seems helpful,

---

passage to some time prior to 586 BCE; Wilson (*Prophecy and Society*, p. 245) considers 7.1–8.3 to be a 'fair representation of Jeremiah's message during the reign of Jehoiakim'.

1.   Holladay, *Jeremiah 1*, pp. 536-37.

2.   Holladay, *Jeremiah 1*, p. 271.

3.   I follow here R.R. Wilson's understanding of the relationship between the prophetic ministry of Jeremiah and the reform of Josiah (*Prophecy and Society*, pp. 242-51). See later in this section.

4.   There is no reason from the text to regard the idolatry as foreign. Rather, that the worship of the sun, moon, stars and Host of Heaven was Yahwistic makes good sense in light of the claim that Judaean royalty, priests, prophets and residents alike were involved in this form of worship.

5.   Although in light of the work of such scholars as Weippert and Nicholson, Deuteronomistic material (what Mowinckel in his classic construal called C material) can no longer be arbitrarily or automatically assigned to Deuteronomistic editors without taking seriously also the relationship of this same material to other parts of Jeremiah, that a relationship between 8.1-3 and Deuteronomic theology nonetheless exists is clear. (On the issue of Deuteronomistic editing in Jeremiah, see, for example, Wilson, *Prophecy and Society*, pp. 231-33.)

namely, that perhaps subsequent to the re-introduction into the Jerusalem establishment of the Anathoth priesthood, Deuteronomistic theology mellowed to the point where it eventually came to differ significantly from the older orthodox Deuteronomistic theology of Josiah and of Jeremiah who stood outside of the royal Jerusalemite establishment.[1]

Also relevant to Jer. 8.1-3 is the significance of the mention of disinterment in the passage. More helpful for understanding the reference to disinterment than either the recognition of irony in the exposure of the dead to the astral bodies once worshipped (as is probable) or the suggestion of grave robbery as a motive for the disinterment (as seems unlikely) are Assyrian parallels noted by M. Cogan.[2] According to Cogan, 'The prophet pictured YHWH's punishment of Jerusalem in terms of an earthly overlord punishing his disloyal subjects, by carrying out, to the letter, the sanctions of their broken oaths'.[3] Particularly noteworthy is the account of the desecration of the royal cemetery of Susa during the eighth campaign of Ashurbanipal:

> The tombs of their former and latter kings, (who had) not revered Ashur and Ishtar, my lords, (who had) harassed my royal ancestors, I (Ashurbanipal) ravaged, tore down and laid open to the sun. Their bones I carried off to Assyria, thus imposing restlessness upon their spirits, and depriving them of food offerings and libations.[4]

The reference to the sun in the Neo-Assyrian parallel reminds the reader that the prophet might have been adding an extra element of irony through his awareness of the role of Shamash as god of justice and the one before whom treaties were often made. Perhaps, too, irony lay in the fact that the sun was the chief means by which corpses left unburied underwent decay, thereby bringing on the horror of

---

1. Wilson, *Prophecy and Society*, pp. 242-51.

2. M. Cogan, 'A Note on Disinterment in Jeremiah', in I.D. Passow and S.T. Lachs (eds.), *Gratz College Anniversary Volume* (Philadelphia: Gratz College, 1971), pp. 29-34.

3. Cogan, 'A Note on Disinterment', p. 32.

4. The translation follows Cogan, 'Note on Disinterment', p. 30, where a brief discussion can also be found. For the text, see M. Streck, *Assurbanipal und die letzten assyrischen Könige bis zum Untergange Nineveh's* (Vorderasiatische Bibliothek, 7; Leipzig: Hinrichs, 1916), 54.70-76.

having one's bones scattered by devouring beasts and birds[1] (although in this instance the disintered were probably little more than bones). In any case, the extended elaboration, 'which they have loved and which they have served and after which they have gone and which they have pursued and which they have worshipped', clearly underlines the disdain that Jeremiah had for the worship of the sun and other astral bodies, just as the further statement, 'they shall not be gathered or buried, but be as dung on the face of the ground', emphasizes the horror that befell the disintered whose bones lay strewn about, thereby preventing anyone from meeting their post-mortem needs.[2]

On the basis of this passage, then, it appears that Jeremiah shared the late Deuteronomistic outlook of disdain towards the worship of the 'sun, moon and all the Host of Heaven' by followers of Yahweh. The worship of these objects was tantamount to idolatry and was thus a breach of Israel's covenant obligations for which a suitable punishment was offered.

Zephaniah

The book of Zephaniah provides important insight into the condition of Judah and the royal court of Jerusalem during the last decades of the southern kingdom, likely during the reign of Josiah (cf. 1.1). It is of particular interest to this discussion because the prophet seems to have had links with both Deuteronomistic theology and the royal Jerusalemite establishment.[3] Moreover, reference is made to the worship of the 'Host of Heaven' which included the worship of the sun. The pertinent passage, Zeph. 1.4-6, reads as follows in the MT:

> 4 I will stretch out my hand over Judah,
> And I will uproot from this place the remnant of Baal,
> And the name of the idol-priests along with the priests,
> 5 And those who bow down upon the roofs to the Host of Heaven,
> And those who bow down, who swear,[4] to the Lord,

---

1. Cf. Jer. 7.33; 2 Sam. 21.10-14.
2. Cf. Cogan, 'Note on Disinterment', p. 30.
3. See the discussion of Wilson, *Prophecy and Society*, pp. 379-82.
4. Several commentators suggest that this first occurrence of *hannišbā'îm*, 'swear', should be omitted because *hannišbā'îm*, 'swear to', is not attested elsewhere. (This is noted by G.C. Heider, *The Cult of Molek: A Reassessment* [JSOTSup, 43; Sheffield: JSOT Press, 1985], p. 333 n. 654.)

And who swear by *malkām*,
6 And those who have turned back from following the Lord,
And who have not inquired of the Lord,
And not sought Him.

According to this passage, the worship of the Host of Heaven was prevalent in Judah and among the inhabitants of Jerusalem at the time of the prophet, and took place on the 'roofs'.

Almost as apparent as what the passage states about the worship of the Host of Heaven is a tension concerning the Host's nature. This tension is evident on two counts. First, reminiscent of the ambiguity noted earlier between idol-priests and Yahwistic priests in 2 Kgs 23.5 is the mention in Zeph. 1.4 of both *kᵉmārîm*, 'idol-priests' (often presumed to be 'foreign') and *kōhᵃnîm*, 'priests' (the normal word for Yahwistic priests). Not surprisingly, here too there is some uncertainty about whether the priests are priests of Yahweh or of 'heathen gods'.[1] And here too, as with the priests in 2 Kgs 23.5, an explanation is readily apparent: the priests were involved in a form of worship that was both Yahwistic and, from the writer's perspective, 'heathen'.

A second factor which points to a tension regarding the Host of Heaven vis-à-vis Yahweh is this: the text places in juxtaposition the worship of Yahweh and the worship of the Host of Heaven (v. 5). Since the worship of Yahweh is commendable in itself, the prophet must be objecting to a specific form of Yahweh worship that was associated with veneration of the Host of Heaven (and the worship of the enigmatic *malkām*, about which more will be said shortly).[2] Here, then, is further clear textual support for the view that the worship of the Host of Heaven (including the sun) was inextricably associated with the worship of Yahweh.[3]

1. Cf. JPSV footnote: '*kemarim*, a term used only of priests of heathen gods'.
2. In other words, if not indistinguishable from the worship of the Host of Heaven, why else would the worship of Yahweh, certainly commendable in itself, be mentioned in this judgment?
3. That Yahweh was included in the worship of the Host of Heaven may also be inferred from the parallel grammatical construction:

> *wᵉ'et hammištahhᵃwîm 'al haggaggôt liṣᵉbā' haššāmāyîm*
> *wᵉ'et hammištahhᵃwîm la YHWH*

> Those who bow down upon the roofs the Host of Heaven,
> And those who bow down to Yahweh . . .

At this point it might be objected that the worship of Yahweh is mentioned also in close association with *mlkm*, traditionally understood to be a foreign (Ammonite) deity, and that, for my argument to hold, Yahweh must be associated not only with veneration of the Host of Heaven but also with the worship of the deity *mlkm*. An appropriate response to the objection, however, is to consider the possible meanings of *mlkm*.

The problem with *mlkm* lies in a tension between the vocalization of MT, *malkām*, 'their king', and the context which requires that *mlkm* refer not to a monarch but to a deity.[1] Plausible explanations offered to date for the referent of *mlkm* include the following: Baal (referred to in v. 5a and sometimes referred to as a 'king'); Milcom (cf. 1 Kgs 11.7, 33); or a wordplay based on the relationship between the name of the god Molek and the root *mlk*, 'to rule as king', from which Molek's name is derived.[2]

A new solution to the impasse that is remarkably straightforward can be found by regarding MT *malkām*, 'their king', as original and as a reference not to an earthly king or to Baal, but to Yahweh who was, after all, 'their king' (that is, the king of these [Yahwistic] worshippers). In favour of the suggestion is the context; Yahweh is mentioned in the immediately preceding context and also many times in the context which immediately follows (vv. 5b, 6a, 6b, 6c, 7a, etc.) Moreover, that the epithet 'king' should be applied to Yahweh in a context which is suggestive of a solar understanding of the deity can hardly be judged surprising in light of the common ancient Near Eastern understanding of the king as 'sun', a (royal) title applied to Yahweh in Ps. 84.12 [11],[3] and in light of the widespread usage of *melek*, 'king' as a title of *yhwh ṣᵉbā'ôt*, 'Yahweh of Hosts'.[4] Further, Yahweh is in fact explicitly referred to as 'king' elsewhere in Zephaniah; in 3.15 we read, *melek yiśrā'ēl yhwh bᵉqirbēk*, 'The King

---

1. The NASB, normally loyal to the MT, reads Milcom. JPSV reads Malcam, but equates the figure with Milcom.

2. For the last option and a clear discussion of the other alternatives mentioned, see Heider, *Cult of Molek*, pp. 332-34.

3. See my discussion of Ps. 84.12 [11] later in this chapter.

4. On the royal nature of the epithet 'Yahweh of Hosts', see the works of Mettinger cited earlier. On the use of *melek*, 'king' in passages specifically suggestive of a solar character for Yahweh of Hosts, see Ps. 24.7, 8, 9, 10; Zech. 14.16 (cf. v. 9). (On both of these passages, see later in this study.)

of Israel, Yahweh, is in your midst'.[1] Contrary to what is traditionally thought, then, *malkām* has been changed secondarily to the name of a foreign deity and not the other way around. The theological problem thus lies not with the variants but with the witness of MT that the 'king' of the worshippers of the Host of Heaven was Yahweh (v. 5; cf. 3.15). To summarize consideration of Zeph. 1.5, this single verse does not refer to three separate cults—Host of Heaven, Yahweh and Milcom—but to one: the Host of Heaven, including its most notable member, 'Yahweh', called 'king' by these Yahwists.[2]

Finally, in light of the Deuteronomistic dictum that one is not to worship Yahweh by facing in the direction of the sun but in the direction of the temple (1 Kings 8), it is at least worth mentioning that in the very next stich, Zeph. 1.6a, the prophet describes those who worship Yahweh incorrectly with possible reference to their orientation, *hann^{e}sôgîm mē'ah^{a}rê yhwh*, literally, 'those who have turned back from after the Lord', an expression used not only figuratively for proving to be faithless but literally for 'turning back'.[3] Thus understood, it is possible (but by no means certain) that both v. 5 and v. 6 describe the offensive manner in which Yahweh was worshipped, the former stating that they bowed to Yahweh and the Host of Heaven from rooftops, and the latter noting that they 'turned back' from following the Lord and did not inquire of him (presumably at the temple).

Although Zeph. 1.4-6 makes it clear that the prophet did not consider it proper to worship Yahweh from the rooftops along with the rest of the Host of Heaven (the Deuteronomistic perspective), it does not follow from this that he did not share a solar perception of Yahweh which was, after all, part of the understanding of Yahweh within the context of the Jerusalem temple with which the prophet also had links (the royal Jerusalemite perspective). Not surprisingly,

---

1. Zeph. 3.15. Here too, the LXX and Syriac offer different readings, but the MT is perfectly intelligible in its context.

2. It might be objected that the reference to Baal in v. 4 argues against an interpretation of vv. 4-6 as references to what to DH are Yahwistic vices. Although one might argue that the reference to Baal alone is to foreign worship, it is possible that reference is made here to some aspect of Baal worship that, like the asherah, made inroads into the cult of Yahweh.

3. BDB, pp. 690-91; cf. 2 Sam. 1.22; Jer. 38.22; 46.5.

therefore, solar language akin to the Jerusalemite perspective is also
found in Zephaniah (3.5, 17):

> 5 The Lord within her is righteous,
> he does no wrong;
> every morning he shows forth his justice,
> each dawn he does not fail...
>
> 17 The Lord, your God, is in your midst,
> a warrior who gives victory;
> he will rejoice over you with gladness,
> he will renew you in his love;
> he will exult over you with loud singing
> as on a day of festival (RSV).[1]

N. Sarna has drawn attention already to the solar character of the language in this context in his important study on Psalm 19 and ancient
Near Eastern sun god literature.[2] According to Sarna, however, the
solar language is being applied here (and in Ps. 19) to the Torah and
for purely polemical purposes. Sarna thus states the following:

> Most remarkably, in chapter III, vv. 4, 5 and 17 he [Zephaniah] mentions
> the Torah and, in the spirit and language of our psalm [Ps. 19], he com-
> pares the moral order that governs the world (*mšpṭ*) to the natural order
> exemplified in the shining forth of the morning sun: *bbqr bbqr mšpṭw ytn
> l'wr...* (Zeph. III:5). He even uses the simile of a 'joyful hero' to
> describe *h´ 'lhyk bqrbk gbwr ywšy' yšyš 'lyk bśmḥh...* (Zeph. III:17).[3]

Although Sarna's basic observation regarding the presence here of
solar language is cogent, his interpretation of the meaning and
significance of this imagery is open to question. To be sure, the Torah
is mentioned in Zeph. 3.4, but the solar imagery is applied not to the
law (mentioned in a different context devoid of solar language), but
specifically to Yahweh himself, mentioned in v. 5. Moreover,
regarding v. 17, although Sarna seems to recognize that the simile of

1.   These last three lines are obscure, but solar imagery is apparent in the first
three lines.

2.   The use of solar imagery in the case of Zeph. 3.5 is obvious. On its presence
also in v. 17, see N. Sarna, 'Psalm XIX and the Near Eastern Sun-God Literature',
Fourth World Congress of Jewish Studies. Papers, Vol. 1 (Jerusalem: World
Union of Jewish Studies, 1967), p. 175 and parallels cited throughout the article
(pp. 171-75).

3.   In citing Sarna, I have used transliterations in place of Hebrew characters.

the 'joyful hero' is not applied to the law here but to God, he nonetheless compares v. 17 with the description of the Torah in Psalm 19B, whereas the real parallel would appear to be with the description of the sun itself in Psalm 19A:

> $w^e h\hat{u}'\ k^e h\bar{a}t\bar{a}n\ y\bar{o}\d{s}\bar{e}'\ m\bar{e}huppat\hat{o}$
> $y\bar{a}\acute{s}\hat{s}\ k^e gibb\hat{o}r\ l\bar{a}r\hat{u}\d{s}\ '\bar{o}rah$
> And it [the sun] as a bridegroom comes forth from his chamber,
> Rejoicing as a hero to run its course...[1]

Psalm 19 will be examined later in this study; suffice it to say here that Zeph. 3.5, 17 point to the use of solar imagery with respect to the deity during the time of Josiah, as Sarna notes. Contrary to Sarna's view, however, the solar imagery in Zeph. 3.5, 17 offers little support for the understanding of Psalm 19 (or Zeph. 3.5, 17) as an 'anti-sun-god polemic'.[2] Rather, the solar language of Zeph. 3.5, 17, like Psalm 19 (see later), seems to reflect a solar understanding of Yahweh.

How can the portrait of solar worship in Zephaniah best be interpreted? The castigation against worshipping Yahweh from the rooftops as a member of the Host of Heaven (Zeph. 1.4-6) is, as observed earlier as well, characteristic of a late-Deuteronomistic perspective. If v. 6 alludes to worshipping Yahweh in the direction of the temple as opposed to the sky (cf. v. 5), continuity is also evident with the Deuteronomistic outlook noted in 1 Kings 8. Regarding Zeph. 3.5, 17, a solar understanding of Yahweh by a prophet linked with the royal Jerusalemite establishment can hardly be judged surprising.

But how does the sympathetic perspective reflected in Zeph. 3.5, 17 relate to 1.4-6? There are several possibilities. First, the apparently different outlooks reflected in Zeph. 1.4-6 and 3.5, 17 are perhaps simply another case of 'the thorough mixing of Deuteronomic and Jerusalemite features in the book',[3] 1.4-6 reflecting the former perspective, 3.5, 17 the latter. Secondly, the prophet's opposition on the one hand to the association between Yahweh and the Host of Heaven (Zeph. 1.4-6) and his advocacy of the association between Yahweh and the sun on the other hand (Zeph. 3.5, 17) might reflect a possible transition in Deuteronomistic thinking during or near the reign of Josiah from a position of relative sympathy towards solar

---

1. Ps. 19.6 [5].
2. Sarna, 'Psalm XIX', p. 175.
3. Wilson, *Prophecy and Society*, p. 281.

Yahwism to one of disdain for it (or a part thereof). Thirdly, since
the late-Deuteronomistic reaction against solar Yahwism may rather
be a reaction only against certain features of it (worship of the sun as
Yahweh and not vice versa, worship of the Host of Heaven, a ban
against the procession of the sun chariot[s], etc.), Zeph. 3.5, 17 are
perhaps consistent with even a late-Deuteronomistic outlook. The
position of Zephaniah as a whole would thus be that, though to some
extent still solar in character (3.5, 17), Yahweh was nonetheless to be
worshipped by facing only in the direction of the temple (1.4-6)
where Yahweh has chosen to dwell in name/glory.[1] Finally, if Zeph.
3.1-17 dates between 612 and 609 BCE, as some scholars believe,[2] the
passage suggests that if Josiah's actions involved an attack against all
aspects of solar Yahwism, their effect was short lived indeed. In any
case, although it is not possible to be too specific about how the
portrait of sun worship in Zephaniah best fits into a historical reconstruction of solar Yahwism, the portrait on the whole is nonetheless
perfectly consistent with the thesis that there was a close relationship
between the worship of the Host of Heaven (including the sun) and
Yahweh and that rejection of the worship of the sun as Yahweh did
not necessarily involve a rejection of all aspects of solar Yahwism.

Zechariah

Although no material relevant to Yahweh and the sun has been
identified by Morgenstern, Stähli or others in the case of Zechariah, it
is nonetheless quite possible that solar elements contributed to the
background of ch. 14.[3] What follows is a case for solar elements
which may lie behind the chapter in its present form.

First and very generally, Zechariah 14 is one of a number of
passages in the Old Testament which deal with the elevation of Zion,
many of which contain the imagery of God as light/solar light, and at
least some of which also have a setting at the Feast of Tabernacles.[4]

---

1.   Cf. 1 Kgs 8.12; Ezek. 8.16, etc.

2.   For example, E. Achtemeier, 'Zephaniah', *HBD*, p. 1161.

3.   A model study on this material is that of B. Otzen, *Studien über
Deuterosacharja* (Copenhagen: Prostant apud Munksgaard, 1964), who discusses
this passage on pp. 199-212. Unfortunately there is no consensus concerning the
date of Zech. 9–14.

4.   See, for example, von Rad, 'City on a Hill', p. 241 and my discussion of
Isa. 60.

Secondly, the appearance of Yahweh on the Mount of Olives 'from the east' (*miqqedem*) in Zech. 14.4 brings to mind the appearance of the glory of the Lord which stood on the Mount of Olives, 'from the east' in Ezek. 11.23.[1] Moreover, immediately following the description of Yahweh's appearance from the east is the following statement which is perhaps relevant for Morgenstern's thesis of an association between sunrise (blocked by the Mount of Olives) and the coming of the glory of the Lord in Ezekiel: 'and the Mount of Olives will be split in its middle, from east to west, a huge valley, so that half of the mountain will move toward the north and half toward the south' (vv. 4b, 5a).[2] Although the forming of a valley through the middle of the Mount of Olives was perhaps to provide an escape route for the residents remaining in Jerusalem, as some suggest,[3] the context which follows this description suggests that the splitting of the Mount of Olives perhaps facilitated the coming of Yahweh westward to Jerusalem: 'and Yahweh my God will come, all the holy beings[4] with

---

1.   Otzen, *Studien*, pp. 202-204. The assumption of some that the reference to the Mount of Olives to the east is for the benefit of members of the diaspora who are ignorant of geography does not account sufficiently for the similarity in language with Ezek. 11.23 and leaves unexplained why the location of the far more obscure Azel (probably a place name) in v. 5 is not specified. This option is mentioned, for example, by R. Mason, *The Books of Haggai Zechariah and Malachi* (The Cambridge Bible Commentary; Cambridge: Cambridge University Press, 1977), pp. 124-25.

2.   Hebrew *wᵉniqba' har hazzêtîm mēhesyô mizrāhâ wāyammâ gê' gᵉdôlâ mᵉ'ōd ûmāš hᵃsî hāhār sāpônâ wᵉhesyô negbâ.*

3.   The problem lies with the threefold occurrence of the verb *nstm* which the MT vocalizes as *nastem*, 'you shall run'. If this vocalization is correct, then the residents of Jerusalem will apparently flee by the valley. Some have questioned, however, whether there will be a need for the residents of Jerusalem to flee at this point in time. (See, for example, E. Achtemeier, *Nahum–Malachi* [Interpretation; Atlanta: John Knox, 1986], p. 165.) Moreover, the LXX understood *nstm* to be a *niphal* perfect of *stm*, 'stop up' and understood the verse to mean that the valley 'will be stopped up', a view followed, for example, by the JPSV. Others (for example, Targum, RSV) understand the first occurrence of the verb to be 'you shall flee' and the last two to be 'will be stopped up'.

4.   There are three possibilities concerning the identity of the 'holy ones': (1) members of Yahweh's heavenly host; (2) earthly 'saints'; and (3) the resurrected. If the first option is correct as most suppose, there is a general similarity between Yahweh's appearance with his attendants and that of the sun god with the Annunaki.

you!'[1] Perhaps, then, just as in Isaiah 60 apocalyptic vision sought to overcome the difficulty of the nightly setting of a symbol for Yahweh, so, too, apocalyptic hope sought to carve a path through the sacred mountain which frustrated the cult by delaying for a few minutes the march of the sun straight into the temple at dawn.[2] As noted, however, this is by no means certain; there are other possible explanations for the splitting of the mountain.[3]

Thirdly, regardless of how one renders the problematic v. 6,[4] it is nonetheless clear from v. 7 that the immediate effect of the coming of Yahweh with his holy beings will be continuous daylight, the obscuring of day and night such that there will be light in the evening.[5] Like the visions in Isaiah 2 and 60, then, Zechariah 14

---

1.   Hebrew *ûbā' yhwh 'elohay kol qedōšîm 'immāk*. Note, for example, the words of Achtemeier (*Nahum–Malachi*, pp. 165-66): 'This [the splitting of the Mount of Olives and the blocking up of the Kidron valley] will have the effect of forming on the east side of the city a level plain stretching into the desert. As the text now stands there is a gloss designating the plain as an escape route for the Jerusalemites, but it really is no such thing. The inhabitants have no reason to flee the city. Instead, the plain is a way provided for God to enter into his holy city (cf. Isa 40:3-5)—a royal processional way on which the Lord with his retinue of heavenly attendants and servants comes to take up his abode in the midst of Jerusalem.'

2.   See later in this section for the reference in Josephus in which this event is associated with the entrance into the temple of the sun, acting as divine judge.

3.   As Otzen notes (*Studien*, pp. 203-204), Jewish tradition linking Zech. 14 and Ezek. 37 understands the Mount of Olives, the point of entry to and exit from the realm of the dead, to be split on the day of resurrection, an interpretation advocated with less caution also by Morgenstern ('The King-God among the Western Semites', *VT* 10 [1960], pp. 180-81).

4.   Following the *kethib* of the MT, the latter part of the verse should be rendered, 'there will be no light; the splendid ones (that is, stars) will dwindle'. Many modern translations are based upon an adaptation of one or another of the early versions which favour the sense, 'there shall be neither cold nor frost'. For a comprehensive survey of the problems associated with the interpretation of this verse, see K.L. Barker, 'Zechariah', in F. Gabelein (ed.), *The Expositors Bible Commentary* (Grand Rapids: Zondervan, 1985), VII, pp. 691-92.

5.   MT: *wehāyâ yôm 'ehād hû' yiwwāda' layhwh lō' yôm welō' laylâ wehāyâ le'ēt 'ereb yihyeh 'ôr*, 'but there shall be continuous day—known only to the Lord—of neither day nor night, and there will be light at evening time'. If the MT *lō'yihyeh 'ôr*, 'there will be no light', should prove correct in v. 6a, there is an apparent contradiction between there being no light and light at eventide. A reasonable solution is that posed by Joyce Baldwin (*Haggai, Zechariah, Malachi* [TOTC, 24; Downers

contains the imagery of God as light in an eschatological passage dealing with a pilgrimage to the elevated Mount Zion, the city from which God reigns in glory and splendour.[1]

Fourthly, the tradition preserved in Josephus concerning the cause of the earthquake in the time of Uzziah appears at least in part to be indebted to the description of the splitting of the Mount of Olives in vv. 4-5 of this passage.[2] In view of the connection between Josephus's understanding of the earthquake and this chapter, it is well worth noting the broader context in which the earthquake is mentioned in this classical source. After describing Uzziah's attempt to offer incense in the temple against the wishes of the priesthood, Josephus says the following:

> In the meantime a great earthquake shook the ground, and a rent was made in the temple, and the bright rays of the sun shone through it, and fell upon the king's face, insomuch that the leprosy seized upon him immediately; and before the city, at a place called Eroge, half the mountain broke off from the rest on the west, and rolled itself four furlongs, and stood still at the east mountain, till the roads, as well as the king's gardens, were spoiled by the destruction.[3]

Although the association between the activity of God in judgment and the activity of the sun cannot be traced back to the imagery of Zechariah 14, as the reference to the earthquake probably can, that

Grove, IL: IVP, 1972], p. 203) who suggests that 'there will be no light' in v. 6a refers to sunlight. If so, there is here the same hint as in Isa. 60.19-20 that Yahweh's coming to Jerusalem in the eschaton will in fact replace or supersede the coming of the sun.

1. At least one other writer has drawn a comparison between the imagery of light in Zech. 14.7 and the role of the sun during the Feast of Booths at the time of the autumnal equinox. Note the words of T.H. Gaster (*Festivals of the Jewish Year*, p. 92): 'It is not difficult to recognize in his words [that is, those of the writer of Zech. 14.7] a projection into mythology of the autumnal equinox at which the Feast of Booths anciently took place (cf. Exod. 34.22)'.

2. This is no doubt because v. 5 compares this event with the earthquake in the time of Uzziah. See, for example, C.H.H. Wright, *Zechariah and his Prophecies* (London: Hodder & Stoughton, 2nd edn, 1879), p. 595, and Mason, *Haggai, Zechariah and Malachi*, p. 126.

3. *Ant.* 9.10.4. (The translation is that by W. Whiston, *The Works of Flavius Josephus* [London: Ward, Lock & Co., n.d.], p. 246.)

divine judgment is brought about by sunlight entering the temple is nonetheless striking.

Fifthly, if the view of many that this chapter is a unit is cogent, the setting of the whole chapter, including the apocalyptic event just discussed, is the Feast of Booths (v. 16).[1] In any case, the reference to the Feast of Booths is noteworthy in this context since this pilgrimage feast was plausibly an important locus for solar elements within the cult of Yahweh.[2]

Sixthly, the suggestion that Yahweh might be associated with the sun in Zechariah 14 offers a new avenue for understanding the enigma of Egypt receiving special consideration in the otherwise blanket statement in vv. 17-19 that any of the families of the earth who do not attend the annual feast will be punished with a lack of rainfall. That the text is clearly garbled and in its present state treats Egypt as both an exception and not an exception welcomes the interpretation that Egypt was originally exempted and that this proved controversial.[3] Moreover, it seems reasonable to suppose that behind the controversy lay a Jewish community in Egypt with a cult centre like that at Leontopolis which was regarded as a suitable substitute for the Jerusalem temple (cf. Isa. 19.18).[4] According to this understanding, then, Egypt was perhaps originally exempted from participation on the grounds that there was an appropriate (solar?) cult centre (or centres) in Egypt to which elements of the diaspora in Egypt could go during the Feast of Booths in place of the journey to Jerusalem.

1.   See, for example, W. Harrelson, 'The Celebration of the Feast of Booths According to Zech xiv 16-21', in J. Neusner (ed.), *Religions in Antiquity* (Leiden: Brill, 1968), pp. 88-96.

2.   See the section 'An Autumn Festival as a Locus for Solar Yahwism?', offered later in this chapter.

3.   The exceptional reference to Egypt is traditionally accounted for on the basis of the fact that Egypt is not dependent upon rainfall but the Nile. According to this view, however, undue emphasis is thereby given to a technicality and there is no way of accounting for the corrupt nature of the text. The view that the verse alludes to a cult place like that established by Onias has also been noted, for example, by E. Sellin, *Das Zwölfprophetenbuch* (2 vols.; Leipzig: A. Deichert, 3rd edn, 1930), II, p. 584 and Venema (as cited by C.H. Wright, *Zechariah*, p. 509).

4.   As argued earlier, Isa. 19.18 bears witness to the notion of an Egyptian city comparable to Jerusalem in which the worship of Yahweh would be such that an appropriate name for the place was 'city of the sun'. See the discussion of Isa. 1–39 offered earlier in this chapter.

Finally, reference is made in this passage to a horse becoming 'Holy to the Lord' (v. 20). To be sure, v. 21 provides some support for the widespread assumption that the horse is an example of something mundane becoming 'Holy to the Lord' and thus sacred, but two things are worth noting: (1) in light of what has been argued in the case both of 2 Kgs 23.11 and the Taanach cult stand, it should no longer be merely assumed that the horse in Zech. 14.20 is mundane and non-cultic, and (2) the immediate context in fact refers to items in the Jerusalem temple cult (cf. 2 Kgs 23.11).[1]

In sum, although Zechariah 14 does not require a solar interpretation, it nevertheless contains a considerable number of features[2] that are consistent with a solar understanding of Yahweh and elements within the cult, especially as it relates to the Feast of Booths.

Malachi 3.20 [4.2]

The text of Mal. 3.20 [4.2] is as follows:

> w^ezār^{e}hâ lākem yir'ê š^{e}mî šemeš ṣ^{e}dāqâ ûmarpē' biknāpêhā
> But there will shine forth for you who fear My name the sun of righteousness, and healing will be in its wings.

The verse describes the fate of the God-fearers[3] on the great Day of Yahweh and stands in sharp contrast to the fate of the arrogant and evil-doers who on this same day, a day 'burning like an oven', will be burned like stubble. The passage is probably not without relevance for

---

1. Although probably a coincidence, it is indeed striking that the priest on whose turban was written the expression 'Holy to the Lord' (whence came the expression in the present context), like this horse, wore 'bells' (see Exod. 28.34-35). The comparison and probably coincidence is made all the more striking by the presence of bell-like ornaments (so-called sun-disks) on the polls of some of the cultic horse figurines examined in the previous chapter. The word for bell, however, is not the same in both cases, and it is of course possible that the bells were part of the trappings for the horse and thus had a different function. In any case, as noted, that the horses had a purely secular function is merely an assumption.

2. It is worth noting as well that reference is made in this passage to Yahweh as *melek yhwh ṣ^{e}bā'ôt*, 'King, Lord of Hosts' (v. 17; cf. vv. 9, 16, 21) both portions of which have been linked with a possible solar understanding of Yahweh elsewhere in this study.

3. On the meaning of 'those who fear Yahweh' here, see P.D. Hanson, *The People Called: The Growth of Community in the Bible* (San Francisco: Harper & Row, 1986), pp. 284-85.

the understanding of the meaning of the Day of the Lord, but here the
focus will be on matters more clearly solar.

The expression *šemeš ṣᵉdāqâ*, 'sun of righteousness', has generated
much discussion. There is little reason[1] to doubt the virtually
unanimous judgment of commentators that the common Near Eastern
depiction of the winged sun disk contributed to the use of the
expression here.[2] In view of the iconography on the royal Judaean
lmlk jar handles, however, Judah itself should be included among the
suggestions about which cultural realm contributed to the image of
Yahweh as winged sun.[3]

In seeking to explain further the significance of the expression 'sun
of righteousness', interpreters often follow one of two approaches,
neither of which necessarily excludes the other. The first understands
the expression in a purely figurative sense by reference to two
features that the sun and the righteousness of Yahweh share in
common, such as their being bright and blessed,[4] or their being
associated with justice,[5] or their affinity with the notion of God as
judge.[6] The second approach understands the expression to associate

---

1.   An important exception is the view which takes *kᵉnāpîm*, 'wings' to refer to
the 'folds' of a garment; cf. BDB, p. 489, §2a, the work of van Gelderen cited by
P.A. Verhoef (*The Books of Haggai and Malachi* [NICOT; Grand Rapids:
Eerdmans, 1987], p. 331), and the JPSV note, 'Lit. "with healing in the folds of its
garments"'. If correct, this interpretation would make less likely a possible indirect
parallel with the winged sun disk, but otherwise does not affect the present
discussion, since solar imagery is still evident in the reference to Yahweh as *šemeš*,
'sun'.

2.   See, for example, B. Glazier-McDonald, *Malachi: The Divine Messenger*
(SBLDS, 98; Atlanta: Scholars Press, 1987), pp. 238-39; Baldwin, *Haggai,
Zechariah, Malachi*, p. 250; J.M.P. Smith, *A Critical and Exegetical Commentary
on the Book of Malachi* (ICC; New York: Charles Scribner's Sons, 1912), p. 80.

3.   For the various options, see, for example, Glazier-McDonald, *Malachi*,
pp. 238-40. Paul Dion first drew my attention to the *lmlk* jar handles as a possible
background to the expression in Mal. 3.20 [4.2]; see already, however, Smith,
Malachi, p. 80, and J. Tigay, *No Other Gods*, p. 95.

4.   Verhoef, *Haggai and Malachi*, 328.

5.   Smith (*Malachi*, p. 80), for example, says, 'The absolute impartiality of the
sun's rays may easily have given rise to the association of justice with the sun. The
phrase "sun of righteousness" does not indicate any personal agent, but is rather a
figurative representation of righteousness itself'.

6.   Baldwin, *Haggai, Zechariah, Malachi*, p. 250.

Yahweh more directly (often in the sense of less figuratively) with the 'sun of righteousness'.[1] A somewhat eclectic outlook which nevertheless emphasizes the second approach is that of Glazier-McDonald:

> The wings symbolize Yahweh's protective presence, a presence which spreads over the earth ensuring its prosperity. The association of the wings (or rays) of the sun (=Yahweh) with healing is significant for it is precisely the sun generating light and warmth which guarantees fertility and thus, life. Further, there is a connection between the sun and world order, cf. *šmš ṣdqh*. In the ancient Near East, the sun god was considered to be the author of the world order. According to Ps 85:12, righteousness, *ṣedeq* (in the sense of world order) goes before Yahweh. Ps 19 suggests an association between the sun and world order (law) when it celebrates the sun (vv. 5-7) and then praises the law of Yahweh which enlightens the eyes (vv. 8-11). In Mal 3:20, the rising of the sun (=Yahweh) ensures the restoration of *ṣdqh*, right order, and thus of harmonious relations between heaven and earth, between Yahweh and man.[2]

To evaluate, without further information on what is regrettably 'a little known period of Judean history',[3] there is no way of verifying that more than mere poetic imagery gave rise to the expression 'sun of righteousness' here. Moreover, as the citation of Glazier-McDonald illustrates, the extent to which one is inclined to see Yahweh as genuinely solar in Mal. 3.20 [4.2] is inevitably determined by the extent to which one sees a more or less concrete understanding of Yahweh as sun elsewhere. In view of these considerations, the passage cannot be used independently as strong evidence in support of a solar understanding of Yahweh. Nevertheless, in illustration of what has just been said with respect to the citation of Glazier-McDonald, my own opinion based on evidence adduced elsewhere in this study is that the expression *šemeš ṣedāqâ* probably reflects an understanding of Yahweh as sun.[4]

---

1. Note, for example, Glazier-McDonald (*Malachi*, p. 236): 'Indeed, Yahweh is called *šemeš ṣedāqâ*, the sun of righteousness'. (Transliteration is used where she cites the Hebrew text.)

2. Glazier-McDonald, *Malachi*, p. 340.

3. Glazier-McDonald, *Malachi*, p. 275.

4. Though far from being strong evidence for a concrete understanding of Yahweh as 'sun of righteousness', the following factors are at least consistent with this view. (1) The prophet uses the expression *yhwh ṣebā'ôt*, known to be a solar epithet in some contexts (but not all and by no means in itself a reliable indicator of

Although at this point it is merely an assumption on my part that a solar understanding of Yahweh lies behind the reference to him as 'sun of righteousness', it is worth observing nonetheless that some of the evidence for solar Yahwism examined elsewhere in this study may open up a fresh avenue for understanding this expression for Yahweh. For example, to judge from the context in which this expression occurs in Malachi—a broad context which is clearly eschatological and a near context in which the ministry of *marpē'*, 'healing', is assigned to the solar figure—there seems to be an affinity between this expression and the eschatological understanding noted earlier of Yahweh as the sublime sun. As may be recalled, one of the roles of Yahweh as eternal sun in the eschaton was healing, as illustrated by Isa. 30.26, mentioned earlier:

> And the light of the moon shall become like the light of the sun, and the light of the sun shall become sevenfold, like the light of the seven days, when the Lord binds up His people's wounds and heals the injuries it has suffered.

The portrait of the sun of righteousness with healing in its wings offered by Malachi is thus consistent with the notion found elsewhere of the coming of Yahweh as the sublime sun, bringing with him a superabundance of attributes associated with the former physical sun, among which are 'righteousness' and 'healing'.

If it is true that Malachi had a solar perception of Yahweh, several implications follow. First, an eschatological understanding of Yahweh as sun on the part of the community which gave rise to the prophecy would be attested in the first half of the fifth century BCE (the time of the prophecy).[1] Secondly, the presence of Deuteronomistic influence(s)

---

solar elements). (2) It is perhaps not coincidental that a different metaphor used to describe the fate of the wicked on the same day of Yahweh, namely, 'a day burning like a furnace' (3.19 [4.1]), is at least amenable to a solar understanding of Yahweh, an understanding which might even be taken to inform an understanding of the significance of the imagery of a calf being released from the stall (3.20c [4.2c], from darkness to sunlight as well as from captivity to freedom). On these two possibilities, see, for example, Baldwin (*Haggai, Zechariah, Malachi*, p. 250) who nonetheless understands the expression 'sun of righteousness' figuratively. Clearly the matter must be left open.

1. P.D. Hanson, 'Malachi', *Harper's Bible Commentary*, p. 753; Glazier-McDonald, *Malachi*, pp. 14-18. (Glazier-McDonald, for example, dates the book to some time between 460 and 450 BCE.)

in the book of Malachi (including probably Mal. 3.20 [4.2])[1] would accord reasonably well with what has been shown elsewhere to be an openness within Deuteronomistic literature to a solar understanding of Yahweh (though not to worship in the direction of the sun or to some cultic practices such as that reflected in 2 Kgs 23.11). And thirdly, the general context in which the expression 'sun of righteousness' occurs, a day of the epiphany of Yahweh, would provide possible support for an association between a solar phenomenon (interpreted Yahwistically) and the expected Day of the Lord.[2]

Finally, since Mal. 3.20 [4.2] possibly offers insight into what notions were conveyed along with Yahweh as sun, a few comments on the meaning of $ṣ^e dāqâ$, 'righteousness', and $marpē'$, 'healing', are in order. First, among the suggested meanings for 'righteousness' here are the senses either of vindication and victory,[3] or of justice and salvation.[4] To evaluate, the latter seems preferable in light of the context in which there is a concern for the restoration of right order involving deliverance for the God-fearers[5] and for the destruction for the wicked.[6] The word $marpē'$ means 'healing', resulting here from the restoration of $ṣ^e dāqâ$,[7] but equally an effect of the coming of Yahweh as sublime sun. This healing could involve the healing of a strained relationship between God and his fearers, and perhaps even

---

1. On Deuteronomistic language and themes within Malachi, see, for example, J. Blenkinsopp, *A History of Prophecy in Israel* (Philadelphia: Westminster Press, 1983), p. 242; R.J. Coggins, *Haggai, Zechariah, Malachi* (OTG; Sheffield: JSOT Press, 1987), pp. 75-76.

2. Malachi's description of the day of Yahweh's epiphany is at points comparable to Amos 5.18, 20; cf. Amos 4.13; 5.8-9. Although the notion of Yahweh as sun perhaps accounts for the imagery of light and darkness often associated with the Day of the Lord, the imagery itself is too general to be of help in this study in which potentially clear cases of solar Yahwism are examined.

3. Note, for example, the rendering of $šemeš ṣ^e dāqâ$ in the JPSV as, 'sun of victory'. For a list of cases in which $ṣ^e dāqâ$ has this meaning, see, for example, Smith, *Malachi*, p. 80.

4. For an extended discussion of this option, see Verhoef, *Haggai and Malachi*, pp. 328-29, and Glazier-McDonald, *Malachi*, p. 236.

5. Mal. 3.20 [4.2]; cf. 3.18.

6. Mal. 3.19, 21 [4.1, 3]; contrast 3.14-15.

7. Glazier-McDonald, *Malachi*, pp. 237-38.

the return of fertility to the land,[1] which was again part of the result of the return of right order.[2] Moreover, Mal. 3.21 [4.3] emphasizes that the coming of the 'sun of righteousness' will clearly result in deliverance and joy, and perhaps also emergence from darkness to light and prosperity.[3]

To conclude, although perhaps reflective of a concrete under-standing of Yahweh as sun within the cult, the Yahweh epithet 'sun of righteousness' could also simply be a case of the use of figurative language for God. Mal. 3.20 thus cannot be used independently as evidence for Yahweh as the sun in ancient Israel. If 'sun of righteous-ness' is a genuinely solar epithet (which is perhaps likely in view of evidence adduced elsewhere in this study), then a number of implica-tions would follow that are consistent with my overall assessment of solar Yahwism. The possible use here of mere poetic language for God (that is, language devoid of reference to a solar cult) nonetheless results in an impasse.

Sun Worship in Job

Job's final speech in ch. 31 contains a series of oaths which serve the legal purpose of clearing him of guilt before God.[4] Included in this list of otherwise moral oaths is Job's claim that he has not succumbed to the temptation of worshipping the sun and the moon and thus has not betrayed God on high.[5] M. Pope translates Job 31.26-28 as follows:

---

1. Glazier-McDonald, *Malachi*, pp. 237-38; cf. Mal. 3.10-11.
2. Glazier-McDonald, *Malachi*, pp. 237-38.
3. Baldwin, *Haggai, Zechariah, Malachi*, p. 250. Glazier-McDonald (*Malachi*, p. 241) plausibly suggests that the imagery of the stall-fed calf denotes prosperity.
4. See N.C. Habel *The Book of Job* (OTL; Philadelphia: Westminster Press, 1985), pp. 428-29 for citation of Egyptian parallels of negative confession depicting the deceased facing judgment at death, and mention of Mesopotamian and biblical parallels suggesting that the oaths are a legal means of justifying innocence.
5. See M.H. Pope, *Job* (AB, 15; Garden City, NY: Doubleday, 3rd edn, 1973), p. 227.

26 If I looked at the shining light,[1]
Or the moon marching in splendor,
27 And my mind was secretly seduced,
And my hand kissed my mouth;
28 That were perfidious sin,
I had betrayed God on high.[2]

Several things may be noted from the passage. First, Job refers to a temptation to which many evidently succumbed (compare, for example, Jer. 8.2, Zeph. 1.4-6). Secondly, this passage alone describes a practice associated with reverence for the astral bodies that apparently involved a gesture of the hand near the mouth.[3] The meaning and nature of the gesture, however, are not well understood.[4] Pope has drawn attention to a Mesopotamian parallel in which Awil-Nannar, portrayed kneeling before Hammurabi, king of Babylon, makes a similar gesture.[5] More recently, an even closer parallel has perhaps come to light in a grafitto-portrait from Kuntillet 'Ajrûd.[6] On Pithos B is depicted a procession of five worshippers with arms extended or bent towards the mouth and with heads in most cases clearly looking upwards (conveying a gesture of adoration towards an object above them).[7] Near the mouth of the leader of the procession is

1. The reference to sun as *'ôr*, 'light', is not without analogy in usage outside the Bible (Pope, *Job*, p. 235). Perhaps the motivation is the same as that which led the writer of Gen. 1.14-16 to refer to sun and moon as *me'ōrōt*, 'lights', although moon is mentioned by name in the case of Job.

2. Pope, *Job*, p. 226.

3. The exact nature of the gesture is unclear. The verse may be translated literally as 'My hand kissed (to/from) my mouth'. NASB translates the verse, 'And my hand threw a kiss from my mouth', which may convey the correct sense. See, however, later in this section.

4. For the difficulties and options, see, for example, Pope, *Job*, p. 235.

5. Pope, *Job*, p. 235.

6. For a drawing of the procession and a description, see P. Beck, 'The Drawings from Horvat Teiman (Kuntillet 'Ajrûd)', *TA* 9 (1982), p. 6, fig. 3, and pp. 36-40 (respectively). For an excellent photograph, see Z. Meshel, 'Did Yahweh Have a Consort?', *BARev* 5/2 (March/April 1979), p. 26.

7. Interestingly, there is a round object crudely drawn immediately above the first two figures, but as Beck notes ('Drawings', p. 39), this might be the head of a processioner, the full drawing of which was abandoned in favour of the two figures below it. Even if not drawn, however, an object located above these processioners (most of whom clearly gaze upwards) seems to have been the object of adoration.

what is appears to be an open hand, although it might also be the
upper extension of a branch or the like.[1] If relevant, this parallel
suggests that the gesture denotes adoration, an attitude which fits well
with the sense of our passage. And thirdly, v. 28 underlines the
Hebrew poet's conviction that veneration of the sun and the moon was
tantamount to denying[2] God and an 'iniquity of judgment',[3] an attitude
akin to that found in Deut. 17.2-5. This passage in Job, then, constitutes evidence from outside of Deuteronomistically influenced circles
for the view that the worship of the sun was a crime against God.
Little more can be gleaned from the passage; many questions remain.

Sun Worship in the Psalms

The Psalms have often played an important role in deliberations about
the relationship between Yahweh and the sun. The reason for this is
obvious: there are a number of passages in which the poetic language
is suggestive that Yahweh might have been associated or even identified with the sun. However, because of the difficulty of distinguishing
between poetic language of God as light or sun which is merely
figurative and that which genuinely reflects a concrete understanding
of Yahweh as sun within the cult, my discussion of the Psalms is
limited to the following considerations: (1) a brief consideration of
Ps. 84.12 [11], the only passage in the Psalter that explicitly refers to
Yahweh as the 'sun'; (2) a full study of Psalms 19 and 104, known to

(Curiously, Beck does not mention the upwards orientation of the leading
processioners.)

1. Beck judges that the leader is holding a walking stick or the like, which
seems to be the case. But since the upper part of the staff and the arm merge in the
drawing, it is impossible to tell whether the hand-like object near the mouth is part of
the stick or the hand itself. Although not drawn, hands on the third processioner
would likewise be near the mouth.

2. BDB, p. 471, renders the verb *kiḥḥēš*, 'to disappoint', 'deny', 'deceive', or
'fail'.

3. A helpful point of comparison may be found in the observation of
F.I. Andersen (*Job* [TOTC, 13; London: Tyndale Press, 1976], p. 243) that the
initial *gam hû'*, 'that also', of v. 28 draws attention to an earlier case of an *'āwôn
pᵉlîlî*, 'judicial iniquity', in v. 11, where the expression is used to describe the sin of
licentiousness. (The expression in v. 11 is *'āwôn pᵉlîlîm*, but, as Pope notes [*Job*,
p. 232], the final *-m* is probably enclitic.)

contain parallels to ancient Near Eastern sun god literature; (3) a brief
study of the clearest cases of possible solar theophanies in Hebrew
poetry, with special attention being given to the notion of seeing the
face of God; and (4) a fresh consideration of Psalm 24, an ark
procession psalm which probably presupposes a solar understanding
of Yahweh.[1]

Psalm 84.12 [11]

What appears to be the clearest case of an association between Yahweh
and the sun in the Psalms is Ps. 84.12 [11], often cited by those who
argue for the presence of solarized Yahwism.[2] The first line of this
verse is *kî šemeš ûmāgēn yhwh*, 'for a sun and a shield is Yahweh'.[3]

To evaluate, Yahweh is explicitly called 'sun' here and some aspects
of the context of the psalm, a song of pilgrimage to Zion in which the
epithet Yahweh of Hosts is used and the altar mentioned, appear to be
amenable to a solar understanding of Yahweh. But a number of other
considerations make it at least as likely that the reference to Yahweh
as sun in Ps. 84.12 [11] is no more than a case of the common royal
epithet 'sun' being applied to Yahweh as king.[4] In light of this latter
possibility, then, and contrary to Stähli,[5] this verse can hardly be

---

1. Pss. 80 and 118 have been discussed already in this study. Ps. 17.15 is also
relevant and will be mentioned in the discussion of seeing God in the Psalms.

2. For example, Stähli, *Solare Elemente*, pp. 42-43; G.W. Ahlström, *Psalm
89*, p. 86.

3. Very different here is the LXX, *hoti eleon kai alētheian agapa Kurios*, 'for the
Lord loves mercy and truth'.

4. Cf. Ps. 89.19 in which *māginnēnû*, 'our shield', occurs together with
malkēnû, 'our king', with reference to Yahweh. In letters at Ugarit (for example,
KTU 2.16.6-10) and el-Amarna (for example, EA 254, 270, 271 [*ANET*, p. 486]),
'sun' commonly occurs as an epithet of the king, and that this may have been the
case in Israel is perhaps implied by 2 Sam. 23.4 in which the benefits of the
religiously proper rule of David are compared with the benefits of the sun. Moreover,
although 'our shield' might be appositional to God in v. 10 [9] of Ps. 84 (so, for
example, KJV, LXX, RV), reference to the 'anointed' in the second line of the colon
suggests that 'shield'—itself parallel to 'sun' in v. 12 [11]—is an epithet of the king
(so, JPSV, RSV). Moreover, Yahweh is explicitly referred to as the psalmist's 'king'
earlier in the psalm (v. 4c [3c]). (For a critique of Dahood's view that 'shield' means
'sovereign' here and elsewhere, see P.C. Craigie, *Psalms 1–50* [WBC, 19; Waco,
TX: Word Books, 1983], p. 71).

5. Stähli, *Solare Elemente*, pp. 42-43. Stähli suggests that, although Kraus's

considered an indubitable and 'highly significant' case in which a solar
understanding of Yahweh has actually given rise to his being called
(literally) 'sun'.

Psalm 19

This well-known and unique psalm in which God's handiwork extols
him and in which the value of the law of the Lord is upheld has
occasioned many difficulties for interpreters. Chief among these
difficulties is its composition. Verses 2-7 [1-6] are often thought to be
in part (or part of) a pre-Israelite creation hymn to El in which, to
judge from its present form, the sun played a major role.[1] To this
hymn has been added a hymn in praise of the Torah of Yahweh.

Relevant to the problem of composition is the relationship between
the two main sections of this psalm, the creation hymn and the Torah
hymn. Although for a long time it was thought that two hymns were
juxtaposed fortuitously, O. Schroeder and L. Dürr argued pursu-
asively earlier in this century that a unifying theme for the psalm as a
whole is the sun, the cosmic role of which is articulated in vv. 5-7 [4-
6] and the judicial role of which is the rationale for the elaboration
upon the justice and law of Yahweh in vv. 8-12 [7-11].[2] Moreover, to

willingness not to reject the text which refers to Yahweh as 'sun' is a step in the right
direction, his adoption of the view that *šmš*, 'sun', is simply an ancient Near Eastern
term for royalty predicated of Yahweh is due to (perhaps even an unconscious)
shyness about a possible solar understanding of Yahweh. However, Kraus's
judgment is almost certainly correct (see the evidence noted in the previous note).
Stähli's only stated bases for objection are the supposed unlikelihood that 'sun'
should refer first to the 'king' and secondarily to 'Yahweh' here (but see elsewhere
in this same psalm where Yahweh is called 'king' [v. 4 (3)]), and the evidence for
an association between Yahweh and the sun based on the solar imagery on the royal
Judaean jar handles.

    1. S. Mowinckel proposes (*The Psalms in Israel's Worship* [2 vols.; Oxford:
Basil Blackwell, 1962], II, p. 267 n. 40) that the extended discussion of the sun
suggests that an earlier version of this poem elaborated on other heavenly bodies. On
the other hand, note the role of the sun goddess *špš* in the Ugaritic texts in which this
deity has a particular affinity with El, perhaps acting as his spokeswoman (*KTU* 1.2
III 15-18; 1.6 VI 22-29).

    2. O. Schroeder, 'Zu Psalm 19', *ZAW* 34 (1914), pp. 69-70; L. Dürr, 'Zur
Frage nach der Einheit von Ps. 19', in W.F. Albright, A. Alt, W. Caspari *et al.*
(eds.), *Sellin-Festschrift: Beiträge zur Religionsgeschichte und Archäologie
Palästinas* (Leipzig: Deichert, 1927), pp. 37-48.

this general insight with respect to the role of sun god as preserver of the law may now be added the more specific observation of Sarna that the attributes applied to the law of Yahweh in Psalm 19B are remarkably similar to attributes assigned to the sun god in ancient Near Eastern sun god literature.[1] Thus, although the question of whether the two sections of the psalm were a unit from the beginning must remain open,[2] a strong case can be made along the lines suggested by these and other scholars for intentional unity at least at a redactional level.[3] Moreover, even if the sun does not hold the key to the psalm's unity, there can be little doubt that the sun plays an important role in both parts of the psalm, vis-à-vis creation in Psalm 19A and vis-à-vis the law of Yahweh in Psalm 19B.

The question remains: what is the function or significance of the high profile given to the sun in Psalm 19? On this issue there is little agreement among scholars. For example, according to Aalen the sun and other created bodies referred to in Psalm 19A reflect the glory of God by obeying the *ḥuqqîm* (that is, the orderly set of principles by which God determined the heavenly bodies should live) referred to in Psalm 19B.[4] But, as Mowinckel notes, that the 'statutes' (*ḥuqqîm*) are not even mentioned in Psalm 19A renders this interpretation somewhat dubious.[5] Or again, for example, according to O. Loretz, there is a correspondence between the shining of the glory of God in nature (Psalm 19A) and the law which, like the rising sun, brings light to humankind (Psalm 19B).[6] However, while this view may be closer to the mark, neither the shining forth of the sun (which by itself has little

1. Sarna, 'Psalm XIX', pp. 171-75. That the correspondences between the psalm and sun god literature are not likely to be coincidental seems clear in light of the prominence of the sun in Ps. 19A and the presence of adjectives applied to the law in Ps. 19B (such as *brh*, 'pure' [v. 9c (8c)], *ṭhr*, 'clean' [v. 10 (9)], and *zhr*, 'admonish' [v. 12 (11)]) which, in addition to their normal form of translation, can have senses tying them with the notion of light. For meanings associated with light in the case of the last two of these Hebrew words see, for example, J. Eaton, 'Some Questions of Philology and Exegesis in the Psalms', *JTS* 19 (1968), pp. 603-609.

2. Against the notion of original unity, see especially the arguments of Mowinckel, *Psalms*, II, p. 267 n. 40.

3. See even Mowinckel, *Psalms*, II, p. 267 n. 40.

4. Cf. Pss. 104.19, 148.3-6. (I know of Aalen's study only through the work of Mowinckel, *Psalms II*.)

5. Mowinckel, *Psalms*, II.

6. O. Loretz, 'Psalmstudien III', *UF* 6 (1974), p. 187.

in common with the Torah) nor the radiance of the glory of God are mentioned specifically in Psalm 19A, and the law is nowhere compared with the rising sun in Psalm 19B.

Finally, according to Sarna, Psalm 19 is an 'anti-sun-god polemic' which was used in the time of Josiah to respond to sun worship, prevalent at this time (cf. 2 Kgs 23.11).[1] To Sarna Ps. 19.5-7 [4-6] serves to show that the sun is not a deity rivalling God, but is created by God; the sun is not something to be praised, but is part of the created realm which lauds the Lord.[2] Moreover, in describing the Torah in language familiar to the sun worshippers, the poet polemically emphasizes the relative merits of the Torah.[3]

An evaluation of the view of Sarna will take the form here of an alternative means of reckoning with the presence of sun god language in the psalm, namely that both parts of the psalm reflect a solar understanding of the Israelite deity to whom praise is offered.

Before considering aspects from both parts of the psalm that suggest a solar character for the deity, it is important to recall that the distinction made between deity and sun in v. 5 [4] in no way requires a polemical interpretation, as is often assumed. As noted earlier, the distinction made here does not imply complete discontinuity between the deity and the disk which he is said to have placed in the heavens. Rather, to take as an analogy the example of the Egyptian material pertaining to Re and the sun which he is said to have generated from himself, God's placement of the sun in the heavens can as easily be judged to imply continuity (though obviously not identity) between God and the sun.[4] In short, Ps. 19.5 [4] does not provide unequivocal support for a conflict between God/El and the sun or a polemic against the latter; rather, the verse can be understood as an articulation of a common Near Eastern concept that a deity, though solar, is nonetheless distinct from the sun disk which he sets in the heavens.

---

1. Sarna, 'Psalm XIX', p. 175.

2. N. Sarna, '*šemeš*', *EncMik*, VIII, p. 189. Sarna notes that although the sun is described in v. 5 [4] using mythological language, the poet distances himself from the Mesopotamian notion that the sun deity had a bridegroom by using the *kaph* of similarity. The sun is thus 'like' a bridegroom which emerges from its pavilion ('*šemeš*', p. 188).

3. Sarna, '*šemeš*', p. 189.

4. See the section 'The Significance of God Setting the Sun in the Heavens' offered earlier, in the discussion of 1 Kgs 8.12.

When considered in light of this clarification and afresh, both Psalm 19A and 19B can be understood to assume an explicitly 'solar' dimension of the character of the God of Israel. Beginning with Psalm 19A, the following points may be noted. First, as Sarna[1] and others[2] have recognized, sun-god language is used with reference to God (or El) the creator in Psalm 19A.[3] Secondly, v. 5c [4c], often taken to imply a conflict between '$\bar{e}l$ and the sun, appears clearly in this context to imply *continuity* between the two entities:

> He placed in them[4] a tent for the sun,
>> 6 who is like a bridegroom coming forth from his chamber,
>> like a hero, eager to run his course.
> 7 His rising-place is at one end of heaven,
>> and his circuit reaches the other;
>> nothing escapes his heat. (JPSV)

Interpreters invariably comment that the sun is singled out for its praise of God but, significantly, that praise never materializes; the sun does not praise God but receives the praise expected of God. Thus, whereas other aspects of creation mentioned earlier in the psalm, such as the heavens, must speak or otherwise specifically declare the praise of God, the sun's praise of God is undeclared and is thus somehow 'self evident' through the praise which it itself receives. This phenomenon of the sun receiving praise which is in continuity with the praise of God can be understood readily by judging that the sun, unlike the other aspects of creation mentioned, must be functioning here in continuity with God, as a kind of symbol of the power and presence of God. In short, to speak proudly of the sun *is* to speak in praise of God. Only in this way can proper sense be made of why this glowing description of the role of the sun (almost half of Psalm 19A

---

1. Sarna refers, for example, to extracts from Hymns from the Egyptian Book of the Dead in which it is written of Re that 'Thou art exalted by reason of thy wondrous works', and 'The stars which never rest sing hymns of praise unto thee and the stars which are imperishable glorify thee' (Sarna, '*šemeš*', p. 189).

2. For example, Gerstenberger, *Psalms*, p. 101; Craigie, *Psalms 1-50*, pp. 179-80; H.-J. Kraus, *Psalms 1–59: A Commentary* (trans. H.C. Oswald; Minneapolis: Augsburg), pp. 272-73.

3. The role of creator is of course not unknown for a sun god in ancient Near Eastern literature (cf. Sarna, 'Psalm XIX', p. 171). Examples include Hermopolitan Re (at least according to some traditions), Theban Amon-Re, and Aten.

4. Presumably 'the heavens'.

and thus sometimes taken to be a 'sun hymn fragment'[1] rather ineptly
inserted into the context) appears in the poem to be a natural extension
of this hymn which clearly focuses on the various ways in which the
created realm extols the glory of God.

A third observation offers further support for the notion of
continuity between God and the sun in Psalm 19A. The word *ḥammâ*,
rendered uniquely in v. 7c [6c] 'heat', but translated everywhere else
in the Old Testament as 'sun', should perhaps be interpreted as it is
elsewhere. Thus understood, Ps. 19.7c [6c] would conclude the first
section of the psalm as follows:

> Nothing is hidden from His [that is, God's/El's] sun.

In sum, no tension can be found in Psalm 19A between *'ēl* and the sun,
but rather continuity which suggests that the sun is a unique
expression of the character of its maker, God.

Turning to Psalm 19B (vv. 8-15 [7-14]) there is obviously some
kind of correspondence between the description of the sun and that of
the law of Yahweh, as Sarna and others have noted.[2] However, that
the correspondence is one of continuity between Yahweh and the sun
rather than one of discontinuity for polemical purposes can be
supported by consideration of the following. First, for Psalm 19B to
have been written in light of 19A (or appended to it), the poet (or
redactor) was probably acquainted with the fact that the god of justice
and law in neighbouring societies was often the sun god.[3] This being
so, is it not possible that the Hebrew poet understood his God of
justice and the law to be 'solar' in character like other gods of justice
and law? While certainty is impossible, this would account for the
application of solar attributes to the law of Yahweh in Psalm 19B.
Secondly, although Sarna claims that appellatives commonly used of a
sun god are specifically applied to the law of Yahweh, closer examination reveals that this is not quite correct. Many of the parallels are
in fact between the *laws* of sun gods and the *laws* of Yahweh.[4] In
other words the correspondence between Yahweh and ancient Near

1. E.g. Kraus, *Psalms 1–59*, p. 272.
2. Even if one assumed the purely fortuitous placement of Ps. 19B after 19A,
the sun god language applied to the Torah would probably still suggest the correspondence.
3. See, for example, Sarna, 'Psalm XIX', p. 173.
4. Sarna, 'Psalm XIX', p. 173. (sections v, vi. b), p. 174 (section f).

Eastern solar deities is not only indirect vis-à-vis Yahweh's law, but is rather more direct, between Yahweh and the sun gods themselves. Thirdly, in addition to the thematic correspondences between Psalms 15A and B, there are clear resonances between the petition in vv. 13-15 [12-14] and the understanding of God as sun in vv. 2-7. Thus, the answer to the question of who can discern errors in v. 13 [12] is logically the god of justice whose circuit of travel extends from one end of the earth to the other (that is, sun, v. 7 [6]). Or again, the psalmist asks that Yahweh clear him of 'hidden things'[1] (cf. v. 7c [6c] where it says that 'no thing is hidden'[2] from the sun's glow).[3]

To conclude, Psalm 19 appears to have been written (or, in the case of Psalm 19A, perhaps adapted) by a devout Yahwist who had a solar understanding of Yahweh. The first part of the psalm upholds what appears to have been a common tenet of solar Yahwism, namely, that the sun which God created was an expression of his character or 'glory' (cf. v. 2 [1]). The second part of the psalm builds upon the notion of continuity between God and the sun but explores this continuity with reference to the law of Yahweh. The laws of Yahweh are thus described with reference to the god of justice (traditionally solar in character). 'Just', 'enlightening' and 'pure', the laws of Yahweh reflect the character of their giver.

Psalm 104

No study of solar elements within ancient Israelite religion would be complete without discussion of Psalm 104, well known for its association with the longer Egyptian Hymn to Aten.[4]

Three things seem reasonably certain in light of current scholarship

---

1.   Hebrew, *nistārôt* (v. 13 [12]).

2.   Hebrew, *'ên nistār*.

3.   Or, on another interpretation, El's/God's sun. Finally, note the words of v. 15 [14]: 'May the words of my mouth and the meditation of my heart be acceptable in thy sight, O Lord, my rock and my redeemer'. It is not unreasonable to suppose that this was perhaps the wish of one who was concerned that the words of his mouth and the meditation of his heart might indeed not be acceptable in Yahweh's eyes. (A distant analogy might be found in the usage of this phrase in the context of a preacher's prayer prior to a sermon.)

4.   See *ANET*, pp. 369-71. When citing the hymn, I use the line numbers found in D. Winton Thomas (ed.), *Documents from Old Testament Times* (New York: Harper & Row, 1958), pp. 145-48.

on Psalm 104. First, although it is doubtful that Psalm 104 is directly dependent upon the longer Aten hymn, it is nonetheless clear that a close relationship of some kind exists between these two hymns. Secondly, a point emphasized most recently by P. Dion,[1] Psalm 104 contains storm-god imagery in addition to the more widely recognized sun-god imagery.[2] And thirdly, a point not unrelated to the first two is that, there can be no doubt that the poetic imagery of storm and sun which the psalmist borrowed has been brought into conformity with the distinctive theological outlook of ancient Israel.[3]

Perhaps the most relevant question for the purpose of this study is how the psalmist dealt with the solar outlook reflected in the Hymn to Aten when he brought this hymnic tradition into conformity with his own theological perspective. The clearest indication of the psalmist's understanding of the sun can be found in vv. 19 and 22 (cited respectively):

> Thou hast made the moon to mark the seasons;
> The sun knows its time for setting.

> When the sun rises, they [lions] get them away
> and lie down in their dens (RSV).

The verses, parallel to the Aten hymn[4] yet distinctive in theology, are instructive for what they do and do not imply. On the one hand, they clearly imply that the psalmist did not share Akhenaten's peculiar understanding that the actual physical form of the sun, 'the disk', was God himself (that is, Aten). Whatever the Hebrew poet's general stance regarding Yahweh and the sun, then, it was clearly far removed from Atenism's specific equation of God and physical sun. On the other hand, however, in making a clear distinction between God and the sun, these verses do not necessarily imply (much less prove, as we

---

1. P.E. Dion, 'YHWH as Storm-God and Sun-God: The Double Legacy of Egypt and Canaan as Reflected in Psalm 104', *ZAW* 103 (1991), pp. 43-71. (My thanks go to Professor Dion for allowing me to see his article in advance of its publication.)

2. On storm god imagery in Ps. 104, see already, for example, P.C. Craigie, 'The Comparison of Hebrew Poetry: Psalm 104 in the Light of Egyptian and Ugaritic Poetry', *Semitics* 4 (1974), pp. 10-21.

3. See, for example, the articles cited in the previous two notes and my discussion of Ps. 104.19, 22 which follows immediately.

4. See respectively, ll. 80, 17.

are sometimes led to believe) that the psalmist's theology was completely devoid of any form of solar perception of the deity.[1] Moreover, it follows from this that neither do these verses necessarily imply, much less demonstrate, that the purpose for adapting the Egyptian hymnic tradition was simply to launch a polemic against sun worship.[2] Thus, while we may be certain that the psalmist did not share Akhenaten's perception of God as a mere object, the sun, the matters of a solar outlook on the part of the psalmist and his purpose for using the Aten hymnic tradition must be left open at least until more than vv. 19 and 22 are considered.

When moving beyond vv. 19 and 22 to consider on the basis of the whole psalm whether the Hebrew poet understood the deity in solar terms, the evidence is conflicting or difficult to interpret, making certainty impossible. To put the matter differently, although it is reasonable to suppose that the psalmist must have identified with at least some aspects of the hymnic tradition in order to make extensive use of it without massive re-working, there is no way of knowing for certain whether those aspects included the concept of a 'solar' deity.[3] While it is often thought that they did not (most often, however, on the dubious polemical interpretation of vv. 19 and 22), that a solar perception of God was shared by both writers can by no means be readily dismissed. Thus, for example, although Dion rightly argues for a relative lack of Aten epithets applied to Yahweh in the psalm, this may reflect a disdain more for Atenism (after all a 'heresy' even in most solar circles) than for solarism per se (or, alternatively, the observation may be of little consequence since at many points the *roles*

1. As noted earlier, solar cults commonly distinguish between the physical form of the sun and the deity who is understood to be solar in character. See, for example, the section on 'The Significance of God Setting the Sun in the Heavens', offered earlier in this chapter.

2. The explanation that Ps. 104 is a polemic against a pagan (that is, foreign) sun cult seems limited by the fact that Atenism was short lived, not typical of sun cults in general, and had been defunct for half a millennium or more. Regarding the possibility, however, that the poem is a polemic against an indigenous *Aten-like* perspective on the relationship between Yahweh and the sun, see later in this discussion.

3. Or whether poetic language of God as the sun, if applied directly to Yahweh here, reflects the use of mere poetic imagery or the notion of a link between God and the sun within the cult.

of Aten and Yahweh are nonetheless parallel).[1] Moreover, although
Dion is correct that references to the deity wrapped in light such as
that found in Ps. 104.2 are not limited to contexts of solar deities, this
language is still appropriate for a solar deity and perhaps particularly
for Aten.[2] Still further to balance Dion's minimalist perspective vis-à-
vis Aten imagery and God himself, an allusion to Yahweh as solar is
perhaps to be found in vv. 28-29 of the psalm. Particularly poignant
here is the line, 'open your hand, they are well satisfied' (v. 28b)
which might recall the well-known iconography of Aten in which the
rays of the sun god end with hands,[3] no less an expression of the
divine provision.[4] The line which follows, 'hide your face, they are
terrified' (v. 29a) is also comparable to 'when you have dawned they
live, When you set they die' (ll. 99-100) especially when one reckons
with a possible correspondence in Hebrew between God hiding his
'face' and the disappearance of the 'sun' (on which see later in this
study). On balance then, whether the psalmist shared the Egyptian
writer's general perception of God as solar must be judged uncertain.
At any rate, the renunciation of Atenism by no means necessarily
entails the renunciation of solar Yahwism.

   A few other considerations point equally to the ambiguous or at
least complex nature of the issue. First, on a methodological note, if it
is acknowledged (as it readily is at least in scholarly circles) that
language of the *storm god* has been employed to contribute to our
understanding of the character of Yahweh here (and if not here at
least elsewhere), there is no reason why the language of the sun god
which functions similarly to that of the storm god should not also be
understood to inform our understanding of a facet of Yahweh's
character. (In other words, there are alternatives to a polemical interpretation of sun-god language.) And secondly, on a comparative note,

   1.   These include, in general, the roles of both Aten and Yahweh as creator and
sustainer of life (*passim*) and, in particular, the one who brings on darkness at
which time beasts roam (Ps. 104.20-23; cf. ll. 11-20) and even the one who marks
the seasons (Ps. 104.19; cf. l. 80). For other similarities between Atenism and
Yahwism, see later in this discussion of Ps. 104.
   2.   See Redford, *Akhenaten*, pp. 176-78.
   3.   See, for example, the drawing in T.H. Gaster, 'Sun', *IDB*, IV, p. 464,
fig. 91.
   4.   Redford, 'Sun-Disc in Akhenaten's Program, I', p. 56. (In the case of the
Egyptian material, the gesture is made specifically before royalty.)

since Psalm 104 appears also to have a close affinity of some kind with Genesis 1, it is reasonable to ask whether these two Hebrew literary works might share a common outlook regarding God and the sun. In light of this it is relevant to note that, as will soon be argued, Genesis 1 upholds a clear distinction between God and the sun (analogous to the discontinuity upheld in Ps. 104.19; cf. Gen. 1.14-18) while *at the same time* upholding a considerable degree of continuity between God and the disk which he created (cf. Gen. 1.3-5).

Regarding the issue of Psalm 104 as a polemic against a foreign sun cult, it will perhaps suffice to point out that such is neither self-evident nor the only possible explanation, and that an alternative explanation according to which the psalmist adopted and adapted the Egyptian hymnic tradition because he could identify with key aspects of the tradition, including perhaps a solar understanding of the deity, accounts at least as well for the presence of this 'sun hymn' in the Hebrew Psalter. Thus, on the assumption that Yahweh was manifest as sun, account can be given for an often-noted tension between Psalm 104 as sun-god literature on the one hand and as perfectly at home within the Hebrew poetic tradition on the other hand.[1] Or again on the assumption of a solar understanding of the deity, account can be given both for the Hebrew writer's use of an Egyptian sun-hymn tradition (peculiar in itself according to a traditional interpretation of the character of Yahweh in ancient Israel) and for the remarkable availability of the Egyptian tradition within the context of the worship of Yahweh half a millennium or more after the time of Akhenaten.[2]

None of this of course rules out a polemical interpretation. The extent to which this interpretation is likely depends on the kind of polemical context theorized. Since Atenism was short lived, had been defunct for half a millennium or more, and was not typical of Near Eastern solar cults in general, the plausible contexts are quite limited. One context well worth considering, however, is a local (that is, Israelite) manifestation of certain 'Atenistic' tenets,[3] including the

---

1. For example, Craigie, 'Comparison of Hebrew Poetry', p. 18.

2. The reasons for the availability of the tradition are of course unclear; in light of the context in which it has surfaced, however, it is not unreasonable to suppose that the Egyptian sun–hymn tradition was preserved (and was thus valued) within Israelite circles, probably within the context of the temple.

3. Craigie ('Comparison of Hebrew Poetry', p. 14) has already cautiously alluded to the possibility of a connection of some kind between Atenism and Israelite

notion of a one-to-one correspondence between God and the physical
form of the sun (which, for example, Gibeonite Yahwism might have
upheld). Though uncertain, a context like this of an ongoing struggle
within ancient Israel regarding what constituted a theologically
acceptable form of solar Yahwism would certainly account well for
both the preservation of the Aten tradition (presumably by those
sympathetic with a simplistic link between God and the sun disk) and
the thoroughly Israelite character of Psalm 104—by any reckoning a
sun hymn adapted to suit the particular needs of a Yahwistic cult.

To conclude, the evidence of Psalm 104 is ambiguous with respect
to the question of a solar understanding of the deity on the part of the
psalmist. We may nonetheless be sure that the psalmist has distanced
himself from the concept within Atenism that God was the same as the
sun as a physical object. Beyond this, however, it is not clear whether
the poetic imagery itself reflects a solar understanding of the deity, let
alone whether, on the assumption of allusions to Yahweh as solar, this
imagery reflects a concrete notion of God as solar within the cult. If a
polemic against sun worship, Psalm 104 was likely directed not
against sun worship in general nor against a foreign cult, but against a
form of solar Yahwism that, like the cult of Akhenaten and perhaps
Gibeon, held to a rather simplistic one-to-one correspondence between
God and the physical form of the sun itself. While neither the notion
of God as solar in Psalm 104 nor the notion that the poem is a polemic
against an indigenous form of Atenism can be established with
certainty, that there was need to react against a simplistic equation of
God and physical sun can at least be argued further on the basis of
Genesis 1 to which the next section is now devoted.

Genesis 1.1-5, 14-18

At this point it is worth diverting our attention from Psalms 19 and
104 to consider another passage in which confusion has arisen over
the claim of the text that the sun was created by God, namely the
account of creation in Genesis 1. Of interest here are vv. 14-18 and
the traditional view that the minimal role assigned to sun and moon in
these verses implies a polemic against Israel's neighbours who held

religion within the context of a discussion of Psalm 104. Many possible points of
similarity come to mind: iconoclasm, 'monotheism', transcendence, complete power,
cosmic regularity, creativity, tendency toward demythologizing, etc.

that the sun and other astral bodies were deities which often played a prominent role in creation.[1] In light of my observation earlier that a distinction between God and the solar orb which he created does not necessarily imply discontinuity between God and the sun, it is worth exploring the possibility that Genesis 1, like 1 Kgs 8.12 and Psalms 19 and 104, may presuppose points of continuity between God and the sun.

First, although Israel was probably not ignorant of its neighbours' beliefs about the astral bodies, there is little indication from the context to suggest that the biblical writer is launching a polemic here against a *foreign* cosmogony. Rather, vv. 14-18 play an integral role within the parallel structure of the chapter as a whole and this suggests that these verses simply contribute towards what appears otherwise to be a rather unselfconscious articulation of a Hebrew understanding of creation.

Secondly, the point of vv. 14-18—that the God of Israel acted alone in creation, that is, without the sun and moon—presupposes a context in which confusion could have arisen regarding the relationship between the God of Israel and the sun and moon. While the clarification of the confusion may have served a polemical purpose vis-à-vis a foreign cult, there is certainly no reason to doubt that the clarification was directed rather towards a point of theology within Yahwistic circles.

Thirdly, Genesis 1 bears testimony to the notion of there being continuity between God and both the sun and moon. For example, the first recorded words of God are $y^e h\hat{\imath}$ *'ôr*, 'let there be light', words so well known that they might elude the fact that, without reference to the sun, these words could perhaps be spoken only by a 'solar' deity. Moreover, in addition to ending the darkness that naturally prevailed before *God* spoke, the words 'let there be light' correspond perfectly with the role of the *lights* in v. 15, namely, 'to give light on the earth'. Moreover, $y^e h\hat{\imath}$ *'ôr*, 'let there be light', is comparable to $y^e h\hat{\imath}$ m^e*'ōrôt*, 'let there be lights', spoken with respect to the heavenly luminaries which God created on day four (v. 14). And still further, there is a clear correspondence between the role of God on day one and the role of the heavenly luminaries on day four (vv. 4, 17-18), namely, to 'separate light from darkness':

1. See, for example, G.J. Wenham, *Genesis 1–15* (WBC, 1; Waco, TX: Word Books, 1987), p. 21.

wayyabdēl bên hā'ôr ûbên hahōšek
And He [God] separated the light from the darkness...

wayyittēn 'ōtām 'ᵉlōhîm birqîa' haššāmayim...
lᵉhabdîl bên hā'ôr ûbên hahōšek
And God set them [the lights] in the firmament of heaven...
to separate the light from the darkness.

There must be some reason for what clearly appear to be links between the activity of God and the heavenly luminaries. Although none of the correspondences are necessarily inconsistent with the traditional polemical interpretation, they are nevertheless perfectly consistent with what we have seen elsewhere to be a conscious attempt to articulate a *distinction* between the God of Israel and the sun that at the same time presupposes *continuity* between God and the sun.

In summary, the inordinate amount of attention given to the role of the sun and moon in Gen. 1.14-18 can be understood as a response to an important theological issue within ancient Israelite religion. The issue arose in light of the common association between God and the sun and moon,[1] and concerned the extent to which God in creation acted independently of the two great lights with which he was closely associated. The biblical writer responds emphatically to this issue by stating that God and his activity are by no means limited by his association with sun and moon. Thus, whereas continuity between God and the sun and moon can be seen through the assignment of roles to God that normally belong to the sun and moon, a clear and emphatic message of discontinuity is evident through God's execution of these roles independently of the sun and its nocturnal counterpart and in fact three days prior to a further act whereby God creates these two 'great lights' (v. 16).

1.   It is beyond the scope of the present study to deal with the role of the moon in ancient Israelite religion. The reference to moon here occasions no difficulty, however; as I have mentioned in passing before, the moon seems to have functioned as the nocturnal counterpart to the sun as a symbol of Yahweh. Regarding the 'stars', these are mentioned in v. 16, almost as an afterthought. The reference is nonetheless appropriate in view of the association between God and the whole Host of Heaven (to use the Deuteronomistic expression) and in view of the writer's purpose to recount how all the various aspects of the created order came into being.

*Theophanies and 'Seeing the Face of God': A Case for a Solar
Dimension*
Consideration is given here to two notions relevant to theophanies,[1]
namely, the possible presence of poetic language of God as sun in
theophanies and the expression 'to see the face of God', an expression
sometimes interpreted with reference to the sun and quite widely
attested in theophanic (and other) contexts.[2] Each of these issues is
examined briefly, then reconsidered after a digression to Gen. 32.23-
33 [22-32], the relevance of which will become clear.

The subject of theophanies can hardly be considered without
recognizing the important work of Cross and Miller[3] on theophanies
involving the manifestation of God through nature.[4] To illustrate this
category of theophanies in such a way as to highlight their nature and
complexities, Deut. 33.2 and portions of Hab. 3.3-15 will be cited.
First, Deut. 33.2:

> Yahweh from Sinai came,
> Dawned from Seir upon them,[5]
> Shone from Mount Paran.
> He came[6] with myriads of Holy Ones[7]...[8]

---

1. For example, Deut. 33.2; Ps. 18[= 2 Sam. 22].8-16 [7-15]; Hab. 3.3-15
(especially vv. 4, 8, 11). On theophanies in general, see in addition to commentaries
on relevant passages, J. Morgenstern, 'Biblical Theophanies', *ZA* 25 (1911),
pp. 139-93; *ZA* 28 (1914), pp. 15-60; J. Jeremias, *Theophanie: Die Geschichte
einer alttestamentlichen Gattung* (WMANT, 10; Neukirchen–Vluyn: Neukirchener
Verlag, 2nd edn, 1977); *idem*, 'Theophany in the OT', *IDBSup*, pp. 896-98; Cross,
Canaanite Myth, pp. 91-111, 147-94. K. Vollers ('Die solare Seite des
alttestamentlichen Gottesbegriffes', *ARW* 9 [1900], pp. 176-84), argues for a solar
origin of Yahweh in his discussion of the expression 'glory of YHWH', but the
argumentation upon which this claim is based was not taken seriously even in its time
(see, for example, Morgenstern, 'Biblical Theophanies [Part 2]', pp. 58-59).

2. See, for example, Ahlström, *Psalm 89*, pp. 85-89, and the cautious remarks
of M.S. Smith, '"Seeing God" in the Psalms: The Background to the Beatific Vision
in the Hebrew Bible', *CBQ* 50 (1988), pp. 171-83.

3. Cross, *Canaanite Myth*, pp. 147-94, and Miller, *Divine Warrior*.

4. See, for example, Jeremias, 'Theophany in the OT', pp. 896-98.

5. The LXX, Syriac, Targum and Vulgate attest to *lānû*, 'upon us'; cf. RSV.
BHS suggests emendation to *lᵉ'ammô*, 'upon his people', or the like.

6. Cf. Aramaic *'th*, 'to come'. Another possibility is *'ittô*, 'with him' (cf.
Syriac, and Miller, *Divine Warrior*, p. 78).

7. LXX *sun muriasin Kades*, 'with myriads of Kadesh'. In light of the context

followed by portions of Hab. 3.3-15:

> 3 God from Teman came,
> The Holy One from Mount Paran.
> His splendour covered the heavens,
> His praise filled the earth.
> 4 Brightness, there was, like light,
> Rays[1] from his own hand;
> Therein His power is concealed...[2]
> 10 The mountains saw you and writhed;
> A torrent of waters crossed over;
> The deep gave forth its cry,
> It lifted its hands on high.
> 11 Sun and moon stood still on high
> At the light of your arrows shooting,
> At the brightness of your flashing spear...
> 15 You trampled the sea with your horses,
> Stirring the mighty waters...

According to Cross, the starting place for the understanding of the theophanic material in Deut. 33.2 and Hab. 3.3-15 (and other passages) is the premise that they are based on theophanies of the storm god Baal and that as such they are 'storm theophanies'.[3] More

and reference to Meribath-kadesh in Deut. 32.51, it is possible that the phrase translated here 'myriads of Holy Ones' is a place name; cf. JPSV.

8.   The last stich is obscure and not translated. Whether this line reflects storm or solar imagery is debated (on which see later in this discussion). To illustrate the nature of the debate and difficulties of translation, the Massoretes vocalize *'ēšdāt* as if two words; cf. Vulgate's *ignea lex*. But we must in this case infer from the second word a Persian loan word *dāt*, 'law', which seems unlikely. Another possibility is an emendation to *'ēš lappidôt*, 'fire of flames', implied, for example, in the rendition of RSV.

1.   The rendering of *qarnayim* as 'rays' is justifiable in light of the context, but must be judged uncertain because this passage is quite obscure and such a meaning is not clearly attested elsewhere in the Hebrew Bible (J.M. Sasson, 'Bovine Symbolism in the Exodus Narrative', *VT* 18 [1968], p. 486).

2.   This verse is very obscure. It is nonetheless clear that the imagery is of God as light and in view of the parallel between v. 3a and Deut. 33.2 it is possible that, to use Gaster's words, 'the poet is comparing the appearance of YHWH *to the sunrise* (cf. vv. 3 and 4ab; cf. Deut 33 2)' (T.H. Gaster, 'On Habakkuk 3 4', *JBL* 62 [1943], p. 345).

3.   Cross, *Canaanite Myth*, p. 157. For Cross's discussion of Deut. 33.2 in this work, see *Canaanite Myth*, p. 101.

specifically, these biblical storm theophanies are viewed as an example of a first kind of genre apparent in the Yahwistic reflex of this mythical material, namely the march of the Divine Warrior into battle.[1] Thus, whereas in the case of Baal, the battle was against the forces of chaos such as Yam, 'Sea', and Mot, 'Death', the battle of Yahweh, though preserving the mythic imagery relating to a conflict with the sea, is thought to have been historicized in contexts of battle in the Exodus and Conquest.[2]

To evaluate, there can be no doubt that much of the biblical material describing the manifestation of God with resultant effects upon nature is indebted to imagery like that associated with Baal as storm god;[3] as is well known, parallels between Baal and Yahweh are clearly evident in the association of both of these deities with the flood,[4] thunder and lightning,[5] riding the clouds,[6] and the language of a cosmic conflict involving the sea.[7]

In my judgment, however, the legitimate recognition of the presence of storm-god imagery in these and other passages has sometimes overshadowed another dimension which also needs to be reckoned with, namely, the presence of sun-god imagery. A clear case in point is Deut. 33.2 in which the verbs used to describe the appearance of Yahweh are *zāraḥ*, 'rise, dawn', and *hôpîa'*, 'shine forth',

---

1. For a definition of this category, see Cross, *Canaanite Myth*, pp. 157, 162-63. Cross considers Hab. 3.3-15 and Deut. 33.2 as examples of the Warrior's march, the latter including 'only the march from Sinai northward, the Conquest proper'. (The other genre focuses on 'the return of the Divine Warrior to take up kingship' [*Canaanite Myth*, p. 162].)

2. Cross, *Canaanite Myth*, p. 157.

3. Note, for example, the effect upon nature resulting from Baal's speaking after a window has been opened in his palace in *KTU* 1.4 VII 25-37.

4. Cf., for example, Ps. 29.10 and RS 24.245 [= *KTU* 1.101] 1-3.

5. Cf., for example, Hab. 3.9 and the same Ugaritic passage cited in the previous note, ll. 3b-4 as well as *KTU* 1.4 V 6-9. On connections between Baal's thunder and both Habakkuk and Ps. 29, see, for example, J. Day, 'Echoes of Baal's Seven Thunders and Lightnings in Psalm XXIX and Habakkuk III 9 and the Identity of the Seraphim in Isaiah VI', *VT* 29 (1979), pp. 143-51.

6. Cf., for example, Hab. 3.11 and *KTU* 1.2 IV 8.

7. Cf., for example, Hab. 3.8 and *KTU* 1.2 I and 1.2 IV. On further possible connections between Hab. 3.5 and Canaanite mythology, see J. Day, 'New Light on the Mythological Background to Resheph in Habakkuk III 5', *VT* 29 (1979), pp. 353-54.

images applicable in the case of the sun but not storm. Not surprisingly, then, Deut. 33.2 has often been interpreted with reference
to the sun (alone).[1] To be sure, as Miller has pointed out, more
general language of fire and light such as that found in Hab. 3.11 is no
less attributable to Baal and other non-solar deities than to a solar
deity,[2] but the language of Yahweh rising and shining in Deut. 33.2
can hardly be aptly described as a 'storm theophany'.[3] In short, there
is a distinctively solar element in some biblical theophanies which
cannot easily be subsumed under the category 'storm theophany'.
Although often mixed with storm language (as we saw for example in
Psalm 104), solar language is so apparent that, at least in the case of
Deut. 33.2, 'storm theophany' is perhaps somewhat misleading.

1. The solar language has recently been noted by M. Smith ('"Seeing God" in
the Psalms', p. 177) and Carol Meyers (*The Tabernacle Menorah: A Synthetic Study
of a Symbol from the Biblical Cult* [ASOR Dissertation Series, 2; Missoula, MT:
Scholars Press for ASOR, 1976], p. 145). A typical interpretation which predates
the work of Cross and Miller is offered by G.E. Wright ('The Book of
Deuteronomy: Introduction and Exegesis', *IB*, II, p. 528): 'In vss. 1–3 it depicts
God as the rising sun, shining upon Israel from Sinai and the wilderness (Seir and
Paran...). With him come the myriads of the heavenly host, worshipping him and
ready to do his bidding.'

2. P.D. Miller, Jr, 'Fire in the Mythology of Canaan and Israel', *CBQ* 17
(1965), pp. 256-61. In the case of Hab. 3.11, the language of light clearly does not
pertain to the physical form of the sun or moon which is distinguished from that
which produces the light, but the language of light might be solar in the case of Hab.
3.4. In light of Miller's point, however, such cannot be simply assumed in the case
of Hab. 3.4, notoriously obscure in any case.

3. In support of Deut. 33.2 as descriptive of the march of Yahweh as Divine
Warrior, Miller (*Divine Warrior*, pp. 76-77) notes the finding at Mari and Ugarit of
names including a verb *ypʻ* together with a theophoric element identifiable with Baal-
Hadad, and cites also *CTA* 3 iii 34//iv 49: *mn.ib.ypʻ.lb'l.ṣrt.lrkb.ʻrpt*, 'What foe has
risen against Baal, Enemy against the cloud rider?' On the basis of this evidence
Miller concludes that 'sparse though the data may be, one is forced to conclude on
this basis that *ypʻ* is a term of battle particularly associated with the deity'. To evaluate, the usage of a verb *ypʻ* with reference to Baal is striking, but (1) in the mythological material cited by Miller, it is not Baal but some enemy who 'rises up' against
Baal and (2) as O. Loretz has argued ('Ugaritische und hebräische Lexikographie',
UF 12 [1980], pp. 279-86), Hebrew *hôpîaʻ*, 'shine forth', is not to be associated
with Ugaritic *ypʻ*, 'rise up'. In any case, that the meaning of the verb in question is
'shine forth' in Deut. 33.2 is virtually assured by its occurrence in parallelism with
zāraḥ, 'rise', clearly attested in non-martial and explicitly solar contexts.

What implications can be drawn from the descriptions of Yahweh as the sun in this early theophanic material? More specifically, does this language of Yahweh as the sun here merely reflect the use of poetic imagery to describe God or should it be related to what we have seen elsewhere to be an understanding of Yahweh as solar within the cult?

A cautious and balanced response seems appropriate in light of several considerations, not the least of which is the clear fact that, with few possible exceptions such as Deut. 33.2, the language of God as sun within this category of theophanies tends to be thoroughly blended with the language of God as storm deity.

The admixture of sun and storm language may be accounted for in one of at least two ways. First, it might be that the mythic tradition(s) which informed the Israelite understanding conveyed the notion of a deity who was identifiable with both the sun and storm, something like a 'solar Baal'. But, as Dion has emphasized recently, it is difficult to find evidence elsewhere in western Asia for a deity who may be characterized as both storm god and sun god,[1] and in the case of a few exceptions (the witness of Philo of Byblos concerning Baal Shamem and of Macrobius concerning Zeus Heliopolis at Baalbek) the solar character of these storm deities is arguably a late development.[2] And secondly, as M.S. Smith has recently stressed, this blending of sun and storm language might simply suggest that God's nature is so great that his appearance cannot be limited to one natural phenomenon, an interpretation with a considerable amount of evidence in its favour.[3]

On the other hand, however, new evidence has been adduced in the

1. See the last few pages of Dion, 'YHWH as Sun-God and Storm-God'.

2. See Smith, *Early History of God*, pp. 43-44, 66-67 (nn. 19-20, 25-27) and Olyan, *Asherah and the Cult of Yahweh*, pp. 62-64.

3. Smith, '"Seeing God" in the Psalms', p. 180. Smith (who notes a similar mixing of sun and storm language in the description of Yahweh's *kābôd* in Ezek. 43.1-5) draws attention to Ps. 50.1-3 in which, according to Aloysius Fitzgerald, Yahweh's procession is described in the language of both the sun (vv. 1b-2) and a sirocco (v. 3). Smith also notes a tile from neo-Assyrian times in which the god Assur is depicted as both riding a sun disk while he aims a bow at his enemies and being accompanied by storm clouds from which rain is falling. Finally, Smith draws attention to several passages in Enuma Elish (I, ll. 101-102, 157; VI, ll. 128-29) in which solar language is applied to Marduk to whom storm language is more often applied. Smith concludes, 'The depiction of Assur and the description of Marduk exalt them by attributing different natural powers to them much as Yahweh is exalted in Ezek. 43.1-5 and Ps. 50.1-3' ('"Seeing God" in the Psalms', p. 180.).

present study which suggests the presence of a solar understanding of Yahweh within ancient Israel. In view of this it is possible that the solarization of storm language associated with Baal may reflect the adaptation of this imagery to the cult of Yahweh. At any rate, given the presence of clear evidence for the notion of Yahweh as sun, it would be unwise to dismiss too readily the possibility that the language of God as sun in early theophanic material[1] involves more than the mere use of poetic imagery for Yahweh.

Once again, then, it has proven difficult to determine whether or not solar language used of God in poetic material reflects a concrete understanding of the deity as sun. Nevertheless, the language of Yahweh as sun in Deut. 33.2 is at least consistent with a solar understanding of the God who marches on Israel's behalf (on which see further the section below on Gen. 33). In sum: although the poetic language of Yahweh as sun in theophanies *may* reflect a solar understanding of Yahweh within the cult, there is nothing in the poetic language itself that requires this understanding.

Turning now to the second issue relevant to theophanies, namely the notion of a possible solar interpretation of expressions for seeing the face of God, Mark S. Smith has recently asked whether references to seeing God's face and the shining of God's face in Psalms such as 17, 27 and 63 might indicate that 'the experience of seeing God was a solar theophany at dawn'.[2] Smith concludes that the language of seeing God does not refer to a solar theophany because 'seeing God' can refer to the divine presence in contexts in which no solar connotations are likely and because 'the experience of God in all these psalms is never reduced to solar language'.[3] Having stated this, however, Smith nonetheless qualifies his judgment and leaves open the possibility of solar influence:

---

1. It is difficult to know from Judg. 5.4-5, perhaps the earliest form of this tradition, whether a solar understanding of the deity is presupposed in the description of the 'going forth' (*yṣ'*) of Yahweh from Seir and his marching from Edom's plain. Such is possible but by no means certain.

2. Smith, '"Seeing God" in the Psalms', p. 175.

3. Smith, '"Seeing God" in the Psalms', p. 181.

As psalms of vigil, Psalms 17, 27, and 63 do not reduce the experience of
God's presence to a solar theophany; but it is possible that the experience
of the dawn after the night vigil helped to evoke the perception of the
luminescent dimension of the divine presence.[1]

To evaluate, Smith is right that in most instances 'the face' of God
simply refers to the divine presence.[2] Similarly, in many cases the
hope that God's face would 'shine' denotes simply the hope for divine
blessing.[3] In most examples no solar context can reasonably be
inferred from expressions for seeing the face of God. Contrary to the
tenor of Smith's argument, however, none of these conclusions in any
way precludes the possibility that there might be *some* cases in which
the sun was associated with the divine presence or even identified with
the face of God. This is because the notion of seeing God's face might
have implied different things through time or to different groups and
because no solar context would normally be expected even if a
concrete solar image lay behind some references to the notion of
seeing the face of God (in the same way for example that one need not
be present, and often is not, when reference is made to the notion of
that one being seen). Of course, for these theoretical possibilities to be
substantiated there must be at least one case in which the divine
presence when actually manifested (as in a theophany) can indubitably
be equated with the presence of the sun. As I shall attempt to argue,
Gen. 32.23-33 [22-32] constitutes such a case.

a. *Genesis 32.23-33 [22-32]*
In my judgment a hitherto unrecognized case of an association
between the sun and the face of God is Gen. 32.23-33 [22-32], the
well-known story of Jacob's encounter with the mysterious *'îš*, 'man'
at the river Jabbok. Leaving aside for the moment the problem of the
identity of the 'man' (I will argue shortly on the analogy of Egyptian

1. Smith, '"Seeing God" in the Psalms', p. 181.
2. See, for example, R.C. Dentan, 'Face', *IDB*, II, p. 221, in which Num.
6.25 is cited as evidence that '"to make the face to shine upon" is an indication of
friendly acceptance', and in which Exod. 10.11 is noted as evidence for 'face' as
'presence'. As M. Fishbane has noted ('Form and Reformulation of the Biblical
Priestly Blessing', *JAOS* 103 [1983], pp. 116-17), there are Mesopotamian parallels
to the priestly blessing in Num. 6.25 which underscore the sense of the bestowal of
favour. (Smith's article drew my attention to the article of Fishbane.)
3. See the previous note.

literature that he is in fact a pre-dawn phase of the sun, a divine figure in human form that makes his way through the waters of the netherworld at night), the following aspects of this familiar story are relevant to the discussion. (1) Jacob detains the *'îš* until the 'breaking of dawn' (*ʿᵃlôt haššāḥar*) (vv. 25, 27; cf. v. 32 [24, 26; cf. 31]). (2) Jacob's having detained the *'îš* at daybreak is in turn clearly linked with his claim, 'I have seen God face to face' (a claim which is clearly difficult to understand by more conventional explanations, since all that Jacob has seen thus far is a 'man' whom he has detained until daybreak) (v. 31 [30]). (3) Immediately following Jacob's declaration that he had seen 'God face to face', the narrator, as if to keep anyone from missing the point, states *wayyizraḥ lô haššemeš kaʾᵃšer ʿābar 'et pᵉnûʾēl*, 'the sun rose upon him as he passed Penuel' (that is, Face-of-God). Here, I suggest, the narrative leaves the reader with no option but to equate the rising of the sun with Jacob's having seen the 'face of God'.

At this point it might be objected that the present explanation is flawed because it is dependent upon there being an association between the face of God (which I consider to be the sun here) and a figure who can hardly be identified with the sun because he encounters Jacob at night and afflicts him at a point which, though admittedly close to daybreak, may not have involved the appearance of the sun. Far from creating a problem, however, the difficulty appears to confirm the equation between God and the sun.

As Gunkel long ago illustrated so well,[1] any attempt to resolve convincingly the problem of the identity of the mysterious *'îš* must reckon squarely with the problem why the shadowy figure must depart by daybreak, twice highlighted as critical to the narrative. An alternative explanation to Gunkel's identification of the man with a night demon[2] is that the figure in question is a pre-dawn phase of the sun who, as in Egyptian literature, travels through the waters of the netherworld en-route to daybreak.[3] The time constraint thus lies in the

1. H. Gunkel, *Genesis übersetzt und erklärt* (Göttingen: Vandenhoeck & Ruprecht, 7th edn, 1910), pp. 359-65.

2. Gunkel, *Genesis*, pp. 359-65.

3. The notion that the sun had a cycle which involved a nightly trek through the netherworld was extremely widespread in the ancient Near East. For example, in Egypt the sun god is attested in three phases: Chepri in the morning, Re during the day, and Atum/Osiris at night. Moreover, representations of this night-time phase of

fact that it was a physical impossibility for two phases of the sun, night and morning, to coexist; the appearance of daybreak thus automatically signalled—even necessitated—the departure of the night phase.[1] Moreover, unlike Gunkel's explanation, that the 'man' is a pre-dawn phase of the sun brings together key elements of the story *as a whole* by providing a common basis upon which to understand the apparently natural yet otherwise inexplicable progression in the story (a) from the 'îš, 'man' to the point of daybreak, (b) from Jacob wrestling with the man at dawn to his having 'seen the face of God', and (c) from discussion of seeing the face of God to mention of 'the sun' rising on Jacob when he crossed 'Penuel' (Face-of-God), limping on his hip. What ties the story together of course is that the 'man', seeing the face of God, and the rising sun are all the same.

In view of the importance of this story and in view of the fact that the best test of an interpretation is its ability to account for the text, the episode is here cited in full. I leave the reader to decide whether the story makes good sense on the basis of a two-part hypothesis according to which (1) the 'man' is understood to be a pre-dawn phase of the sun and (2) the sun itself is presumed to be the face of God:

> 23 The same night he arose and took his two wives, his two maids, and his eleven children, and crossed the ford of the Jabbok. 24 He took them and sent them across the stream, and likewise everything that he had. 25 And Jacob was left alone; and a man wrestled with him until the breaking of the day. 26 When the man saw that he did not prevail against Jacob, he touched the hollow of his thigh; and Jacob's thigh was put out of joint as he wrestled with him. 27 Then he said, 'Let me go, for the day is breaking'. But Jacob said, 'I will not let you go, unless you bless me'. 28 And he said to him, 'What is your name?' And he said, 'Jacob'. 29 Then he said, 'Your name shall no more be called Jacob, but Israel,

the sun are essentially human in form, though clearly divine (solar) in nature. Moreover, that Jacob was at a river might have meant that he was thought to have been particularly susceptible there to a visit from the divine figure who was making his way through the watery realm below en route to the horizon to the east.

1. A possible exception, of course, is at critical transitional points between phases such as daybreak, a tension upon which the storyteller capitalizes to provide a context in which Jacob, like no other, actually saw God face to face by tenaciously holding on to the 'îš at the very point of its transition to the sun, and yet lived—no doubt because his direct contact with God's face, that is, the sun, was prior to the time of its fully-damaging intensity. (Note the obvious parallel between the impossibility of looking at the sun and seeing the face of God.)

for you have striven with God and men, and you have prevailed'.
30 Then Jacob asked him, 'Tell me, I pray, your name'. But he said,
'Why is it that you ask my name?' And there he blessed him. 31 So
Jacob called the name of the place Penuel, saying, 'For I have seen God
face to face, and yet my life is preserved'. 32 The sun rose upon him as
he passed Penuel, limping because of his thigh. 33 Therefore to this day
the Israelites do not eat the sinew of the hip of the thigh, because he
touched the hollow of Jacob's thigh on the sinew of the hip. (RSV)

Clearly there is far more to this wonderful story than the two-part
interpretation here.[1] For our purposes, however, it is sufficient to
suggest that Gen. 32.23-33 [22-32] provides not only a clear case in
which the notion of seeing the face of God is synonymous with seeing
the sun,[2] but a clear case also of a theophany to an individual in which
the divine is manifested as a 'solar' being.

b. *Seeing the Face of God in the Psalms Reconsidered*
To return briefly to the notion of seeing God in the Psalms, in light of
the evidence adduced above which strongly suggests an association
between the sun and seeing the face of God at least in some contexts
(and in light also of Ps. 24.6 which will be considered shortly), that
there are cases in the Psalms in which seeing the face of God refers to
a solar theophany at dawn is far more likely than Smith has implied.
As reasonable a candidate as any is Ps.17.15:[3]

---

1.   Elsewhere I plan to argue that this story and other elements in the conflict
between Jacob and Esau have a clear parallel in the conflict of the two brothers in the
Egyptian 'Tale of Two Brothers'. Suffice it to note in support of my hypothesis that
in both stories the deity who facilitates the reconciliation of two brothers who find
themselves on opposite sides of a river (and in each case at the time of 'dawn',
'when the sun disk rises') is solar in character.

2.   Egyptian literature is of course familiar with the understanding that the sun is
the face of Re. Note, for example, words of those who tow the boat of the sun god
Re through the netherworld at night: 'We follow Re towards heaven. Mayest thou
have power over thy great face, oh Re. Mayest thou be satisfied with thy mysterious
face, oh Re. Re's face is opened [that is, his disk begins to spread light]'. The
translation is by J. Zandee, 'The Book of Gates', *Liber Amicorum: Studies in
Honour of Professor Dr C.J. Bleeker* (Leiden: Brill, 1969), pp. 316-17.

3.   Ps. 17.15 was suggested by Smith as a possible case of a solar theophany
('"Seeing God" in the Psalms', p. 175), but later rejected on the grounds that
tᵉmûnâ, 'form', is similar to *pānîm*, 'face', in denoting the divine presence ('"Seeing
God" in the Psalms', p. 181). In response, the argument I used earlier in the case of

'ᵃnî bᵉṣedeq 'eḥzeh pānêkā
'eśbᵉ'â bᵉhāqîṣ tᵉmûnātekā
As for me, I shall behold thy face in righteousness;
When I awake, I shall be satisfied with beholding your form. (RSV)

c. *Deuteronomy 33.2 Reconsidered in Light of Genesis 33.1-16*
Finally, to return to the matter of whether the solar imagery of Deut.
33.2 reflects a solar understanding of the deity, a further argument
which bears on this matter arises from the interpretation of Gen.
32.23-33 [22-32] offered above, but includes consideration of the
broader narrative framework of Genesis 33–34.

It has long been noted that there must be some kind of direct
correspondence between Jacob having seen the face of God and his
statement to Esau in the chapter which immediately follows, 'for to
see your face [Esau's] is like seeing the face of God, with such favour
you have received me'.[1] To be sure, the correspondence can be
accounted for in part on the basis of the fact that, like God, Esau
responded favourably to Jacob.[2] However, in light of the obvious
significance attributed to Jacob's having, incredibly, seen God 'face to
face' on the night before this suspense-filled human encounter, and in
light also of the relative rarity of the expression 'to see the face of
God' elsewhere in Genesis, it would be surprising if there were no
more significance to the claim that seeing Esau's face was like seeing
the face of God beyond the mere fact that Esau, like God, bestowed
favour. As I hope to show, the significance of the comparison between
seeing Esau's face and seeing the face of God lies in a parallel between
the march of Esau from Seir (for example Gen. 32.4) and the theophanic tradition of the march of Yahweh as sun from Seir (Deut. 33.2).

pānîm equally applies in the case of *tᵉmûnâ*: that the noun denotes the divine presence
does not exclude possible occasional reference to the sun as a tangible sign of that
presence. Moreover, in Deut. 4 the prohibition against the worship of the sun occurs
in the context of the claim that Yahweh at Horeb had no *tᵉmûnâ* 'form'. This seems
to imply that the covenant community whom the writer addresses understood the sun
to be a 'form' of Yahweh. For a criticism of the alternative explanations for the
meaning of seeing God in Ps. 17 (and elsewhere), see Smith, '"Seeing God" in the
Psalms', pp. 173-76. See also my discussion of Deuteronomy offered earlier in this
chapter.
   1. That is, *kî 'al kēn rā'îtî pāneykā kir'ôt pᵉnê 'ᵉlōhîm wattirṣēnî* (Gen. 33.10).
   2. This is in fact a good example of the usage of 'to see the face of God' as an
expression of divine favour.

According to Gen. 32.4, Esau marches northward from the land of Seir of Edom (cf. 33.1, 12-17), accompanied by his army. Moreover, the march of Esau with his entourage is mentioned in the verse that immediately follows the description of Jacob's encounter with the divine-solar figure, 'And Jacob lifted up his eyes, and saw Esau coming and with him four hundred men...'[1] Further, following the description of the encounter with Esau in which seeing his face is equated with seeing the face of God, the text twice mentions 'Seir'.[2]

The point is no doubt clear by now: there is a parallel between the poetic tradition of the march of Yahweh as the sun from Seir and the narrative tradition of the march of Esau as the 'face of God' from Seir. In other words, Yahweh as *sun* in Deut. 33.2 does exactly what Esau as the 'face-of-God' does in Gen. 32-33; as 'sun' and on account of Israel, he marches northward from the land of Seir of Edom (Deut. 33.2; cf. Hab. 3.3-4), accompanied by an army host.[3]

Finally, to consider this narrative parallel in light of the question whether the march of Yahweh as sun from Seir as reflected in Deut. 33.2 is genuinely solar, the parallel of course cannot be adduced in favour of such a notion since its validity is dependent upon a solar understanding of the poetic material. The impasse thus remains. The parallel nonetheless appears to be consistent with the notion that Yahweh's march from Seir as sun was understood to convey more than mere poetic imagery and thus perhaps a genuinely solar understanding of the deity. Moreover, the parallel offers a clear explanation for the otherwise obscure but unmistakable allusion in Gen. 33.10 to 'seeing the face of God' in 32.23-33 [22-32].

Psalm 24 and the Procession of the Ark
Psalm 24, and with it the ceremony of bringing the ark into the Jerusalem temple which it recounts,[4] also appear to show signs of an

1. Gen. 33.1.
2. Gen. 33.14, 16.
3. Whether MT *m^erib^ebōt kōdeš* in Deut. 33.2 refers to a heavenly host or not (so Cross, *Canaanite Myth*, p. 101, RSV, NIV) is less than clear. This interpretation is highlighted for the purposes of the parallel. That Yahweh in his march would be accompanied by a host of attendants might be assumed in any case; cf. Judg. 5.20, Hab. 3.5.
4. Although its nature is debated, in all probability an ark procession underlies the psalm (see, for example, Kraus, *Psalms 1–59*, p. 312). I do not find convincing

association between the sun and Yahweh. Although none are particularly compelling in themselves, the indicators when considered as a whole render it highly plausible that Psalm 24 presupposes a solar understanding of Yahweh of Hosts, the King of Glory. The indicators of this are as follows, beginning with a few general considerations based upon what has been adduced elsewhere in this study concerning the loci of solar Yahwism.

First, evidence examined earlier in this study (including for example Ps. 80) pointed to a possible solar connotation to the expression *yhwh ṣᵉbā'ôt*, 'Yahweh, Sublime Host', or the like. It is perhaps no coincidence then that this epithet, rare in the Psalms, occurs as a kind of climax within Psalm 24 (v. 10).[1] Secondly, that *yhwh ṣᵉbā'ôt* should be interpreted with reference to the sun in this psalm receives further support from the occurrence of the epithet in parallelism with the expression 'the King of Glory', both elements of which have at times similarly been interpreted with reference to the sun.[2] And thirdly, many have argued that the setting for the ark procession described in this psalm is the autumnal Feast of Booths.[3] If so, it is relevant in light of an apparently solar dimension to the Feast of

the alternative explanation of Cooper, according to whom Ps. 24.7-10 is a fragment of a myth in which the high God confronts the gatekeepers of the netherworld either upon the deity's entrance to or return from the netherworld (A. Cooper, 'Ps 24:7-10: Mythology and Exegesis', *JBL* 102 [1983], pp. 37-60). Cooper's interpretation, however, may be no less amenable to a solar understanding for the character of the deity, Yahweh of Hosts, who emerges triumphantly from the netherworld (see Cooper, 'Ps 24:7-10', p. 44 n. 37).

1. See Cooper, 'Ps 24:7-10', p. 52. Incidentally, although I am not convinced by Cooper's interpretation of Ps. 24.7-10, it can nonetheless be seen to imply a solar understanding for the character of *yhwh ṣebā'ôt* which is compatible with my own view (Cooper, 'Ps 24:7-10', pp. 44, 52-55; cf. my discussion, 'The Epithet "Yahweh of Hosts"').

2. For reference to Yahweh as 'king' by solar Yahwists, see for example, Zeph. 1.6 and the interpretation of *malkām* 'their King', offered earlier in this study. On the notion of light and even sunlight associated with 'glory', see respectively G. von Rad, *Old Testament Theology* (2 vols.; New York: Harper & Row, 1962 [German, 1957]), II, p. 240, and Ezek. 43.2 (on which see my discussion earlier in this chapter); cf. also Isa. 60.1-3. The many works of J. Morgenstern advocate a solar interpretation of the glory of the Lord (see throughout this study).

3. I refer to the well-known theory of an autumnal festival of the enthronement of Yahweh. See further, the next section of this book.

Booths (on which see both later and earlier in this study) to note by implication a possible[1] solar context for this 'enthronement psalm'.

A few observations of Morgenstern also lend some force to a possible solar understanding of the deity in Psalm 24. Concerning reference in this psalm to the *š⁰'ārîm*, 'gates' of the temple and its *piṯḥê 'ôlām*, 'eternal doors', Morgenstern makes two comments, the second of which is dependent upon the validity of the first for its relevance here. First, Morgenstern concludes that an early Christian tradition and perhaps one reflected in the Talmud as well imply that the gates referred to in Psalm 24 were in fact the eastern gates of the temple.[2] And secondly, Morgenstern notes that this eastern gate had names (for example 'Golden Gate', and even 'Sun Gate')[3] as well as traditions associated with it that are clearly amenable to a solar understanding of Yahweh.[4]

A few other factors are relevant to the question of a solar perception of Yahweh in Psalm 24. First, a solar understanding of Yahweh of Hosts, King of glory, makes good sense of the problematic imagery of v. 7:[5]

---

1.   No great weight should be placed on the last point, however, since the biblical material nowhere explicitly links the Feast of Booths with an ark procession beyond the original coincidence of these events in 1 Kgs 8.2-5 (perhaps only a one-time occurrence and thus not descriptive of later practice). See further, de Vaux, *Ancient Israel*, pp. 505-506.

2.   Morgenstern, 'Gates of Righteousness', pp. 14-15. Even if it could be established that both traditions clearly reflect an understanding that the gates mentioned in Ps. 24 were the eastern gates of the temple, the traditional understanding might not have been correct. Morgenstern mentions also that the designation of the eastern gate today as 'The Eternal Gate' might evoke recollection of Ps. 24.7, but the same point applies in this case.

3.   Morgenstern, 'Gates of Righteousness', p. 20. The talmudic term for the eastern gate, *š⁰'r hrysyt*, 'Sun Gate', occurs in *y. 'Erub.* V 22c.

4.   See Morgenstern, 'The Gates of Righteousness', pp. 1-37.

5.   For example, Kraus (*Psalms 1–50*, p. 315) suggests that the verse probably reflects a tension concerning the relationship between the earthly and heavenly temples (which were one) and concerning the dimensions of the former in view of its being also the latter. Cross (*Canaanite Myth*, pp. 91-99) suggests that the city wall is described figuratively as if the divine council of Yahweh who, like the divine assembly on one occasion in the Baal cycle, raise their heads from their knees at the coming of the deity. Though possible, it is open to question whether a wall is likely as a figure for the divine council. In any case, the emphasis in the verse seems clearly

> Lift up your heads, O gates,
> Be lifted up, O ancient doors,
> That the King of Glory may enter!

To understand the significance of the imagery one needs only to imagine worshippers putting words to the wish that the 'King of glory' (that is, Yahweh of Hosts *as sun*) might be able, quite literally, to fit under the eastern temple gates along with his throne, the ark, and for this to happen, of course, the doors and gates would have to be higher.[1] (On what other basis is it possible to explain the emphasis in the verse on the doors/gates being heightened as a means of permitting the King of Glory to enter? Though it might be merely poetic, the imagery of Yahweh as celestial if not specifically solar seems clear.)

Secondly, a solar understanding of Yahweh of Hosts, King of Glory, may be adduced from v. 6 (to which brief reference was made in connection with Gen. 32-33). Virtually every commentator has noted of the MT of v. 6, *zeh dôr dōrᵉšāyw[2] mᵉbaqqᵉšê pānêkā yaᵃqob*, 'This is the generation of those who seek Him, who seek your face, O Jacob', that the second line makes little sense in the context;[3] since Yahweh is referred to in the first line ('those who seek Him'), Yahweh and not Jacob must be referred to in the second line. In spite of the apparent corruption of the MT, the original form of the second line can nonetheless probably be identified on the basis of the LXX which reads, *zētountōn to prosōpon tou theou Iakōb*, 'those who seek the face of the God of Jacob'.[4] In view of the interpretation of Gen. 32.23-33 offered earlier and what it meant for Jacob to see the face of God, it is possible that the expression 'the face of the God of

---

to fall not on the wall so much as on the gates/doors, and particularly on their need to be higher in order to permit the King of Glory to enter.

1. This explanation accounts for why particular emphasis is placed upon the gates/doors and in particular upon their height (and the need for this height to permit the entry of the King of Glory). Interestingly, the interpretation offers a possible solution to the problem of the apparent lack in Israel of a cultic symbol with which to celebrate/re-enact Yahweh's enthronement (on which see further the following section).

2. *Qere. Kethib* reads *dršw*.

3. For example, Kraus (*Psalms 1–59*, p. 311) judges the MT reading 'hardly possible according to the parallelism and the context'.

4. This is the reading followed, for example, in the RSV.

Jacob' was taken to be a rather explicit allusion to Yahweh as the sun, in which case it is easy to account for the alteration of the MT of v. 6b (and perhaps also for the fact that the expression 'face of the God of Jacob' is not found elsewhere in the Old Testament). In this passage, then, the psalmist's description of the faithful pilgrims as a generation of those who 'seek the face of the God of Jacob' strongly implies that these worshippers shared a solar understanding of Yahweh of Hosts,[1] the King of Glory about to enter the gates of the sanctuary.[2] Like Psalm 80, this psalm probably identifies *yhwh ṣᵉbāʾôt* with the sun. Moreover, it suggests that the sun played an important role in a cultic setting in which Yahweh's ark was understood to enter his sanctuary (possibly on the occasion of an autumnal festival, to which consideration is given below).

An Autumnal Festival as a Locus for Solar Yahwism?

Throughout this study a number of factors have pointed to a possible connection between the Feast of Booths and solar elements within Yahwism as practised at the Jerusalem temple.[3] The purpose of this section is to draw together these factors as a means of supporting a hypothesis to the effect that an autumnal festival of the Feast of Booths was an important locus for solar Yahwism in ancient Israel.[4] First, however, a word of clarification is in order.

By referring to an autumnal festival of the Feast of Booths I refer, but do not commit myself, to the well-known theory according to

1.   In further support of a solar perception of Yahweh of Hosts in Ps. 24, it is interesting to compare the reference in v. 8 to Yahweh as a *gibbôr*, 'hero' with the notion of the sun god as a 'hero' (cf. for example, Ps. 19.6 [5]).

2.   Cf. Ps. 118.19-20, 26-29, the possible relevance of which is highlighted later in this study, in the discussion of the autumn festival as a possible locus for solar Yahwism.

3.   In view of the purpose of this book, I do not propose to discuss this feast beyond pointing to a solar dimension to it. For detailed discussions of the feast, see, for example, de Vaux, *Ancient Israel*, pp. 495-502; Gaster, *Festivals*, pp. 80-104; R. Martin-Achard, *Essai biblique sur les fêtes d'Israël* (Geneva: Labor et Fides, 1974), pp. 75-92; J.C. Rylaarsdam, 'Booths, Feast of', *IDB*, I, pp. 455-58.

4.   A similar judgment, though based for the most part on different (and often inadequate) evidence, has been reached by J. Morgenstern in his 'Gates of Righteousness', pp. 1-37. My hypothesis was formulated independently of Morgenstern. Since having arrived at a similar conclusion, I have nonetheless gleaned relevant evidence from the work of Morgenstern.

which the Feast of Booths should be understood within the broader context of a New Year festival at which time, for example, the ark was processed and the kingship of Yahweh of Hosts was celebrated or even re-enacted.[1]

There are reasons for expressing ambivalence toward this rather 'full-blown' Autumn Festival of Yahweh's Enthronement.[2] On the one hand, a number of unsubstantiated assumptions are often made with respect to this festival in pre-exilic Israel (for example the notion of an autumnal 'New Year' in pre-exilic Israel,[3] and the celebration specifically of Yahweh's kingship).[4] On the other hand, however, a surprising number of features which scholars often associate with the Autumnal Festival have been shown in this study to possibly reflect the outlook of solar Yahwism,[5] and this leads one to suggest that if there was an Autumnal Festival of Enthronement, it bore the marks of solarized Yahweh worship. Moreover, solar Yahwism offers a clear solution to one of the chief criticisms of the theory of the cultic celebration of Yahweh's kingship, namely that in Israel there was no tangible cultic symbol with which to celebrate/re-enact the enthronement of Yahweh.[6] Thus, for example, the horses and chariot(s) of the sun must have had some role within the cult of Yahweh and in light of

---

1. See, for example, S. Mowinckel, *The Psalm in Israel's Worship* (2 vols.; Oxford: Basil Blackwell, 1962) and J. Eaton, *Kingship and the Psalms* (The Biblical Seminar; Sheffield: JSOT Press, 2nd edn, 1986).

2. For a fair and thorough analysis of the pros and cons vis-à-vis an autumnal New Year festival in ancient Israel, see, D.I. Block, 'New Year', *ISBE*, III, pp. 529-32.

3. On the uncertainty of an autumnal New Year in pre-exilic Israel, see Clines, 'Autumnal New Year in Pre-exilic Israel Reconsidered', pp. 22-40; *idem*, 'New Year', pp. 625-29.

4. De Vaux, *Ancient Israel*, pp. 505-506, who also evaluates the theory in general (pp. 504-506). For a similarly helpful evaluation, see also Kraus, *Psalms 1–59*, pp. 86-89.

5. For example, the time of the autumnal equinox, the worship of *yhwh ṣᵉbā'ôt*, the procession of the ark, and the incorporation of elements associated with the Feast of Booths (cf. for example, Zech. 14).

6. H.-J. Kraus, for example, states the problem as follows: 'How could an enthronement of Yahweh in Israel have been carried out in the first place? There is here no divine image that could have been lifted up to a throne, nor is any cultic symbol familiar to us that might have represented Yahweh' (Kraus, *Psalms 1–59*, 87).

such passages as Ps. 24.7, it is not difficult to imagine that the march of the ark through the gates of the temple perhaps coincided with the westward march of the sun.[1] Thus, while I reserve judgment on the exact nature of the autumnal festival beyond what may be reasonably judged about the Feast of Booths, in setting forth the hypothesis I nonetheless include elements linked with the great Autumn Festival as interpreted more broadly by Mowinckel and others.[2] In either case, my hypothesis is the same: the autumnal festival of Booths appears to have been a locus for solar Yahwism in ancient Israel. Having highlighted an important point of uncertainty, we may now consider several points which support the hypothesis. Though no one point is conclusive, a combination of factors outlined below supports the hypothesis.

1. A tradition in the Mishnah relates that during the Feast of Booths two priests, accompanied by a multitude, assembled at dawn at the eastern gate of the temple area and at sunrise confessed the following as they faced the temple to the west:

> Our fathers when they were in this place turned with their backs to the temple and their faces toward the east, and they worshipped the sun toward the east; but as for us, our eyes are turned toward the Lord.[3]

The clear allusion to Ezek. 8.16 falls short of proving that it was on this same occasion of the Feast of Booths that, at an earlier period, the solar rite to which the Mishnah and Ezekiel refer took place, but it certainly welcomes this conclusion as a possibility.[4]

---

1. On Ps. 24.7, see the interpretation suggested in the previous section.

2. On the assumption that the festival included the elements of sun and cultic procession involving both deity (as sun) and affirmation of the king's reign, a rough analogy might be something like the Egyptian *sd*-festival at the time of Amenophis IV/Akhenaten (on which see Redford, *Akhenaten*, pp. 122-30).

3. *M. Suk.* 5.4.

4. Others have made similar judgments about the implications of this particular rite (called the Rejoicing at the Beth Ha-Shoebah) for our understanding of the Feast. For example, Gaster in stating, 'this ceremony... was originally a magical rite, its purpose being to rekindle the decadent sun at the time of the autumnal equinox and to hail it when it rose at dawn', assumes a connection between this practice and an original aspect of the significance of the Feast (T.H. Gaster, *The Festivals of the Jewish Year* [New York: William Sloane Associates, 1953], p. 83). Martin-Achard (*Essai biblique*, p. 87 n. 46) writes in a somewhat similar vein stating that, although solar, the rite has been redirected by the rabbis with reference to the one God.

2. Also attested in the Mishnah is a spectacular rite which took place during the night previous to the rite just described and which involved lights.[1] The light from this rite, said to have been so brilliant that it lit up every court in Jerusalem, came from four enormous candelabra lit with wicks made from priestly garments and from burning torches juggled by pious men who danced before a merry throng.[2] Though not certain, an ancient connection of some kind between this spectacular light show and either the motion of the sun at the time of the autumnal equinox[3] or the full moon at harvest[4] is possible, as others have observed.[5]

3. That the solar rite referred to in Ezek. 8.16 took place during the Feast of Booths is also suggested by the fact that a setting 'at the Feast'[6] (clearly the Feast of Booths) is assigned to the ceremony of the dedication of the temple in 1 Kings 8, a passage with which Ezek. 8.16 has several parallels.[7]

4. Although the biblical text does not unambiguously assign a time for the solar rite described in Ezek. 8.16,[8] a time at the Feast of Booths is suggested still further by v. 17 with which v. 16 is

---

1. *M. Suk.* 5.2-4; cf. Gaster, *Festivals*, pp. 82-83, Hillyers, 'Feast of Tabernacles', pp. 49-50, N.H. Snaith, *The Jewish New Year* (London: SPCK, 1947), pp. 89-90.

2. *M. Suk.* 5.4.

3. See, for example, Gaster, *Festivals*, p. 83.

4. See, for example, Snaith, *New Year Festival*, pp. 89-91. The notion of a connection with the full moon of harvest complicates the hypothesis, but does not undermine it, since I have tentatively assumed throughout this study that the moon probably functioned as the nocturnal counterpart to the sun as a cultic manifestation of Yahweh. Celebrants thus might well be expected to take advantage of timing of the feast both at the time of the harvest moon (reputed to be the brightest of all full moons) and at or near the time of the autumnal equinox. Moreover, as noted earlier, the time of the Feast of Booths is ideal for a solar-lunar Yahwistic rite, since the bright harvest moon appears at the time of the setting of the equinoctial sun. (Analogues may be found, for example, in the role of the moon as representative of the 'solar' Horus of Edfu and as the eye of Re.)

5. See the previous two notes.

6. 1 Kgs 8.2; cf. 8.65.

7. See my section on Ezek. 8.16-18, offered earlier in this chapter.

8. As noted earlier, it is not clear whether the date given in Ezek. 8.1 (late September, near the time of the autumnal equinox) is relevant to the rite of vv. 16-18.

probably to be associated. Ezek. 8.17 makes reference to a rite
involving the extending of branches which is comparable at many
points with the well-known practice of branch-waving during the
Feast of Booths.[1]

5. The exact time for the beginning of the Feast of Booths was set at
some point in time with reference to the full harvest moon (Tishri
15), and the general date of the Feast of Booths was set with reference
to the autumnal equinox.[2] The date of the autumnal festival is thus
ideally suited for a cultic celebration in which sun and perhaps also
moon (the sun's nocturnal counterpart) were understood as
manifestations or symbols of Yahweh.

6. As noted earlier, Zech. 14.16 assigns a setting at the Feast of
Booths for the annual pilgrimage that is to follow the apocalyptic-like
scene described earlier in the same chapter. In addition to its well-
known role as a 'proof-text' for a connection between the Feast of
Booths and the celebration of Yahweh as king,[3] v. 16 is not without
relevance to the present hypothesis for one or more of the following
reasons: (1) the apocalyptic scene in the preceding context (vv. 1-15)
which plausibly reflects the outlook of a solar Yahwist is perhaps
similarly set at the Feast of Booths;[4] (2) according to at least one
scholar, several elements within the chapter as a whole (for example
'living waters', v. 8; 'no rain', v. 17) play on imagery relating to the
Feast of Booths;[5] and (3) the possibly cultic (and more specifically

1. See *m. Sukk.* 3.9, 4.5. See my earlier discussion of Ezek. 8.16-18.
2. Exod. 23.14-17; 34.18-26. Whereas the setting of months and exact dates
within the month were made with reference to the moon within the framework of a
lunisolar calendar, equinoxes (and solstices) were pivotal for regulating the year and
seasons within the year, including the beginning of autumn and harvest time which
the Feast of Booths commemorates. On the relevance of the equinox for the date of
the feast, see, for example, D.F. Morgan, 'Calendar', *ISBE*, I, pp. 575, 576.
Regarding the apparently general nature of the relationship between the Feast of
Booths and the exact time of the equinox, there is no way of knowing whether this is
significant to the hypothesis without knowledge of the exact orientation of the temple
and without a better understanding of the nature of the calendar in ancient Israel.
3. Also well known are the limitations of the verse as a proof text; see, for
example, the negative assessment of de Vaux, *Ancient Israel*, p. 506.
4. See my earlier discussion of Zechariah, including the reference to the work of
Harrelson.
5. Gaster, *Festivals*, pp. 92-93. On assumption of a connection between the
Feast of Booths and the procession of the ark (from the east gate), other possible

solar) nature of the horse referred to in v. 20 (cf. 2 Kgs 23.11).

7. Also noted earlier and relevant for an autumnal festival which includes celebration of Yahweh as king and the procession of the ark is the possible link between a solar understanding of Yahweh and each of these elements: the ark and its procession, and Yahweh epithets 'King', 'King of Glory', and *yhwh $s^eb\bar{a}$'ôt*.

8. Language that associates God with light is often used in passages which have as their stated or commonly supposed setting the Feast of Booths.[1] One of the more intriguing of these passages is Ps. 118.26-27, located towards the end of the Egyptian Hallel (Pss. 113-18)[2] and immediately following the cry of v. 25 (whence came the name of the rite of the Feast of Booths, Hoshianah):

---

elements include the procession of Yahweh (from the east) (vv. 1-5) and the notion of Yahweh as 'king' (v. 9). Gaster (*Festivals*, p. 92) includes reference also to a possible connection between the language of sun (v. 6) and the autumnal equinox.

1. The passages are as follows (specific verses mentioning light are in parentheses): 1 Kgs 8 (v. 53 LXX); Isa. 2.1-5 (v. 5), 60 (vv. 1-3); Ezek. 8 (vv. 16-18); Zech. 14 (vv. 6c-7); Pss. 113 (v. 3?), 118 (v. 27). (See further the discussion of these passages in this chapter.) A passage with less certain connections with the Feast of Booths and mentioning light in its broader context is Isa. 30.29 (cf. vv. 26, 27, 30). It is interesting in light of what has been argued in this study concerning the significance of Solomon's prayer that 1 Kgs 8.2-21, 54-66 are chosen as the readings from the prophets on the second and eighth day of the festival (Gaster, *Festivals*, p. 94). Martin-Achard (*Essai biblique*, p. 92) notes that in rabbinic tradition the book of Ecclesiastes (in which the refrain with sun repeatedly occurs) is customarily read at Sukkoth.

2. The imagery of light occurs also at the beginning of the Egyptian Hallel in the expression *mimmizraḥ šemeš 'ad $m^eb\hat{o}$'ô $m^ehull\bar{a}l$ šēm yhwh*, 'from the rising of the sun to its setting, praised be the name of Yahweh' (Ps. 113.3). Here, however, it is possible that the reference to the sun has no significance beyond its clear use in a common expression of extended space (cf. Mal. 1.11 and the Phoenician Karatepe inscription [*KAI* 26 I.4-5]). In light of the absence of the article on *šemeš* here (but also elsewhere in the expression), its position at the beginning of the Hallel, and the language of the God of glory in heaven in the next three verses of Ps. 113, it is possible that this psalm subtly reflects an association between Yahweh and the sun, but this is far from certain.

> Blessed is he who enters in the name of the Yahweh;
> We bless you from the house of the Yahweh.
> God is Yahweh, He has given light to us;[1]
> Bind the festal (procession) with branches,[2]
> Up to the horns of the altar![3]

Although in each passage the imagery of light obviously does not necessarily imply a solar dimension to the character of Yahweh, the references in this passage to the altar of burnt offering, to a public procession involving branches and to the 'Gates of Righteousness'[4] (v. 19) are clearly amenable to the notion of Yahweh manifested as sun.[5]

9. There are a few suggestive links between the Festival of Sukkoth

---

1. The expression *'ēl yhwh wayyā'er lānû* can be translated a number of ways, especially in light of the Syriac, Targum and Vulgate which omit the conjunction and presuppose the jussive *yā'ēr*. Examples of other ways in which the passage could be understood include, 'El is Yahweh, He has given us light', 'The Lord is a god, and he has given us light' or 'Supreme Lord, give us light!'

2. Or 'cords'. The sense offered here is essentially that of the RSV. For the meaning, 'branches' (so RSV), see Ezek. 19.11 and BDB, p. 721. At the Feast of Booths, the priests and people held branches during ceremonies associated with the altar. Two alternatives are that the festal offering was to be bound with cords, or, that perhaps the festal *lulab* was to be bound with cords. (There is some discussion in *m. Sukk.* 3.8 about whether the *lulabs* should be bound with branches or cords. Also, according to R. Meir, 'It is a fact that men of Jerusalem used to bind up their *lulabs* with golden threads'.)

3. That the verse is suggestive of 'solar symbolism' has also been noted by May ('Solar Aspects', p. 278) who renders the verse 'El is Yahweh, And he gives us light' and who compares the verse with Ezek. 43.2 in which it says of Yahweh who comes from the east, entering the eastern gate of the temple, *wᵉhā'āreṣ hē'îrâ mikkᵉbōdô*, 'and the earth shone from his glory'.

4. Morgenstern, 'Gates of Righteousness', pp. 1-37, esp. p. 34. Ps. 24 suggests to me that Morgenstern's thesis should be accepted, *though only in part.*

5. In the case of some other passages, connection of a sort between this feast and solar elements has been suggested by means other than the language of Yahweh as providing light, such as association with the sanctuary of 'Yahweh of Hosts' at Shiloh or use of the language of the God of heaven possibly reflecting a concrete understanding of God as sun. On Yahweh of Hosts at Shiloh, see 1 Sam. 1.3, 21 (cf. also Judg. 21.16-21), the discussion of Yahweh of Hosts offered earlier in this study, and the discussion of Shiloh offered by Rylaardsam, 'Booths', p. 456. On the plausibly suggestive nature of the language of the God of heaven, see 1 Kgs 8.2, 65 (LXX) and Neh. 9.6.

and the place 'Succoth' in the Transjordan which seems to have had some connection with the feast beyond the mere correspondence in name.[1] The biblical explanation for Succoth occurs in Gen. 33.17 which states that Succoth was so named because when Jacob travelled there he built 'booths' for his livestock. Perhaps more significantly, however, this description of Jacob's journey to 'Succoth' occurs in the verse that immediately follows the description of Jacob's encounter with Esau, a passage for which a solar interpretation has been offered and that in part plays upon the solar connotation of another place name, Penuel, 'face-of-God'.[2] Moreover, the place Succoth is located in an area in which other place names with solar connotations occur, including *ma'ᵃlê ḥeres*, 'ascent of the sun', clearly known to the inhabitants of Succoth,[3] and, to judge from Gen. 32.23-33 [22-32], both Penuel and Jabbok as well. Further, according to the writer of 1 Kgs 7.46, it was in the ground near Succoth that Solomon himself cast all the bronze implements which Hiram had made for the temple of Jerusalem. (As argued earlier, Solomon, the temple of Solomon, and at least the bronze altar were all inspired at least to some extent by a solar cult.)

To conclude, while no single line of evidence in itself is sufficient to warrant the conclusion that an autumn festival was an important locus for the cultic celebration of Yahweh as (manifested in the) sun, the cumulative evidence makes the hypothesis a reasonable one.

Conclusion

The combined evidence of both the archaeological and biblical data will be considered in the next chapter. Suffice it to note here that the biblical material appears to bear witness in many places to the integration of solar and Yahwistic elements and indeed at several

1.   That there must be some connection between the name of this place in the Transjordan and the feast bearing the same name has long been recognized. Cohen, for example, suggests that 'this is an old Canaanite place for the observance of the harvest festival which came to bear the same name' (S. Cohen, 'Succoth', *IDB*, IV, p. 449).

2.   See my earlier section on Gen. 32.23-33 [22-32] and the section 'Deuteronomy 33.2 Reconsidered in Light of Genesis 33.1-16'.

3.   Judg. 8.13-17; see the discussion of place names at the beginning of this chapter.

points to a rather more direct association between Yahweh and the sun than has often been thought. The association is nonetheless one of discontinuity as well as continuity. Not unlike most other concepts of deity influenced by solar elements in the ancient Near East, the discontinuity lies in an outright rejection of the 'Atenistic' notion of the identification of the deity with the physical form of the sun, to Israel a mere object created by God (for example Gen. 1.14-18; Pss. 19A, 104). The continuity on the other hand is upheld with equal vigour and is attested in many of the same passages that emphasize discontinuity (Gen. 1.1-4, Pss. 19B, 104). A conclusion based upon consideration of these and other passages is that the sun functioned as a manifestation or symbol of the God of Israel. Continuity between Yahweh and the sun was probably enhanced by the historical influence of the cult of Yahweh-in-Gibeon (that is, the sun) and by several points of commonality between Yahweh and the sun, such as the common association of the solar deity with creation, light, justice, law and royalty.

Chapter 4

CONCLUSIONS

The purpose of this book has been to examine in detail various lines of
evidence bearing on sun worship in ancient Israel, with a view to
answering the question: What was the relationship, if any, between
Yahweh and the sun? Whilst it has not been possible to answer the
question fully, the nature of the relationship has been clarified
considerably, and several lines of evidence are now much better
understood than before.

My basic thesis can be stated simply. Several lines of evidence, both
archaeological and biblical, bear witness to a close relationship between
Yahweh and the sun. The nature of that association is such that often a
'solar' character was presumed for Yahweh. Indeed, at many points
the sun actually represented Yahweh as a kind of 'icon'. Thus, in at
least the vast majority of cases, biblical passages which refer to sun
worship in Israel do not refer to a foreign phenomenon borrowed by
idolatrous Israelites, but to a Yahwistic phenomenon which
Deuteronomistic theology came to look upon as idolatrous. In the
summary which follows I shall elaborate upon sun worship as a
Yahwistic phenomenon, summarize lines of evidence upon which new
or different light has been shed, and offer some explanations and
implications.

To elaborate in general terms, an association between Yahweh and
the sun was not limited to one or two obscure contexts, but was
remarkably well integrated into the religion of ancient Israel. Thus,
for example, some form of association between the sun and Yahweh is
evident in most of the traditional sources J, E, D and P and is evident
(though not necessarily in a continuum) from early in the monarchy
to the exilic period and (probably) beyond. Solar Yahwism during the
monarchy was a feature of royal religion. Opposition to solar
Yahwism during this time appears in fact to have been the exception,

limited for the most part to Deuteronomistic theology. Even the DH, however, attributes a form of solar Yahwism to figures which it does not condemn (for example, Joshua and, by strong implication, probably Hezekiah as well) and welcomes the notion of a direct correspondence between the actions of Yahweh and the sun at more than one point in the History (Josh. 10.12-14, 2 Kgs 20.8-11). It nonetheless reacts negatively to at least certain manifestations of solar Yahwism during the reign of Josiah, leaving the impression that even Deuteronomistic opposition was late. The Deuteronomistically influenced passages Jer. 8.1-3 and Zeph. 1.4-6 suggest that the worship of the sun and other members of the Yahwistic Host of Heaven was practised not only within royal Jerusalemite circles but also among the inhabitants of Jerusalem (Jer. 8.1) and Judah in general (Zeph. 1.4). Jeremiah's understanding of this worship as a breach of covenant thus seems to have been consistent with a relatively late 'hard-line' Deuteronomistic opposition to solar Yahwism reflected in 2 Kgs 23.11. A similarly negative attitude is evident in Zeph. 1.4-6, but 3.5, 17 constitute evidence that an understanding of Yahweh as still in some sense solar in character nonetheless remained (and perhaps was not included in the purging of solar cult elements from the temple referred to in 2 Kgs 23.11). In any case, a solar understanding of God lived on past the fall of the southern kingdom, as did perhaps the horses and chariots of the sun, something of which there *might* be a hint in Zech. 14.20.

Several additional aspects of the nature of sun worship in ancient Israel may be outlined as follows.

1. It is important to clarify at an early point in the discussion of the relationship between Yahweh and the sun a common misconception concerning several relevant biblical passages. Passages such as Genesis 1, Psalm 19, and 1 Kings 8.53 LXX which refer to Yahweh (or God) setting the sun in the heavens do *not* deny the possibility of any form of relationship between God and the sun as a kind of polemic against sun worship, as is often argued. Rather, since sun cults typically distinguish the sun god from the physical form of the sun itself (the cult of Aten being the notable exception), and similarly attribute the creation of the sun to the sun god, these passages are at least as likely to presuppose or uphold some form of relationship between God and the sun. Ironically, then, these passages which are often taken as forceful polemics against sun worship are almost

tantamount to an admission of the solar nature of the deity within their ancient Near Eastern context.

Indeed in the case of each of these passages a strong case can be made for the notion of a presupposition of continuity between deity and sun. Thus, in Ps. 19.5c-7 [4c-6], the action of the *sun* is described for its own sake as if this was tantamount to declaring the 'glory of *God* ' (in contrast to other entities such as the firmament which must actually make declaration of God's glory, vv. 2-5b [1-4b]). As is well known, Psalm 19 continues by applying solar epithets to the law of Yahweh (vv. 8-12 [7-11]). Or again, for example, in Gen. 1.3-5, God performs exactly the same functions that the sun does in vv. 14-18, such as creating light and separating light from darkness. As a 'polemic' against an *Israelite* perception of God, the passage thus clarifies that Yahwists should not equate God with the physical bodies sun and moon, since, as a 'solar' creator deity, he naturally performed the functions of sun and moon prior to their creation. And finally, 1 Kgs 8.53 LXX, almost certainly the more complete poetic form of the excised v. 12 of the MT, clarifies the relationship between Yahweh and the sun in a way that would not be necessary if some form of relationship were not thought to have existed between them.

2. Although, like God's setting of the sun in the heavens, the common notion in apocalyptic literature that Yahweh will replace the sun might appear at first to preclude the possibility of a historical association between Yahweh and the sun, such an association is probably presupposed by the very notion of replacement. In keeping with their apocalyptic contexts, passages that describe Yahweh's replacement of the sun point to a time in the new world order when Yahweh as the sublime sun (that is, 'sun of righteousness') will replace the mere symbol or icon of his power and presence in the old world order.

3. The Deuteronomistic association of the worship of 'the sun, moon, stars, all the Host of Heaven' may be taken at face value. The worship of these entities belong together and to the same religion: Yahwism. The sun—and probably also the moon, the sun's nocturnal counterpart[1]—was understood to be a tangible expression of Yahweh

---

1. The relationship between Yahweh and the moon goes beyond the scope of the present study. I have tentatively suggested several times in passing, however, the possibility that the moon also served as a symbol for Yahweh, the nocturnal counterpart to the sun as an icon of Yahweh. (Comparison may be drawn with the

in ancient Israel, and the Host of Heaven indicative of his heavenly entourage. Moreover, in itself this association between Yahweh and the sun, Host and entourage, appears to pose no great difficulty for Deuteronomistic theology (e.g. Josh. 10.12-14, 1 Kgs 22.19) at least prior to the reforms of Josiah. Rather, that to which Deuteronomistic theology objected was the reverse phenomenon when brought to cultic expression, namely, *the worship of an object,* the sun, as Yahweh, or the actual veneration of stars as members of his entourage. In other words, the issue was not whether the sun was an icon of Yahweh— after all *he* created this powerful symbol and at more than one point in Israel's historical tradition the actions of sun and Yahweh miraculously coincided—but whether the icon itself could be worshipped. In the DH the answer is no, a no which is rationalized in Deut. 4.19 on the basis of the fact that when Yahweh appeared amid fire at Sinai he assumed no 'form'. The DH further portrays this no as normative from the time of the inception of the temple of Solomon. Thus in 1 Kings 8, conscious of a transitional period between Gibeon and Jerusalem as the main high place (the former of which advocated a radical solar theology which the latter sought to qualify), Solomon is portrayed now for the last time extending his hands *in the direction of the heavens* in prayer to the God of heaven. His prayer on the occasion of the dedication of this new temple is in reality a message to the effect that the God with whom the sun is admittedly associated (1 Kgs 8.53 LXX) should nonetheless *now* be prayed to through the offering of prayers *in the direction of the temple,* since the God of heaven had himself determined to dwell amid darkness (1 Kings 8; contrast Ezek. 8.16 which attests to the presence in the late pre-exilic period of an abiding tendency *not* to follow this prescription, probably in connection with the celebration of the Feast of Booths).

4. There is a considerable amount of evidence to warrant a new hypothesis to the effect that the well-known expression Yahweh of Hosts early (and probably originally) had solar connotations. A logical explanation for this phenomenon is that Yahweh Sebaoth (best translated 'Yahweh Host Sublime' or the like) denoted Yahweh as the pre-eminent member of the Host of Heaven (that is, the sun).

5. The horses and chariot(s) of the sun removed from the Jerusalem temple (2 Kgs 23.11) were neither Assyrian nor late. Rather, they

notion of the sun and moon as the two 'eyes' of Re in Egyptian literature.)

were Israelite and traditional (as one normally expects of cultic items in the context of a national shrine) and with antecedent dating to no later than the late tenth century BCE (see pl. 1d and the discussion of the Taanach cult stand).

6. The four- and two-winged emblems on the royal Judaean *lmlk* jar handles, both solar symbols, are not emblems of the northern and southern kingdoms respectively (or vice versa), but are equivalent alternative representations of the falcon-headed Horus of Behdet (that is, Horus of Edfu) who is attested as both winged disk and winged beetle. Mythic tradition associates Horus of Behdet with royalty and identifies this god with both the king himself (as the image of Horus of Edfu on earth) and the sun god (most often as Re-Harachte's son who takes the form of the winged disk). Moreover, the winged sun and flying scarab are mentioned etiologically in the mythic tradition as signs of Horus of Behdet (king, god and sun) who vanquishes the enemies of his father, Re, the sun god. This significance of this new understanding of the imagery on the royal Judaean jar handles for the present thesis is this: because these symbols appear as the royal emblem of the kingdom of Judah during the time of Hezekiah, Hezekiah must have identified with at least some aspects of the imagery. While it is impossible to say exactly what the symbols meant within the Judaean context, a balance must be struck between a minimalist's perspective according to which the symbols might simply denote, say, protection (which seems not to reckon sufficiently with the presence of no less than three solar motifs in the royal emblem and their highly specific background vis-à-vis king as sun, and god as sun) and a more radical interpretation which might claim the status, say, of both deity for Hezekiah and sun for God. In any case, the dominant motif of this imagery—which must for some good reason have been adopted as the royal emblem of the kingdom of Judah—was that the king as a divine solar hero acts as protector of the territory on behalf of his father, the sun god Re Harachte.

7. A rather full study of the orientation of Yahwistic and selected other temples leaves little or no reason to suspect that Solomon's temple was aligned to the sun (thus, for example, the 'Solar Shrine' at Lachish is almost certainly a misnomer). There is, however, far more biblical evidence in support of a Yahwistic solar theology that was influential at the time of the founding of the temple than has often been acknowledged (for example, 1 Kgs 8.53 LXX, and several

passages which suggest that the worship of Yahweh-in-Gibeon as the sun lay behind the controversial theology of the Gibeonite high place which the temple replaced). The specifically solar backdrop against which the Jerusalem temple was founded might thus be sufficient to explain the apparent lack of analogue among other temples. It nevertheless remains an open matter whether the solar theology of the Jerusalem temple, evidently a corrective to the excesses of Gibeonite solar Yahwism, included a concern for such elements as would make alignment of the temple to the sun important for the cult (for example, the ability of the sun to shine into the temple where, after all, Yahweh had now determined to dwell in *darkness* [but in association nonetheless with his radiant 'glory']). Certainly there is nothing to suggest that the temple could not theoretically have been aligned towards the sun for an important occasion within the year[1] (the most likely candidate being the Feast of Booths which, timed with reference both to the autumnal equinox and harvest moon, was very plausibly an important locus for solar Yahwism). Thus, although the sun played a role in the founding of the temple, whether it affected specifically the orientation of the temple remains uncertain.

8. The well-known story of Jacob wrestling with a 'man' at the river Jabbok (Gen. 32.23-33 [22-32]) makes remarkably good sense on the basis of a two-part hypothesis to the effect that (1) the 'man' is a nocturnal manifestation of the sun who was en-route via the waters of the netherworld to the eastern horizon where he would of necessity assume an alternative manifestation as the rising sun at dawn, and (2) that the writer of the story equates the rising sun with seeing the 'face of God' (Peniel). The hypothesis effectively resolves most of the tensions in the story and seems to make good sense of the story as a whole. Moreover, by clearly equating the sun with seeing the face of God, the passage provides some basis for seeing in certain other contexts a connection between the sun and the face of God (for example, Ps. 17.15 and Gen. 33.10 where Esau's march from Seir symbolizes the theophanic march of Yahweh as sun from Seir [cf. Gen. 33.1; Deut. 33.2]).

9. It is doubtful that several Iron Age horse figurines identified by Kenyon and Holland bear 'sun disks' between their ears: the cone-

---

1. I.e. when such matters as astronomy, topography and the biblical description of the architecture of the temple are considered.

shaped protrusions are not without close parallels in Cyprus and can be accounted for more reasonably by means other than connection with a sun cult (for example, exaggerated manes only the top portion of which was represented due to the presence of riders).

10. On the assumption that Psalm 24 alludes to a rite in which the ark was processed through an eastern gate of the temple v. 7, which states 'Lift up your heads, O gates/ Be lifted up, O ancient doors, that the King of Glory may come in', gives ritual expression to the wish that 'Yahweh of Hosts' (that is, Yahweh as the *sun*) might be able to accompany the ark by, quite literally, fitting through (that is, under the heads of) the gates and into the temple complex. Several other aspects of this ark-procession psalm are similarly amenable to interpretation as solar-Yahwistic.

11. Psalm 104 clearly seeks to distance itself from the cult of Aten from which the psalm ultimately derived some inspiration. However, since to reject Atenism is not to reject solarism per se, it cannot be concluded from this that the psalm denies the notion of any affinity between Yahweh and the sun. The matter remains unresolved, but that memory of an ancient sun hymn would somehow be preserved and then used with only modest adaptation is perhaps suggestive of a poet for whom the link between God and the sun was meaningful.

Prior to considering implications, a few questions arise from the preceding discussion. First, how could the Israelites who had an early and deeply entrenched aniconic tendency vis-à-vis images of God have worshipped the sun? The worship of the sun was clearly exceptional and the exception may be explained on the following basis: since the sun was made by *God*, its veneration as an icon of Yahweh may technically have fallen outside iconic prohibitions such as the second commandment which prohibits *humans* from making images of God (Exod. 20.4-5, Deut. 5.8-9).[1] (Perhaps the tenet of solar Yahwism that Yahweh set the sun in the heavens functioned in some contexts as an apologetic in defence of the apparent 'loophole' in the second commandment, although no cases of this appear to have been preserved).

---

1. Despite the popularity of the sun *itself* as an icon of Yahweh, we should not be surprised in light of the second commandment to find relatively few humanly crafted representations of the sun as Yahweh in the archaeological record, unless as a mere icon the sun was considered a safe step removed from the deity.

Secondly, should Yahweh be viewed as a 'sun god'? Certainly not, at least not any more than Yahweh should be considered, say, a storm god on the basis that the Old Testament borrows imagery of Baal and applies it to Yahweh. Thus, whereas I have attempted here to argue for a largely unrecognized category of language and indeed iconic symbolism for Yahweh, it must be remembered that a wide range of other (non-solar) forms of language for the deity in fact render solar language *alone* for God a rarity. Further, I have in many cases for the purposes of argument brought to the foreground a solar aspect which the biblical writers themselves have been rather more content to leave in the background (as in the case, for example, of DH subtly alluding to the presence of solar elements during the reign of Hezekiah). To put the matter differently, an overwhelming impression based upon the portrait of Yahweh in the Old Testament as a whole (and indeed the consensus of theologians for millennia!) is that the God of Israel must be understood in categories and terms that extend far beyond the limits of an ancient Near Eastern sun god.

Finally, if correct, the notion that Yahweh was associated with the sun will undoubtedly have implications for the study of the religion of ancient Israel[1] and beyond. One particularly striking example from beyond the parameters of ancient Israelite religion is Mk 15.33-34 (cf. Mt. 27.45-46, Lk. 23.44-45a) which describes an extraordinary solar phenomenon at the time of the crucifixion of Jesus:

> At the sixth hour darkness came over the whole land until the ninth hour.[2] And at the ninth hour Jesus cried out in a loud voice. '*Eloi, Eloi, lama sabachtani?*'—which means, 'My God, my God, why have you forsaken me?' (NIV)

---

1. For example, the close link between God and the sun perhaps explains why J. Tigay could find little evidence among personal names in Israelite onomastica for the claim of the prophets that idolatry (that is, the worship of *foreign* deities) was widespread among the Israelites (Tigay, *No Other Gods*, pp. 37–38). To judge from the case of the sun as an icon of Yahweh, many of the religious practices deemed idolatrous by the prophets were not associated with the veneration of foreign gods but with the worship of Yahweh.

2. Luke adds, 'for the sun stopped shining' (Lk. 23.45a), but does not make explicit the connection known to Mark and Matthew between the disappearance of the sun and God-forsakeness.

When a connection is seen between Jesus' complaint of God-forsakeness and this solar phenomenon, new light is shed on the theological significance of both the failure of the sun and the cry; suffice it to note here, however, that the link is consistent with the thesis of this book that the Old Testament bears witness to a rather direct correlation between the activity of God and the sun. Simply put, Israel's struggle with the sun was this: Is it appropriate to venerate so magnificent an icon of Yahweh which no human had created, but rather God himself? Whereas the tendency for Deuteronomistic and other canonical biblical literature was to say no, many Israelites (including, later, the Essenes) apparently said yes.

Appendix A

SOLAR ALIGNMENT: ARAD TEMPLE (IRON II) (AHARONI)

Latitude of Temple: 31.30
Angle of Temple: 90 (Aharoni)[1]

Days Past Winter Solstice	Angle of Sun to Horizon	Angle of Sun to Equator
0–84	negative value	negative value
91 (spring equinox)	-0.25	-0.13
98	5.28	2.73
105	10.75	5.56
112	16.14	8.29
119	21.40	10.92
126	26.47	13.39
133	31.31	15.65
140	35.83	17.70
147	39.97	19.48
154	43.61	20.99
161	46.66	22.19
168	48.99	23.07
175	50.48	23.61
182 (summer solstice)	51.05	23.82
189	50.65	23.67
196	49.32	23.19
203	47.13	22.37
210	44.21	21.22
217	40.66	19.77
224	36.60	18.03
231	32.14	16.04
238	27.36	13.80

1.   Calculations are based on the assumption that the compass point in the published report (Aharoni, 'Arad: Its Inscriptions', figs. 12, 15) points to true north. If Aharoni's compass mark reflects magnetic north, the angle of the temple (assuming a directional reading taken in 1965, mid-way through the excavations) would be 92.43 degrees. In this case the angle of the sun in the horizon on equinoctial days 91/273 at sun declination –0.13/0.38 would be 3.75/4.74 degrees.

245	22.32	11.37
252	17.09	8.78
259	11.72	6.05
266	6.25	3.24
273 (fall equinox)	*0.74*	*0.38*
280–365	negative value	negative value

Appendix B

SOLAR ALIGNMENT: ARAD TEMPLE (IRON II) (HERZOG)

Latitude of Temple: 31.30
Angle of Temple: 91 (Herzog *et al.*)[1]

Days Past Winter Solstice	Angle of Sun to Horizon	Angle of Sun to Equator
0–84	negative value	negative value
91 (spring equinox)	1.40	−0.13
98	6.91	2.73
105	12.39	5.56
112	17.78	8.29
119	23.03	10.92
126	28.11	13.39
133	32.94	15.65
140	37.46	17.70
147	41.59	19.48
154	45.24	20.99
161	48.28	22.19
168	50.61	23.07
175	52.10	23.61
182 (summer solstice)	52.67	23.82
189	52.27	23.67
196	50.94	23.19
203	48.75	22.37
210	45.83	21.22
217	42.28	19.77
224	38.23	18.03
231	33.77	16.04
238	28.99	13.80

1.   Calculations are based on the assumption that the compass point in the published report (here, Herzog *et al.*, 'Israelite Fortress', fig. 6) points to true north. If the compass mark reflects magnetic north, the angle of the temple (assuming a directional reading taken in 1987) would be 94.5 degrees. In this case, the angle of the sun in the horizon on equinoctial days 91/273 at sun declination -0.13/0.38 would be 7.11/8.09 degrees.

245	23.95	11.37
252	18.73	8.78
259	13.37	6.05
266	7.90	3.24
273 (fall equinox)	*2.39*	*0.38*
280–365	negative value	negative value

Appendix C

Solar Alignment: 'Solar Shrine' at Lachish

Latitude of Temple: 31.56
Angle of Temple:101.5[1]

Days Past Winter Solstice	Angle of Sun to Horizon	Angle of Sun to Equator
0–63	negative value	negative value
70	2.33	−8.54
77	7.39	−5.8
84	12.54	−2.99
91 (spring equinox)	*17.75*	*−0.13*
98	22.95	2.73
105	28.11	5.56
112	33.18	8.29
119	38.11	10.92
126	42.85	13.39
133	47.34	15.65
140	51.51	17.70
147	55.28	19.48
154	58.58	20.99
161	61.31	22.19
168	63.37	23.07
175	64.68	23.61
182 (summer solstice)	*65.18*	*23.82*
189	64.83	23.67
196	63.66	23.19
203	61.73	22.37
210	59.11	21.22
217	55.91	19.77

1. Calculations are based on the assumption that the compass point in the published report (Aharoni, *Lachish V*, pl. 56) points to true north. If Aharoni's compass mark reflects magnetic north, the angle of the temple (assuming a directional reading taken in 1966) would be 103.52 degrees. In this case the angle of the sun in the horizon on equinoctial days 91/273 at sun declination −0.13/0.38 would be 21.08/21.99 degrees.

224	52.21	18.03
231	48.11	16.04
238	43.67	13.80
245	38.97	11.37
252	34.07	8.78
259	29.03	6.05
266	23.88	3.24
273 (fall equinox)	*18.68*	*0.38*
280	13.47	−2.48
287	8.30	−5.31
294	3.22	−8.06
301–365	negative value	negative value

Appendix D

Solar Alignment: 'Basement House' at Beer-Sheba

Latitude of Temple: 31.24
Angle of Temple: 90^{1}

Days Past Winter Solstice	Angle of Sun to Horizon	Angle of Sun to Equator
0–84	negative value	negative value
91 (spring equinox)	*−0.25*	*−0.13*
98	5.28	2.73
105	10.76	5.56
112	16.16	8.29
119	21.42	10.92
126	26.50	13.39
133	31.34	15.65
140	35.88	17.70
147	40.11	19.48
154	43.67	20.99
161	46.72	22.19
168	49.01	23.07
175	50.55	23.61
182 (summer solstice)	*51.12*	*23.82*
189	50.72	23.67
196	49.39	23.19
203	47.20	22.37
210	44.26	21.22
217	40.71	19.77
224	36.65	18.03
231	32.18	16.04
238	27.39	13.80

1. Calculations are based on the assumption that the compass point in the published report (Herzog, Rainey and Moshkovitz, 'The Stratigraphy at Beer-sheba', fig. 1) points to true north. If the compass mark reflects magnetic north, the angle of the temple (assuming a directional reading taken in 1970) would be 92.68 degrees. In this case the angle of the sun in the horizon on equinoctial days 91/273 at sun declination –0.13/0.38 would be 4.17/5.15 degrees.

245	22.34	11.37
252	17.11	8.78
259	11.73	6.05
266	6.26	3.24
273 (fall equinox)	*0.74*	*0.38*
280–365	negative value	negative value

Appendix E

SOLAR ALIGNMENT: HELLENISTIC SHRINE AT BEER-SHEBA

Latitude of Temple: 31.24
Angle of Temple: 66[1]

Days Past Winter Solstice	Angle of Sun to Horizon	Angle of Sun to Equator
0–91	negative value	negative value
98	−29.46	2.73
105	−24.92	5.56
112	−20.48	8.29
119	−16.18	10.92
126	−12.08	13.39
133	−8.24	15.65
140	−4.71	17.70
147	−1.56	19.48
154	1.16	20.99
161	3.38	22.19
168	5.01	23.07
175	6.06	23.61
182 (summer solstice)	6.45	23.82
189	6.18	23.67
196	5.25	23.19
203	3.71	22.37
210	1.59	21.22
217	−1.04	19.77
224	−4.12	18.03
231	−7.59	16.04
238	−11.38	13.80
245	−15.43	11.37

1. Calculations are based on the assumption that the compass point in the published report (Aharoni, 'Fifth and Sixth Seasons', fig. 8) points to true north. If Aharoni's compass mark reflects magnetic north, the angle of the temple (assuming a directional reading taken in 1974) would be 68.9 degrees. In this case the angle of the sun in the horizon during the time of summer solstice would be 11.31 or even higher in the sky than if the angle was 66 degrees.

252	−19.70	8.78
259	−24.11	6.05
266	−28.64	3.24
273 (fall equinox)	*−33.22*	*0.38*
280–365	negative value	negative value

Appendix F

SOLAR ALIGNMENT: TELL TA'YINAT

Latitude of Temple: 36.25
Angle of Temple: 83.5

Days Past Winter Solstice	Angle of Sun to Horizon	Angle of Sun to Equator
0–84	negative value	negative value
91 (spring equinox)	−8.99	−0.13
98	−4.20	2.73
105	0.54	5.56
112	5.18	8.29
119	9.68	10.92
126	13.98	13.39
133	18.03	15.65
140	21.75	17.70
147	25.10	19.48
154	28.00	20.99
161	30.36	22.19
168	32.13	23.07
175	33.25	23.61
182 (summer solstice)	33.67	23.82
189	33.38	23.67
196	32.38	23.19
203	30.72	22.37
210	28.46	21.22
217	25.65	19.77
224	22.38	18.03
231	18.72	16.04
238	14.73	13.80
245	10.47	11.37
252	6.00	8.78
259	1.37	6.05
266	−3.35	3.24
273 (fall equinox)	−8.13	0.38
280–365	negative value	negative value

Appendix G

SOLAR ALIGNMENT: SOLOMONIC TEMPLE (MORGENSTERN)

Latitude of Temple: 31.78
Angle of Temple: 58.20[1]

Days Past Winter Solstice	Angle of Sun to Horizon	Angle of Sun to Equator
0–91	negative value	negative value
98	−36.43	2.73
105	−32.33	5.56
112	−28.34	8.29
119	−24.38	10.92
126	−20.83	13.39
133	−17.42	15.65
140	−14.30	17.70
147	−11.54	19.48
154	−9.18	20.99
161	−7.28	22.19
168	−5.86	23.07
175	−4.98	23.61
182 (summer solstice)	−4.65	23.82
189	−4.88	23.67
196	−5.67	23.19
203	−6.99	22.37
210	−8.81	21.22
217	−11.09	19.77
224	−13.78	18.03
231	−16.84	16.04
238	−20.20	13.80
245	−23.81	11.37
252	−27.64	8.78
259	−31.61	6.05

1.   This angle is based on that offered by Parunak ('Solomon's Temple', p. 32) for the line from the Sacred Rock to the present-day Golden Gate which Morgenstern ('Gates of Righteousness', p. 1) takes to be the location of the ancient Eastern Gate.

266	−35.69	3.24
273 (fall equinox)	−39.83	0.38
280–365	negative value	negative value

Appendix H

SOLAR ALIGNMENT: SOLOMONIC TEMPLE (HOLLIS)

Latitude of Temple: 31.78
Angle of Temple: 83.93[1]

Days Past Winter Solstice	Angle of Sun to Horizon	Angle of Sun to Equator
0–91	negative value	negative value
98	–4.56	2.73
105	–0.76	5.56
112	–5.99	8.29
119	–11.09	10.92
126	–15.99	13.39
133	–20.65	15.65
140	–25.00	17.70
147	–28.95	19.48
154	–32.42	20.99
161	–35.30	22.19
168	–37.49	23.07
175	–38.89	23.61
182 (summer solstice)	–39.42	23.82
189	–39.05	23.67
196	–37.80	23.19
203	–35.75	22.37
210	–32.98	21.22
217	–29.61	19.77
224	–25.73	18.03
231	–21.45	16.04
238	–16.84	13.80
245	–11.98	11.37
252	–6.91	8.78

1.   The angle used here is based on Parunak's revised estimation ('Solomon's Temple', p. 32) of the angle of the line of site from the Sacred Rock and perpendicular to the eastern wall. (Hollis [*Archaeology of Herod's Temple*, p. 133] had incorrectly estimated this angle to be 5 degrees north of east.)

259	−1.70	6.05
266	−3.60	3.24
273 (fall equinox)	*−9.00*	*0.38*
280–365	negative value	negative value

Appendix I

SOLAR ALIGNMENT: SOLOMONIC TEMPLE (THEORETICAL)

Latitude of Temple: 31.78
Angle of Temple: 90

Days Past Winter Solstice	Angle of Sun to Horizon	Angle of Sun to Equator
0–84	negative value	negative value
91 (spring equinox)	−0.24	−0.13
98	5.20	2.73
105	10.59	5.56
112	15.90	8.29
119	21.08	10.92
126	26.07	13.39
133	30.82	15.65
140	35.25	17.70
147	39.29	19.48
154	42.85	20.99
161	45.81	22.19
168	48.07	23.07
175	49.52	23.61
182 (summer solstice)	50.06	23.82
189	49.68	23.67
196	48.39	23.19
203	46.27	22.37
210	43.43	21.22
217	39.97	19.77
224	36.01	18.03
231	31.64	16.04
238	26.94	13.80
245	21.99	11.37
252	16.84	8.78
259	11.55	6.05
266	6.16	3.24
273 (fall equinox)	0.73	0.38
280–365	negative value	negative value

Appendix J

YAHWISTIC PERSONAL NAMES WITH POSSIBLE SOLAR ELEMENTS FROM EPIGRAPHIC SOURCES[1]

Name	Date (BCE)	Provenance	Number
'wryhw	L 7th–E 6th	Arad	47.13[2]
'ryhw	M 7th–E 6th	En Gedi	48.17
[']ryh/[w]	E 7th	Jerusalem O	48.18
[']ryh/[n] ryhw	L 7th–E 6th	Lachish	48.19
'ryhw	E 6th	Arad	48.20
'ryhw	M 8th	Kh. el-Qôm	48.21
'ryhw	L 8th–7th		48.22
'ryhw	6th		48.23
'ryhw	7th		48.24
'ryw	M 8th	Samaria	48.25
yhwz[r]ḥ	L 8th–E 7th		54.15
yhwzrḥ	L 7th–E 6th		54.16
yw'r	L 8th[3]		55.9
[n]ryhw	E 6th	Lachish	58.6
nryhw	E 6th	Lachish	58.7
nryhw	L 7th–E 6th	Arad	58.8
nryhw	L 8th	Beer-sheba	58.9
nryhw[4]	ca. 700[5]	Gibeon	58.10
nryhw	L 7th–E 6th	Jerusalem D	58.11
nryhw	ca. 700		58.12
nryhw	?		58.13
nr[y]hw	7th		58.14

1. The list of personal names from inscriptions is taken from Appendix A, 'Yahwistic Personal Names in Inscriptions', in Tigay, *No Other Gods*, pp. 47-63. (For biblical names with possible solar elements, refer to Chapter 3 of the present book.)

2. The numbers before and after the period in this column refer respectively to the page and order of listing in Tigay's Appendix A (*No Other Gods*).

3. This is the date given by L.G. Herr, *The Scripts of Ancient Northwest Semitic Seals* (HSM, 18; Missoula, MT; Scholars Press, 1978), p. 127, no. 102.

4. See Tigay, *No Other Gods*, p. 58 n. 12.

5. The date and reading are that of N. Avigad, 'Some Notes on the Hebrew Inscriptions from Gibeon', *IEJ* 9 (1959), pp. 132-33.

nryhw	7th	58.15
nryhw	8th	58.16
nryhw	L 7th–E 6th	58.17
nryhw	M 7th[1]	58.18
nryhw	L 7th–E 6th	58.19
[nr]yh[w]	L 7th–E 6th	58.20
nryhw	L 7th–E 6th	58.21
nryhw	L 7th–E 6th	58.22
nryhw	L 7th–E 6th	58.23
[n]r[y]h[w]	L 7th–E 6th	58.24
nryhw	L 7th–E 6th	58.25
nryhw	L 7th–E 6th	58.26
nryhw[2]	L 7th–E 6th	58.27
nryhw	L 7th–E 6th	58.28

1. Herr, *Scripts*, p. 144, no. 151.
2. Tigay (*No Other Gods*, p. 58) notes that this name may refer to the same person above this entry.

Plate 1a. *Taanach cult stand, discovered by Paul Lapp during the 1968 excavations at Tell Taanach (late tenth century BCE). Front view of stand as originally found.* (Israel Antiquities Authority.)

Plate 1b. *Taanach cult stand. Front and side view of stand (with parts reconstructed; cf. pl. 1a).* (Israel Antiquities Authority.)

Plate 1c. *Tier three (from top) of Taanach cult stand (cf. pls. 1a and 1b).* (Israel Antiquities Authority.)

Plate 1d. *Top tier of Taanach cult stand showing quadruped below sun disk (cf. pl. 1a).* (Israel Antiquities Authority.)

P.547

19.289

Plate 2. *Royal Judaean jar handle with rosette (late seventh century BCE).* (Israel Antiquities Authority.)

Plate 3. *Side view of horse with cornucopia-shaped 'disk' between its ears, Jerusalem Cave 1 (seventh century BCE).* (Israel Antiquities Authority.)

Plate 4. *Front view of horse with cornucopia-shaped 'disk', Jerusalem Cave 1; cf. pl. 3 (same horse).* (Israel Antiquities Authority.)

Plate 5. *Horse figurine from Iron II period showing typical odd-shaped object between its ears (Holland's 'forelock' type) and noseband.* (Israel Antiquities Authority.)

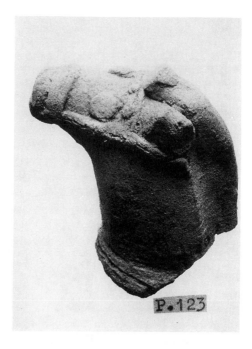

Plate 6. *Horse figurine from Iron II period showing abrupt disk-like ending to prominent mane and bridle.* (Israel Antiquities Authority.)

Plate 7. *Horse figurine from Iron II period showing prominent mane.* (Israel Antiquities Authority.)

Plate 8. *Horse figurine from Iron II period with odd-shaped headpiece and mane ending abruptly.* (Israel Antiquities Authority.)

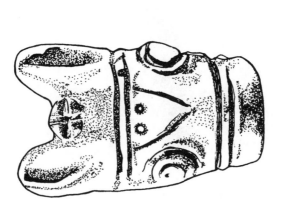

Figure 1. *Horse figurine from Hazor (late tenth century BCE).*

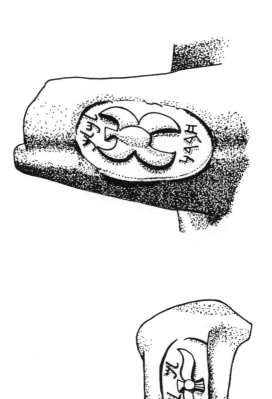

Figure 2. *Royal Judaean jar handle with two-winged emblem (late eighth century BCE). Inscription:* lmlk, *'for the king'.*

Figure 3. *Royal Judaean jar handle with four-winged scarab (late eighth century BCE). Inscription:* lmlk, *'for the king', and* hbrn, *'Hebron'.*

Figure 4. *Phoenician seal with falcon and boat in Egyptian style, published by W.A. Ward (JEA 53 [1967], pp. 69-74).*

Figure 6. *Amulet with four-winged scarab, rosette and winged sun disk from same date, context, and source as fig. 5 (cf. Dows Dunham,* El Kurru, *pls. 53A: 1101; 55A: 997-98).*

Figure 5. *Amulet with four-winged scarab and rosette from royal (twenty-fifth dynasty) tomb at El Kurru, Nubia (late eighth century BCE), published by Dows Dunham (*El Kurru: The Royal Cemeteries of Kush, *Vol. 1 [Cambridge, MA: Harvard University Press for the Museum of Fine Arts, 1950]; cf. pl. 49A: 1256/57).*

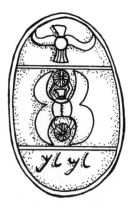

Figure 7. *The royal insignia of the kingdom of Judah in the eighth to seventh centuries* BCE *(reconstructed tentatively on the basis of Nubian exemplars of the twenty-fifth dynasty and the royal Judaean* lmlk *jar handles).*

Figure 8. *Rider and horse, both broken, Jerusalem Cave 1 (seventh century* BCE*). Side view showing pie-shaped 'disk', 'disk' support, and other trappings on the horse's nose and cheeks.*

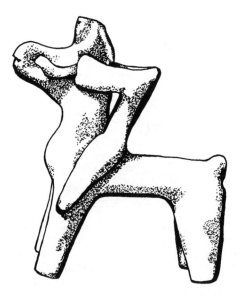

Figure 9. *Horse with headless rider, Tomb 106, Lachish (late seventh to early sixth centuries* BCE*).*

Figure 10. *Head and neck fragment of horse with 'disk' and bridle pieces, Hazor (mid eighth century* BCE*).*

Figure 11. *Horse figurine from Amathus, Cyprus, with rider and 'disk' (Cypro-Archaic Period) (cf. A.C. Brown and W.W. Catling,* Ancient Cyprus *[Oxford: Ashmolean Museum, 1975], p. 53).*

BIBLIOGRAPHY

Achtemeier, E.R., 'Zephaniah', *HBD*, pp. 1161-62.

—*Nahum–Malachi* (Interpretation; Atlanta: John Knox, 1986).

Ackerman, S., 'Baal, Anat and the Song of Deborah' (paper read at the annual meeting of the Society of Biblical Literature, November, 1990).

Aharoni, Y., 'Excavations at Ramath Raḥel: Preliminary Report', *IEJ* 6 (1956), pp. 137-57.

—'Excavations at Ramath Raḥel', *BA* 24 (1961), pp. 98-118.

—*Excavations at Ramat Rahel: Seasons 1959 and 1960* (Rome: Centro di studi semitici, 1962).

—*Excavations at Ramat Rahel: Seasons 1960 and 1961* (Rome: Centro di studi semitici, 1964).

—'Arad: Its Inscriptions and Temple', *BA* 31 (1968), pp. 2-32.

—'The Horned Altar of Beer-sheba', *BA* 35 (1974), pp. 2-5.

—'Excavations at Tel Beer-sheba. Preliminary Report of the Fifth and Sixth Seasons, 1973–1974', *TA* 2 (1975), pp. 146-68.

—'Tel Beersheba', *EAEHL*, I, pp. 160-68.

—*Investigations at Lachish: The Sanctuary and the Residency (Lachish V)* (Tel Aviv: Institute of Archaeology, 1975).

—'Ramat Raḥel', *EAEHL*, IV, pp. 1000-1009.

—*The Land of the Bible* (Philadelphia: Westminster Press, rev. edn, 1979).

—Aharoni, Y. (ed.), *Beer-sheba I: Excavations at Tel Beer-sheba, 1969–1971 Seasons* (PIA, 2; Tel Aviv: Institute of Archaeology, 1973).

Ahlström, G.W., *Psalm 89: Eine Liturgie aus dem Ritual des leidenden Königs* (Lund: Gleerup, 1959).

—*Aspects of Syncretism in Israelite Religion* (Horae Soderblominae, 5; Lund: Gleerup, 1963).

—'An Archaeological Picture of Iron Age Religions in Ancient Palestine', *StudOr* 55 (1984), pp. 117-57.

Albright, W.F., Review of S.H. Hooke (ed.), *Myth and Ritual, JPOS* 14 (1934), pp. 152-56.

—*The Excavations of Tell Beit Mirsim. III. The Iron Age* (AASOR, 21-22; New Haven: ASOR, 1943).

—'The Psalm of Habakkuk', in H.H. Rowley (ed.), *Studies in Old Testament Prophecy Presented to Professor Theodore H. Robinson* (Edinburgh: T. & T. Clark, 1950), pp. 1-18.

Allen, L.C., *The Books of Joel, Obadiah, Jonah and Micah* (NICOT; Grand Rapids: Eerdmans, 1976).

—*Psalms 101–150* (WBC, 21; Waco, TX: Word Books, 1983).

Amiran, R., 'A Note on Figurines with "Disks"', *EI* 8 (1967), pp. 99-100.

Andersen, F.I., *Job* (TOTC, 13; London: Tyndale Press, 1976).

Anderson, B.W., 'Hosts, Host of Heaven', *IDB*, II, pp. 654-56.

— 'Lord of Hosts', *IDB*, III, p. 151.

Anderson, R.T., 'The Elusive Samaritan Temple', *BA* 54 (1991), pp. 104-107.

Assmann, J., 'Chepre', *LÄ*, I, pp. 934-40.

— 'Sonnengott', *LÄ*, V, pp. 1087-94.

Auffret, P., *Hymnes d'Egypte et d'Israël: Etudes de structures littéraires* (OBO, 34; Göttingen: Vandenhoeck & Ruprecht, 1981).

— 'Note sur la structure littéraire du psaume 104 et ses incidences pour une comparaison avec l'hymne à Aton et genèse 1', *RevScRel* 56 (1982), pp. 73-82.

— 'Note sur la comparaison entre l'hymne à Aton et le Ps 104 à partir de leurs structures littéraires d'ensemble', *RevScRel* 57 (1983), pp. 64-65.

Avigad, N., 'Some Notes on the Hebrew Inscriptions from Gibeon', *IEJ* 9 (1959), pp. 130-33.

— 'A Seal of "Manasseh Son of the King"', *IEJ* (1963), pp. 133-36.

— *Hebrew Bullae from the Time of Jeremiah* (Jerusalem: Israel Exploration Society, 1986).

Baldwin, J.G., *Haggai, Zechariah, Malachi* (TOTC, 24; Downers Grove, IL: IVP, 1972).

Barkay, G. 'Northern and Western Jerusalem in the End of the Iron Age: Volume 2' (unpublished PhD dissertation, Tel Aviv University, 1985).

Barker, K.L., 'Zechariah', in F. Gaebelein (ed.), *The Expositors Bible Commentary* (Grand Rapids: Zondervan, 1985), VII, pp. 595-697.

Barnett, R.D., *A Catalogue of the Nimrud Ivories* (London: British Museum Publications, 2nd edn, 1975).

Barta, W., 'Der Greif als bildhafter Ausdruck einer altägyptischen Religionsvorstellung', *JEOL* 23 (1973–74), pp. 335-57.

Beck, P., 'The Drawings from Ḥorvat Teiman (Kuntillet 'Ajrûd)', *TA* 9 (1982), pp. 3-86.

Beek, G.W. van, 'Jemmeh, Tell', *EAEHL*, II, pp. 545-49.

Bernhardt, K.-H., 'Amenophis IV und Psalm 104', *MIO* 15 (1969), pp. 193-206.

Biran, A., 'Two Discoveries at Tel Dan', *IEJ* 30 (1980), pp. 89-98.

— 'Tel Dan Five Years Later', *BA* 43 (1980), pp. 168-82.

Bisi, A.M., *Il grifone: Storia di un motivo iconografico nell'antico oriente meditteraneo* (Studi semitici, 13; Rome: Centro di studi semitici, 1965).

Blackman, A.M., and H.W. Fairman, 'The Myth of Horus of Edfu—II', *JEA* 28 (1942), pp. 32-38; *JEA* 29 (1943), pp. 2-36; *JEA* 30 (1944), pp. 5-22.

Blenkinsopp, J., *Gibeon and Israel* (SOTSMS, 2; Cambridge: Cambridge University Press, 1972).

— *A History of Prophecy in Israel* (Philadelphia: Westminster Press, 1983).

Block, D.I., 'New Year', *ISBE*, III, pp. 529-32.

Boling, R.G., and G.E. Wright, *Joshua* (AB, 6; Garden City, NY: Doubleday, 1982).

Börker, J, 'Greif', *Reallexicon der Assyriologie*, III, pp. 633-39.

Bram, J.R., 'Sun', in M. Eliade (ed.), *Encyclopedia of Religion* (New York: MacMillan, 1987), XIV, p. 134.

Braun, R.L., *1 Chronicles* (WBC, 14; Waco, TX: Word Books, 1986).

Bright, J., *Jeremiah* (AB, 21: Garden City, NY: Doubleday, 1965).

— *A History of Israel* (Philadelphia: Westminster Press, 3rd edn, 1981).

Brown, A.C., and H.W. Catling, *Ancient Cyprus* (Oxford: Ashmolean Museum, 1975).

Brownlee, W.H., *Ezekiel 1–19* (WBC, 28; Waco, TX: Word Books, 1986).

Bruce, F.F., 'Chamberlain', *NBD*, p. 182.

—'Zadok', *NBD*, pp. 1272-73.

Buck, A. de, 'La fleur au front du grand-prêtre', *OTS* 9 (1951), pp. 18-29.

Bull, R.J., 'The Excavations of Tell er-Râs on Mt. Gerizim', *BA* 31 (1968), pp. 58-72.

—'A Tripartite Sundial from Tell Er Râs on Mt. Gerizim', *BASOR* 219 (1975), pp. 29-37.

—'Er-Ras, Tell (Mount Gerizim)', *EAEHL*, IV, pp. 1015-22.

Bull, R.J., and E.F. Campbell, 'The Sixth Campaign at Balâṭah (Shechem)', *BASOR* 190 (1968), pp. 1-41.

Buren, E.D. van, 'The Sun-god Rising', *RA* 49 (1955), pp. 1-14.

Busink, T.A, *Der Tempel von Jerusalem, von Salomo bis Herodes* (2 vols.; Leiden: Brill, 1970, 1980).

Cazelles, H., 'David's Monarchy and the Gibeonite Claim', *PEQ* 86 (1955), pp. 165-75.

Charlier, C.V.L., 'Ein astronomischer Beitrag zur Exegese des Alten Testaments', *ZDMG* 58 (1904), pp. 386-94.

Chassinat, E., *Le Temple d'Edfou* (8 vols.; Cairo: L'institut français d'archéologie orientale, 1934–78).

Clements, R.E., *Isaiah 1–39* (NCB; Grand Rapids: Eerdmans, 1980).

Clifford, R.J., 'Bull', *HBD*, pp. 144-45.

Clines, D.J.A., 'The Evidence for an Autumnal New Year in Pre-exilic Israel Reconsidered', *JBL* 93 (1974), pp. 22-40.

—'New Year', *IDBSup*, pp. 625-29.

Cogan, M., and H. Tadmor, *II Kings* (AB, 11; Garden City, NY: Doubleday, 1988).

Cogan, M., 'A Note on Disinterment in Jeremiah', in I.D. Passow and S.T. Lachs (eds.), *Gratz College Anniversary Volume* (Philadelphia: Gratz College, 1971), pp. 29-34.

—*Imperialism and Religion* (SBLMS, 19; Missoula, MT: Scholars Press, 1974).

Coggins, R.J., *Haggai, Zechariah, Malachi* (OTG; Sheffield: JSOT Press, 1987).

Cohen, S., 'Succoth', *IDB*, IV, p. 449.

Cooper, A., 'Ps 24:7-10: Mythology and Exegesis', *JBL* 102 (1983), pp. 37-60.

Corney, R.W., 'Zadok the Priest', *IDB*, IV, pp. 928-29.

Craigie, P.C., 'The Comparison of Hebrew Poetry: Psalm 104 in the Light of Egyptian and Ugaritic Poetry', *Semitics* 4 (1974), pp. 10-21.

—'Deborah and Anat: A Study of Poetic Imagery (Judges 5)', *ZAW* 90 (1978), pp. 374-81.

—*Psalms 1–50* (WBC, 19; Waco, TX: Word Books, 1983).

Crenshaw, J.L., *Samson: A Secret Betrayed, A Vow Ignored* (Macon, GA: Mercer University Press, 1978).

Cross, F.M., Jr, *Canaanite Myth and Hebrew Epic* (Cambridge, MA: Harvard University Press, 1973.)

Crowfoot, J.W., G.M. Crowfoot and K.M. Kenyon, *The Objects from Samaria. Samaria-Sebaste: Reports of the Work of the Joint Expedition in 1931–1933 and of the British Expedition in 1935, no. 3* (London: Palestine Exploration Fund, 1954).

Dahood, M., 'La Regina del Cielo in Geremia', *RivB* 8 (1960), pp. 166-68.

—*Psalms II* (AB, 17; Garden City, NY: Doubleday, 1968).

—*Psalms III* (AB, 17A; Garden City, NY: Doubleday, 1970).

Day, J., 'Echoes of Baal's Seven Thunders and Lightnings in Psalm XXIX and Habakkuk III 9 and the Identity of the Seraphim in Isaiah VI', *VT* 29 (1979), pp. 143-51.

—'New Light on the Mythological Background to Resheph in Habakkuk III 5', *VT* 29 (1979), pp. 353-54.

—'Asherah in the Hebrew Bible and Northwest Semitic Literature', *JBL* 105 (1986), pp. 385-408.

Davies, P.R., *Behind the Essenes: History and Ideology in the Dead Sea Scrolls* (BJS, 94; Atlanta: Scholars Press, 1987).

Davies, T.W., 'Temple', *HDB*, IV, pp. 695-716.

Delitzsch, F., *Isaiah* (repr. edn; Grand Rapids: Eerdmans, n.d.).

Dempster, S.G., 'Mythology and History in the Song of Deborah', *WTJ* 41 (1978), pp. 33-53.

Dentan, R.C., 'Face', *IDB*, II, p. 221.

Dever, W.G., 'Material Remains and the Cult in Ancient Israel: An Essay in Archeological Systematics', in C.L. Meyers and M. O'Connor (eds.), *The Word of the Lord Shall Go Forth: Essays in Honor of David Noel Freedman in Celebration of his Sixtieth Birthday* (Winona Lake, IN: Eisenbrauns, 1983), pp. 571-87.

—'Asherah, Consort of Yahweh? New Evidence from Kuntillet 'Ajrûd', *BASOR* 255 (1984), pp. 21-37.

Diebner, B., 'Die Orientierung des Jerusalemer Tempels und die "Sacred Direction" der frühchristlichen Kirchen', *ZDPV* 87 (1971), pp. 153-66.

Dion, P.E., 'YHWH as Storm-god and Sun-god: The Double Legacy of Egypt and Canaan as Reflected in Psalm 104', *ZAW* 103 (1991), pp. 43-71.

Diringer, D., 'The Royal Jar-Handle Stamps of Ancient Judah', *BA* 12 (1949), pp. 70-86.

Donner, H., and W. Röllig, *Kanaanäische und aramäische Inschriften* (3 vols.; Wiesbaden: Otto Harrassowitz, 1973–79).

Dunham, D., *El Kurru* (The Royal Cemeteries of Kush, 1; Cambridge, MA: Harvard University Press, 1950).

Dürr, L., 'Zur Frage nach der Einheit von Ps. 19', in W.F. Albright, A. Alt, W. Caspari *et al.* (eds.), *Sellin–Festschrift: Beiträge zur Religionsgeschichte und Archäologie Palästinas* (Leipzig: Deichert, 1927), pp. 37-48.

J. Dus, 'Gibeon—Eine Kultstätte des Šmš und die Stadt des benjaminitischen Schicksals', *VT* 10 (1960), pp. 353-74.

Eaton, J., 'Some Questions of Philology and Exegesis in the Psalms', *JTS* 19 (1968), pp. 603-609.

—*Kingship and the Psalms* (The Biblical Seminar; Sheffield: JSOT Press, 2nd edn, 1986).

Edwards, I.E.S., 'A Relief of Qudshu-Astarte-Anath in the Winchester College Collection', *JNES* 14 (1955), pp. 49-51.

Eggebrecht, E., 'Greif', *LÄ*, II, pp. 895-96.

Eichrodt, W., *Old Testament Theology* (trans. J.A. Baker; 2 vols.; OTL; Philadelphia: Westminster Press, 1967 [1959]).

—*Ezekiel* (trans. C. Quin; OTL; Philadelphia: Westminster Press, 1970 [1965–66]).

Eissfeldt, O., 'Jahwe Zebaoth', in R. Sellheim and F. Maass (eds.), *Kleine Schriften III* (Tübingen: Mohr, 1966), pp. 103-23.

Emerton, J.A., 'New Light on Israelite Religion: The Implicaions of the Inscriptions from Kuntillet 'Ajrûd', *ZAW* 94 (1982), pp. 2-20.

Fairman, H.W., 'The Myth of Horus at Edfu—I', *JEA* 21 (1935), pp. 26-36.

Fairman, H.W. (ed.), *The Triumph of Horus* (London: B.T. Batsford, 1974).

Faulkner, R.O., *A Concise Dictionary of Middle Egyptian* (Oxford: Griffith Institute, 1962).

Fishbane, M., 'Form and Reformulation of the Biblical Priestly Blessing', *JAOS* 103 (1983), pp. 115-21.

Flagge, I., *Untersuchungen zur Bedeutung des Greifen* (Sankt Augustin: Hans Richarz, 1975).

Fohrer, G., *Ezechiel* (HAT, 13; Tübingen: Mohr, 1955).

—*Das Buch Jesaja. III. Kapitel 40–66* (Zürich: Zwingli Verlag, 1964).

Franken, H.J., 'The Excavations at Dier 'Allā', *VT* 10 (1960), pp. 386-93.

Frankfort, H., *The Art and Architecture of the Ancient Orient* (Harmondsworth: Penguin, 4th edn, 1970).

Freedman, D.N., 'The Name of the God of Moses', *JBL* 79 (1960), pp. 151-56.

—*Pottery, Poetry and Prophecy: Studies in Early Hebrew Poetry* (Winona Lake, IN: Eisenbrauns, 1980).

—'Yahweh of Samaria and his Asherah', *BA* 50 (1987), pp. 241-49.

Fritz, V., *Tempel und Zelt* (WMANT, 47; Neukirchen–Vluyn: Neukirchener Verlag, 1977).

Gall, A.F. von, 'Ein neues astronomisch zu erschließendes Datum der ältesten israelitischen Geschichte', in K. Marti (ed.), *Karl Budde zum siebzigsten Geburtstag am 13 April 1920* (BZAW, 34; Giessen: Töpelmann, 1920), pp. 52-60.

Gardiner, A.H., 'Horus the Beḥdetite', *JEA* 30 (1944), pp. 23-60.

Garfinkel, Y., '2 Chr 11:5–10: Fortified Cities List and the *lmlk* Stamps—Reply to Nadav Na'aman', *BASOR* 271 (1988), pp. 69-73.

Gaster, T.H., 'Ezekiel and the Mysteries', *JBL* 60 (1941), pp. 289-310.

—'On Habakkuk 3 4', *JBL* 62 (1943), pp. 345-46.

—*Festivals of the Jewish Year* (New York: William Sloane Associate Publishers, 1953).

—'Sun', *IDB*, IV, pp. 463-65.

—*Thespis* (New York: Gordian, 2nd edn, 1975).

Gerstenberger, E.S., *Psalms, Part 1: With an Introduction to Cultic Poetry* (FOTL, 14/1; Grand Rapids: Eerdmans, 1988).

Gevirtz, S., 'A New Look at an Old Crux: Amos 5:26', *JBL* 87 (1968), pp. 267-76.

Gibson, J.C.L., *Syrian Semitic Inscriptions*. III. *Phoenician Inscriptions* (Oxford: Clarendon Press, 1982).

Giveon, R., 'Skarabäus', *LÄ*, V, pp. 968-70.

Gjerstad, E., J. Lindros, E. Sjöqvist and A. Westholm, *The Swedish Cyprus Expedition* (6 vols.; Stockholm: The Swedish Cyprus Expedition, 1935–48).

Glazier-McDonald, B., *Malachi: The Divine Messenger* (SBLDS, 98; Atlanta: Scholars Press, 1987).

Glock, A.E., 'Taanach', *IDBSup*, pp. 855-56.

—'Taanach', *EAEHL*, IV, pp. 1138-47.

Gold, V.R., 'En-shemesh', *IDB*, II, p. 106.

Gomaà, F., 'Sile', *LÄ*, V, pp. 945-47.

Goodenough, E.R., *Jewish Symbols in the Greco-Roman Period* (13 vols.; Bollingen Series, 37; Princeton, NJ: Princeton University Press, 1953–68).

Graham, W.C., and H.G. May, *Culture and Conscience: An Archaeological Study of the New Religious Past in Ancient Palestine* (Chicago: University of Chicago Press, 1936).

Grant, M., and J. Hazel, *Who's Who in Classical Mythology* (London: Weidenfeld & Nicolson, 1973).

Gray, G.B., *The Book of Isaiah I–XXVII* (ICC: Edinburgh: T. & T. Clark, 1912).

Gray, J., *I and II Kings* (OTL; Philadelphia: Westminster Press, 2nd edn, 1970).

—*Joshua, Judges and Ruth* (NCB; Greenwood, NC: Attic Press, 1967).

Greenberg, M., *Ezekiel 1–20* (AB, 22; Garden City, NY: Doubleday, 1983).

Griffith, F.L., 'Oxford Excavations in Nubia', *Liverpool Annals of Archaeology and Anthropology* 10 (1923), pp. 73-136.

Griffiths, J.G., 'The Interpretation of the Horus Myth of Edfu', *JEA* 44 (1958), pp. 75-85.

—'Horusmythe', *LÄ*, III, pp. 54-59.

Gröndahl, F., *Die Personennamen der Texte aus Ugarit* (Studia Pohl, 1; Rome: Pontifical Biblical Institute, 1967).

Gunkel, H., *Genesis übersetzt und erklärt* (Göttingen: Vandenhoeck & Ruprecht, 7th edn, 1966).

Habel, N.C., *The Book of Job* (OTL; Philadelphia: Westminster Press, 1985).

Haines, R.C., *Excavations in the Plain of Antioch II* (OIP, 95; Chicago: University of Chicago Press, 1971).

Hanson, P.D., *The People Called: The Growth of Community in the Bible* (San Francisco: Harper & Row, 1988).

—'Malachi', in J.L. Mays (ed.), *Harper's Bible Commentary* (San Francisco: Harper & Row, 1988), pp. 753-56.

Haran, M., 'The Disappearance of the Ark', *IEJ* 13 (1963), pp. 46-58.

Harden, D., *The Phoenicians* (Harmondsworth: Penguin, 1971).

Harrelson, W., 'The Celebration of the Feast of Booths According to Zech xiv 16-21', in J. Neusner (ed.), *Religions in Antiquity* (Leiden: Brill, 1968), pp. 88-96.

Hayward, R., 'The Jewish Temple at Leontopolis: A Reconsideration', *JJS* 33 (= Yadin Festschrift) (1982), pp. 429-43.

Heider, G.C., *The Cult of Molek: A Reassessment* (JSOTS, 43; Sheffield: JSOT Press, 1985).

Heller, J., 'Der Name Eva ', *ArOr* 26 (1958), pp. 636-56.

—'Die schweigende Sonne', *Communio Viatorium* 9 (1966), pp. 73-78.

Herr, L.G., *The Scripts of Ancient Northwest Semitic Seals* (HSM, 18; Missoula, MT: Scholars Press, 1978).

Hertzberg, H.W., *I and II Samuel* (OTL; Philadelphia: Westminster Press, 1964).

Herzog, Z., M. Aharoni and A.F. Rainey, 'Arad: An Ancient Israelite Fortress with a Temple to Yahweh', *BARev* 13 (1987), pp. 16-35.

Herzog, Z., M. Aharoni, A.F. Rainey and S. Moshkovitz, 'The Israelite Fortress at Arad', *BASOR* 254 (1984), pp. 1-34.

Hestrin, R., 'Canaanite Cult Stand', in J.P. O'Neill (ed.), *Treasures of the Holy Land: Ancient Art from the Israel Museum* (New York: Metropolitan Museum of Art, 1986), pp. 161-63.

—'The Cult Stand from Ta'anach and its Religious Background', in E. Lipiński (ed.), *Studia Phoenicia V: Proceedings of the Conference Held in Leuven from the 14th to the 16th of November 1985* (OLA, 22; Leuven: Peeters, 1987), pp. 61-77.

Hillers, D.R., 'The Goddess with the Tambourine', *CTM* 41 (1970), pp. 606-19.

Hillyers, C.N., 'First Peter and the Feast of Tabernacles', *TynBul* 21 (1971), pp. 39-51.

Hoffmann, H.-D., *Reform und Reformen: Untersuchungen zu einem Grundthema der deuteronomistischen Geschichtsschreibung* (ATANT, 66; Zürich: Theologischer Verlag, 1980).

Holladay, J.S., Jr, 'The Day(s) the *Moon* Stood Still', *JBL* 87 (1968), pp. 166-78.

—'Religion in Israel and Judah under the Monarchy: An Explicitly Archaeological Approach', in P.D. Miller, Jr, P.D. Hanson, S.D. McBride (eds.), *Ancient Israelite Religion: Essays in Honor of Frank Moore Cross* (Philadelphia: Fortress Press, 1987), pp. 249-99.

Holladay, W.L., *Jeremiah 1* (Hermeneia; Philadelphia: Fortress Press, 1986).

Holland, T.A., 'A Typological and Archaeological Study of Human and Animal Representations during the Iron Age' (2 vols.; unpublished PhD dissertation, The University of Oxford, 1975).

—'A Study of Palestinian Iron Age Baked Clay Figurines, with Special Reference to Jerusalem: Cave 1', *Levant* 9 (1977), pp. 121-55.

Hollis, F.J., 'The Sun-Cult and the Temple at Jerusalem', in S.H. Hooke (ed.), *Myth and Ritual* (London: Oxford University Press, 1933), pp. 87-110.

—*The Archaeology of Herod's Temple* (London: J.M. Dent and Sons, 1934).

Huffmon, H.B., *Amorite Personal Names in the Mari Texts* (Baltimore: The Johns Hopkins University Press, 1965).

Iwry, S., 'The Qumrân Isaiah and the End of the Dial of Ahaz', *BASOR* 147 (1957), pp. 27-33.

Jastrow, M., *A Dictionary of the Targumim, the Talmud Babli and Yerushalmi, and the Midrashic Literature* (Brooklyn: Traditional Press, n.d.).

Jeremias, J., 'Theophany in the OT', *IDBSup*, pp. 896-98.

—*Theophanie: Die Geschichte einer alttestamentlichen Gattung* (WMANT, 10; Neukirchen–Vluyn: Neukirchener Verlag, 2nd edn, 1977).

Jones, G.H., *1 and 2 Kings* (2 vols.; NCB; Grand Rapids: Eerdmans, 1984).

Kaiser, O., *Isaiah 1–39* (trans. R.A. Wilson; OTL; Philadelphia: Westminster Press, 1974 [1973]).

Kallai, Z., *Historical Geography of the Bible* (Jerusalem: Magnes; Leiden: Brill, 1986).

Kapelrud, A.S., 'Temple Building, a Task for Gods and Kings', *Orientalia* 32 (1963), pp. 56-62.

Kaufman, A.S., 'Where the Ancient Temple of Jerusalem Stood', *BARev* 9 (1983), pp. 40-59.

Kearney, P.J., 'The Role of the Gibeonites in the Deuteronomic History', *CBQ* 35 (1973), pp. 1-19.

Kenyon, K.M., 'Excavations in Jerusalem, 1962', *PEQ* 96 (1964), pp. 7-18.

—'Excavations in Jerusalem, 1967', *PEQ* 100 (1968), pp. 97-109.

—*Jerusalem: Excavating 3000 Years of History* (New Aspects of Antiquity; London: Thames & Hudson, 1967).

—*Royal Cities of the Old Testament* (New York: Schocken Books, 1971).

—*Digging Up Jerusalem* (London: Ernest Benn, 1974).

Kessler, W., 'Aus welchem Gründen wird die Bezeichnung "Jahwe Zebaoth" in der späteren Zeit gemieden?', *Wissenschaftliche Zeitschrift der Martin-Luther Universität, Halle* 7/3 (1957–58), pp. 767-71.

Köhler, L., *Theologie des Alten Testaments* (Tübingen: Mohr, 1947).

Kraeling, E.G.H., 'The Early Cult of Hebron and Judges 16:1-13', *AJSL* 41 (1925), pp. 174-78.

Kraft, C.F., 'Samson', *IDB*, IV, pp. 198-201.

Kraus, H.-J., *Theology of the Psalms* (trans. K. Crim; Minneapolis: Augsburg, 1986 [1979]).

—*Psalms 1–50: A Commentary* (trans. H.C. Oswald; Minneapolis: Augsburg, 1988 [1978]).

Lambert, W.G., *Babylonian Wisdom Literature* (Oxford: Clarendon Press, 1960).

Lance, H.D., 'The Royal Stamps and the Kingdom of Judah', *HTR* 64 (1971), pp. 315-32.

Lapp, P.W., 'The Second and Third Campaigns at 'Arâq el-Emîr', *BASOR* 171 (1963), pp. 8-39.

—'The 1963 Excavation at Ta'anek', *BASOR* 173 (1964), pp. 4-44.

—'Taanach by the Waters of the Megiddo', *BA* 30 (1967), pp. 2-27.

—'Late Royal Seals from Judah', *BASOR* 158 (1968), pp. 11-22.

—'A Ritual Incense Stand at Taanak', *Qadmoniot* 2 (1969), pp. 16-17 [Hebrew].

—'The 1968 Excavations at Tell Ta'anek', *BASOR* 195 (1969), pp. 2-49.

La Sor, W.S., 'Beth-shemesh', *ISBE*, I, pp. 478-79.

Legrain, L., *Seal Cylinders* (Ur Excavations, 10; London: Oxford University Press, 1951).

Lemaire, A., 'Les inscripions de Khirbet el-Qôm et l'ashérah de YHWH', *RB* 84 (1977), pp. 595-608.

L'Hour, J., 'Une législation criminelle dans le Deutéronome', *Bib* 44 (1963), pp. 1-28.

Lipiński, E., 'The Goddess Atirat in Ancient Arabia, in Babylon, and in Ugarit', *OLP* 3 (1972), pp. 101-19.

Lohfink, N., 'The Cult Reform of Josiah of Judah: 2 Kings 22-23 as a Source for the History of Israelite Religion,' in Miller *et al.* (eds.), *Ancient Israelite Religion*, pp. 459-75.

Long, B.O., *1 Kings: With an Introduction to Historical Literature* (FOTL, 9; Grand Rapids: Eerdmans, 1984).

Loretz, O., 'Der Torso eines kanaanäisch-israelitischen Tempelweihspruches in 1 Kg 8, 12–13', *UF* 6 (1974), pp. 478-80.

—'Psalmstudien III', *UF* 6 (1974), pp. 175-210.

—'Ugaritische und hebräische Lexikographie', *UF* 12 (1980), pp. 279-86.

Maag, V., 'Jawhäs Heersscharen', *Schweizerische Theologische Umschau* 20 (1950), pp. 27-52.

McCarter, P.K., Jr, *II Samuel* (AB, 9; Garden City, NY: Doubleday, 1984).

McCown, C.C., *Tell En-Nasbeh* (Berkeley: The Palestine Institute of Pacific School of Religion; New Haven: American Schools of Oriental Research, 1947), I.

McKay, J.W., 'Further Light on the Horses and Chariot of the Sun in the Jerusalem Temple', *PEQ* 105 (1973), pp. 167-69.

—*Religion in Judah under the Assyrians* (SBT, 2/26; Naperville, IL: Allenson, 1973).

Mackenzie, D., *Excavations at Ain Shems (Beth-Shemesh)* (Palestine Exploration Fund Annual, 1912–13; London: Harrison and Sons, n.d).

Maier, J., 'Die Sonne im religiosen Denken des antiken Judentums', *ANRW*, II, 19/1, pp. 346-412.

Maier, W.A. III, *'Ašerah: Extrabiblical Evidence* (HSM, 37; Atlanta: Scholars Press, 1986).

Malamat, A., 'Doctrines of Causality in Hittite and Biblical Historiography: A Parallel', *VT* 5 (1955), pp. 1-12.

Mallowan, M.E.L., *Nimrud and its Remains* (2 vols.; London: Collins, 1966).

Margalit, O., 'More Samson Legends', *VT* 36 (1986), pp. 397-405.

Martin-Achard, R., *Essai biblique sur les fêtes d'Israël* (Geneva; Labor et Fides, 1974).

Mason, R., *The Books of Haggai, Zechariah and Malachi* (The Cambridge Bible Commentary; Cambridge: Cambridge University Press, 1977).

May, H.G., *Material Remains of the Megiddo Cult* (OIP 26; Chicago: University of Chicago Press, 1935).

—'The Departure of the Glory of Yahweh', *JBL* 56 (1937), pp. 309-21.

—'Some Aspects of Solar Worship at Jerusalem', *ZAW* 55 (1937), pp. 269-81.

Mayes, A.D.H., *Deuteronomy* (NCB; London: Oliphants, 1979).

—'Deuteronomy 4 and the Literary Criticism of Deuteronomy', *JBL* 100 (1981), pp. 23-51.

Mays, J.L., *Micah* (OTL; Philadelphia: Westminster Press, 1976).

Mazar, A., *Archaeology of the Land of the Bible, ca. 10,000–586 BCE* (ABRL; New York: Doubleday, 1990).

Mazar, A., and E. Netzer, 'On the Israelite Fortress at Arad', *BASOR* 263 (1986), pp. 87-91.

Mazar, B., T. Dothan and I. Dunayevsky, *En-Gedi: The First and Second Seasons of Excavatons: 1961–1962* ('Atiqot, 5, English Series; Jerusalem: Department of Antiquities and Museums, 1966).

Mazar, E., 'Archaeological Evidence for the "Cows of Bashan" who are in the Mountains of Samaria', in B. Akzin *et al.* (eds.), *Festschrift: Rëuben Hecht* (Jerusalem: Korén Publishers, 1979), pp. 151-52.

Mendelsohn, I., 'Guilds in Ancient Mesopotamia', *BASOR* 80 (1940), pp. 17-21.

Meshel, Z., 'Did Yahweh Have a Consort?', *BARev* 5/2 (March–April 1979), pp. 24-35.

Mettinger, T., 'The Veto on Images and the Aniconic God in Ancient Israel', in H. Biezais (ed.), *Religious Symbols and Their Functions* (Uppsala: Almqvist & Wiksell, 1979).

—'YHWH SABAOTH—The Heavenly King on the Cherubim Throne', in T. Ishida (ed.), *Studies in the Period of David and Solomon* (Winona Lake, IN: Eisenbrauns, 1982), pp. 109-38.

—*In Search of God: The Meaning and Message of the Everlasting Names* (trans. F.H. Cryer; Philadelphia: Fortress Press, 1988 [1987]).

Metzger, M., 'Himmlische und irdische Wohnstatt Jahwes', *UF* 2 (1970), pp. 139-58.

Meyers, C.L., The Tabernacle Menorah: A Synthetic Study of a Symbol from the Biblical Cult (ASOR Dissertation Series, Missoula, MT: Scholars Press, for the ASOR, 1976).

Milgrom, J., 'Challenge to Sun-Worship Interpretation of Temple Scroll's Gilded Staircase', *BARev* 11 (1985), pp. 70-73.

Millard, A.R., 'An Israelite Royal Seal?', *BASOR* 208 (1972), pp. 5-9.

Miller, P.D., Jr, 'Fire in the Mythology of Canaan and Israel', *CBQ* 17 (1965), pp. 156-61.

—*The Divine Warrior in Early Israel* (HSM, 5; Cambridge, MA; Harvard University Press, 1973).

Mommsen, H., I. Perlman and J. Yellin, 'The Provenience of the *lmlk* Jars', *IEJ* 34 (1984), pp. 89-113.

Montgomery, J.A., *The Book of Kings* (ICC; Edinburgh: T. & T. Clark, 1951).

Morgan, D.F., 'Calendar', *ISBE*, I, pp. 574-78.

Morgenstern, J., 'Biblical Theophanies', *ZA* 25 (1911), pp. 139-93; *ZA* 28 (1914), pp. 15-60.

—'The Book of the Covenant, I', *HUCA* 5 (1928), pp. 1-151.

—'The Gates of Righteousness', *HUCA* 6 (1929), pp. 1-37.

—'The Chanukkah Festival and the Calendar of Ancient Israel (Continued)', *HUCA* 21 (1948), pp. 365-496.

—'Two Prophecies from 520–516 BC', *HUCA* 22 (1949), pp. 356-431.

—'The King-God among the Western Semites and the Meaning of Epiphanes', *VT* 10 (1960), pp. 138-97.

—*The Fire upon the Altar* (Chicago: Quadrangle Books, 1963).

—'The Cultic Setting of the Enthronement Psalms', *HUCA* 35 (1964), pp. 1-42.

Moscati, S. (ed.), *An Introduction to the Comparative Grammar of the Semitic Languages: Phonology and Morphology* (Wiesbaden: Otto Harrassowitz, 1980).

Mowinckel, S., *The Psalms in Israel's Worship* (2 vols.; Oxford: Basil Blackwell, 1962).

'The Mystery of the Horses of the Sun at the Temple Entrance', *BARev* 4/2 (June 1978), pp. 8-9.

Na'aman, N., 'Sennacherib's Campaign to Judah and the Date of the LMLK Stamps', *VT* 29 (1979), pp. 61-86.

—'Hezekiah's Fortified Cities and the LMLK Stamps', *BASOR* 261 (1986), pp. 19-21.

—'The Date of 2 Chronicles 11.5-10—A Reply to Y. Garfinkel', *BASOR* 271 (1988), pp. 74-77.

Nelson, R.D., *The Double Redaction of the Deuteronomistic History* (JSOTSup, 18; Sheffield: JSOT Press, 1981).

Nicholson, E.W., *Preaching to the Exiles* (Oxford: Basil Blackwell, 1970).

Noth, M., *Die israelitischen Personennamen im Rahmen der gemeinsemitischen Namengebung* (BWANT, 3/10; Stuttgart: Kohlhammer, 1928).

Oldenburg, U., *The Conflict between El and Baal in Canaanite Religion* (Leiden: Brill, 1965).

Olyan, S., *Asherah and the Cult of Yahweh in Israel* (SBLMS, 34; Atlanta: Scholars Press, 1988).

Oswalt, J.N., *The Book of Isaiah, Chapters 1–39* (NICOT; Grand Rapids: Eerdmans, 1986).

Ottosson, M., *Temples and Cult Places in Palestine* (Boreas, 12; Uppsala: n.p., 1980).

Otzen, B., *Studien über Deuterosacharja* (Copenhagen: Prostant apud Munksgaard, 1964).

Overholt, T.W., 'Jeremiah', in J.L. Mays (ed.), *Harper's Bible Commentary* (San Francisco: Harper & Row, 1988), pp. 597-645.

Parrot, A., *The Temple of Jerusalem* (trans. B.E. Hooke; Studies in Biblical Archaeology, 5; New York: Philosophical Library, 1955).

294 Yahweh and the Sun

Parunak, H. Van Dyke, 'Was Solomon's Temple Aligned to the Sun?', *PEQ* 110 (1978), pp. 29-33.

Petrie, W.M.F., *Hyksos and Israelite Cities* (London: Office of School of Archaeology, 1906).

—*Egypt and Israel* (London: SPCK, 1911).

—*Gerar* (London: British School of Archaeology in Egypt, 1928).

—'Supposed Sun Worship at Jerusalem', *Syro-Egypt* 3 (1938), pp. 11-13.

Pettinato, G., 'Is. 2,7 e il culto del sole in Giudea nel sec. VIII av. Cr.', *OrAnt* 4 (1965), pp. 1-30.

Physick-Sheard, P.W., Letter to the author, 19 November 1986.

Polzin, R., 'HWQY' and Covenantal Institutions in Early Israel', *HTR* 62 (1969), pp. 227-40.

Pope, M.H., *El in the Ugaritic Texts* (VTSup, 2; Leiden: Brill, 1965).

—*Job* (AB, 15; Garden City, NY: Doubleday, 3rd edn, 1973).

Porada, E. (ed.), *The Collection of the Pierpont Morgan Library* (Corpus of Ancient Near Eastern Seals in North American Collections, 1; The Bollingen Series, 14; New York: Pantheon Books, 1948).

Porten, B., 'The Structure and Orientation of the Jewish Temple at Elephantine—A Revised Plan of the Jewish District', *JAOS* 81 (1961), pp. 38-42.

—*Archives from Elephantine* (Berkeley: University of California Press, 1968).

Pritchard, J.B, *Palestinian Figurines in Relation to Certain Goddesses Known through Literature* (New Haven: American Oriental Society, 1943).

—*The Water System of Gibeon* (Museum Monographs; Philadelphia: The University Museum, University of Pennsylvania, 1961).

Pritchard, J.B. (ed.), *The Ancient Near East in Pictures* (Princeton, NJ: Princeton University Press, 1954).

—*Ancient Near Eastern Texts* (Princeton, NJ: Princeton University Press, 3rd edn, 1969).

—*The Harper Atlas of the Bible* (Toronto: Fitzhenry & Whiteside, 1987).

Pumpelly, R. (ed.), *Explorations in Turkestan: Carnegie Institute of Washington Publication No. 73, Volume 1* (Washington; Carnegie Institute of Washington, 1902).

Quellette, J., 'Temple of Solomon', *IDBSup*, p. 872.

Rad, G. von, *Old Testament Theology* (2 vols.; New York: Harper & Row, 1962 [1957]).

—*Deuteronomy* (trans. D. Barton; OTL; Philadelphia: Westminster Press, 1966 [1964]).

—*The Problem of the Hexateuch and Other Essays* (London: SCM Press, 1984).

Rainey, A.F. 'Beer-sheba', *ISBE*, I, pp. 448-51.

Redford, D.B., 'The Sun-disc in Akhenaten's Program: Its Worship and Antecedents, I', *JARCE* 13 (1976), pp. 47-61.

—'The Sun-disc in Akhenaten's Program: Its Worship and Antecedents, II', *JARCE* 17 (1980), pp. 21-38.

—*Akhenaten: The Heretic King* (Princeton, NJ: Princeton University Press, 1984).

—*Pharaonic King-Lists, Annals and Day-Books: A Contribution to the Study of the Egyptian Sense of History* (Mississauga, ON: Benben Publications, 1986).

Reed, W.L., 'Timnath-heres', *IDB*, IV, p. 650.

Rehm, M.D., 'Zadok the Priest', *IDBSup*, pp. 976-77.

Renaud, B., 'La structure du Ps 104 et ses implications théologiques', *RevScRel* 55 (1981), pp. 1-30.

—'Note sur le psaume 104: Réponse à P. Auffret', *RevScRel* 56 (1982), pp. 83-89.

Rendsburg, G., 'Hebrew *'šdt* and Ugaritic *išdym*', *JNSL* 8 (1980), pp. 81-84.

Roberts, J.J., 'Zaphon, Mount', *IDBSup*, p. 977.

Rose, H.J., and C.M. Robertson, 'Apollo', *OCD*, p. 82.

Rylaarsdam, J.C., 'Booths, Feast of', *IDB*, I, pp. 455-58.

Sarna, N., 'Ezekiel 8:17: A Fresh Examination', *HTR* 57 (1964), pp. 347-52.

—'Psalm XIX and the Near Eastern Sun-god Literature', *Fourth World Congress of Jewish Studies, Papers I* (Jerusalem: World Union of Jewish Studies, 1967), pp. 171-75.

—'*šemeš*', *EncMik*, VIII, pp. 182-89 [Hebrew].

Sasson, J.M., 'Bovine Symbolism in the Exodus Narrative', *VT* 18 (1968), pp. 380-87.

Schmitt, R., *Zelt und Lade* (Gütersloh: Gütersloher Verlagshaus, 1972).

Schnutenhaus, F., 'Das Kommen und Erscheinen Gottes im Alten Testament', *ZAW* 76 (1964), pp. 1-22.

Schroeder, O., 'Zu Psalm 19', *ZAW* 34 (1914), pp. 69-70.

Sellin, E., *Das Zwölfprophetenbuch* (2 vols.; Leipzig: Deichert, 2nd and 3rd edns, 1930).

Selms, A. van, 'Timnath-serah', *ISBE*, IV, p. 856.

Shiloh, Y., 'Iron Age Sanctuaries and Cult Elements in Palestine', in F.M. Cross (ed.), *Symposia Celebrating the Seventy-Fifth Anniversary of the American Schools of Oriental Research (1900–1975)* (Zion Research Foundation, 1–2; Cambridge, MA: ASOR, 1979), pp. 147-57.

—*The Proto-Aeolic Capital and Israelite Ashlar Masonry* (Qedem, 11; Jerusalem: The Institute of Archaeology, The Hebrew University of Jerusalem, 1979).

Sloley, R.W., 'Primitive Methods of Measuring Time', *JEA* 17 (1931), pp. 166-78.

Smith, J.M.P., *A Critical and Exegetical Commentary on the Book of Malachi* (ICC; New York: Charles Scribner's Sons, 1912).

Smith, M., 'Helios in Palestine', *EI* 16 (1982), pp. 199-214.

—'The Case of the Gilded Staircase: Did the Dead Sea Scroll Sect Worship the Sun?', *BARev* 10/5 (September–October 1984), pp. 50-55.

Smith, M.S., Review of H.P. Stähli, *Solare Elemente im Jahweglauben des Alten Testaments*, *JBL* 106 (1987), pp. 513-15.

—' "Seeing God" in the Psalms: The Background of the Beatific Vision in the Hebrew Bible', *CBQ* 50 (1988), pp. 171-83.

—*The Early History of God: Yahweh and the Other Deities in Ancient Israel* (San Francisco: Harper & Row, 1990).

—'The Near Eastern Background of Solar Language for Yahweh', *JBL* 109 (1990), pp. 29-39.

Snaith, N.H., *The Jewish New Year* (London: SPCK, 1947).

Snijders, L.A., 'L'orientation du temple de Jérusalem', *OTS* 14 (1965), pp. 214-34.

Soggin, J.A., *Joshua* (OTL; London: SCM Press, 1972).

Spieckermann, H., *Juda unter Assur in der Sargonidenzeit* (FRLANT; Göttingen: Vandenhoeck & Ruprecht, 1982).

Spiegelberg, W. (ed.), *Der ägyptische Mythus vom Sonnenauge nach dem Leidener demotischen Papyrus I 384* (2 vols.; Strassburg: R. Schultz, 1917).

Stager, L.E., 'The Archaeology of the East Slope of Jerusalem and the Terraces of the Kidron', *JNES* 41 (1982), pp. 111-21.

Stager, L.E., and S.R. Wolff, 'Production and Commerce in Temple Courtyards', *BASOR* 243 (1981), pp. 95-102.

Stähli, H.-P., *Solare Elemente im Jahweglauben des Alten Testaments* (OBO, 66; Freiburg: Universitätsverlag, 1985).

Stern, E., *'ma'alôt 'āḥāz'*, *EncMik*, VIII, p. 197.

—'Seal-Impressions in the Achaemenid Style in the Province of Judah', *BASOR* 202 (1971), pp. 6-16.

—*Material Culture of the Land of the Bible in the Persian Period 538–332 BC* (Warminster: Aris & Phillips, 1982 [1973]).

Streck, M., *Assurbanipal und die letzten assyrischen Könige bis zum Untergange Nineveh's* (Vorderasiatische Bibliothek, 7: Leipzig: Hinrichs, 1916).

Tallqvist, K.L., *Assyrian Personal Names* (Leipzig: August, 1914).

Taylor, J.G., 'The Song of Deborah and Two Canaanite Goddesses', *JSOT* 23 (1982), pp. 99-108.

—'Yahweh and Asherah at Tenth Century Taanach', *Newsletter for Ugaritic Studies* 37-38 (April–October 1987), pp. 16-18.

—'The Two Earliest Known Representations of Yahweh', in L. Eslinger and J.G. Taylor (eds.), *Ascribe to the Lord: Biblical and Other Essays in Memory of Peter C. Craigie* (JSOTSup, 67; Sheffield: JSOT Press, 1988), pp. 557-66.

—Review of H.-P. Stähli, *Solare Elemente im Jahweglauben des Alten Testaments*, *JAOS* 111 (1991), pp. 128-31.

Thackeray, H.StJ. (trans.), *Josephus II: The Jewish War, Books I–III* (LCL; London: William Heinemann, 1956).

—*Josephus. III. The Jewish War, Books IV–VII* (LCL; London: Heinemann, 1957).

Thomas, D.W. (ed.), *Documents from Old Testament Times* (New York: Harper & Row, 1958).

Thompson, J.A., *Deuteronomy* (TOTC, 5; Leicester: Inter-Varsity Press, 1974).

Tigay, J.H., *You Shall Have No Other Gods: Israelite Religion in the Light of Hebrew Inscriptions* (HSS, 31; Atlanta: Scholars Press, 1986).

Tufnell, O., *Lachish III: The Iron Age* (The Wellcome-Marston Archaeological Research Expedition to the Near East, 3; London: Oxford University Press, 1953).

Tushingham, A.D., 'A Royal Israelite Seal (?) and the Royal Jar Handle Stamps (Part One)', *BASOR* 200 (1970), pp. 71-78.

—'A Royal Israelite Seal (?) and the Royal Jar Handle Stamps (Part Two)', *BASOR* 201 (1971), pp. 23-35.

Ussishkin, D., 'The Destruction of Lachish by Sennacherib and the Dating of the Royal Judaean Storage Jars', *TA* 4 (1977), pp. 28-60.

—'Excavations at Tel Lachish 1973–1977: Preliminary Report', *TA* 5 (1978), pp. 76-81.

—'Excavations at Tel Lachish 1978–1983: Second Preliminary Report', *TA* 10 (1983), pp. 97-175.

—'The Date of the Judaean Shrine at Arad', *IEJ 38* (1988), pp. 142-57.

Vandier, J., 'Iousâas et (Hathor)-Nébet-Hétépet', *Revue d'Egyptologie* 17 (1965), pp. 89-176.

Vaux, R. de, *Ancient Israel. II. Religious Institutions* (New York: McGraw–Hill, 1965).

—'Post-Scriptum' to 'Le temple d'Onias en Egypte', by M. Delcor, *RB* 75 (1968), pp. 204-205.

—*The Early History of Israel* (trans. D. Smith; Philadelphia: Westminster Press, 1978 [1971, 1973]).

Verhoef, P.A., *The Books of Haggai and Malachi* (NICOT; Grand Rapids: Eerdmans, 1987).

Vollers, K., 'Die Solare Seite des alttestamentlichen Gottesbegriffes', *ARW* 9 (1900), pp. 176-84.

Volz, P., *Jesaja II* (KAT; Leipzig: A. Deichertsche Verlagsbuchhandlung, 1932).

Vries, S.J. de, 'Calendar,' *IDB*, I, pp. 483-88.

Ward, W.A., 'Three Phoenician Seals of the Early First Millennium BC', *JEA* 53 (1967), pp. 69-74.

Watts, J.D.W., *Isaiah 1–33* (WCB 24; Waco, TX: Word Books, 1985).

Weddle, F., 'Heres', *ISBE*, II, p. 684.

Weinfeld, M., 'The Worship of Molech and the Queen of Heaven and its Background', *UF* 4 (1972), pp. 133-54.

Welten, P., *Die Königs-Stempel: Ein Beitrag zur Militärpolitik Judas unter Hiskia und Josia* (Abhandlungen des Deutschen Palästinavereins; Wiesbaden: Otto Harrassowitz, 1969).

Wenham, G.J., *Genesis 1–15* (WBC; Waco, TX: Word Books, 1987).

Westerholm, S., 'Temple', *ISBE*, IV, pp. 759-76.

Wevers, J., *Ezekiel* (NCB; London: Nelson, 1969).

Whiston, W., *The Works of Flavius Josephus* (London: Ward, Lock & Co., n.d.).

Williamson, H.G.M., *1 and 2 Chronicles* (NCB; Grand Rapids: Eerdmans, 1982).

Wilson, R.R., *Prophecy and Society in Ancient Israel* (Philadelphia: Fortress Press, 1980).

—'Ezekiel', in J.L. Mays (ed.), *Harper's Bible Commentary* (San Francisco: Harper & Row, 1988), pp. 652-94.

Wiseman, D.J., 'Calendar', *NBD* (1982), pp. 157-97.

Woude, A.S. van der, '*ṣābā*', *THAT*, II, pp. 498-507.

Wright, C.H.H., *Zechariah and his Prophecies* (London: Hodder & Stoughton, 2nd edn, 1879).

Wright, G.E., 'Solomon's Temple Resurrected', *BA* 4 (1941), pp. 20-21.

—'The Book of Deuteronomy: Introduction and Exegesis', *IB*, II, pp. 311-537.

—'Beth-shemesh', *EAEHL*, I, pp. 248-53.

Würthwein, E., *Das erste Buch der Könige* (ATD; Göttingen: Vandenhoeck & Ruprecht, 1977).

—*Die Bücher der Könige: 1 Kön. 17–2. Kön. 25* (ATD, 11.2; Göttingen: Vandenhoeck & Ruprecht, 1984).

Yadin, Y., 'The Dial of Ahaz', *EI* 5 (1958), pp. 91-96 [Hebrew].

—'Ancient Judaean Weights and the Date of the Samaria Ostraca', *Scripta Hierosolymitana* 8 (1961), pp. 9-25.

—'The Fourfold Division of Judah', *BASOR* 163 (1961), pp. 6-12.

—*Hazor: The Head of all those Kingdoms. The Schweich Lectures of the British Academy, 1970* (London: Oxford University Press, 1972).

—*Hazor: The Rediscovery of a Great Citadel of the Bible* (New York: Random House, 1975).

—'Beer-sheba: The High Place Destroyed by King Josiah', *BASOR* 222 (1976), pp. 1-17.

—'The Temple Scroll: The Longest and Most Recently Discovered Dead Sea Scroll', *BARev* 10/5 (September–October 1984), pp. 33-49.

Yadin, Y., (ed.), *The Temple Scroll* (3 vols.; Jerusalem: Israel Exploration Society, 1983 [1977]).

Yadin, Y., Y. Aharoni, R. Amiran, T. Dothan, I. Dunayevsky, J. Perrot and S. Angress, *Hazor II* (Jerusalem: At the Magnes Press of the Hebrew University, 1960).

Younker, R.W., 'Israel, Judah, and Ammon and the Motifs on the Baalis Seal from Tell el-'Umeiri', *BA* 48 (1985), pp. 173-80.

Zandee, J., 'The Book of Gates', in *Liber Amicorum: Studies in Honour of Professor Dr C.J. Bleeker* (Leiden: Brill, 1969), pp. 282-324.

Zimmerli, W., *Ezekiel 1* (trans. R.E. Clements; Hermeneia; Philadelphia: Fortress Press, 1979 [1969]).

—*Ezekiel 2* (trans. J.D. Martin; Hermeneia; Philadelphia: Fortress Press, 1983 [1969]).

INDEXES

INDEX OF REFERENCES

Entries in bold indicate important references or key passages which are given new interpretations.

BIBLE